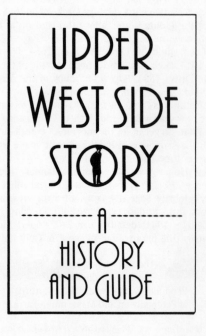

UPPER WEST SIDE STORY

A

HISTORY AND GUIDE

PETER SALWEN

ABBEVILLE PRESS

PUBLISHERS

NEW YORK LONDON PARIS

Jacket: J. S. Johnston, "Skaters in Central Park, Dakota Apartment Building," ca. 1890 (detail). *Frontispiece:* Sleighing in Central Park, 1886, under the gaze of the recently completed Dakota Apartments. *Dedication page:* A picturesque ravine at West 90th Street in Riverside Park, 1880. *Page 12:* Van de Water's Heights—today's Morningside Heights—looked deceptively peaceful in 1781, the fifth year of the Revolution. View is north from the approximate site of Grant's Tomb, in Riverside Park at West 123rd Street. *Page 22:* The Battle of Harlem Heights, September 16, 1776—as seen by *Harper's Weekly* a century later. *Page 30:* Springtime in Bloomingdale: back yard of the Eidlitz home, above the Hudson at 87th Street, c. 1876. *Page 54:* Squatter shanties near Central Park, 1869. *Page 62:* The Dakota (1886 drawing). *Page 78:* The fashionable Oliver A. Olson Co.—"The Store of Service"—at Broadway and 79th, 1914. *Page 128:* Third annual parade of the League of American Wheelmen, Riverside Drive, 1883. *Page 134:* Lobby of the Ansonia Hotel, c. 1910. *Page 146: The Wizard of Oz,* a legendary musical extravaganza, inaugurated the new Majestic Theatre on Columbus Circle in 1902. *Page 178:* December 31, 1905: Lillian Russell welcomes the new year with friends Enrico Caruso and Cornelius Vanderbilt. *Page 186:* "Oh, how I hate to get up in the morning," complains Irving Berlin in the 1943 war film *This Is the Army*—reprising the song he made famous on the stage of Central Park West's Century Theatre in 1918. *Page 196:* Artist Robert Henri and students in their new Upper West Side quarters, January 1909. New York *World* drawing by Cesare. *Page 210:* The earnestly morbid Edgar Allan Poe, the Upper West Side's earliest literary celebrity. *Page 224:* Polly Adler, the West Side's favorite madam, joins a companion for a little outdoor fun. *Page 240:* "Freedom of Speech, Columbus Circle," by Don Freeman, 1941 (detail). *Page 270:* Robert Moses and the city he reshaped. (*Fortune* magazine photo, 1938.) *Page 276:* Columbus Avenue street fair, 1983.

Editor: Alan Axelrod
Designer: Julie Rauer
Production supervisor: Hope Koturo
Photo research: Peter Salwen and Massoumeh Farman-Farmaian

First paperback edition.

Published in the United States of America in 1989 by Abbeville Press, Inc.

Library of Congress Cataloging-in-Publication Data
Salwen, Peter.
Upper West Side story: a history and guide/Peter Salwen.
p.   cm.
Bibliography: p.
Includes index.
ISBN 1-55859-429-9
1. Upper West Side (New York, N.Y.)—History.   2. Upper West Side (New York, N.Y.)—Buildings, structures, etc.—Guide-books.   3. Upper West Side (New York, N.Y.)—Description—Tours.   4. New York (N.Y.)—History.   5. New York (N.Y.)—Description—1981—Tours.   6. New York (N.Y.)—Buildings, structures, etc.—Guide-books.   7. Architecture—New York (N.Y.)—Guide-books.   1. Title.
F128.68.U67S35   1989   88-32729
974.7'1—dc19   CIP

For Franklyn and Peggy Sue
who helped with this
and so much more.

CONTENTS

Preface   8

PART III · THE UPPER WEST SIDE

ANNEX A : WHO WAS WHERE

ANNEX B : WEST SIDE WALKING TOURS

PREFACE

I've decided to blame this whole thing on the goat.

When I came to the Upper West Side in the 1950s, she had been standing for decades in the window of Friedgen's Pharmacy, at Amsterdam Avenue and West 118th Street. Stuffed. If you asked what a stuffed nanny goat was doing in a drugstore window (everyone did, once), you learned that she had been a historic figure—the last goat in the neighborhood, lived into the 1920s or 1930s. And if you were properly impressed (most people were), Mr. Friedgen would top that by pointing to a framed photo behind the counter. It showed a wooded setting and two young men with shotguns, grinning and leaning against a sign that read NO HUNTING. That, he said, was Morningside Heights a half century before.

The idea that my intensely urban neighborhood had sprung up out of farmland, and within living memory at that, was intriguing, and like most intriguing thoughts it was forgotten. Twenty-some years later, though, that photo and that goat were in the back of my mind when I set out to learn a little more about my neighborhood, present and past. I was living then near Riverside Drive on West 89th (some of us don't cover a lot of distance). All I wanted then was a half page of local history for a block association newsletter, and just as an aside I would like to suggest that books on New York history should carry a warning label: CAUTION, ADDICTIVE MATERIAL. A few weekends' research at the Historical Society and I was hooked—and I'd fallen in love all over again with Manhattan's Upper West Side, the quirky, sordid, hustling, grandiose, hopelessly *over*articulate hodgepodge of a neighborhood bounded by Morningside, Riverside, and Central parks and stretching from Columbus Circle to Morningside Heights. The first result of that addiction was a series of articles in the late, lamented *Columbus Ave* magazine, where Sue Berkman and Mary Frances Shaugnessy, the editor and publisher, very kindly allowed their local historian free rein. The second is this book.

Like most kids exposed to an American education, I had had the general idea that history began in 1776. Rooting around among old books and manuscripts, I found myself among some neighbors who had been carrying on remarkably like today's New Yorkers, a good century before the Revolution. I also came to the somewhat startled realization that my little corner of New York had a population well over a quarter of a million— roughly equal to that of Sacramento or Akron, or of Hartford and New Haven combined—i.e., it was a fair-sized city in its own right, and one that had never really been written about, unless you counted a couple of parish histories that came out in 1905 and 1907. I became fascinated with how the onetime riverbank suburb got swallowed up by the burgeoning metropolis—and even more by the fact that it apparently stuck, undigested, in the city's craw. Like an unsubdued colony, the Upper West Side often

seems, as an earlier writer, Lloyd Morris, put it, like a city unto itself, with its own distinctive social tone.

With a few obvious differences, a biography of the Upper West Side could be the story of almost any American town. One difference, of course, is that any American town would not have boasted—or endured—the throng that has made the Upper West Side one of New York's most vital neighborhoods. A collage of West Side faces would include Lillian Russell and Anna Held; William Tecumseh Sherman and Florenz Ziegfeld; Charles Evans Hughes and Bruno Richard Hauptmann; Humphrey Bogart and Richard Rodgers; F. Scott Fitzgerald and Theodore Dreiser; Caruso and Toscanini; Walter Winchell and his pal Frank Costello; Gertrude Stein and Mae West; Leonard Bernstein and John Lennon; Elizabeth Cady Stanton and Polly Adler. And luckily for the storyteller, most of them were up to something worth mentioning when they were here. You'll also meet a number of their relatively unknown neighbors, some of them sufficiently celebrated or notorious in their own day, but never, until now, trapped between the covers of a book.

When the townsfolk of New Amsterdam first turned their attention to the undeveloped West Side, they called it Bloemendaal, after a town in Holland's tulip region. Gentrification, as we now call it, started in the 1760s, when the wealthiest Colonial merchants and power brokers chose this area, with its grand river views, for their lavish country seats. In the nineteenth century the name Bloomingdale was familiar to all New Yorkers. The Bloomingdale Road (later renamed the Boulevard or Western Boulevard) was the main western route in and out of town and a favorite with sleighing parties; we call it Broadway. There were three different Bloomingdale Squares on the map at different times, and the Bloomingdale Lunatic Asylum—where Columbia University is now—was a prime tourist attraction.

For most of this century the name "Upper West Side" has been familiar and thoroughly *un*fashionable; the area's most recent gentrification was preceded by a half century when it became home to an unsurpassed mix of classes, races, and ways of life, which was stimulating or alarming, depending on your point of view.

My archetypal East Side–West Side story (old-style) is about the Fifth Avenue dowager who admits that yes, she actually had been to the West Side once, "but only to board the *Ile de France* for Cherbourg, my dear." The people in this book would mostly have been outside the lady's circle of acquaintance: promoters, eccentrics, writers, socialists, scientists, madams, artists, a counterfeiter and a poisoner or two, lots of actors, musicians, and theater people. But then at times it also was a place of high social aspirations, a district of fine homes and noble public boulevards. At certain carefully selected epochs in the neighborhood's checkered past, I would wager, the Cherbourg-bound lady would have felt right at home.

But then, so would the goat.

PART
I
BLOOMINGDALE

1

THE SWEET RURAL VALLEY

*They pranced it through the
pastoral scenes of Bloemen Dael;
which in those days was a sweet
and rural valley, beautified with
many a bright wild flower,
refreshed by many a pure
streamlet, and enlivened here and
there by a delectable little Dutch
cottage, sheltered under some
sloping hill, and almost buried in
embowering trees.*

—Washington Irving,
*Knickerbocker's History
of New York,* 1809

I n the closing years of the seventeenth century Theunis Idens could look out from his home above the cove on a scene that would make any pioneer proud: land recently wild, now tamed and fecund, cleared with his own and his son's hands and harrowed to pasture, tillage, and orchard.

The same scene, with variations, would be repeated endlessly in the coming decades and centuries, as settlers fanned out across the new American continent. But the river outside Theunis's door was not the Mississippi or the Platte; it was the Hudson. The geographic coordinates of his sturdy stone farmhouse would be designated today as West End Avenue and West 97th Street, and the wilderness he had conquered with such effort was the Upper West Side of Manhattan, an area he and the other Dutch settlers of New Amsterdam referred to, with considerable poetic license, as Bloemendaal, "valley of flowers."

Seven miles south, the city of New-York (so renamed by the marauding English when they seized it in 1664) was still a straggling settlement of fifteen hundred souls, part seaport, part brawling frontier town. Its handful of crooked, dusty streets, overrun with cattle, swine, and goats, met at seemingly random angles, reflecting a time not long before when each settler erected his cabin more or less where he chose. Most of the three

hundred or so houses were wooden, a handful were yellow-and-black Dutch brick; one in five was a tavern.

At the edge of town a rickety wooden palisade — the wall of Wall Street — ran from river to river. Beyond, Bloemendaal (which the English soon corrupted to Bloomingdale) and the other upland regions had scarcely changed since the end of the Ice Age. Of New York's ruler-straight streets and avenues, not an inkling; they wouldn't exist, even on paper, for another century and a half. In their place was virgin forest where the Wickquaskeek people — the so-called Indians — hunted beaver, bear, mountain lion, deer, and small game: meadows and hills clad in hemlock and oak-hickory forest, dozens of ponds and clear streams. (The Indians, the original commuters, only hunted here; their permanent village was near present-day Yonkers.) The riverfronts were edged with scores of coves, like the one below Theunis's home, and wide stretches of alder and red oak swamp.

The first Christians (their names, for the record, were Johannes van Brugh, Thomas Hall, Jacob Leenders, Egbert Woutersen, Jan Vinje, and Isaac Bedlow) took formal possession of property on the Upper West Side in 1667. To European eyes it was simply hostile wilderness. London was already a fifteen-hundred-year-old metropolis, where Isaac Newton had recently completed his first measurements of the moon's orbit and Milton had just published *Paradise Lost*. As pioneers sank their axes into virgin timber above the banks of the Hudson, a twenty-two-year-old Antonio Stradivari was affixing his name to a violin for the first time. Even by New World standards the place was raw. Boston and Philadelphia were younger, but both eclipsed New York in size and wealth; in Mexico City, already a century and a half old in 1667, they were celebrating the completion of the great cathedral, after ninety-six years of construction.

There had been a handful of earlier settlers. Back in the 1630s Jan Cornelissen, from Rotterdam, had set out a tobacco plantation on the north bank of the Great Kill, a broad stream that wound through swampy flatland and emptied into the Hudson at what is now Eleventh Avenue and West 42nd Street. He hung on until February 1643, when he was killed in an Indian war, and his fields returned to wilderness, "unmanured and un-planted." And so they stayed for another quarter century, until the first English governor, Sir Richard Nicolls, started handing out portions of the duke of York's outlying territory, "to the End," as he put it, "some good Improvem^t may be made thereupon."

The first grant, signed by Governor Nicolls February 13, 1667, went to Bedlow, a merchant and speculator whose holdings at one time included Bedloe's (Liberty) Island and most of the Bronx. It included nearly a mile of riverfront property, reaching, in modern terms, from 89th to 107th streets and back to the boundary of Harlem Village, roughly in the middle of Central Park.

Later that year, a syndicate organized by van Brugh, Hall, Leenders,

Woutersen, and Vinje got title to the thirteen hundred acres between 89th Street and the Great Kill. The lower three hundred went to van Brugh and Vinje; the remaining thousand acres were laid out in ten equal rectangles, numbered south to north, and distributed, two per man, among the five owners.

If history has forgotten the original masters of the Ten Lots, they were well enough known to their townsmen. Van Brugh and Vinje were the colony's leading brewers; Hall was a prosperous tobacco planter (New Yorkers already drank and smoked copiously). All speculated with typical Dutch ferocity in fur, livestock, drink, food, nails, powder, cloth, and land. Vinje liked to claim he was the first European born in the colony of New Netherlands. Thomas Hall was one of the first two Englishmen to settle on Manhattan: he had arrived as a prisoner, captured by the Dutch in a raid against a Swedish settlement on the South (i.e., Delaware) River, and by 1667 he was a wealthy man with a large plantation on ground now occupied by the United Nations headquarters.

These real-life New Amsterdammers were not a whit less corrupt than the venal burghers of *Knickerbocker Holiday* and were considerably less lovable. In fact, the average God-fearing Gothamite of that day seemed to be forever insulting and cheating, cuckolding, assaulting, and suing his neighbor, and incidentally making the court records of the time a mine of abuse and anecdote for future researchers.

For instance, Jan Vinje kept a pea patch between Wall Street and Maiden Lane. One day Franz Clasen's boy and some playmates got into it and "did much damage with their footprints etc." Did Vinje take them aside like a Dutch uncle, and explain the error of their ways? No. He beat them black-and-blue, sued Schoolmaster Clasen for damages, then assumed his role as city magistrate to sit in judgment on his own case. The court records also tell of one Wolfert Webber, who ran a tavern in what is now Chatham Square and whose descendants would be prominent among Bloomingdale families, suing his neighbor Judith Verleth, who happened to be an in-law of Governor Stuyvesant. She had come with her sister to his home, Webber said, beaten him, and thrown stones at him. This Judith would seem to have been an interesting character; among other things, she had once been jailed in Hartford for witchcraft. The record does not, alas, disclose just what it was she had against Mijnheer Webber.

Around the same time, Isaac Bedlow was being haled into court by Joost Goderis, a somewhat slow-witted laborer at the public weighhouse. Joost's complaint was that Bedlow and a gang of his friends had labeled him a cuckold, shouting for everyone on the Battery to hear that "Joost Goderis ought to wear horns, like the cattle in the woods!" and "Allard Anthony has had your wife down on her back!" and loudly demanding the same privileges for themselves. To make matters worse, Bedlow, when confronted, pulled a knife and cut poor Joost in the neck. It may or may

not have affected the disposition of the case that Bedlow and Allard Anthony both were magistrates of the court (which sat, appropriately enough, in the City Tavern). At all events, Goderis seems to have gotten no satisfaction. His case was in court for months, but its main effect seems to have been to provide his neighbors with entertainment.

Bedlow & Co. were basically land speculators, but after them came some real settlers. One of the earliest was Hendrick Hendrickson Bosch, a "sword-cutler" from Leyden, who arrived in 1677 with his third wife, several small children, and title to the triangle of high ground on Morningside Heights now occupied by Columbia University, Riverside Church, and Grant's Tomb. His handsomely wrought swords were prized by the militia, and he seems to have prospered. He also seems to have shown an appropriate steeliness of character: in his "extreme old age" Bosch disinherited two of his daughters—aged thirty-five and forty and both married—for their "stubborn and disobedient conduct toward me these many years," and sold his property to one Thomas Tourneur, constable of Harlem Village.

Our friend Theunis Idens, Bosch's downtown neighbor, arrived a few years later. An industrious yeoman, Theunis Idens van Huyse, to use his full name, interests us for several reasons. Not only did he manage to accumulate a very major spread of Upper West Side farmland, but in the process he acquired a nicely documented case history of vintage worka-holism and achieved a notable first: the earliest recorded nervous breakdown in New York City history.

That had been back in the mid-1680s, when Theunis and his family—his wife Annetje and their six children—had a farm in what is now Greenwich Village. Theunis was then thirty-five, ambitious ("extraordinarily covetous," neighbors said), overworked, quarrelsome, and depressed. He purchased some Bloomingdale property from Issac Bedlow's widow and put in what spare time he had working "like a mole," as one observer put it, "to make tillable soil out of rough woods." He nearly lost his life doing it: he carelessly tried to free a half-fallen tree and had his hand nearly crushed when it slipped.

Hard luck seemed to plague him, he complained. In one year alone his favorite slave was killed by a horse, *two* of his daughters were seriously hurt (the narrative seems to hint at one of them suffering a miscarriage), his best canoe was smashed in a storm—and not a single neighbor raised a hand to help or warn him. By winter Theunis felt "as though the Devil were after him."

Came the spring, and Theunis hitched up the plough and went to his fields. But as he lurched along behind his team the horses, for no reason, suddenly began to bellow, leaping and tearing the harness as though the devil really *were* in them—an idea that was taken quite literally in those days. Next thing he knew, Theunis was scrambling blindly through fields

and woods, in desperate flight from God knew what terror. Somehow he made it home, torn and hatless, where he swore that he could live no longer and called loudly for a rope to hang himself with. A modern wife might have broken out the Valium and phoned the psychiatrist. Annetje did the seventeenth-century equivalent: she sent for a pair of Dutch missionaries who were visiting nearby.

"Friends," said Theunis when he saw them, "is there still grace with God? Is there still grace for me with God?" The priests assured him there was. They prayed together, and soon the worst of Theunis's hysteria had passed. In the days that followed, in fact, he seemed a changed character. "It is as if it were Sunday," he said. "I know that the cattle must be taken care of and other things must be done, but that concerns me not. I have no work, and will not work again as I have done before. God will take care of me."

In the end, of course, he seems to have taken excellent care of himself, though we can hope for his sake he learned to moderate his work habits. In old age Theunis and Annetje apportioned their land among their six children, giving possession, after the ancient usage, "by turf and twig." When the property was surveyed, they turned out to have amassed the largest chunk of Upper West Side property—460 acres—ever held by one family. And they had brought the sounds of hearth and plough to the "rough woods" of Bloomingdale.

The children of Bloomingdale followed their parents' pastoral ways. Of Theunis Iden's five daughters, for example, Dinah, Maria, and Catalina all married the sons of nearby farmers: Marinus Roelofse, Jurien Rynchout, and George Dyckman, a cousin of the Dyckman family whose 1783 farmhouse on upper Broadway is still a Manhattan landmark. Sarah married Myndert van Evera, a local blacksmith; Rebecca, more cosmopolitan, married Abraham Delamontaine, a master weaver, while Eide, the son, inherited the family home, barns, and orchard as a matter of course.

By now there were plenty of neighbors. Most had Dutch or Flemish names (Webbert, Harsen, Somerindyck, Hooglandt, De Key), but New York was incorrigibly cosmopolitan from the start (seventeen languages were spoken in the colony by the 1650s, according to an official), and others were French (De Lancey, Le Roy, Delamontaine), English (Fletcher, Bayard, Jones) and Portuguese (Van Angola). Considering the future ethnic history of the Upper West Side, it's interesting to note that in the late 1600s, a large property near present-day 75th Street belonged to one Anthony Jan Evertse, "a ffree negrow"; he inherited it from Thomas Hall's widow, whose possessions previously had included both the land and Anthony Jan Evertse.

By 1703 the governor's council decided the Hudson River sloops couldn't handle Bloomingdale's output of tobacco and produce. They ordered a new road laid out—a proper highway, four rods wide: the Bloomingdale Road.

It branched off northwest from the Boston Post Road at around today's 23rd Street, near John Horn's farm, and kept to the high ground, following an old Indian hunting trail until it ended, four miles north, at Adrian Hooglandt's barn on the Hudson River at 114th Street. The obvious reason for building it was the need to move goods, but there was also another: the area had caught the eyes of downtown aristocrats, and a new phase of development was about to start. By the end of the colonial era, when New York had grown into a thriving town of twenty thousand, Bloomingdale had become well and truly "gentrified."

If an Upper West Sider of, say, 1775 wanted to show you his neighborhood, he would drive you up "the Road." The first sign of Bloomingdale was near today's 50th Street: Andrew Hopper's Dutch-style stone house, its steep sloping roof and rounded gables almost hidden among willows and Lombardy poplars. The trees had been planted by Andrew's father John, and the Hopper farm extended another third of a mile up the road, on both sides; if you peered west through the foliage, you could just make out the ancient homestead of Matthys Adolphus Hoppe, the original settler.

A little farther north was Little Bloomingdale, the three-hundred-acre estate where James De Lancey, Jr., bred his celebrated racehorses. By the time of our visit the De Lancey family had dominated New York politics for two generations. Etienne De Lancey, a French Huguenot refugee, had come to New York in 1686, married into the powerful Van Cortlandt family, and became one of the city's great merchants. He changed his name to Stephen, built a fine home at Broad and Pearl streets, bought New York its first fire engine and town clock, and sired a political dynasty. James De Lancey, Stephen's first son, became the colony's chief justice at thirty and frequently served as acting governor. He also, shortly before his death in 1760, presided over an extraordinary congress of representatives from the thirteen colonies, making him, in an obscure sense, the first American president. James Jr. was more interested in horseflesh. It would later be claimed that most of the great thoroughbreds of pre–Civil War America were descended from James De Lancey's stud. Another of his stallions, True Briton, was sire of the famous Morgan horses that today are used by New York City's mounted police.

Continuing up the Road, the next landmark was Jacob Harsen's Dutch-style house, on a hill to the left at the future line of West 70th Street. A few steps more, and Harsen's Lane branched off to the right, one of the few cross lanes to the island's east shore. At 75th Street came the cottage of Teunis Somerindyck, an overseer for the De Lanceys, and at 79th was the old house built by James De Lancey's grandfather as his country seat sometime before 1729. James's uncle Oliver (of whom more later) had used the house for a time, then sold it to his neighbor Charles Ward Apthorpe; now it was the home of Apthorpe's widowed sister, Mrs. James McEvers.

Beyond, the Road led through Oliver De Lancey's large estate, with its grand manor house looking down on the river from a bluff near today's West 87th Street and Riverside Drive. This De Lancey was no gregarious sportsman, but a tough soldier, leader of the expedition against Ticonderoga in the French and Indian Wars. In his youth he had been something of an upper-class lout, yet enough of a romantic to have eloped with the lovely Jewess Phila Franks. This came as a "shock" and an "affliction" to Phila's mother, but she allowed that at least her new son-in-law was "a man of worth and Charector." By 1775 the De Lancey children were grown, the daughter well married, and the sons following their father—now sixty, plump, and gouty—into military careers.

Beyond De Lancey's was Elmwood, the large property of Charles Ward Apthorpe, whose mansion stood on a height a hundred feet west of what is now Columbus Avenue and 91st Street. When Apthorpe had declared his intention to build there eleven years earlier, an associate, John Watts, had written to a mutual friend, "If you incline to see sheer industry come hither & see how he Toils, he has bought a lott beyond Blomandall something like Rome with seven Hills & is going to build a house on the highest of them." Work on the house had been briefly interrupted when one M'Intosh, a Scottish laborer, was killed in a fistfight with a Dutchman named Loudon. But the finished house, with its two-story-high Ionic columns, was conceded to be the finest on the island.

The last mile of the Road led across rolling country past several well-known landmarks. Directly across the Road from Apthorpe was Judge Robert Bayard's new estate, purchased just a year earlier, and at what is now 97th Street you came to Striker's Bay Farm. Gerrit Striker had bought a small tract of riverfront land from Apthorpe, the same lot where Theunis Idens had lived over a half century before. He built on the foundations of the old farmhouse and gave his own name to the pretty cove on the Hudson at 96th Street. The cove is long since filled in, but Striker's Bay is one of the very few place names from that era still used today.

At about 102nd Street the Road swerved left (as Broadway does to this day) where a stream flowed south toward Striker's Bay. A raised causeway, flanked with cherry trees, led westward toward Humphrey Jones's large rough stone house, its gardens enclosed by neat picket and board fences. Nearby, Jones's son Nicholas had his own house and stone-walled gardens west of what is now West End Avenue between 106th and 107th streets— landmarks that would soon figure in local folklore.

Almost at the river, near modern 115th Street, the end of the Road was marked by Adrian Hooglandt's barn—it was still called that, though it now belonged to a schoolmaster named Richard Fletcher—but your host surely would have pointed out the many cross lanes leading to other fine mansions and homesteads, such as Nicholas and James De Peyster's estates nearby, and Van de Water's Heights (now Morningside Heights), crowned

by Harman Van de Water's excellent stone house and his large orchards of apples and grafted pears. Beyond the line of modern 123rd Street, the land fell away sharply in a steep bluff overlooking a geological fault valley, and you were at Bloomingdale's natural northern boundary.

If you were a visitor of the right sort, you might have been invited to pause on your way back to the city at Charles Apthorpe's Elmwood, a Palladian mansion known for its lavish hospitality. Born in Boston, Apthorpe was the very model of the Colonial gentleman of affairs. Apart from shipping and immense up-colony land speculations, he imported Spanish and Portuguese gold for transfer to the army paymasters, then, as contractor for the army, arranged for the purchase of food, clothing, arms, and munitions, taking the customary percentage on both transactions.

In this last year before the Revolution, Apthorpe was around fifty, quiet and somewhat scholarly. He and four others made up Governor William Tryon's Royal Council, though he had little stomach for the political intriguing that went with the job. He also was one of the governors of King's College (now Columbia University), which he had helped to found. As befit a gentleman, he dabbled in architecture (including designs for his own elegant home); his signature appeared prominently on a circular for the promotion of the arts, and no less an artist than John Singleton Copley gratefully mentioned visits to Apthorpe and "the widow McEvers" during a stay in New York in 1771.

"Elmwood," Charles Ward Apthorpe's mansion, near Columbus Avenue and West 91st Street.

A description of Apthorpe's place from a 1780 newspaper advertisement offers as good a glimpse as we may hope to get of the Upper West Side in

this, its first golden age. Even allowing for advertising hype, it conjures up a world almost unimaginably far from today's reality:

> about 300 acres of choice rich land, chiefly meadow, in good order, on which are two very fine orchards of the best fruit, one of them in its prime, and the other beginning to bear plentifully. An exceedingly good house, elegantly finished, commanding beautiful prospects of the East and North-Rivers, on the latter of which the estate is bounded.
>
> Also, a two story brick house, for an overseer and servants, a wash house, cyder house and mill, corn crib, a pidgeon house, well stocked, a very large barn, and hovels for cattle, large stables and coach houses, and every other convenience.
>
> About the dwelling house is a very handsome pleasure garden, in the English taste, with good kitchen gardens well furnished with excellent fruit trees, of most kinds.

"In short," our copywriter concludes, "nothing is wanting to make it a most agreeable and profitable estate for a gentleman."

There was just one catch. By the time those lines were written, that "most agreeable estate" happened to be located in a war zone.

2

BATTLE FOR BLOOMINGDALE

The pursuit of a flying Enemy was
so new a Scene that it was with
Difficulty our Men could be
brought to retreat.

—Adjutant General Joseph Reed,
Continental Army,
September 16, 1776

I t would be pleasant to report that Bloomingdale played this or that heroic role in America's struggle for liberty. But the Revolution, alas, found most of the locals firmly on the other side.

The loss of Boston to the rebels in March 1776 made New York the key British stronghold in America, and in the view of Bloomingdale's first families, that was just fine. A month or so earlier, Judge William Smith, a De Lancey cousin, had urgently advised General Howe that "this city and Province is the only spot for carrying on the war with effect against the Rebels . . . for all the principal inhabitants are, at heart, with the Crown." But in the meantime, "as the mob now commands, prudence forbids them [the Loyalists] declare without a military force." In other words: send reinforcements!

Judge Smith's fear of the mob was well founded. Attempts to enforce the Stamp Act ten years earlier had provoked such rioting that Stamp Commissioner James McEvers (Apthorpe's brother-in-law) quit the job, fearing "the greatest risk to my person and future." In the early seventies New York had its share of liberty pole riots, tea parties, and hangings in effigy, and when news of the rebel victories at Concord and Lexington reached New York in 1775, it touched off three days of joyous parades, rallies, bonfires, and fireworks. Still, the Sons of Liberty knew Smith was right: in a real war the city would prove to be Loyalist at heart.

Oliver De Lancey was an inevitable target for the mob's attentions. As a young man, he distinctly showed the qualities of an overprivileged thug.

Then-Governor George Clinton (admittedly no friend of the De Lanceys) recounted a couple of incidents—one when Oliver and some cronies attacked a poor Dutch Jew and his wife, smashing their windows and swearing "they would lie with the woman," another when he had fatally stabbed a Dr. Colchoun in a drunken brawl—and complained bitterly that "no Lawyer in the place will undertake to prosecute him" for fear of his brother James, the chief justice.

James's death in 1760 left Oliver as head of the aristocratic, Episcopalian "De Lancey faction," rivaled in local politics only by their hereditary enemies, the Presbyterian, independence-minded Livingstons. After Concord and Lexington the revolutionary press loudly blamed the De Lanceys and others of New York's "worst Tories" for inciting the British to fire on the Minutemen. "Fly for your lives," they thundered; "the blood of your unfortunate British and American fellow-subjects . . . calls to Heaven for vengeance." James De Lancey, Jr., had been fairly active in support of Colonial interests, but these warnings persuaded him the time had come to sell his stables and sail for England. His uncle Oliver characteristically waded into an enraged mob, swore his innocence, and emerged unharmed.

By the summer of 1776 the rebels had, in fact, taken over New York. Governor Tryon had fled town in March and set up headquarters on a frigate, the *Dutchess of Gordon*, anchored in the Narrows. In June De Lancey and several other "dangerous" Tories were summoned before the revolutionary Conspiracies Committee, and he, too, finally fled. The night of June 19 he boarded a canoe at Striker's Bay with his neighbors (and fellow Councillors) Apthorpe and Robert Bayard, and slipped down the Hudson to join the governor. There De Lancey took a commission as a brigadier general—making him the highest-ranking officer among Loyalist troops—and made plans to raise three battalions to put down what he called "the present unprovoked rebellion." Once, in the French and Indian Wars, he had been able to recruit an entire regiment in only ten days; surely he could do so again.

Meanwhile Congress, with sublime disregard for reality, had ordered General Washington to hold New York City against the British. It was a dubious proposition. The main force of Continental troops was still on Long Island, for one thing. And even as a crowd gathered at Bowling Green July 9 to hear the Declaration of Independence, an armada of British warships was crowding into New York Harbor.

Rebel troops spent the summer constructing earthworks, redoubts, forts, gun emplacements, and trenches at key points, across Manhattan Island. But by the end of August, Washington's senior officers were still urging him to abandon the city or burn it (most of it was Tory property anyway), when a joint assault by British, Hessian, and Loyalist forces— including a contingent led by Oliver De Lancey, Jr.—drove the Continentals out of Queens and Brooklyn and back across the East River. Manhattan

had suddenly become a trap, which the British could snap shut at will, and Bloomingdale, for a few interesting days, was the critical setting for the American Revolution.

On Thursday, September 12, Washington began his retreat. From temporary headquarters in the Apthorpe mansion (unharmed, though the lead window weights had been melted down for bullets) he started shifting troops northward out of the city. Just north of Van de Water's (now Morningside) Heights was a rocky bluff known as Harlem Heights. Between the two was a swampy valley, a natural moat known as the Hollow Way, now traversed by West 125th Street. If his troops could regroup on Harlem Heights, Washington reasoned, they might be able—untrained, ill-fed, and badly disciplined as they were—to check the British advance. So while the sick and wounded were evacuated to New Jersey, every available boat and wagon was drafted to ferry weapons, ammunition, food, tents, and blankets to the new position. But more than half of Washington's twenty thousand soldiers were still miles to the south when the British invasion of Manhattan started on the hot, clear Sunday morning of September 15.

The first move was a feint. Three British men-of-war (the *Renown*, the *Repulse*, and the *Pearl*) moved up the Hudson to Striker's Bay, where the rebels had been frantically landing supplies at Gerrit Striker's wharf in the little cove. The sudden appearance of the British flotilla shut off that vital route, and worse: an invasion in force would certainly have cut Washington off from half his troops, with interesting consequences, at least, for history.

The real attack came on the opposite side of the island at Kip's Bay, near the foot of present-day East 34th Street. Unfortunately, the Continentals assigned to hold the position were untrained recruits from Colonel William Douglas's Connecticut brigade. Few of them had guns; none had eaten since early the previous day. We can imagine their terror as five British frigates drew up to the beach, decks crowded with cannon and well-armed soldiers—the most awesome war machine in the world. The assault began a little before eleven with a simultaneous broadside from eighty-six cannon. The roar was heard in New Jersey; the American defenders barely stayed long enough to hear the echo.

The city was lost, but instead of immediately following up this rout, the British paused to consolidate their beachhead. By now the American leaders were fairly expert at retreating (General Israel Putnam and Major Aaron Burr, his twenty-year-old aide, emerged as the day's heroes), and almost all the troops still in the lower city managed to escape to Harlem Heights. There were even two brief skirmishes with the advancing British, one at McGown's Pass in what is now upper Central Park, the other near 91st Street, where Apthorpe Lane met the Bloomingdale Road—delaying actions that allowed the last American regiments to escape the trap.

By nightfall, two regiments of British light infantry and one of Black Watch Highlanders were bivouacked along Apthorpe Lane and in the woods

to the north. Lieutenant General Sir Henry Clinton now occupied the Apthorpe home, while Washington and his staff were quartered in the elegant Roger Morris house, which still stands, two-hundred-odd years later, at Edgecombe Avenue and 161st Street.

Writing to John Hancock that night, Washington was understandably bitter about his soldiers' "disgraceful and dastardly conduct." He even questioned whether they would ever "show themselves worthy of the blessings of freedom." Still, he said, "I have sent out some reconnoitering parties, to gain intelligence of the disposition of the enemy." Perhaps his troops, if given the opportunity, might yet "behave with tolerable bravery."

The reconnoitering party was Knowlton's Rangers, an elite unit of volunteers led by thirty-six-year-old Lieutenant Colonel Thomas Knowlton, a handsome, inspiring commander. They specialized in dangerous, often secret, assignments. (One Ranger, a Connecticut schoolteacher named Nathan Hale, was not with them this morning; Washington had called him to the Apthorpe mansion a day or so earlier and dispatched him on his ill-fated intelligence mission behind the British lines. There are now *four* sites in Manhattan described in guidebooks and on historic markers as the place where Hale regretted that he had but one life to give for his country.)

First light on the sixteenth found the Rangers advancing stealthily through the woods of Van de Water's Heights. By daybreak they had reached Nicholas Jones's farm, near 106th Street, with still no sign of the enemy, when suddenly there was a burst of rifle fire from a detachment of British pickets a hundred yards down the Road. The rebels had been spotted.

Their recon mission was accomplished, but Knowlton, one of the heroes of Bunker Hill, was in no hurry to withdraw. The Jones farmhouse was a largish stone building, conveniently located on a rise, and as the four hundred or so British reinforcements advanced up the Road, the Rangers took positions behind the house and stone garden walls and returned their fire. For half an hour both sides held their ground, each losing about ten men. Then Knowlton saw more enemy troops closing in from the east— the much-feared Black Watch Highlanders, to judge by the skirling of bagpipes—and ordered his men back. This retreat, unlike Sunday's, was orderly and deliberate, the Rangers covering one another's movements as they backtracked northward up the Road, over the steep hill known as Claremont (where Grant's Tomb now stands) and across the Hollow Way. By nine they were back at their own lines.

Their general was of course heartened beyond all expectation. Washington had decided long ago that a taste of victory, however small, was essential, just enough to convince his troops that the British really were not invincible. Would Van de Water Heights provide that victory? As he pondered, the derisive tones of a British bugle sounded—the well-known hunting call signaling that a fox had gone to ground. He decided to attack.

A hundred-fifty or so troops would cross the Hollow Way, as though making a frontal charge. As the British advanced to meet them, Knowlton and the Rangers would lead a second force around to the left; screened by the trees, they would complete a flanking movement to cut off the British advance guard. A simple enough ruse, but considerably more ambitious than anything the Continentals had ever tried before.

It nearly worked. The flanking movement was aborted when some overeager soldiers fired their weapons too quickly, but even so, the rebels managed to force the British back up the Heights, where the sortie became a pitched battle between British and Continental riflemen, centered around a buckwheat field owned by the Van de Water and Hooglandt families. The Americans drew their lines across the upper end of the field, at about where Teachers College is now, on West 120th Street, while generals Putnam and Greene rode back and forth behind them, shouting encouragement. After two hours, the British gave way, some of the more ebullient Americans chasing them nearly a mile down the Road before prudently returning to quarters.

In tactical terms, the so-called Battle of Harlem Heights accomplished little or nothing: no ground was gained, four fine officers (including the brilliant Knowlton) were dead, and within a month the Continental Army would be driven from Manhattan for the war's duration. But it accomplished a great deal for the men's spirits. "These troops charged the enemy with great intrepidity, and drove them from the wood into the plain," Washington wrote to Hancock soon afterwards. "This affair, I am in hopes, will be attended with many salutary consequences, as it seems to have greatly inspirited the whole of our troops."

Just days after the British took it back, almost a third of New York went up in flames. Trade and manufacturing virtually ceased, replaced by the debauchery, waste, and graft that go with military occupation. (Some writers have speculated that the Crown would easily have won the war, if not for the twenty million or so pounds sterling that went into the pockets of crooked quartermasters in New York.)

Bloomingdale was at the outskirts of the British defenses. Cannon were posted at Judge (now Major) Bayard's house, to be fired four times if the rebels should attempt a landing from the North River. Apthorpe's home was used as a military headquarters for much of the war, by Washington and Clinton first, and later by generals Cornwallis and Carleton.

Bloomingdale had its patriot families as well, mostly small landowners and lesser gentry, and of course they got the worst of it. Hopper, Striker, Mott, Dyckman, Van de Water, Kortright, Webbers, Post—many a name that would be familiar in later Bloomingdale lore was also to be found on the rolls of Washington's New York regiments.

The Strikers' case was fairly typical. At the start of the war James Striker, Gerrit's son, was twenty, his father dead. Drafted into De Lancey's

Second Regiment, he deserted at the first opportunity and—more or less over his mother's dead body, one gathers—joined Washington's army in New Jersey just in time for the Battle of Trenton on Christmas night 1776. He served honorably until the summer of 1780, when he got hold of a boat at Fort Lee, disguised himself as a yeoman, and slipped secretly back home.

But home—now in "enemy territory"—had changed. Skirmishes were frequent, such as the one in which a patriot and two Tories were killed on the lane and buried where they fell. Twice, officers were quartered in the house, and at least one party of prisoners was billeted there on their way to the deadly British prison ships. As one indignant Striker later recalled, the British took over the house a second time, the year after James's return, and "the slaves and servant men were driven off and the women compelled for days to cook and attend to the wants of their captors."

At that, the Strikers were better off than some of their neighbors. The Somerindycks, down the Road near present-day 75th Street, were forced to hide in their own garret for two weeks when Hessian troops took the place over. When they emerged, "every particle of wood"—furniture, moldings, doors—had been chopped up for firewood. And there was suffering on both sides. Charles Apthorpe lost his wife to fever in September 1779, and his young brother William, a refugee from Boston, where the rebels had imprisoned him on a counterfeiting charge, died the following month.

The De Lanceys remained as conspicuous as ever, but their time was coming, too. The three battalions headed by Brigadier General Oliver acquitted themselves well, if not always with complete honor. One incident for which they were never forgiven involved the American General Nathanael Woodhull, who died after being captured in the battle of Long Island; Oliver's son was widely believed to have engineered his murder. Meanwhile another De Lancey, Oliver's nephew James, was rampaging through rebel-held Westchester with a force of volunteer Tory light horse. Plundering rebel homesteads and stealing horses and cattle in hit-and-run raids, they were known variously as "De Lancey's Refugees" or (by the other side) "those damned Cowboys," and they made the territory a virtual no-man's-land.

Rebel bands calling themselves "Skinners" made similar guerrilla-style incursions against Westchester farmers suspected of Loyalist sympathies, and one November night in 1777, when De Lancey's Cowboys had been making themselves particularly obnoxious along the Saw Mill River valley, the Skinners decided that personal revenge was in order. "In the dead of night," according to yet another De Lancey relation, about twenty rebels, led by Abraham Martling of Tarrytown, slipped down the Hudson past the anchored British men-of-war to the landing at Bloomingdale, captured the guards, and destroyed Oliver De Lancey's splendid home at 87th Street.

Only ladies and children were there, sleeping. The sound of voices

outside roused them and, assuming it was some of the slaves, who should have been indoors by then, sixteen-year-old Charlotte De Lancey opened a window and called, "Who is there?"

"Put in your heads, you bitches!" came a man's voice, and instantly the front and rear doors were burst in. The rebels

> broke into the house and plundered it [the chronicle continues], abused and insulted the General's lady in a most infamous manner, struck Miss Charlotte DeLancey, a young lady of about sixteen, several times with a musket, set fire to the house, and one of the wretches attempted to wrap up Miss Elizabeth Floyd (an intimate acquaintance of Miss DeLancey's about the same age) in a sheet all in flames, and, as she ran down the stairs to avoid the fire, the brute threw it after her.

The De Lancey home and its contents were destroyed; Phila De Lancey hid under the stoop until the rebels left; the girls, dressed only in nightgowns and carrying an infant nephew, fled into the swampland that one day would be Central Park. They were found there at eight the next morning and were carried to Apthorpe's house.

Washington and his troops reentered New York in 1783, and it was the Strikers, Somerindycks, and their kith who inherited, if not the earth, at least this corner of it. Oliver De Lancey died in England in 1785, stripped of his American property, "his body wasted to a skeleton," as an old friend said, "his mind the same." Today, the names of Delancey and Oliver streets in lower Manhattan are almost the only clues that his family was ever here. (Orchard and Stanton streets are named, respectively, for an orchard and a foreman on the De Lancey's city estate.) But by a neat trick of fate, Oliver De Lancey's birthplace on Pearl Street is still standing, though much altered. It's a national shrine, in fact. As Fraunces Tavern, it was where George Washington delivered the Farewell Address to his officers.

Other Bloomingdale Loyalists were luckier. De Lancey's brother-in-law (and former business partner) John Watts became a founder of the New-York Historical Society; the De Peysters, vigorous Loyalists though they were, went on to prominence in New York affairs after a brief sojourn in New Brunswick. Judge Bayard, on the other hand, was another who forfeited his property after the war, and his neighbor Charles Apthorpe was also indicted for treason, but never tried; he lived on in his great home until 1797. Downtown in the teeming city, there was the usual acrimonious tumult, as new classes and parties shouldered their way to power. Up in the suburbs, meanwhile, Bloomingdale was entering its most pastoral era.

3

"WOODMAN, SPARE THAT TREE!"

*Bloomingdale . . . was the Newport
of New York in the olden time—
the watering-place of the blue-
blooded, the resort of
distinguished strangers, and the
place above all others near the
city, where social delights were
the study and business of summer
life.*

—Martha J. Lamb, "Riverside
Drive, The Fashionable Drive
of the Future," 1884

Bloomingdale was just as alluring to America's own aristocrats as to their Loyalist predecessors. When New York was the nation's capital and George Washington its president in 1789–90, the chief magistrate's favorite drive was "the Fourteen Miles Around," a popular coaching route that led from Cherry Street up the Post Road to Apthorpe Lane, thence west and back to town via the Bloomingdale Road.

The Road was still the principal link with the city. A stage line from the lower part of the city was established in 1819, and four years later another from the Bull's Head Tavern in the Bowery up to Manhattanville. Private lanes ran off to the right and left, leading to expansive, landscaped estates and elegant mansions, many the summer homes of well-to-do New Yorkers and visitors: Harsen's Lane, McVickar's Lane, Livingston's, Striker's Bay, Apthorpe's (later Jauncey's), Clendenning's, De Peyster's lanes.

There was no village of Bloomingdale as such—the name referred loosely to the whole western district up to present-day Morningside Heights—but the Road wound through or past half a dozen hamlets: Harsenville and Striker's Bay and, beyond them, Manhattanville, Carmans-

ville, and Inwood Village, each with its smithy and stables, grocer, shoe-maker, school, and village church. Like Greenwich Village in lower Manhattan, these communities owed their existence partly to their natural charm and partly to the pestilences—malaria, cholera, and especially yellow fever—that struck reliably every other summer or so and sent the downtown population fleeing to the suburbs, where some eventually stayed.

The largest village was Harsenville, near what is now Lincoln Center. The name derived from the Harsen family, Dutch farmers who had arrived there in 1763 and married into the local Dyckman clan. The name Harsenville was never official, but was almost universally used. Almost. A Harsen descendant once protested when a neighbor, without authority, started using the name Treaceyville for his own property near Eighth Avenue; Treacey's response was to prod poor Harsen's shoulder and demand, "Misther Harsen, Misther Harsen, tell my by what right your father gave it the name of Harsenville?" (The *real* old-timers, in fact, were the Dyckmans, who had come in 1701 and bought 188 acres for the fairly hefty price of £450. Perhaps the village should have been called Dyckmanville.)

At its modest peak, Harsenville numbered perhaps five hundred people in sixty to a hundred houses scattered for a mile or so along the Road, with a single cross street, Harsen's Lane, following the general line of the future West 71st Street. (The city's numbered streets and avenues were plotted in 1811, but most of them existed only on paper until late in the century.) There were two chief landmarks: Jacob Harsen's rambling Dutch-style farmhouse, which sat on a rise west of the Road between today's 70th and 71st streets, and the thrifty stone building of the Harsenville Dutch Reformed Church, on a hill near 68th. This noble institution had been founded in 1807 by Jacob Harsen (who donated the land) and his neighbors Andrew Hopper, James Striker, and Philip Webbers. (Later, in the 1820s and 1830s, Webbers had grieved his friends by lapsing into the Baptist heresy, but after fourteen years he renounced his error and was welcomed back to the fold.) The bell in its open cupola was a gift from one of the village's wealthiest men, the French-born merchant Stephen Jumel, who had a country home near today's 78th and Amsterdam. Jumel's name survives today in one of the city's most venerable landmarks, the Morris-Jumel mansion in Harlem—and in the legend of Betsy Jumel, his beautiful widow, who had a brief and sensational marriage to the seventy-eight-year-old Aaron Burr (he married her, they said, principally for Jumel's money) and lived on to enjoy a scandalous old age.

Harsen's Lane marked the center of the village, and as late as 1849, Tenth (Amsterdam) Avenue ended right there at the village firehouse, forming a V with the Bloomingdale Road at what is now Sherman Square. Facing the Road was "Pop" Griffin's Pelican Inn, which doubled as a stagecoach stop. Across the way, where the Nevada Tower apartments now stand, was Harsenville's first brick building; the owner, John Jasper, used

Bloomingdale Lane, 1862.

Top:
View north from junction of Eighth Avenue and Bloomingdale Road—today's Columbus Circle—1861. Drawing by George Hayward shows then-new Central Park at right, village of Harsenville, with steeple of Reformed Church, at left.

Valentine Mott's summer home in 1853 or 1854. The great doctor built it in 1835 beside the Bloomingdale Road, at a spot now in the center of Broadway, just above West 93rd Street.

Top:
In the late 1860s, General Ulysses Grant and publisher Robert Bonner were conspicuous among the sportsmen on the Bloomingdale Road.

Streetcar passengers bound for the Upper West Side changed cars at "the old Halfway House," Eighth Avenue and 59th Street.

A gloriously corrupt ex-mayor,
Fernando Wood, was an ardent
friend of West End development.

Right:
Brigadier General Egbert L. Viele.
The city applauded his sanitary
engineering schemes, not his
park designs.

John Back's cottage, Tenth
Avenue and West 98th Street.
Back ran a tavern two blocks
uptown in the 1870s and early
1880s, but was listed as a
carpenter in later directories.

Top:
Looking west from 94th Street and
Eleventh (West End) Avenue on a
Sunday morning in June 1890.

Bird's-eye view of Central Park
toward the Upper West Side and
New Jersey, 1863. Blocks on near
(east) side of Fifth Avenue are
filling with houses, while beyond
the park the Upper West Side
still lies fallow.

American Museum of Natural
History and Manhattan Square,
1878: "We could only wait and
hope that the elevated train
company would soon extend its
lines north to 77th Street."

the ground floor for his grocery and variety store and rented out the second as the local police station.

Of the village shops, the children of the 1840s recalled Mr. Bonesteel's grocery and Jacob Tripp's general store and, most vividly, Aleck White's shop on the east side of the Road near 76th Street, where a youngster was hard put to choose between the chocolate balls called "bull's-eyes" and the cylindrical packets known as "hundreds and thousands," sealed with a gold paper band and filled with aromatic, candy-coated seeds.

There was also a certain amount of industry. One of the Harsenville church deacons, Duncan Macfarlan, operated a silk mill at 81st and West End Avenue that was supposed to have turned out the first silk ribbons made in America; another, Peter Rennie, had a calico print factory by the river. Also by the water were the Bloomingdale (Flint) Glass Works, the Sanger soap mill, and one of the leading U.S. ironworks, the Hamersley Forge. The Peacemaker, a massive cannon designed by the Swedish-born engineer John Ericsson, was forged at the Hamersley; unfortunately, it blew up during trials on the Potomac in 1844, pulverizing two cabinet secretaries and nearly killing President Tyler.

Few of the villagers were notable enough to leave any trace today. We do know from memoirs that Anna Park and Annie Cargill were considered the village belles, and that Murphy, the village blacksmith, had his shop at what is now the southwest corner of Amsterdam and 69th. One of Murphy's boys, Ned, stirred up "quite a touse" when he experimented on the church weathervane with his new rifle. Another son, Joe, had a successful stage career and was the composer of "A Handful of Earth from My Dear Mother's Grave," a hit song of the post–Civil War era.

Near what would become 68th and Tenth Avenue also lived a person known to us only as "queer old Granny H— —," who ran a private school for very small children, hated boys, and loved cats. It was Granny's delight to appear unannounced in a neighbor's kitchen and chirp, "I have come to see you. I want to make some pies." As the dish in her hand was invariably empty, her hostess would ask good-naturedly, "What are you going to make them with, Granny?" "Oh," Granny would say, "I thought you would give me a little flour and some apples." These were never refused, the old lady would make her pies, and, after a little chat, be on her way.

Early in the century, Harsenville enjoyed a French invasion of sorts— a sudden influx of aristocratic fugitives waiting out the restoration of the monarchy. A Mme. d'Auliffe, onetime *dame d'honneur* to Marie Antoinette, was an early arrival. She held court in a pretty house west of the Road at 72nd Street, where her guests included Talleyrand and Jean Victor Moreau, formerly one of Napoleon's most honored generals but now en route to exile in Trenton, New Jersey. Supposedly the young Duc d'Orleans, later to reign as France's "Citizen King" Louis Philippe, also stayed awhile in Harsenville, where (local tradition said) he taught school in the old

Somerindyck house beside the Road at what is now the middle of Broadway just above West 75th Street. The house stood, with royal classroom preserved intact, until the Road was widened in 1868.

This influx of continental blue bloods lent the village a social gloss that was warmly remembered decades later, but it's easy to believe that something about the place would have made the Frenchmen feel at home, too. Pictures of the French village of Honfleur, near Versailles, a favored haunt of Monet and Renoir some decades later, show a place that could be the image of Harsenville, right down to the square belfry on the village church.

The bluest blood in Bloomingdale flowed in the veins of the Livingstons—ancient enemies of the De Lanceys—and the most prominent of Bloomingdale Livingstons (as well as the most belligerent) was the lawyer Henry Brockholst Livingston, whose country seat, Oak Villa, was one of the most stately portions of what had been the De Lancey estate, on a broad bluff east of today's Riverside Drive at 91st Street. ("I miss the thousand delights of Bloomingdale," he wrote to his wife, Catharine, while on official business in upstate Geneva in 1806.)

In the Revolution, Brockholst, the oldest son of Governor William Livingston of New Jersey, had been a colonel (serving with Benedict Arnold at Saratoga) and later an envoy to the court of Spain, where he instantly antagonized the Spanish nobility. Back in New York, he mixed it up enthusiastically in the violent politics of the 1790s. A rabid anti-Federalist, Livingston was on hand during the 1795 riots against the unfortunate Jay treaty with Spain, in which his cousin John Jay was burned in effigy and Alexander Hamilton wounded (in person) by a stone.

He was also the target of an assassination attempt and fought several duels, a practice still tolerated though not encouraged. His final effort in that line involved one James Jones, who had been the victim of Livingston's caustic pen: "Mr. Jones was so much hurt [said an acquaintance], that irritating words passed, Livingston told him he might take satisfaction when & how he pleas'd, on which Jones caught him by the nose & struck him. To day a challenge was given by Livingston, accepted by Jones, they crossed to Hobuck in New Jersey, Livingston's shot took effect, & Jones is dead." "Hobuck," or Hoboken, had long been the favored venue for such contests.

Livingston's nose ("a regular Roman triumph") was noted by his contemporaries, as was his "explosive temprement and rambunctious sense of humor." But he was also a brilliant, persuasive lawyer, an accomplished classical scholar, and, when he wanted to be, a genial and witty companion. He had the honor of delivering the first Independence Day oration under the Constitution at St. Paul's Chapel in 1789 to an assembly that included George Washington and the members of Congress. He also was a lawyer for the defense in New York's first sensational murder trial. On January 2,

1800, the body of Juliana Sands had been found in the city well. Levi Weeks, her supposed lover (some said fiancé), was charged with her murder and acquitted after a trial in which seventy-five witnesses were heard and the jury was out only five minutes. The verdict may have been a tribute less to Weeks's innocence than to the eloquence of his attorneys; Livingston's cocounsels were Aaron Burr and Alexander Hamilton, who would have their own fatal meeting across the Hudson just three years later.

When his party finally came to power, Livingston was named to the New York State Supreme Court and later to the United States Supreme Court. One of his first actions on the bench was to issue a restraining order—against dueling.

The elevated area of Bloomingdale that included Oak Villa was generally called Striker's Bay, and was the heart of the wealthy suburb. It reached roughly from merchant John McVickar's sixty-acre estate at modern 86th Street, with its winding drive and large Palladian house, to St. Michael's Episcopal Church, Bloomingdale's second church (1807), which stood above a pretty stream at 99th and Amsterdam Avenue.

Just above McVickar's, a deep ravine fell away sharply to the river at about the present line of West 87th Street. Leopold Eidlitz, America's first major Jewish architect and a leader of the Gothic Revival movement, erected a handsome chalet there in 1850, possibly on the charred foundations of the old De Lancey home; the deeply wooded setting must have seemed much like his native Bavaria. (Eidlitz's credits include the State Capitol at Albany and St. George's Church on Stuyvesant Square, as well as the original portion of West Park Presbyterian Church, still standing on West 86th Street; Cyrus L. W. Eidlitz, his son, was the architect of the New York Times Tower and the New York Bar Association Building on West 43rd–44th streets.)

The old Apthorpe home at 91st Street had by now descended to Colonel Herman Jauncey Thorne, who maintained it as his country seat, coming and going in an expensive coach and four until his death in 1859. Thorne spent many years in Paris living in princely style, which astonished the Parisians. They could not figure out how an American had acquired such refined tastes.

In the summers Dr. Valentine Mott, who had a large colonnaded house west of the Road at today's 93rd Street, could be seen in polished white top boots and a low-crowned, broad-brimmed hat, driving daily to the Columbia Medical School far downtown on Park Place. A Quaker, he was a cousin of James and Lucretia Mott, the great Philadelphia abolitionists, and an internationally famous surgeon. (Touring Europe once, he had been hastily summoned to operate on the sultan of Turkey.) Mott was a master of the bold, rapid technique needed before the era of anesthetics, and was said to have performed "more of the *great* operations than any man living,

or that ever did live." He was also ambidextrous, which probably helped.

North of Striker's Bay another dozen or so fine houses lined the bluff above the river. At what is now 100th Street stood William P. Furniss's mansion, with its oval dining room and Corinthian columns. Furniss was a lawyer and a poet as well, and published at his own expense a collection of odes to the beauties of Bloomingdale, *Tetra-Chordon*. A hundred-fifty yards on, Humphrey Jones's farmhouse had become the Abbey Hotel and now boasted a rather grand entrance via Cherry Lane, a tree-bordered, raised causeway supported by stone walls. Nicholas Jones's farmhouse, where Colonel Knowlton and the Hessians had traded musket fire, was now the gracious suburban home of William and Sarah Heyward, who called it Woodlawn. And Willow Bank, at present-day 118th Street, was the orchard-strewn riverfront estate of Caspar Meier, sometime consul to Bremen and head of what would become North German Lloyd, the world's largest steamship company.

Another hundred rods up the shore you came to Claremont, beyond doubt the favorite "resort" of Mrs. Lamb's "distinguished strangers," and the one with the longest history. A large, graceful wooden edifice similar to the slightly later structure now known as Gracie Mansion, it stood as recently as 1953 just north of Grant's Tomb on the high knoll once known as Strawberry Hill.

This region was hallowed by still-green patriotic traditions—in fact, Washington, as president, once led a party that included Vice President Adams and secretaries Jefferson and Hamilton up the Road to revisit the military landmarks of upper Manhattan—and during the War of 1812 a line of defenses was thrown up from river to river above the high land above Harlem Plain; a small stone fortress from that period survives in Central Park today, and another stood near 123rd Street and Amsterdam Avenue until the late 1960s. At the same time, a strong gate was built across the Road at the top of Morningside Heights, which remained in position until 1824. By one account, Strawberry Hill, with its magnificent views up and down the Hudson, had been "one of the sites suggested by Washington for the capital of the nation." Instead, an English linen merchant, George Pollock, built his family home there in the early 1790s.

In short order, Pollock, like many another mansion-builder, went broke and had to sell out. But he left behind one of the city's most affecting landmarks. His four-year-old boy, St. Clair, had died on July 15, 1797, possibly on a fishing trip nearby, and was buried in what was intended as the family graveyard. A few years later Pollock wrote to his former neighbor, Cornelia Verplanck: "There is a small inclosure near your boundary fence within which lie the remains of a favorite child covered by a marble monument. . . . You will confer a peculiar and interesting favor upon me by allowing me to convey the enclosure to you, so that you will consider

it as a part of your own estate, keeping it, however, always inclosed and sacred." You can still find the "small inclosure" and St. Clair Pollock's grave, with its monument "To the Memory of an Amiable Child," a few steps from Grant's Tomb in Riverside Park.

The name Claremont was bestowed on Pollock's house by a subsequent owner, the Irish sea captain Michael Hogan, who named it for the Roehampton castle of his long-time friend William, duke of Clarence, the future "Sailor King," William IV of England. Hogan came to New York in 1804 with two trophies from the Orient: his wife, described as "a dark Indian princess," and her dowry of forty thousand pounds in gold. A plaque in Greenwich Village's Grace Church describes Hogan as "a bold and successful navigator and discoverer, in seas then almost unknown," and his house was decked out royally with imported furniture and the largest plate-glass mirrors yet seen in the city.

After Hogan came other eminent occupants: in 1809 Lord Courtenay, earl of Devon, who lived eccentrically with but one manservant and a cook, and who watched from the veranda as his old friend Robert Fulton captained the world's first successful steamboat up the Hudson; in 1811 Joseph Alston, a future governor of South Carolina, and his wife Theodosia, Aaron Burr's beautiful, beloved daughter, who died at sea in 1813; in 1815 Joseph Bonaparte, brother of Napoleon and former king of Spain. The Joel Post family acquired the place in 1829 (George B. Post, architect of the New York Stock Exchange, spent his early boyhood there) and later still the house became a famous inn and outing spot—but that will keep till a later chapter.

There were humbler settlements as well. In the valley below Claremont, the Hollow Way that had figured so largely in the Battle of Harlem Heights, was the village of Manhattanville, described simply as "a hamlet of about fifteen houses, the centre of a somewhat larger population, chiefly of poor people" and centered around the huge Tiemann paint factories at present-day 126th to 127th streets. The little brick church of St. Mary's, together with its two-story, wooden 1840s rectory and the graves of the Tiemann family, still survive on 126th Street.

Another small settlement was found in Clendenning (or Clendening) Valley (now sometimes called Manhattan Valley), around the equivalent of today's 96th to 101st streets west of Central Park. There, though, the old homes, like that built by John Clendening before the War of 1812, were overshadowed by the great hulk of the Croton Aqueduct. This was the engineering marvel of the age. Since Colonial days, New York had complained of an inadequate water supply. A cholera outbreak in 1832 and the Great Fire of 1835 drove the point home, and a modern water system was finally started in 1837 and completed five years later. It ranked as the city's grandest public works project ever: the Croton River in Westchester was

dammed to form a huge reservoir; forty-plus miles of aqueduct and water mains led through the Bronx and over High Bridge (then the longest in the world) to Manhattan, thence down the western side of the island to a rectangular, thirty-one-acre receiving reservoir located at what is now the Great Lawn in Central Park (a second, one hundred-five-acre reservoir, still in use, was added in 1860); from there, underground pipes led to a distributing reservoir at 42nd Street and Fifth Avenue, the future site of the New York Public Library.

Bloomingdale's portion of the works was imposing enough: a masonry aqueduct thirty feet wide at the top, with massive, outward-sloping walls. It began at the 110th Street gatehouse (which marked the downtown end of a twelve-hundred-foot water tunnel) and ran parallel to and a hundred feet west of the future Ninth (Columbus) Avenue, then curved east at 89th Street, and entered the future park at 85th. Between 101st and 96th streets, where the ground fell away fairly sharply, the section known as Clendening Bridge stood as high as fifty feet aboveground to maintain a uniform fall of thirteen inches to the mile. There were thirty-foot-wide arches for traffic at 98th, 99th, and 100th streets, each flanked by two smaller openings for foot traffic. (Passages had been planned for every street, but the thrifty water commissioners decided to eliminate those at 96th, 97th, and 101st, and if they'd thought about it earlier they would have omitted them all. Bloomingdale's streets existed only on paper, they reasoned, and probably wouldn't be opened "for a century or two to come.")

Next to the reservoir was a more obscure community—all but invisible, in fact: Seneca Village. Another one of those strictly local appellations, this name turns up tantalizingly in a handful of old maps and documents as the name of a down-at-heels, multiracial settlement that survived in some form or other until the land it stood on was condemned to become part of Central Park in the 1850s.

That land originally belonged to the Stillwell family, long active in Methodist church affairs. (General "Vinegar Joe" Stillwell of Burma Road fame was a twentieth-century descendant.) In 1825, according to city records, several parcels of the Stillwells' land were sold to several men from downtown: Epiphany Davis, a "black laborer" (the city directories of that era obligingly listed race as well as occupation), John Carter, a "colored grocer," their neighbor Andrew Williams, a bootblack, and the Trustees of the Corporation of the African Methodist Episcopal Church. Similar purchases were made nearby in following years, and by the late 1840s short stretches of what had been designated as West 83rd, 84th, 85th, and 86th streets had been cut through as narrow lanes east of Eighth Avenue.

The terrain was—still is—among the steepest and rockiest on the West Side. Even so, the streets ran east for a full city block from Eighth Avenue to the reservoir, and were lined with over seventy houses and outbuildings, among them two small churches and a schoolhouse. One of the churches,

labeled on various maps as Zion Church and Free African Church, was perched at an angle above 85th Street and was possibly the small brick church built in 1843 and identified as Little Zion in Jonathan Greenleaf's 1850 *History of the Churches of New York.*

No record seems to have survived of the village in its happier days. Reverend Thomas McClure Peters of St. Michael's Church brought his ministry there in the 1840s or 1850s, and found the people a diverse and unsavory lot: "White and black and Indian, American, German, and Irish; the believers and practitioners in monogamy and those who troubled themselves about no *gamy* at all; gentle folk deteriorated and rough lovers of a free and easy life; saints the most exalted and sinners the most abandoned, lived and multiplied and died." The houses, he said, "were built largely of old boxes, thrown out as rubbish, and timbers salvaged from the river, on which were nailed tin cans beaten out flat. The settlement was intersected by a labyrinth of lanes into which it was dangerous for a stranger to venture alone, not so much on account of the people as on account of the dogs." These roved in packs, feasting on decomposing pigs and occasionally bringing down a spavined horse that had been turned out on the commons to die.

Conditions had not improved in 1856, when the land was surveyed for the new park. "A suburb more filthy, squalid and disgusting can hardly be imagined [said the Central Park Commissioners]. A considerable number of its inhabitants were engaged in occupations which are nuisances in the eye of the law, and forbidden to be carried on so near the city. They were accordingly followed at night in wretched hovels, half hidden among rocks, where also heaps of cinders, brick-bats, potsherds, and other rubbish, were deposited by those who had occasion to remove them from the city."

The only problem with all this is that the city assessors' maps, prepared at the same time, depicted many of the structures in Seneca Village as substantial two- and three-story dwellings, including one with a fifty-foot piazza on three sides. It would be interesting to know more. New York had slavery until 1830, but there had long been colonies of free blacks here and there, in Yorkville and on the Lower East Side. Was this another—and if so, how and when did it become a "filthy, squalid and disgusting" shantytown? For that matter, how degenerate was it, really? Did it get bad press because a multiracial neighborhood was offensive to pre-Civil War sensibilities—and/or because the land was needed for the new park? There is still in Central Park a small stone foundation, just about where the maps show the Zion Church to have stood. Perhaps some future Ph.D. candidate will dig deep enough (in the earth or in the archives) to tell us more.

Bloomingdale was known for its eleemosynary institutions—orphanages, asylums, houses of refuge that naturally gravitated to where land was cheap. In the 1850s, Mrs. William Richmond, wife of the rector of St. Michael's

Church, made over the McVickar mansion, overlooking the Hudson near 86th Street, into the House of Mercy, a Protestant Episcopal home for "abandoned women who found no hand outstretched to help them." The New York Orphan Asylum, in Harsenville, was a Presbyterian institution, the first of its type in the city, founded in 1806 by a group of prominent ladies and directed by Eliza Hamilton, Alexander's widow. A large, not-too-grim brownstone-fronted building, it stood far back from the Road behind a low stone wall, above modern 73rd Street. A broad carriageway, shaded by horse chestnuts, led through the grounds, which, until the railroad came, ran down to the shore. There was a bathhouse by the water, and in the early summer evenings the neighborhood children were allowed to use it freely.

Bloomingdale's other big orphanage came into existence by a fluke. John G. Leake, a lawyer, had left a substantial fortune to Robert Watts, son of an old friend. But he insisted that either Watts change his name to Leake, or the money would go to found an orphanage in Leake's name. Watts died before he could comply, so fifty acres of land were purchased on a high, commanding site above 110th Street, and in 1843 the trustees of the Leake & Watts Orphan Asylum (they tactfully split the honors) erected a large Greek Revival building on wooded grounds at 113th Street, with two high, square pavilions flanking a broad central wing, which sheltered some two hundred boys and girls, ages three to twelve. From the 1860s on, they attended St. Michael's Church at Amsterdam and 99th Street, the girls in green checked gingham, the boys in blue smocks. The rector there organized some of them into New York's first boys' choir, and two of the boys ended up as Episcopal ministers, one becoming a missionary to Alaska and the other the next superintendant of the orphanage. In the 1890s, the largest Gothic church in the world, the still-unfinished Cathedral of St. John the Divine, began to rise on the imposing site (the orphanage having relocated to White Plains), but one wing of the Leake & Watts building still survives. Used for a time as a cathedral gift shop, it is by far the oldest building on the Upper West Side and one of the city's best examples of Greek Revival architecture—which unfortunately may have to be destroyed to make way for the cathedral's soon-to-be-built south transept.

Slightly northwest of Leake & Watts was Bloomingdale's best-known charitable institution, the Bloomingdale Lunatic Asylum. In nineteenth-century New York, you didn't call your neighbor crazy when his eccentricities got out of hand; you said he was "ready for Bloomingdale." Originally a branch of New York Hospital, the asylum moved uptown in 1818 to a group of imposing stone and brick buildings on eighty acres—now occupied by Columbia University—with a farm and gardens, and broad lawns with winding avenues; patients of all classes were admitted, with accommodations available for servants.

New Yorkers and tourists greatly enjoyed an outing to the asylum and

its grounds (nineteenth-century cemeteries like Woodlawn often served the same purpose). Of Bloomingdale, one guidebook noted, "It occupies a most beautiful and commanding site, and its approach and surroundings are admirably fitted to lighten the sense of depression and gloom which we instinctively associate with every establishment of the kind." The central building, it added, "is always open to visitors, and the view from the top of it, being the most extensive and beautiful of any in the vicinity of the city, is well worthy of attention."

The resident physician, Dr. Macdonald, had introduced the latest "moral and mental treatments" from Europe, and conditions seem to have been remarkably humane—at first, anyway. In the 1830s the artist-play-wright-historian William Dunlap noted his impressions: "The widow of Brockholst Livingston was here, a little old woman who I remember a beauty, full of health, tall & proud of deportment. A strange and melancholy scene, though most of the inmates appear happy." On another visit, he said, "a tall young man with great glee invited everyone to toss coppers 'head or tail' with him. I was told that he became insane in electioneering, with its attendant drinking & would soon be well." Delia Bacon, the writer who first ascribed Shakespeare's plays to Francis Bacon, was a guest for awhile, and some years later Cornelius Vanderbilt had his wife confined in Bloomingdale when her complaining annoyed him. It probably wasn't hard to get her committed: she objected to living on Fifth Avenue and pined for the Vanderbilt farm on Staten Island—obvious signs of dementia.

The brilliant actor Edmund Kean (watching Kean perform, Coleridge said, was "like reading Shakespeare by flashes of lightning") made quite an impression when he paid a visit in 1820. He'd been touring the States, and an admirer, Dr. John Wakefield Francis, had arranged for a drive out to Bloomingdale. Kean toured the buildings, attending closely to explanations of the patients' disorders and treatment, then climbed to the roof. After a few moments he suddenly announced dramatically, "I'll walk the ridge of the roof and take a leap. It's the best end I can make of my life!" and started for the gable; his hosts had to seize him by the arms to force him back. Afterwards, one suspects, the management kept an eye on visitors as well as inmates.

The social delights of Bloomingdale, extolled by Mrs. Lamb in our epigraph, came in public and private versions. A favorite New York excursion was a drive up the Bloomingdale Road. "The country on either side of it was so fresh and rural," one frequent visitor recalled, "the houses so charming, and the glimpses of the Hudson!—sometimes at the foot of a narrow lane, where the water was but a point of lightness closing the vista, sometimes a broad expanse showing a large and noble view of the grand river."

Sunday road driving became a popular sport, first among marketmen and small tradesmen (butchers, especially, prided themselves upon their

fast-stepping trotters hitched to carts). Driving became a gentleman's recreation when Robert Bonner, publisher of the New York *Ledger*, took it up for his health. "And," said another chronicler, "when snow covered the landscape . . . high carnival reigned on the Road, and Burnham's, Striker's Bay, and the Abbey were thronged with gay crowds. An old resident informs us that during the winter of 1847, his family, while sitting on their piazza, had counted eleven hundred and sixty sleighs which passed along the Road in one hour."

In other words, traffic was about what you'd expect today. So were the accommodations. The poet Fitz-Greene Halleck, whose statue now adorns the Mall in Central Park, might have been in one of those carriages. He enjoyed sleighing parties to Bloomingdale and Manhattanville, he reported, even though "the public houses on those roads are so thronged, that a person can hardly elbow one's way into the house."

"Pop" Griffin's place in Harsenville was the oldest in the region, built sometime in the 1790s. One Thomas Palmer took it over in 1797 and operated it as the Old Bloomingdale Inn and Tea Garden. He invited the public for "breakfasting and tea parties," offering wine, ale, punch, "syllabubs," and jelly and fruit from his orchards. A later proprietor, Daniel Mayer, kept a carriage to run guests to and from town (at five shillings a head) and another pre-Griffin owner, Thomas Rogers, advertised in the *Evening Post* that his liquors and accommodations "are such as to give general satisfaction to those gentlemen who may favor him with their company." An added note—"N.B. No ladies admitted without a gentleman"—attested to the high moral tone of the place.

The areas now roughly bounded by 64th to 66th streets, and 79th to 85th, and up around 96th, were famous for woodcock and snipe shooting. About 1831 a Mr. Foley rented an open place between the Road and Ninth Avenue at about 80th Street and furnished pigeons for trapshooting. Soon after, a Mr. Batterson, proprietor of a hotel that had been an old country seat, did the same at 88th and the river.

A favored destination, also with its own pigeon ground, was Burnham's Mansion House in Harsenville, just west of the Road below today's 79th Street. Built at the turn of the nineteenth century as the home of John Cornelius and Charlotte Apthorpe van den Heuvel, it had a gable roof and four great columns of white cedar, cut on the estate. Inside, a twenty-foot-wide marble-floored hall opened into rooms with tiled fireplaces and window seats with small, square Dutch-style window lights. From the rear porch there was a glorious view of the Hudson, and a path led through an old-fashioned garden with boxwood borders to a charming little summer-house perched on the bank, just overhanging the river. (At the turn of the *next* century the van den Heuvels' grandson, William Waldorf Astor, would tear the building down and put up the Apthorp Apartments in its place.)

Some of the roadhouses on the outskirts of the city were "notorious

for their evil character," but the Burnhams (who had also run "Pop" Griffin's for a while) kept a genteel or "family type" establishment. One memoirist of the 1880s reminded his readers of "the many gambols they enjoyed in childhood on Burnham's lawn," and of "the kind old host and his motherly wife," who were always at the door to greet their guests with a smile of welcome. Another whose childhood had been spent nearby remembered the pump near the house, where the lemonade pitchers were replenished and the squeezed-out fruit discarded—and sometimes, if the kids were quick enough, attacked greedily by passing schoolchildren. "We fear the lemons sometimes contained something stronger than lemon-juice," one of them recalled happily, "but the temperance people were not so strong in the middle of the last century."

The other great outing place on the Road was Striker's Bay Tavern at 97th Street, formerly the Striker farmhouse, but since converted to a "secluded little snuggery" at the foot of a steep lane, with a dock and, in later days, a small station of the Hudson River Railroad. The lawn by the river made a fine dance floor, and behind the house there were targets for shooting parties.

In 1841 the landlord was the inventor Joseph Francis, who took advantage of the waterside location to perfect his designs for a new type of metal lifeboat that would later save thousands of lives. Guests sometimes tended toward the literary. Edgar Allan Poe, who spent the summers of 1843 and 1844 in Bloomingdale, was a frequent visitor. Likewise Halleck, Samuel Woodworth (author of "The Old Oaken Bucket"), Thomas Dunn English ("Ben Bolt"), William Ross Wallace ("The hand that rocks the cradle / Is the hand that rules the world"), and George Pope Morris, whose most memorable work begins,

> Woodman, spare that tree.
> Touch not a single bough!
> In youth it sheltered me,
> And I'll protect it now.

This sentimental ditty, set to music by Henry Russell, became a universal hit, sung in every modern language and reportedly even in Greek and Latin—and it came straight out of a visit to Striker's Bay. In 1837, Morris said, he and a companion came upon a tenant of the property about to cut down a "grand old elm" for firewood. They asked what the felled tree would be worth to him and paid ten dollars for his promise, in writing, not to molest the tree further; it was still standing, Morris said, in 1862.

In short, Bloomingdale was famed for its beauty and conviviality. Even the acerbic Mrs. Trollope, whose *Domestic Manners of the Americans* (1832) seemed mainly an attempt to prove they had none, fairly gushed after a visit with the Heywards at Woodlawn: "To describe all its diversity of hill

and dale, of wood and lawn, of rock and river, would be in vain; nor can I convey an idea of it by comparison, for I never saw anything like it. How far the elegant hospitality which reigns there may influence my impressions, I know not; but, assuredly, no spot I have ever seen dwells more freshly in my memory, nor did I ever find myself in a circle more calculated to give delight in meeting and regret at parting, than that of Woodlawn."

But nothing lasts forever, especially in New York. "Up to 1853," said an old resident, "no more charming spot than Bloomingdale could be found. Then suddenly there came a change. Squatters came, and from 59th to 68th Street, west of the Road, there were miniature farms." Soon, it seemed, some "foreigner" was building a jury-rigged shack on every outcrop, and goats, pigs, poultry, and unwashed children were running loose everywhere.

What was happening? A population explosion, for one thing; the city that had numbered thirty-three thousand or so in 1790 had grown to over half a million by 1850, most confined to airless, pestilential tenement buildings. Many squatters were simply honest working poor, too independent or fastidious for tenement life. When some five thousand of these were ejected in the 1850s to make way for Central Park, many just shifted west a few blocks, with the result that several thousand unwelcome newcomers suddenly appeared in Bloomingdale's hitherto bucolic landscape.

Despite their alarming appearance and unconventional housing, many of them actually held respectable jobs. Others worked at honest, if humble, trades, collecting rags and cinders, picking up bones to boil for hog feed. All too many, of course, were exactly the ruffians and thieves the old-time villagers took them for.

Most of the old families—the Meiers, Le Roys, Posts, McVickars—"took up their luggage and crossed over the river," as William Furniss put it. Furniss and a few others stuck it out; until his death in 1872, he and his family closed their city home in Bond Street to spend every May to November in their country house at 100th Street—though, he complained, "it is somewhat hard for the rest of us to stay here and shiver." At Claremont, the Post family watched as "the growth of the city pushed ahead of it a moraine of rowdyism and lawlessness, which settled in what had become a sort of no-man's-land, between the city police and rural tranquility." The city police in this instance was no more than Captain Thompson and his five-man constabulary, in their rented quarters in Harsenville. No wonder, as one of the Post family put it, "there was no protection against vandalism of every kind": "Fruit, flowers and vegetables were stolen, with impunity. At one time, in the early '50s, [Post's] dogs were shot before his eyes on the lawn. Claremont was thereafter rented as a roadhouse, and the beauty of the place much injured by the cutting of trees, the erection of sheds, bowling alleys, etc. Shortly before 1873 a large portion of the property on the river side was taken by the city, and the work of devastation completed

by squatters, timber thieves, etc."

So much for sparing trees. New York City was growing, in its usual chaotic, headlong fashion. "Day by day," complained one who had known the Road in greener days, "the shanties and cheap villas crowded in along its sides." Mr. Post thought of it as a glacial movement; "flood" might have been more like it—enough, either way, to wipe a quiet, old-fashioned village off the map.

Soon the time-blackened milestone at 73rd Street, with its inscription "Five Miles from New York," would be a meaningless relic. The villages of the Upper West Side, or what was left of them, would falter through the years of the Civil War (when troops were drilled on the lunatic asylum grounds) and languish though the seventies, finally to be swallowed, with barely a hiccup, by the growing metropolis.

INTERLUDE

"IT IS A BURNING SHAME!"

*Every street should be sewered
and paved with solid stone block
pavement under one contract; so
that when buildings are erected,
their value will not be impaired
by the malaria which arises from
unfinished streets and the
upturning of soil.*

—John McClave, *Engineer's Report
to the West End Association in the
City of New York,* 1871

On a gloomy November afternoon in 1878, the members of the West Side Association assembled in the handsome new building of the American Museum of Natural History on West 77th Street for one of their most important meetings since the group was formed nearly fifteen years before. The Honorable Fernando Wood called them to order. More than once the former mayor had proclaimed his faith that the West Side would soon be "the most healthy, the most enchanting and the most desirable section of this emporium," and the property owners, investors, and real estate operators in the room shared his great expectations. At least, they had back in 1864, when the group was organized to "protect and advance" their interests. What they wanted was quick action that would open up the West Side to development. What they got was an endless Victorian melodrama, replete with heroes and villains.

By the early 1870s, they were expecting development to start any day. Like hopeful parents, they even chose place names for their new district. The avenue along Central Park would be known simply as Westbourne. Other street names would be poetic or historic: Sunset Terrace, Livingstone Terrace, Knickerbocker Avenue, and Claremont Avenue (one of the few

that actually stuck). Clendenning Avenue would honor a family of eigh-teenth-century farmers; Knowlton Place, the hero of Harlem Heights. Some marketing genius even had the happy thought of calling the whole area "the West End," a name with overtones of London gentility.

At first, land prices were equally fancy. Four inaccessible lots at the (future) intersection of 81st and Riverside Drive went for $75,000, an undeveloped half-block at 66th and the Boulevard for $110,000. Then the Panic of 1873 hit, and for the next five years almost every effort to develop the Upper West Side was stymied, while inferior East Side and Harlem properties were built up by the mile with brownstone houses.

What was holding up the West Side? There were hardly any streets, for one thing, although the area, like the rest of Manhattan, had been officially laid out in 200-by-600-foot blocks nearly seventy years before. (Some blocks on the West Side, such as Ninth to Tenth avenues, were actually considerably longer—over 900 feet.) Admittedly, the West Side was a road builder's nightmare, with deep glaciated furrows running north to south between massive, sharply tilted ledges of tough schist. To make a properly graded street, outcrops of thirty or more feet had to be blasted and vast amounts of fill trucked in to build up the hollows. But according to John McClave, an engineer who prepared a report for the association, the few streets that had been built were nothing to be proud of. Eighth Avenue, for instance, was being graded and rebuilt for the third time, and West 79th, the main cross street to the Hudson River wharves, was "ruinous": at the shore it was so steep that a builder would pay an extra 15 percent for materials that were landed there, and between Ninth and Tenth avenues, where there should have been a gentle nine-and-a-half-foot slope, the builder had actually left a twenty-one-foot hill in the middle of the block. (It's still there, by the way.)

Where nature didn't block the way with stone, she used water. Just a few yards from the museum, a two-acre pond sprawled over what is now 79th Street and Central Park West; others nearly as large were found at 64th Street and Tenth (Amsterdam) Avenue, 84th near Riverside Park, and along the Boulevard at 72nd and 83rd streets—the latter still used for skating in the 1890s. A major east-flowing stream rose at 79th Street and Ninth Avenue and another, called Arch Brook, at 87th and Tenth; numerous rills emptied into the Hudson at Striker's Bay and at 67th, 69th, 81st, and 115th streets. They may have been picturesque, but all—especially Arch Brook, which spread out in wet weather into a half-mile-wide swamp—were first-rate breeding grounds for cholera, malaria, and the occasional outbreak of yellow fever.

Most members of the West Side Association would readily have told you that the real villain of the piece had been "Boss" William Marcy Tweed and his notorious Ring, who, until Tweed's arrest in 1871, had operated City Hall like a closely held (and vastly profitable) company. As reports to

the strongly Republican West Side Association had demonstrated, the city couldn't even acquire land for a new street unless the Democratic bosses of the Ring got their cut: for property along West 65th Street, valued at no more than twenty-three dollars, the city had paid out $5,267.14 in clerical and related expenses. Similar "expenses" for opening West 77th Street were $6,827.76; for 124th Street, $15,428.21; and so on.

Herman H. Cammann, chairman of the building committee, talked about the "squatter nuisance," which he called "the direct cause of the slow building up of the West Side," and which he also blamed on Tammany Hall. Shanty dwellers had arrived in huge numbers after the 1873 crash, many of them at first renting land from the legal owners. Some had even set up as landlords themselves, building whole rows of hovels and renting them out in turn. Now there were ten thousand of them, mostly Irish and German squatters (there was even a colony of Hollanders camped on an ash dump at 81st Street, with their own Dutch-speaking schoolhouse and chapel), and they seemed to think they owned the place. Cammann had evicted several hundred from his own property, he said, but it was notorious that they had backing from the Democratic political organization, and they weren't going without a fight. Around 79th Street especially, well-dressed strangers were apt to be roughly handled; one deputy marshal, serving papers around 81st Street, was seized, and a milk can, half full, was turned over his head like a hat.

With Tweed and his successors controlling the surface transit lines, transportation was another major problem. How could anyone (unless he kept a private carriage) get to and from a home on the Upper West Side when the only way there was the Eighth Avenue horsecar (for which you had to change cars at the little Half-Way House at 59th Street) or the old Bloomingdale Road stagecoach, whose drivers were coarse, abusive men notorious for passing off counterfeit coins? Finally, and most hopeless of all, fashion, that remorseless tyrant, had turned its face against the West Side; the "best people" had never lived there, and never would. So sewers were left unfinished, cross streets remained unopened or unfinished, and, as one of the would-be builders complained bitterly, "the Riverside Park and Morningside Park, which give value to the west side of town, are in a wild and desolate condition."

Of course it wasn't true that *nothing* had been done; it just felt that way. To begin with, an ambitious system of parks and drives had taken shape, on paper, at least, that would garland the whole Upper West Side with greenery. And of all of them, Central Park was the first and the greatest.

As early as 1844 William Cullen Bryant, the beloved poet and editor of the *Evening Post*, had warned that commerce was devouring Manhattan Island "inch by inch." "If we would rescue any part of it for health and recreation," he urged, "it must be done now." A lively parks movement

grew up, and starting in 1853 the city acquired some seventy-five hundred lots of mostly empty land between Fifth and Eighth avenues, 59th to 106th streets (subsequently extended to 110th); total price: $5,169,369.90. Fernando Wood, then mayor, named a group of eminent citizens, headed by Washington Irving, to provide aesthetic guidance. He also urged them to adopt a design by a young man he had taken under his wing, Lieutenant Egbert L. Viele, a West Point–trained engineer who would be one of the heroes of West End development, and who was making a name for himself with occasional talks at the Geographic Society.

But first there was a crisis. The common council, succumbing to the blandishments of well-connected landowners, had shamelessly rolled back the park's lower boundary, from 59th to 72nd Street. Mayor Wood, it must be admitted, was running an administration that was remarkably corrupt even by twentieth-century standards. (In 1857 the state legislature had gone so far as to abolish Mayor Wood's police force and appoint a new one reporting directly to the governor. Wood resisted, and the two rival police forces battled in front of City Hall until the Seventh Regiment surrounded the building and the mayor himself finally submitted to arrest.) But on the park issue he turned out to be incorruptible. His veto saved for New York the two-hundred-odd acres that now include the Swan Lake, the Sheep Meadow, the Mall, the zoo, and Wollman Rink. "Mr. Wood's public record is in every way so unhandsome," said a contemporary, "that we are glad to be able to give him credit for at least one creditable act." Only a cynic would point out that the mayor's own extensive holdings, including a large mansion and grounds at West 77th Street, stood to benefit considerably from the action.

Construction got under way in 1856, with Lieutenant Viele as chief engineer. But to Viele's disgust, his design was dropped, largely at the instigation of an English-born architect, Calvert Vaux, who had been proclaiming the defects of the lieutenant's plan, as he said, "whenever I got the chance." A new plan was submitted, drawn up by Vaux and his partner Frederick Law Olmsted, who happened to be Viele's own second-in-command. (The Vaux-Olmsted Greensward plan is now acknowledged as a sort of Sistine Chapel of landscape design, but Viele always considered himself the park's real creator and eventually won a court judgment of $8,625 for the design he claimed Vaux and Olmsted had stolen.) In 1857, a depression year with plenty of unemployed labor handy, Olmsted was named architect-in-chief and placed at the head of a public works army of up to thirty-eight hundred men, removing rocks, draining swamps, grading, fertilizing, planting, and building.

Soon all New York was coming to the park. They came to mingle democratically—"poor and rich, young and old, Jew and Gentile," in Olmsted's words—to experience the civilizing benefits of nature in the arcadian Sheep Meadow (complete with shepherd and flock), the romantic,

densely planted thickets and winding paths of the Ramble, and the rugged hills and outcrops of the upper park. You went to Central Park for boating, pony or goat-cart rides, or just to stroll along the Mall, a stately quarter-mile esplanade lined with double rows of elms that led to the Terrace, the park's stately centerpiece, elaborately embellished with stone carvings designed by another Englishman, Jacob Wrey Mould. In winter there were sleighing parties and skating, and nighttime ice carnivals in the glare of brilliant calcium lights. In warm weather, the parade of equipages on the East Drive every afternoon from five o'clock to half past seven was one of New York's great sights: young ladies in victorias and phaetons, dowagers in stately barouches, the handsome coaches of the Four-in-Hand Club, and wealthy men in sulkies pulled by fast trotters—the fleetest and costliest animals in the country—on their way to settle a wager with a race along Harlem Lane. By 1867 the number of park visitors passed ten million.

At the end of the 1860s, work began on the West End's second great improvement: an ambitious program to widen and straighten the Bloomingdale Road, making it a grand European-style boulevard, suitable for palatial mansions.

The idea actually originated with Andrew Haswell Green, head of the Central Park Commission, but it soon became a pet project of Boss Tweed, who also owned large amounts of West Side land himself. A Grand Circle was laid out at the southwest corner of Central Park, where the Bloomingdale Road crossed Eighth Avenue at 59th Street, and from there the Grand or Western Boulevard ran north to Washington Heights: twin roadways, 160 feet wide overall, with two rows of elms along the curbs and two more lining the grassy, thirty-foot-wide central mall. Like all the Tweed Ring's public works projects, the Boulevard was, as a contemporary put it, "a gigantic steal." Every bill was outrageously padded; unsupervised "laborers," each representing one or more Democratic votes on election day, might spend hours working a single pebble back and forth a few feet. Many older families, impoverished by sky-high assessments for the improvements, lost their land to Tweed and his cronies. And then, the downfall of the Ring a few years later slowed the work considerably, so that it wasn't paved until the nineties. But even in its unpolished state—mud bath or dust bowl, as weather dictated—the Boulevard was a welcome sign of progress.

In the seventies, a lot of work was also done on what we would now call the West Side's "infrastructure," and here General Viele (he had been promoted to brigadier rank during the Civil War) was a prime mover. Early in his career, Viele had noticed that cholera and malaria seemed to be discouraged by well-drained camps and boiled drinking water; this led him to set up in the 1850s as one of the first sanitary engineers in the country (the first, he said) and to lobby for the Metropolitan Health Law of 1866, which established the city's first health department. Having moved in 1872

to a red brick villa overlooking the Hudson at 88th Street, he naturally took a keen interest in local sanitation. At his urging the sewer department set to work in 1874—another depression year—and with his colleague Stevenson Towle as chief engineer, *two* sewer systems were excavated and built beneath the main streets and avenues of the barely occupied district: a network of six-inch pipes just below street level to carry off household wastes, with deeper drains, as much as forty feet underground, to handle the natural runoff. A stone wall was set into every major streambed—uncemented, to permit free inflow—and covered with sturdy flagstone, and ditches loosely filled with broken stone were run out to drain swampy areas. By 1876, when there were hardly a dozen modern buildings planned, let alone built, the West End already boasted some three hundred thousand dollars' worth of sewers.

It also boasted at least the beginnings of its second scenic boulevard, the much-debated "Riverside-avenue." In 1865 William R. Martin, an early president of the West Side Association, had first suggested the idea. Instead of the ruler-straight Twelfth Avenue plotted on the official maps, why not build a combined drive and park: an ornamental drive that would wind along the West Side's rocky spine north from 72nd Street to a turnaround loop at Claremont, and commanding the grand sweep of the sail-dotted Hudson. As usual, it took years to get started, and then the first design, drawn up in the early seventies, was not only unaesthetic but unbuildable. Martin and Viele offered a revised plan, but the design finally adopted, in 1873, was by Olmsted. Viele's comment is not recorded.

Construction finally started, under direction of the parks department, in the spring of 1877, and the experience seems to have been remarkably unpleasant for all. Leopold Eidlitz, a highly respected architect-engineer who lived beside the new avenue, inspected the work and found it "carelessly and improperly done." Essential rock and landfill were missing, and the parapet was so high you could hardly see the river; apparently the contractors, the former canal builders Decker and Quintard, expected to be paid according to the amount of material used.

A more persuasive sign of progress was the museum where the November 26 meeting was being held. Its director, Albert S. Bickmore, had dreamed of founding an American Museum of Natural History when he was studying under the famed naturalist Louis Agassiz at Harvard; by 1867 his sheer persistence had enlisted such powerful backers as Alexander T. Stewart, owner of the world's largest retail store, copper magnates Isaac N. Phelps and A. G. Phelps Dodge, bankers Morris K. Jesup (a future museum president) and J. P. Morgan, Theodore Roosevelt, Sr. (father of the future president), and—most important—then-State Senator William M. Tweed. In 1877 the museum moved from temporary quarters in the Central Park Arsenal to its permanent home on West 77th Street. Designed by Calvert Vaux and Jacob Wrey Mould, the original building (now barely discernible

among later additions) was bright red brick with high arched windows, embellished with slender columns and varied stone trim, and topped with a gaily colored roof of red, white, and blue slate. Its dedication on December 22nd was the West Side's social event of the decade, with a band playing and President and Mrs. Rutherford B. Hayes in attendance.

But the neighborhood was still remote and desolate. After the dedication, Bickmore noted miserably, attendance at the museum dropped to almost nothing: "We could only wait and hope that the elevated train company would soon extend its lines north to 77th Street." And as the West Side Association members remarked pointedly and often, Manhattan Square, the sixteen acres of so-called park surrounding the museum, was a disgrace. The four blocks from 77th to 81st streets, Eighth to Ninth avenues, had been acquired by the city a full thirty years ago. Yet, as one speaker grumbled, "There is not a man in this assembly that could be hired to walk across it today in a straight line for a five dollar bill."

"This square ought to be the central point around which, and from which, should radiate some of the finest and most expensive private residences of the city," said another. This was Samuel B. Ruggles, who, many years earlier, had conceived and built Gramercy Park. "But look at it!" he continued. "It is a disgrace to the city. It is in some places forty feet below the grade, and well characterized as 'a pestilential hole of stagnant water.' And yet we've put this fine museum here, and invite strangers to come and see it. It is a burning shame that such a thing can be."

Still, the mood at the November meeting was optimistic. Even the "miasmatic frog pond" outside the windows was only a minor irritant. Mayor Ely, it was reported by a committee, had assured the association of his hearty concurrence in its efforts. Other committees were appointed: to get after the legislature to push improvements to Manhattan Square; to get on with the completion of "Riverside-avenue"; to thank the board of aldermen for moving ahead with the completion of Ninth Avenue; and to ask them to move forward with providing high-pressure water service. And Cyrus Clark of the Rapid Transit Committee had the best news of all: a contract had been let that very day for the extension of the elevated steam railroad up the West Side to the Harlem River, to be completed within another year.

By the time the meeting broke up, several owners were declaring that they would start construction immediately. Christian Blinn, who was just finishing off five houses on 71st Street and Ninth Avenue, said he had already let three of them to persons who had been trying for a long time to get back to the city from New Jersey, but could find no good houses within their means—until now. He contemplated more building, and did not doubt that if the whole district were suitably built up he would find immediate occupants.

4

"A HIGHER ORDER OF DOMESTIC ARCHITECTURE"

*With its Riverside Drive and Park,
Manhattan Square and
Morningside Park, and its wide
streets opening into Central Park,
"The West Side" offers in this
respect an attractiveness rarely
found within the limits of a great
city. Considered from every point
of view, "The West Side" bids fair
to excel in attractiveness,
convenience of location, and
elegance of surroundings, every
other residential part of the city.*

—Title Guarantee and Trust Co.,
"The West Side," 1895

Professor Bickmore's prayer was finally answered on the mild, late-spring morning of June 9, 1879, when the New York Elevated Railroad carried its first passengers up Ninth—later Columbus—Avenue.

The new line ran from 53rd Street (the end of the Sixth Avenue line, already in operation for several years) to the Harlem River at 145th. At 110th Street it swung over from Ninth to Eighth Avenue in a high S-curve that was called "one of the most audacious and skillful specimens of engineering to be found on the globe." The public called it Suicide Curve, and it so impressed one otherwise courageous visitor, the explorer Eugene Schuyler, that he begged to be returned to the city some other way rather than ride Suicide Curve twice.

The el was opulent. It had to be, to lure fashionable folk out to the hinterland. The steam locomotives (replaced by electric engines in the nineties) were painted pea green; the carriages were variants on the Pullman Palace Car, a dainty light green outside, with oak and mahogany woodwork, plate-glass windows with adjustable blinds, Morocco leather seats, and Axminster carpeting. Stations, designed by a popular landscape artist, Jaspar Cropsey, resembled little Alpine chateaux, with pavilion roofs and wrought-iron crestings and finials.

Viele, who had once called the elevated trains "unsafe and dangerous to life" (he happened to be involved in a competing underground scheme at the time), was exultant. "Steam transit has accomplished in a year," he declared in a lengthy article in the *Herald*, "what a decade would have failed to do without it. The admirable service on the elevated roads has shown with what comfort and facility a home in this vicinity can be reached." It proved, he said, that the West End plateau had "undoubtedly" been "held intact for the development of a higher order of domestic architecture than it has been the good fortune of New York hitherto to possess."

EGBERT L. VIELE

If there is a heaven for engineers, Egbert Viele is there, cursing his ill-deserved obscurity and his lifelong rival Frederick Law Olmsted.

Educated at West Point (class of 1847), Egbert Ludovicus Viele followed the twin careers of soldier and civil engineer. He served with Winfield Scott in the Texas Indian wars, and in the Civil War, as a brigadier general, he accompanied Lincoln to Norfolk after its fall and was the city's military governor for two years. But civic improvements were his passion. In New York from 1853 on, Viele threw himself into schemes for parks (including the original layouts for Central, Prospect, and Riverside parks), drainage and sanitation (he claimed to be the country's first sanitary engineer, and helped to create New

York's first board of health), mass transit (his 1872 Arcade Railway was a sort of primitive subway system), and, above all, the development of what he called "the West End Plateau" or "the Transvaal of New York." His 1865 *Hydrographic and Topographical Map of Manhattan* is still consulted by builders; he was a key backer of the Harlem River Ship Canal project, served in Congress and as parks commissioner, and was invited to address the English House of Lords in 1894 on "the science of municipal improvement."

He came of one of the oldest Knickerbocker families. "Knickerbocker" itself was a Viele family name, come to that; Washington Irving borrowed it from Viele's uncle Herman Knickerbacker and

used it to personify New York's old Dutch stock (whence the names of Father Knickerbocker, Cholly Knickerbocker, Knickerbocker Beer, and the New York Knicks). But history has relegated Viele to a footnote: Olmsted and Vaux bumped him from the Central Park project and, later, from Prospect and Riverside parks. (Olmsted declared himself "shocked" when Viele was named a park commissioner, protesting that "it has for twenty-five years been his principal public business to mutilate and damn the park.")

His private life was scarcely less turbulent. In the early '70s Viele divorced his first wife—the beautiful Theresa Griffin, described by her daughter as a "brilliant, dashing society woman, surrounded by a small admiring court whom she kept in peals of laughter by her wit"—to marry a younger woman. Theresa thereupon returned to the unguarded Viele house with several companions—including one mysteriously described in the press as "of prominent position in the army, well-known by name throughout the country"—and absconded with two

of their four children to Paris, where the eldest, Egbert, Jr., became a leading Symbolist poet as Francis Viele-Griffin. Another son, Herman Knickerbocker, followed his dad into engineering, then became a painter and novelist.

The general died at his Riverside Drive home in 1902, as workmen were putting the finishing touches on the Soldiers and Sailors Monument a block away. His tomb is one of the more striking features of West Point's Old Cadet Cemetery: a thirty-one-foot-high granite pyramid, with bronze doors flanked by pairs of ornate Egyptian columns and carved sphinxes and an inscription—in Etruscan!—proclaiming "EGBERT LUDOVICUS VIELE HIS BODY OCCUPIES THIS SEPULCHER WITH JULIET HIS WIFE AND BELOVED COMPANION." The general, terrified of being buried alive, also took the unusual precaution of installing an electric buzzer in his marble sarcophagus, in case he should revive. Connected to the cemetery caretaker's house, it was occasionally rung by prankish plebes. An "eternal" light illuminated the gold-leafed ceiling for forty years, but even that was blacked out during World War II.

By the end of the year builders were at work near the el stations at 59th, 72nd, 81st, 93rd, and 104th streets. Their first ventures, understandably, were tentative and conventional. The developers may have dreamed of a luxury district, "exclusively reserved for the very wealthy," but what they actually built was generally some version of the basic three- to five-story, high-stooped, single-family row house, with a handful of tenements or flats along Ninth and Tenth avenues. At the northeast corner of 82nd Street and Tenth Avenue, Herman Cammann put up a group of five four-story brick apartment houses with Bedford stone (marble) trim and named them the Bedford Apartments. They would have stores at street level and

fifteen apartments, one per floor, for "families of gentlemen of moderate incomes, such as book-keepers, confidential clerks and secretaries."

Boldest of the developers was Edward Clark, head of the giant Singer Sewing Machine Company, who invested nearly five million dollars in the area. He started with an almost full block of buildings on 73rd Street west of Central Park: a row of twenty-seven four-story private homes, with a small apartment building at the Ninth Avenue corner, overlooking the el. Designed by Clark's favorite young architect, Henry J. Hardenbergh (who later did the Plaza Hotel and the Art Students League building), they were, for elegance, the equal of anything in their class downtown, with chateau-esque fronts of red and buff brick and carved stone. They were for rent, not for sale. Clark, a financial genius who had virtually invented installment buying to promote his company's products, believed in holding on to a good thing; and though they didn't do well at first, rumor had it that Clark was not discouraged and would soon begin work on a "mammoth, magnif-icent hotel" nearby.

Other builders picked up the pace. The three Hudson River landings at 59th, 79th, and 125th streets were so crowded that vessels sometimes waited for days to unload timber, iron, brick, and stone. By mid-decade a cable car line was running up Tenth Avenue and another along the Boulevard; in September 1886 the building bureau reported no fewer than 778 buildings going up between 59th and 110th streets, and the *Times*, under the heading SETTLING THE WEST SIDE, reported that "about 20,000 men, carpenters, masons, plumbers, painters, and other artisans, are steadily employed, and in them about $20,000,000 is being invested." At this rate, "it will not be long before the west side of the city will present the same lines of fine streets and the same unbroken array of houses that are now seen on the east side below Harlem Bridge."

Until recently, failure to own one's own home had been a confession of shabby antecedents or disreputable habits. As one old-school East Sider had put it, "Gentlemen will never consent to live on mere shelves under a common roof!" But on the West End, well-to-do and perfectly respectable people were actually living in apartments—or French flats, as they were called. And in 1881 an imaginative builder, John C. Thompson, Jr., started work on a hotel, the Inca, at 62nd and the Boulevard, explaining that it would "supply a want that is catered to in Europe, but little attended to in this country—a hotel in which families may reside and have their meals served in their own private dining rooms, directly from the hotel kitchen."

Edward Clark's million-dollar family hotel on the park at 72nd Street was something along the same lines, but an order of magnitude grander. Four years in the building, the Dakota, as it was called, was a 200-by-200-foot edifice with a high, arched carriage entrance opening into a central courtyard, and a three-story mansard roof that could be seen from either river. Architect Henry Hardenbergh gave it a profusion of bay and octagonal

windows, niches, balconies, and balustrades, with elaborate terra-cotta spandrels and panels and heavy cornices decorating three sides (the fourth, west side was plain red brick); inside were apartments with columned rooms up to forty-nine feet long, fourteen-foot ceilings, floors of oak, cherry, hazelwood, and mahogany, public dining rooms with inlaid marble floors and hand-carved oak ceilings and paneling. The Dakota's baptism—associates intimated to Clark that he might just as well have built in Indian territory—may be the best-known anecdote in New York real estate lore. Clark could take a joke, and not only gave his building its ironic name but also decorated the wall high above the entrance with the terra-cotta portrait of an Indian chief.

Clark died suddenly in 1882, before he could see the Dakota finished, but his influence on the West Side had been profound. Following the Dakota's success (every apartment was rented by opening day) other apartment hotels sprang up nearby, especially on Central Park West: the eleven-story Majestic, facing the Dakota across West 72nd Street, the San Remo at 74th, the Beresford at 81st, and the Rutledge at 82nd. Two almost equally successful opened on Columbus Avenue: the Endicott at 81st-82nd (1889) and the Brockholst at 85th (1890). Clark's row of town houses on 73rd Street also set a pattern for hundreds of later West Side row houses, which attained a new level of style and workmanship.

Electric lighting had come to Eighth Avenue in 1884, and the part of the avenue above 59th Street was officially renamed Central Park West on April 22, 1890. Ninth and Tenth were baptized Columbus and Amsterdam, respectively, the same day. (Eleventh Avenue had already become West End on February 10, 1880.) By 1895 two *hundred* million dollars had been invested in buildings, a fact proclaimed by the *Times* in a long article that opened with a series of triumphal heads and subheads:

WEST SIDE IS ITSELF A GREAT CITY

QUARTER NORTH OF FIFTY-NINTH STREET WEST OF CENTRAL PARK A MODEL COMMUNITY

PURE AIR AND PERFECT SANITARY CONDITIONS

SURROUNDED BY PLEASURE GROUNDS, CROSSED BY FINE BOULEVARDS AND WIDE STREETS LINED WITH ARTISTIC BUILDINGS

ITS RESIDENTS LIVE LONG IN COMFORT AND HAPPINESS

And so on.

A well-defined social geography soon took shape, though not quite what the planners had foreseen. Riverside Drive was starting to get its grand mansions—though for many years it would continue to sport a distressing

number of decrepit wood houses and undeveloped lots, many of the latter crowned with the usual jerry-built shanties and livestock.

The other avenues and streets were also acquiring their permanent characters—permanent in the New York sense of lasting twenty or thirty years. Central Park West had a handful of first-class private homes, some fine churches, and its famous hotels and apartment houses. The Dakota itself remained one of the most distinctive addresses in town. The early tenants included the piano manufacturer Theodor Steinway and his friend the music publisher Gustave Schirmer, who liked to fill his salon with such brilliant guests as Mark Twain, William Dean Howells, Herman Melville, and Peter Ilyich Tchaikovsky, who came to town in 1891 to conduct the opening night concert at Carnegie Hall. (A charming and extremely unreliable anecdote has the bewildered Tchaikovsky mistaking the Dakota for his host's private home—and Central Park for its garden—and grumbling afterward, "No wonder we composers are so poor!")

Columbus Avenue was largely dedicated to providing the West End with life's necessities and comforts: coal, lumber, beer, meat, vegetables, bread, and flowers. Acker, Merrill & Condit, at 335 Columbus Avenue, was the state's oldest licensed package store, having purveyed liquor since 1820. Most shopkeepers toiled in obscurity, but one, Richard Hellmann, became a household word. In the years after 1905, when he opened his shop at 84th and Columbus, he sold his wife's mayonnaise from a blue-ribboned jar on the countertop. By 1912, Nina Hellmann's mayonnaise had become a neighborhood staple and today, of course, you can find it anywhere, still proudly wearing the blue ribbon on its label.

The avenue's buildings were tenements or at best middle-class apartments, but even these had pretentious facades. Their ornate moldings and bay windows usually started at the *second* floor, though, where they could be seen from the el, and their fancy arched entrances were placed judiciously around the corner, well away from the sparks and hot oil that showered down from passing trains. Many also bore elegant names, a favorite West End affectation: La Rochelle at 75th, by Lamb & Rich, with its two-story restaurant on the avenue, complete with a grand stairway, large potted palms, and a Japanese garden; the Aylesmere, with its porticoed fourth-story windows; and the Sylvia, both at 76th. All these survive today. So does the elegant building at the southwest corner of 72nd and Columbus designed by McKim, Mead & White for the Park & Tilford grocery chain (whose president lived around the corner on West 74th).

At 77th Street, the Museum of Natural History now had new architects, Cady, Berg & See, and was adding a massive, block-long front along 77th Street in full-blown Romanesque Revival style. The new design called for three more identical facades and a tremendous central tower, which would fill the square and make the museum the largest building on the continent. Another nearby survivor, the red brick Evelyn apartment house at the

northwest corner of Columbus and 78th, is a tangible reminder of the area's late-nineteenth-century ups and downs. The original 1883 design by Emile Gruwe was for a *seven*-story building, not the nine now there. Lack of funds stopped work on the building, and when construction resumed in 1885 the project had acquired two new architects (D. & J. Jardine) and two additional stories—which may explain why the eighth and ninth floors don't quite match the rest of the building. For reasons never made clear (but which may have involved the bosomy terra-cotta figures over the windows) the building was very popular with millionaires from the Colorado silver country.

Continuing up Columbus, you would leave the prosperous district behind somewhere above 96th Street, where the ground fell away to what was known as Manhattan or Clendenning Valley, with the spindly legs of the el high overhead and the venerable Lion Brewery and its adjacent picnic grounds and dance hall at 108th.

Amsterdam Avenue was destined for small shops and low-rent tenements except for the blocks around Sherman Square, where Christ Church and the Colonial Club were among the district's finest buildings. Here, as on parts of Columbus, you found the poorer classes—the cabmen, clerks, mechanics, and seamstresses—and the lumberyards, truckers, iron foundries, and other rude enterprises. Lacking wealthy residents, Amsterdam seemed an easy target for the new electric streetcar companies, which were in the midst of a franchise war at the time. At one point it looked as though the avenue would get *four* competing lines, but Reverend John Peters of St. Michael's Church, "a little fighting terrier of a man," launched a movement—inevitably tagged the Trolley War by the press—and fought them off.

West End Avenue also began with an unsavory district—breweries, silk works, stables, feed stores, saloons—that extended uptown to about 68th Street. West End had been intended as a street of shops and small businesses to serve the mansions of Riverside Drive and the Boulevard. Instead it became a residential street for prosperous families: the two miles from 68th to 106th had more private houses than any other avenue in town, fronting broad sidewalks edged with grass and planted with a double row of saplings. The houses, semisuburban rather than citified, wore an air of solid upper-middle-class comfort and permanence and many had "important claims architecturally." The *Architectural Record*, in its first issue, praised the Romanesque Revival design of several West End Avenue homes and called attention to their "successful color treatment" and Richardsonian and "Provencal" details.

The Grand Boulevard was the great question mark. Intended to receive the finest private residences, instead it had hotels (the Marie Antoinette and the Tecumseh at 66th and 67th streets, the Sherman Square at 71st, the St. Andrew's at 72nd) and apartment houses (the Nevada, Lyonhurst,

Antwerp, Amidon, and others), the 22nd Regiment Armory at 67th Street, the elegant Colonial Club at 72nd, and a sprinkling of opulent new churches (Bloomingdale Reformed at 68th, Rutgers Riverside Presbyterian at 73rd, First Baptist at 79th *et al.*). Meanwhile, owners held tight to their Boulevard properties, waiting for prices to go even higher, and great stretches were empty or covered with shanties. Still, all the Boulevard needed to become "the most famous, beautiful and costly residence thoroughfare in the world," opined the *Real Estate Record & Builder's Guide*, was an architect "of real genius, who could plan a house that would be artistic, novel and appropriate to the surroundings."

And where was that architect? Like as not, in the 1880s he was designing row houses, not mansions—though it was sometimes hard to tell them apart.

In the 1860s and 1870s, speculative row-house builders had filled block after block of the East Side with the stolid, uniform, Italianate brownstone fronts that suited the taste of that sober epoch. By the eighties, when the tide of development finally reached the West Side, the style had changed: prosperous New Yorkers wanted their homes individualistic and preferably flamboyant.

Architects and builders were more than happy to oblige. They turned out housefronts by the score in a profusion of "revival" styles, wielding a lively palette of colors and materials. Row houses of the late eighties and nineties were colorful brick, from red and tawny brown to orange and cream, lavishly trimmed with polychrome stone, tile, terracotta, and copper, and sporting bay windows, dormers, arched doorways, finials, crests, and gargoyles—an ebullient eclecticism that provoked considerable, mainly favorable comment.

Many of these homes were designed or at least inspired by well-known architects and by such firms as McKim, Mead & White, Lamb & Rich, and Babb, Cook & Willard. On Riverside Drive, an enterprising architect-builder, Clarence F. True, erected a great number of fine speculative row houses in the 1890s that were indistinguishable in quality from real mansions. On and near Riverside Drive, from West 105th Street north, was an enclave of similarly opulent town houses that cost up to $50,000 (even in 1900), designed by True, Robert D. Kohn, Janes & Leo, and others in full-blown French Beaux Arts style. A single block, like the block of West 76th Street from Central Park West to Columbus Avenue, could become a virtual showcase of popular architectural styles, with smatterings of English Gothic, French Renaissance, French Neo-Grec, neo-Italian Renaissance, Romanesque Revival, the so-called "Queen Anne" style, and French Beaux Arts. (The architects there included William A. Potter, who designed the original Teachers College building, and John H. Duncan, architect of Grant's Tomb.)

This 1890s surge of exuberant, variegated construction has been called "the swan song of the upper-middle-class, urban row house." Probably the very last row houses to be built on the West Side (or anywhere in New York, for that matter) for nearly eighty years were the long row of high-fronted, vaguely Georgian houses on the south side of West 74th Street. Designed by Percy Griffin for the heirs of Edward Clark and built in 1902–04, they stand back-to-back with the first Henry Hardenbergh row of 1879–80, bringing the story of the West End row house to an improbably neat finish. But by the time they were completed it was already clear that the apartment house would be the wave of the future.

In the end, all this opulent architecture says less about good design than it does about the pretensions of well-to-do New Yorkers of the late nineteenth century, the era for which Mark Twain and Charles Dudley Warner had coined the mocking phrase "the Gilded Age." It was the age of the factory, the telephone, and the electric light; engineering geniuses like Telford, Paxton, and Brunel had devised brilliant new construction technologies; steel-frame construction was about to bury downtown Manhattan in skyscrapers. But the architect's patrons seemingly had eyes only for the past. Homes, schools, stables, churches—even skyscrapers—were encrusted with pseudohistoric battlements, columns, arches, stone balconies, gargoyles. Lewis Mumford, whose architectural studies began with boyhood walks along the streets of his native West Side, would later complain of the "hypocrisy and concealment that the eclectic architects used to practice," deriding their lavish ornamentation as so many "tourist souvenirs." Those of us who have survived the heyday of the stripped-down International Style are less inclined to purism; we enjoy the chaotic exuberance of those designs, smile indulgently (or perhaps wistfully) at the nostalgic yearnings they seem to embody, and envy their craftsmanship.

The craftsmanship was nowhere more evident than in the West End's splendid churches. West End Avenue alone boasted the ebullient, Dutch-style West End Collegiate Church at 77th Street, All Angels' at 81st, the Church of St. Paul (later St. Paul and St. Andrew) with its octagonal belfry at 86th, and the Fourth Presbyterian Church (later the Church of the Annunciation) by Heins & La Farge at 91st. The huge church of St. Paul the Apostle at Columbus and 59th, home of the Paulist Fathers, was the largest noncathedral church in the country. Begun in 1876 and built partly of stone from the dismantled Croton Aqueduct, it included large stained glass windows by John La Farge, the architect's father, and an altar designed by Stanford White. St. Agnes's Chapel, near the Boulevard on West 92nd, was judged one of the handsomest new churches on the east coast, with a Romanesque design by William A. Potter in warm shades of brownstone and buff granite. The churches of the West End "represent the best models of church architecture," said a writer in the nineties, "and their rich facades and graceful towers add greatly to the imposing streets that characterize

this part of the city." Alas, churchmen, like other developers, being prone to overoptimism, most of these grand buildings were half-empty from the day they opened.

Most ambitious of all was the Cathedral Church of St. John the Divine, on the site of the Leake & Watts orphanage, which had relocated to White Plains. The original design, by Heins & La Farge, called for a magnificent Romanesque structure 520 by 192 feet, and 445 feet high to the top of its crowning cross. Later, that plan would be dropped in favor of a Gothic design by Cram & Ferguson, and in the tradition of the great medieval cathedrals, St. John would still be incomplete nearly a century after it was begun. But they didn't know that on St. John's Day, December 17, 1892, when Bishop Henry Codman Potter laid the cornerstone, and the cathedral's rising arches, visible from the riverside or even from far downtown, were literally the West End's crowning glory.

The "Riverside-avenue" (to backtrack a bit) had finally been opened in 1880, and in a suitably dramatic fashion.

Work on it was more or less done by the start of that year, but the contractors were unpaid (or so they claimed) and they and everyone from the landowners to the mayor and the board of aldermen were the target of someone else's lawsuit. The contractors posted guards on "their" road and blocked off the few existing cross streets with derricks, timbers, and heaps of stone; and there matters rested, while General Viele (as he complained bitterly) groped his way home at night among the surrounding shanties, "at the imminent risk of being bitten by the vicious dogs the shanty-dwellers kept to harrass the bailiffs."

The next spring, the contractors' guards made the mistake of actually laying hands on a property owner, Christopher R. Robert, when he tried to enter his own property at 116th Street. Furious, he went to court, got an injunction to keep the guards off the premises, and on Thursday, May 6, the contractors' barricades were unprotected for the first time. That night, some time after midnight, about a hundred men entered the avenue quietly at 72nd Street and tore up the obstructions. The derricks were hurled from the wall, some of them rolling into the river and some remaining on the hillside. Timbers, toolhouses, and fences were tossed after them, and by 3 A.M. the drive was cleared. The next day the *Times* reported, "The sun rose upon Riverside-avenue yesterday open, for the first time, from one end to another. The citizens along the avenue were jubilant and all of them conveniently ignorant as to the man under whose orders the barriers had been destroyed."

Would the West Side now get the "imperial avenue" that Viele insisted would be "the equivalent of the Chiaja of Naples and the Corso of Rome"? The *Real Estate Record and Builder's Guide* thought so. Forget Fifth Avenue, it urged; on Riverside Avenue "any ordinary millionaire" could afford to

construct what the *Record & Guide* considered a proper millionaire's home: "a fashionable edifice surrounded by grounds and having such approaches in the way of lawns and walks that will heighten the architectural ensemble."

The first arrivals had tried to set an example—though, granted, they had bought when land was cheap. General Viele's red brick, ivy-covered "suburban villa," which dated from 1872, commanded a half-block of well-planted lawn at the southeast corner of 88th. Cyrus Clark, the "Father of the West Side" (whose portrait and honorific can be found today on a bronze plaque in Riverside Park at 83rd Street), had bought the Brockholst Livingston house—actually in the bed of the future West 90th Street—in 1866. Around twenty years later he sold it to John H. Matthews, the "Soda-Water King," whose bottling works took up two full blocks in the East 20s. Matthews built a huge, rambling storybook mansion at the northeast corner of 90th Street, designed by Lamb & Rich, with numerous ells and ample porches, an immense tiled roof, stained-glass windows, and voluptuous caryatids gazing toward New Jersey. Neighborhood children told each other the Matthews house contained that wonder of wonders, a private soda fountain! At least one would hang about the elaborate wrought-iron fence, angling for an invitation (which, alas, never came). Clark, meanwhile, had built his new home facing the Matthewses across West 90th, a turreted, high-ceilinged, gray-granite mansion, also with a half-block of Riverside frontage.

Farther uptown, Peter Doelger, one of the more successful brewers of the era, had a large square brick house at 99th Street, overlooking Striker's Bay; William Foster, who had made two fortunes in the glove business (the first, in Chicago, wiped out by the fire of 1871), had a great stone house on a high, grassy knoll at 102nd, much abused by the critics for the cast-iron frieze above the third floor. At 108th Street, Samuel Gamble Bayne, who had started out peddling equipment in the oil fields of Pennsylvania and ended up heading the Seaboard Bank, had a colorful Romanesque chateau designed by the great Brooklyn architect Frank Freeman; across 108th, the broker Henry F. S. Davis had an equally handsome home on the same scale, also by Freeman. And at 113th the restaurant man George Noakes had a large English Victorian granite mansion on a terraced lawn at the top of three flights of stairs, with corbelled windows and tower and an eighteen-foot-high conservatory—all a few yards from where the Bloomingdale Road had once dwindled away to a footpath beside Adrian Hooglandt's barn.

Rumors abounded that the city's aristocrats would soon descend on the area, and a few upper-crust families—the Altmans, Cuttings, Schiffs—went so far as to actually buy land. But the invasion never materialized, and soon other trends intervened. Clarence True's mansion rows headed off the inevitable, for awhile, but the appearance of the first apartment house, at 83rd Street, in 1895 was the writing on the wall. In an amazingly

short time, Riverside Avenue—or Riverside Drive, as it became in 1908—turned into a street of apartment houses. One observer noted the pace with astonishment in 1898: "West 91st Street is built up with fine new houses not a year old. The ledge of rock on Riverside Drive at 92nd Street that I climbed up on with some difficulty about four months ago, and which was twenty-five feet high, is nearly all blasted away now."

The age of mansion-building was not quite over, though. At 89th Street, on the north side, Mrs. Elizabeth Scriven Clark, whose father-in-law had built the Dakota, built a large, square Beaux Arts mansion of red brick, lavishly frosted with marble, surrounded with formal gardens and an impressive wrought-iron fence with stately carriage gates. The architect was the prolific Ernest Flagg, who, as the family's favorite architect, also got the commission for the Singer Building, once the world's tallest. While her home was under construction, Mrs. Clark went to court to restrain the city from building the long-delayed Soldiers and Sailors Monument at 89th Street. It would "interfere with the flow of light and air and obstruct the view and prospect from her house," she said through her lawyers, and diminish the value of her property. The dispute was finally put in Mayor Van Wyck's hands. He came for a look, said he saw no problem, and that was the end of that. Soon afterward, Mrs. Clark married Henry Codman Potter, Episcopal Bishop of New York and founder of the Cathedral Church of St. John the Divine, and her landmark home was henceforth known as Bishop Potter's Residence.

Facing the Potters across 89th Street was Villa Julia, built by railroad lawyer and chess enthusiast Isaac Leopold Rice and named for his wife. The house, today one of the Drive's two surviving freestanding mansions, was designed by two future theater architects, Henry Herts and Hugh Tallent. They blended Beaux Arts and Georgian Revival with a hint of the then-new Prairie Style in the ample tiled roof, and the Rice children loved the grand front doorway ("It gave scope for posing that appealed to us," one of them recalled). Other features included a porte cochere on the 89th Street side and a soundproof Chess Room carved out of the bedrock, where Rice hosted cable matches, with the Cornell, Dartmouth, and Princeton teams pitted against Oxford and Cambridge.

Meanwhile, the financier Jacob Schiff had bought the grounds of the New York Orphan Asylum, a full block, from 73rd to 74th. But he had not reckoned with Mrs. Schiff; convinced she would never see her fashionable friends again if she had to live on the Drive, she pleaded tearfully until he relented and sold the land.

The buyer, Charles Schwab, had once been a dollar-a-day stake driver and now headed United States Steel, the world's first billion-dollar corporation. He cared less than Mrs. Schiff about social geography. In the middle of his new block he erected Riverside, a six-million-dollar, seventy-five-room mansion of cream-colored granite with 116-foot-high pinnacles,

designed by Maurice Ebert and based on the three Loire Valley chateaux of Chenonceaux, Blois, and Azay-le-Rideau: probably the largest and most lavish private home Manhattan ever saw. Schwab's mentor was Andrew Carnegie, whose Fifth Avenue home is now the Cooper-Hewitt Museum. "Have you seen that place of Charley's?" Carnegie asked a friend when Riverside was completed. "It makes mine look like a shack."

But Riverside really was the last of the breed. The real estate operators who hoped to lure the Four Hundred west had missed a crucial point: New York's elite got all they wanted of nature's majesty at Bar Harbor or in the Adirondacks, and if they wanted grand houses with a view, that's what Newport was for. At home, what they wanted to see when they came and went was not the broad sweep of the Hudson, but other millionaires, suitably domiciled. In other words, the truly elite had no intention of budging from their natural habitat: Fifth Avenue and points east.

Even in its golden years the West End suffered from fairly spotty development. Owners along the Boulevard were still holding on until prices went up. A fairly typical block along the Boulevard (west side, 67th to 68th streets) looked like this at the start of the nineties: "Five buildings on four lots of the northwest corner comprising four four-story brick, with a liquor saloon, an undertaker's, a bakery and a vacant store, all with apartments above, and a four-story frame, with a butcher's store and apartments. A lot adjoining, vacant. The 75 feet on the southwest corner covered with three-story high stoop frame stores and apartments built on a few feet of rock above grade."

Riverside Drive was still marred by commercial wharves and coal pockets, stables and feed stores, truck gardens and roadhouses that were as shabby as they were homey. "The streets had mostly—not all—been cut through at grade," a journalist recalled, "but the blocks between remained at their original level. So some of the streets were shallow open canyons, flanked by plateaus and mesas ten, fifteen, or twenty feet above them, and upon these rock-girt eminences were perched the houses of the squatter sovereigns, like Swiss chalets or medieval strongholds," most surrounded with barrels and crates, broken-down carts, discarded furniture, and similar junk. Out of nearly two miles of frontage from 72nd Street to Claremont, the *Real Estate Record* reported in 1902, more than half was vacant.

But to the men—and women—who built the West End, these were details, empty patches on a splendid canvas that was nearing completion. Most residents would have agreed. Clark, Cammann, Viele, True, and their brethren had done no less than build a new quarter of the city, and its houses, grand hotels, apartment houses, and even tenements proclaimed the energy and optimism of the astonishing century that gave them birth.

PART
········· II ·········
THE
WEST
END

5

THE CITY BETWEEN THE PARKS

*People who like to live amid life
and movement, and yet to have
pure air and quiet and to be near
some of the great parks, naturally
gravitate to Upper Broadway.*

—New York *American,*
"Renting Guide to
High Class Apartments," 1911

Summer evenings, after the lamplighter had come, West End families pulled out straw mats from the hall and joined their neighbors to chat comfortably on the high stoops, the men in shirtsleeves, the ladies in white shirtwaists. Everyone knew everybody else. "Through fluttering lace curtains," Lewis Mumford recalled, "a lonely piano might be pleading the cause of love. But except for that and the rumble of the elevated or the clop-clop of a cab horse on the cobblestones, the human voice struck the dominant note: chuckling, laughing, just idly talking, sometimes whistling and even singing."

Climb the brownstone stoop of 586 West End with young Helen Worden, who lived there in the nineties and could have led you blindfolded through every foot of it or any similar home:

You went into a little vestibule, where the straw mats were kept behind the storm door, and then on into the front hall. A very formidable stairway went up to the second floor, long and steep, with a little niche near the top for a piece of statuary. The parlor was on the main floor, with walls panelled in satin, little gilt "impossible" chairs scattered around, and the piano, with its vases and framed photographs on top. Everybody played.

The dining room, in the rear, usually had a Tiffany lamp on a vanity table, and an elaborate, built-in oak sideboard, with stained

glass cut-outs and fancy mirrors, and off of that was the butler's pantry with a dumbwaiter. The second floor front was the library, with the large master bedroom at the rear; off the master bedroom was the only "complete" bathroom in the house, above the butler's pantry. Between the front room on the third floor and the back bedroom there was a passageway with a sink in it, and closets. The bedroom off the end of the hall was for Maggie, the hired girl. We got her straight off the boat. She was part of the family. The basement had the kitchen, and the kitchen opened out on the backyard, and there was a clothesline in the back yard, and grandfather planted roses. And the front room was a billiard room; everybody had a billiard table. That was *status*.

One easy way to enjoy this, in those simpler days, was as a boarder. You just looked in the paper under BOARDERS WANTED:

68TH ST., 56 WEST — Newly furnished and decorated; private bath; dressing room; electric lights; private residence; attentive service; elegant home surroundings.

80TH WEST, 108 — Lady having beautiful home will accommodate parties desiring refined atmosphere; excellent board, use handsome parlor and piano.

83RD ST., 136 WEST — Large and single rooms; white American house; excellent food; references.

81ST ST., 138 WEST — Beautiful, comfortable rooms; excellent table; high-class Jewish house; table guests.

118TH, 400 WEST — Large corner rooms overlooking Morningside Park; celebrated table; rooms, $5.50–$7.50.

Some offered room and board, or you could have your own place, and then you'd go across to Mrs. Babcock's or Miss Fawcett's for dinners. The better boarding houses were in the West End, and well into the twentieth century quite a few people "of quality " enjoyed very pleasant and genteel arrangements such as these.

Many West End homes were built on the new "American basement" plan. Instead of a high stoop and narrow hall, you entered a wide reception hall one or two steps above street level, suitable for "thronged receptions and dancing-parties." Lloyd Morris, a historian and social critic, knew the style well. "A curving staircase," he recalled, "led to a high-ceilinged library or salon, music room, and dining room on the parlor floor above. Most of these luxurious homes had 'extensions' built out into the rear yard; these provided a butler's pantry on the ground floor, a smoking room or 'den' behind the dining room and large 'boudoir bathrooms' on the upper stories."

A score or so of Riverside Drive homes built in the nineties by Clarence True, Charles Buek, and others were technically in the row-house category (i.e., spec-built, in groups, sharing common "party" walls), but the builders had every right to call them, as they did, mansions. Consider no. 42, a forty-foot-wide, five-story "double American basement house" still standing near 76th Street, built by Charles Buek "in the style of Francis I." It had ten family bedrooms, each with its own gas-equipped fireplace, five "luxurious" baths, five servants' bedrooms (and one bath), and such details as quartered oak paneling and a timbered ceiling in the entrance hall. There were mahogany columns and a seven-foot-high arched mirror in the drawing room and stained-glass windows in the conservatory. The dining "hall," Buek boasted, was "really a work of art," with a massive mantle supported by carved figures and a built-in display cabinet "for the exhibiting of cut glass." The 1898 asking price was $110,000.

Houses large and small were filled with a rich, variegated clutter of settees, wicker chairs, hangings, William Morris wallpaper, Anglo-Japanese "art furniture," Arabian swords and cymbals, Rogers genre groups, and anything else that would fit. A mania for things Oriental expressed itself in the turn-of-the-century "Turkish corner," which featured an overstuffed divan, gongs, scimitars, "mosque" lamps, and (since you didn't have to be a purist about it) Japanese masks, Venetian glass, and Chinese ceramics.

"Maggie" and other new arrivals were helping to ease New York's perennial servant problem. Even a middle-class family might keep a live-in cook, housemaid, and waiter; in what was termed a prosperous home you also expected to see—or rather, not to see—a parlor maid, upstairs maid, houseman, laundress, coachman, and so on. The West End, it was claimed, offered "more home life" than other parts of town. "Wives, mothers and sisters vie with each other in making the interiors of the homes as charming as the exteriors are delightful to the eye. Husbands, sons and brothers prefer the home circle to the distractions of the lower part of town. When they crave the society of their fellow-men they invite them to dinner. There are more little dinners given in the West End than in any other two square miles of territory in the world." The local tradesmen offered the best meats and groceries at moderate prices. "The dining room," said the writer complacently, "is a wonderful civilizing medium. It is a great recruiting station for 'white' people."

The social pages of the *Herald*, the *Daily Tribune*, and the *World* began to carry columns of "Uptown Notes," to chronicle the weddings and engagements of West End families, the at-homes of newly engaged couples, the theatrical productions of Barnard undergraduates, sorties to and from Patchogue, Far Rockaway, Sea Girt, Ocean Grove, or Lake Placid.

The prosperous business class was settling in nicely. Herman Westinghouse, chairman of Westinghouse Electric Manufacturing, lived at 86th

and Broadway. Meyer Guggenheim, founder of the mining and financial dynasty, had a mansion facing the Museum of Natural History across West 77th. On just one block of West 76th the residents included financiers Murry Guggenheim (Meyer's second son), Charles H. Lowerre, and Henry Goldman; Orlando Harriman, the transit and real estate operator; Daniel M. Brady, who made railway equipment; and pioneer adman "Commodore" J. Walter Thompson—a rank bestowed by the New York Yacht Club, not the Navy. Thompson's brilliant innovations are still very much with us. He was the first to place advertising on the back of a magazine, he created the "Rock of Gibraltar" logo for Prudential Insurance and the first nationwide ad campaign (for Mennen talcum powder), and he published the first book on the black art now known as demographics. He only fell down seriously as a prophet. Selling out his business in 1916, when billings had grown to three million dollars, he boasted, "No one will ever make as much money out of advertising as I have!" By the 1980s the J. Walter Thompson agency was billing over 2.3 *billion* dollars a year.

Isidor Straus and his brother Nathan were just starting to build R. H. Macy's into The World's Largest Store in 1884, when he and his wife Ida left the respectable East 50s for a roomy, cupola-topped house on semirural West End Avenue at 105th, with an apple orchard and barn on the grounds. After the blizzard of 1888, the two oldest boys had to trek over to Amsterdam Avenue for supplies with Pat MacDermott, the coachman, wearing skis fashioned from barrel staves.

Isidor's brothers soon followed him to the West End. All were noted philanthropists and civic leaders. Nathan, a patron of children's milk funds and of the new public library system, would eventually be voted Most Valuable Citizen of Greater New York's first quarter century, 1898–1923, and is still commemorated by the Nathan Straus Young Adult Library on West 53rd Street. Oscar, the youngest brother and the designated family scholar, went to Columbia and was later appointed to major posts by every president from Cleveland to Wilson.

General William Tecumseh Sherman retired to West 71st Street in 1886, looking for peace and quiet, which he said could be had only in the forest or in a great city. He soon was one of New York's great toastmasters and first-nighters, taking the el, which he preferred to a private carriage, to the theater district (then at 23rd Street) or to The Players, the theatrical club on Gramercy Park, which he helped to found in 1888. After his death in 1891, the nearby junction of Amsterdam Avenue and the Boulevard was named Sherman Square.

The West End's other great first-nighter, at 7 West 86th, was James Buchanan Brady, known to all as Diamond Jim, a one-man personification of the Gilded Age. He had made millions selling railroad equipment (not brother Daniel's, though; they never spoke) and speculating on Wall Street, and he enjoyed his money, taking front-row seats for every Broadway

THE CHARITABLE WEST END

Partly because land was still cheap around the Straus farm, the area continued to have more than its share of the charitable and "sanitary" organizations for which Bloomingdale had been famous—literally dozens by the mid-nineties. Some predated the area's rebirth, such as the House of Mercy and the 1865 New York Infant Asylum, in its large L-shaped wood building at Amsterdam and 61st. Roosevelt Hospital, which occupied a full city block at 59th Street and Ninth Avenue, was opened in 1871 with a bequest from James H. Roosevelt. Later came the turreted, block-long New-York Cancer Hospital at Central Park West and 106th, the country's first institution exclusively for cancer patients (two-thirds of the patients admitted free, others paying seven to thirty dollars a week); Woman's Hospital at Amsterdam and West 109th to 110th; the Pasteur Institute at 1 West 97th (first U.S. clinic to offer Pasteur's

antirabies treatment); and St. Luke's Hospital, facing Morningside Park at 113th Street. Charitable institutions included the Protestant Society for the Relief of Half-Orphan and Destitute Children (Manhattan Avenue, 104th to 105th), the Society for the Relief of the Destitute Blind (104th and Amsterdam), the Home for the Aged of the Little Sisters of the Poor (135 West 106th), and the Home for Aged and Infirm Hebrews (125 West 105th). The New-York Home for Convalescents at 433 West 118th offered "gratuitous temporary care to worthy Protestant poor people." The Association for the Relief of Respectable, Aged, Indigent Females (Amsterdam Avenue, 104th to 105th streets) had a chapel with Tiffany ornaments and stained glass; clientele was restricted to "persons of refined sensibilities"—the qualification serving to exclude any former servant with the temerity to seek a place there.

opening and hosting large lobster-palace parties after the show. Dinner might start with four dozen oysters and a dozen hard-shell crabs, followed by six or seven giant lobsters, a large steak, a tray of French pastry, and coffee, all washed down with gallons of orange juice. To the great restaurateur George Rector, Brady was simply "the best twenty-five customers we had." True to his sobriquet, Diamond Jim always wore a full set of blazing diamonds—or emeralds, rubies, sapphires, or other precious stones—and had thirty such sets. He may have become a touch more conservative toward the end of his life, when he was quoted as saying, "I consider that twenty-eight rings are enough for any man to wear at one time. The others may be carried in the pocket and exhibited as occasion requires."

One of the few who could (almost) keep up with Diamond Jim at the dinner table was Lillian Russell, reigning beauty of the musical stage and

Brady's frequent companion on nights and days out. Russell had what one reporter described as a "cosey nest" just off Riverside Drive on West 78th in the 1890s, where she gathered a brilliant company around her bird's-eye maple piano, including Mme. Nordica, Nellie Melba, John Drew, and that up-and-coming young promoter, Florenz Ziegfeld. When she returned from a tour, reporters would rush to her intimate press conferences, breathlessly report her mood and decor, her delight in strolling on the sunny drive, and the latest news of her frequent and stormy marriages.

With so many hospitals nearby, doctors were naturally plentiful. Dr. Simon Baruch of West 70th Street was the first surgeon to save a patient by making an accurate diagnosis of appendicitis—*before* the operation. His son Bernard grew up to be the renowned financier and advisor of presidents. Dr. Abraham Brill, who lived at several West End locations, was the founder of the New York Psychoanalytic Society and an earnest disciple of Sigmund Freud: he even named his daughter Gioia—"joy," the literal meaning of the German *freude*. When Freud first came to the United States in 1909, he visited Brill on Central Park West, approved the location, and commanded, "Stay here, don't move from this spot; it is the nicest part of the city"—which may help explain why the area has been so popular with the psychoanalytic fraternity ever since. Dr. Philip F. O'Hanlon of 191 West 95th is still remembered—or rather his daughter is: it was to Virginia O'Hanlon that the New York *Sun* addressed an editorial in 1897 that included the immortal words, "Yes, Virginia, there *is* a Santa Claus." Herman L. Collyer, M.D., of 153 West 76th was a prominent gynecologist who had left his strong-willed wife and two sons in Harlem. Decades later the sons would be enshrined in New York legend as the reclusive Collyer brothers, found dead in their upper Fifth Avenue brownstone amid truckloads of old newspapers, five pianos, a dismantled automobile, broken machinery and toys, and other trash. Dr. Belmont DeForest Bogart of 241 West 103rd is also remembered for his progeny. When his first child came home from the maternity hospital Dr. Bogart realized that his son's strong grip destined him to become a surgeon. He immediately made plans to send young Humphrey to Yale.

A West End medical student of a slightly later era was the future multibillionaire Armand Hammer, who entered Columbia University before the First World War and studied medicine while helping to run a family pharmaceutical company. This left no time for attending classes, so Hammer rented a room in his West 77th Street apartment to an impoverished classmate, who provided him with copious notes in lieu of rent. This worked nicely until Hammer came home one afternoon to find the pretty nurse he'd been dating in bed with his lodger. Even without the roommate, he made Alpha Omega Alpha, the medical honor society, and at the same time built up his father's near-bankrupt company into a fifteen-hundred-man concern. The month after graduation he sold it and banked his first

JULIA RICE:
"THE WOMAN WHO STOPPED NOISES"

The boats in New York's harbor and rivers, with their deafening whistles and sirens, were a well-known nuisance, but when Julia Rice, one of the city's first woman doctors, learned that the racket was actually driving hospital patients into a state of acute dementia, she determined to launch what the papers promptly dubbed an "anti-noise war."

Soon an army of notebook- and stopwatch-wielding student volunteers from Columbia Law School (where Mr. Rice was a former professor) were poking around the harbor in small boats. Armed with data showing that the rivermen were serenading their fellow citizens with over twenty-five hundred whistle-blasts a night, Dr. Rice's group, the Society for the Suppression of Unnecessary Noise, was ready to proceed against the Shamrock Line and other tug owners. A typical skirmish, reported in the *Times* under the heading HAULS UP ANOTHER TOOTER, was the hearing against Captain James Black of the tug *Primrose* before the Local Board of Steamboat Inspectors. The charge: sounding "unnecessary and obnoxious shrieks" near Bellevue

Hospital. Dr. Rice herself was unfailingly gracious. She said nothing at the hearing, but afterwards, the *Times* recounted, "she took in hand the offending Captain, and explained in detail the reasons why she brought the charges." The captain's reaction is not recorded, but within a few years, the S.S.U.N. had won a federal law to regulate noise from rivercraft, and had gone on to create the now-familiar "quiet zones" near hospitals and, through Mr. Rice's magazine, *The Forum*, had helped formulate New York City's first noise code.

But the rivermen were not done with their adversary. In those days the Rice residence was a very conspicuous Riverside Drive landmark. One neighbor of that era has told me, with wicked glee, of New Year's Eve 1908, when seemingly every boat in the Hudson came to the foot of West 89th, "to fill the midnight air with foghorns, sirens, bells and whistles." And in case anyone missed the point, one big steamer switched on a searchlight and played it across the brick-and-marble front of Dr. Rice's home. After all, who could object to a little extra noise on New Year's Eve?

two million dollars.

The miserly financier Hetty Green, allegedly the richest woman in America, frequently stayed (and eventually died) at her son's home at 7 West 90th. She confined her affections to a rather unpleasant mongrel dog called Cupid Dewey, saying, "*He* loves me, and he doesn't know how rich I am."

By contrast, it would be hard to imagine a more congenial home life than that of Charles Evans Hughes, future New York governor and United States Chief Justice. The Hugheses' house was a brownstone at 75th and West End. When bicycling was the rage Charles enjoyed cycling to Grant's Tomb and back before breakfast. Sunday afternoons were for trips to Central Park with his wife and children, the Museum of Natural History, sleigh rides in the winter, victoria rides in warm weather, ferry trips to Fort Lee, and, one memorable day, when the fleet came up the river after the Spanish-American War, a visit to the battleship *Indiana*. The study, said Hughes's biographer, Merlo J. Pusey, was the favorite room. "In this second-floor retreat looking out over West End Avenue, the walls banked with bookcases and a large portrait of Gladstone giving a legal touch, Charles and Antoinette Hughes spent many an evening together; she in an easy chair with a book, he at a great central desk covered with manuscripts, letters, and telegrams." This lasted until 1905, when Hughes was asked to head a sensational investigation of the insurance industry. Concentrating on the Big Three—the Mutual, Equitable, and New York life insurance companies—he exposed large-scale mismanagement, graft, and corruption, and found himself launched into a political career. The next year he left the West End for the governor's mansion—after defeating another West Ender, William Randolph Hearst, in the bitterest campaign ever fought in the state up to that time.

Considerably less effective politically was the socialist publisher H. Gaylord Wilshire of West 93rd Street, who not only failed to win a congressional seat in New York but also entered—and lost—elections in California, England, and Canada. Wilshire's brand of socialism seems to have left plenty of leeway for the profit motive. When not editing *Wilshire's Magazine* and turning out such tomes as *Socialism Is Inevitable*, he busied himself with land development and stock promotion schemes and marketed something he called an "electric health belt." This last got him a little trouble from the Rockefeller Institute for Medicine when somebody there noticed that they were being mentioned in his advertising, but he eventually made enough to buy up much of downtown Los Angeles, where the name Wilshire Boulevard still testifies to his industry.

Just as radical, in their way, were Frank and Lillian Gilbreth, the pioneer industrial engineers later portrayed by Clifton Webb and Myrna Loy in the film *Cheaper by the Dozen*, whose first home together was on West 94th near Riverside Drive. To the alarm of some factory owners, they insisted that workers should share in the profits of improved efficiency. Later, as the Gilbreth family grew, Frank applied the Gilbreth System at home, assigning each child a file number and process chart, e.g., "7:00 A.M.—Rise and shine; 7:01—Your turn in bathroom; 7:02—Play German records while brushing teeth; 7:07—Weigh self and post on weight chart; 7:11—Play French records in bedroom while dressing; 7:18—Make bed;

WILLIAM RANDOLPH HEARST

The biggest apartment in West Side history, and probably the most cluttered, was William Randolph Hearst's. In 1907 the newspaper tycoon took over the top three floors of the twelve-story Clarendon apartment house at 137 Riverside Drive (86th Street) but soon needed more space for his statuary and armor, furniture, tapestries, paintings, and other *objets*, including Millicent Hearst and their five sons. When the owner balked at W.R.'s plans (which included evicting the eighth- and ninth-floor tenants and tearing out the ceilings to make a baronial reception room with thirty-five-foot-high windows overlooking the Hudson), he simply bought the building.

Hearst's special brand of yellow journalism reached its shameless acme in 1898, when the U.S. warship *Maine* blew up in Havana Harbor. Though there was never any real evidence of Spanish sabotage (it was probably an internal explosion, not a torpedo, that sank her), Hearst's papers whipped up war sentiment with screamer headlines: THE MAINE WAS DESTROYED BY TREACHERY, HAVANA POPULACE INSULTS THE MEMORY OF THE MAINE VICTIMS, and THE WHOLE COUNTRY THRILLS WITH THE WAR FEVER. The resulting Spanish-American War was deeply gratifying to W.R.'s patriotic soul and sold a million copies a day of the *Journal*. (For a while, the "ears" on the paper's front page carried the smug question, "How do you like our war?" But this must have been judged in dubious taste, and was soon dropped.)

It was common knowledge that W.R.'s heart belonged to the lovely comedienne Marion Davies, a seventeen-year-old Ziegfeld girl when they met. His papers carried rapturous reviews of her performances in the 1916 *Follies* and 1917's *Oh, Boy!*; a little later his film company, Cosmopolitan Productions, was starring her in *Little Old New York*, *When Knighthood Was in Flower*, and similar fluff; he gave them extravagant openings at his Cosmopolitan Theatre (formerly the Majestic) on Columbus Circle, then published rave reviews in his papers—all of which effectively killed her career. He also gave her the brick-and-marble town house at 331 Riverside Drive, and another nearby for her father, and spent a reported million dollars for a palatial renovation that included a marble fountain with two cupids for the sitting room. (Anita Loos, author of *Gentlemen Prefer Blondes*, once lunched with W. R. and Davies at 331, then joined him and Mrs. Hearst that evening for dinner at the Clarendon. "And when I took my place beside W.R. at his wife's table," Loos recalled, "he observed, with a naughty twinkle, 'Well, young lady, we seem to be sitting next to each other in rather diverse locations, don't we?' ") Eventually the lovers moved west to Hearst's Xanadu, the San Simeon estate in California; Millicent Hearst stayed at the Clarendon until 1937, when it was sold and carved up into smaller apartments—the kind an ordinary millionaire could afford.

7:21—Straighten room; 7:31—Eat breakfast," and so on. There was even a Gilbreth method for soaping yourself in the bath. "This may sound about as gay and informal as a concentration camp," Frank, Jr., admitted, "but it really seemed more like a game at the time."

By 1904, the Sunday "Society at Home & Abroad" column in the *Times* was including West End gentry without remark:

> Mrs. Daniel O'Day and Miss O'Day at 128 West 72nd Street, who have been giving Tuesday afternoon teas, will have a series of luncheons during the month of February.

> Mrs. William Henry Oakley, who has been quite ill this winter, is much better and has cards out for a reception at 269 West 73rd Street on Thursday.

> Mrs. Elmer A. Miller of 32 West 95th Street will give an entertainment on Saturday afternoon for members of the College Women's club.

> Mrs. Roxanna A. Hampton, cousin of the late Gen. Wade Hampton, will give a series of musicales during Lent in her apartments at the Belleclaire Hotel. Brilliant entertainer she is, and somewhat known as a clever writer of special articles and dainty poetry.

Here and there you saw someone who evoked a more distant and exotic past. At the Soldiers and Sailors Monument, an aged G.A.R. veteran, faded as his Union blues, served as a sentry-*cum*-guide. And when the subway opened a few years later, the ticket-taker at the 103rd Street station was a figure calculated to put awe into a schoolboy's heart: he was John Martin, originally Giovanni Martini, the cavalry bugler who was the sole survivor of Custer's regiment.

The West End's schools were a source of pride. The two oldest in the United States, Collegiate and Trinity (founded in 1638 and 1709), had moved up to the West End in the nineties. Public School 165, on 108th Street east of Broadway, was the most up-to-date public school in Manhattan, modeled after the Hotel de Cluny in Paris and designed by another West End resident, C. B. J. Snyder, New York City's long-time superintendent-architect for school buildings. By the time Snyder was done, dozens of New York schools—and hundreds more across the country—would resemble the chateaux he'd admired on European vacations. When Prince Henry of Prussia came to town on a state visit, they took him to P.S. 165 to admire it, and Jacob Riis, the antislum reformer, called it "a palace for the people" and declared "I cannot see how it is possible to come nearer perfection in the building of a public school." (Lewis Mumford could, though; he attended third grade there in 1903 and remembered it as "prisonlike.")

The choice of local schools was lavish: the De Lancey School, LeBaron Drumm School, Columbia Institute, West Side School for Boys, Mrs. Smart's "school for exceptional children," and a score more. The Cathedral School for Boys offered "the advantages of a private school under church influence," including military drill. Schoolmaster Joseph C. Groff assured parents that he employed "no YOUNG and INEXPERIENCED teachers to EXPERIMENT with students." At the Misses Ely's School, which occupied the large house on the Drive built by John McVickar in 1800 (and used in the interim as a home for unwed mothers), the "million-heiress" daughters of western silver kings and cattle barons learned to swish a silk train, toy with a teacup, and talk to a nice young man at the same time. How effective some of them were could be debated. Elmer Rice, the playwright, and George Gershwin, then an aspiring piano-pounder, both dropped out of the High School of Commerce on West 66th Street, with no noticeable ill effects. Dorothy Parker, *née* Rothschild, had gone to the Blessed Sacrament Convent near Sherman Square, until she was sent home with a note suggesting her parents "find a more suitable educational establishment" for their precociously irreverent daughter. "The only thing I ever learned in school that ever did me any good in later life," she claimed, "was that if you spit on a pencil eraser, it will erase ink."

A "civic Acropolis" began to take form on the West End in 1892, when Teachers College established itself in a tall red brick building at 120th and Amsterdam. The next year the Bloomingdale Lunatic Asylum relocated to White Plains, and Columbia University, then in the East 50s, took over the seventeen and a half acres for its campus and began its evolution from a respectable local college into one of the world's great institutions. Charles Follen McKim of the McKim, Mead & White firm provided a master plan for the new university: a relatively open lower campus (114th to 116th streets) with playing fields and tennis courts, and an upper campus laid out in a series of small, closed courtyards, approached via broad granite stairs, centered around the great dome of Low Library—named for Seth Low, formerly mayor of Brooklyn and president of the university during its great growth surge. Under President Nicholas Murray Butler, the former asylum grounds swarmed with such celebrated scholars as Edward L. Thorndike, Gilbert Murray, Franz Boas, Harlan Stone, and John Erskine. (Even so, as Erskine liked to point out, the gardeners for many years insisted on referring to the faculty as "the inmates.") John Dewey laboriously expounded his "instrumentalist" theories of ethics and education, and Melvil Dewey (no relation) founded the world's first library school, then was fired by the trustees for admitting women to it. Charles A. Beard's iconoclastic view of American history ("The seat of the American government was first established at the corner of Broad and Wall streets; it has remained there ever since") brought him into head-on collision with

President Butler, and he was fired, too. (Decades later the university's presidency would devolve upon General Dwight D. Eisenhower, who found his official residence there uncomfortably palatial. The faculty cringed at his hopeless naivete, while he, used to dealing with the likes of Churchill and Stalin, felt cut off from the real world. Both sides were relieved when he moved on to the White House in 1953.)

The scientific faculty was likewise stellar, with Henry Fairfield Osborn (who also headed the American Museum of Natural History *and* the New York Zoological Society), Frank M. Chapman, and Hans Zinsser (bacteriologist author of *Rats, Lice, and History*). Among others, Thomas H. Morgan, Harold Urey, Willis E. Lamb, Jr., Polykarp Kusch, and Willard F. Libby earned Nobel Prizes, and one Nobel Laureate, Enrico Fermi, also had an element named for him (fermium). The student body was fairly productive also, including among many others Richard Rodgers, Oscar Hammerstein II, J. D. Salinger, William O. Douglas, Lionel Trilling, Jacques Barzun, Richard Hofstadter, Paul Robeson, and Lou Gehrig.

Early in the century, the Juilliard School of Music, Union Theological Seminary, and Jewish Theological Seminary all followed Columbia to Morningside Heights, while Barnard College, Columbia's college for women, set up shop across the Boulevard at 116th Street. Other notable neighborhood institutions included the National Academy of Design, located at Columbus and 109th from 1899 to 1915; the American Geographic Society on West 81st; the New-York Historical Society around the corner on Central Park West; and the American Museum of Natural History.

Since Bickmore's day the American Museum had blossomed into one of the world's great research institutions, and it would continue to grow vigorously throughout the twentieth century, employing over two hundred scientists and housing some twenty-three hundred habitat groups and thirty-four million artifacts and specimens, from the *Tyrannosaurus* skeletons under the roof to the full-size model of a blue whale, the Hall of Man in Africa, the world's largest meteorite, the Hope diamond, the four-story-high Naturemax movie screen, and an annual *origami*-festooned Christmas tree. From the north or west its twenty-two interconnected buildings look like the working end of a New England mill town—though Cady, Berg & See's pink granite 77th Street facade is a glorious block-long range of Romanesque Revival arches and turrets, and John Russell Pope's Theodore Roosevelt Memorial on Central Park West and Trowbridge & Livingston's Hayden Planetarium are landmarks in their own right. In a sixth-floor office in the southwest turret, the late anthropologist-guru Margaret Mead worked for over half a century on the twenty-odd books that made her a quoted authority on everything from primitive cultures (her nominal specialty) to sex, war, and the generation gap. She lived twelve years at the Beresford Apartments on 81st Street, which she said was "like sleeping in the office." (In bad weather, she told a visitor, "you

can walk through the subway to the Museum if you put a token in the turnstile.") A portion of the park surrounding the museum has since been renamed in her honor: Margaret Mead Green.

The museum's naturalists and explorers often lived nearby, but they seemed to escape at every opportunity to the farthest corners of the earth. Or under them. William Beebe, a long-time West 67th Street resident, was the first human to descend (in a bathysphere of his own design) three thousand feet underwater, returning to the surface with weird specimens of fish life. Dr. Frank M. Chapman, the greatest birdwatcher since Audubon, was generally on his way to or from the jungles of Central America; Carl Akeley roamed Africa to bring back (among other trophies) the elephants that greet visitors to the museum's main floor; Robert E. Peary, with museum backing, discovered the North Pole and also brought back (from Greenland) the Ahnighito, the world's largest meteorite; it took thirty horses to haul it up Broadway to the museum. Vilhjalmur Stefansson, the "blonde Eskimo" whose books introduced temperate-zone folk to the facts of arctic life, shared a place with Akeley at 1 West 89th; Margaret Mead covered thousands of miles on research trips to the South Seas, then millions more to lecture in almost every major town and university. Through the museum and its neighboring institutions, the American Geographic Society and the Explorers Club (then on Central Park West), the West Side literally reached out to the world.

The dining room generally got a rest on Sunday. As the *New York Daily Tribune* explained, "Many servants insist on having Sunday afternoon 'out,' and would rather give up their places than cook an elaborate evening meal." A prudent employer gave her cook "all possible liberty" and planned a Sunday dinner at La Rochelle's "sumptuous French restaurant," with its famous Hungarian orchestra, or at the Manhattan Square Hotel on West 77th, or perhaps at some family hotel such as the Majestic, where the popular roof garden was enlivened with fountains and green arbors.

For the West End gentlemen, there was dinner at the club—or rather, at one of his clubs, since there were over three hundred social clubs in New York, and "no self-respecting society man," as *Scribners* noted, "limits his expenditure and attendance to a single one." General Viele's clubs, for instance, included the Loyal Legion, the Holland Society, and the Sons of the Revolution; his son Herman joined the Union, Metropolitan of Washington, University, and Church clubs. Cyrus Clark was in the Union League, Columbia, and Republican clubs; Charles Evans Hughes in the University, Lawyers, National Arts, and Republican clubs; W. E. D. Stokes, a major West End developer (of whom much more later), listed as his affiliations the Union League, Manhattan, Country, Down Town, New York Yacht, Meadowbrook, and the Seawanhaka and Corinthian Yacht clubs, as well as the St. Nicholas Society and the Sons of the Revolution.

The West End's premiere club was the Colonial at 72nd and the Boulevard, named for its supposed proximity to the Harlem Heights battlefield and boasting a fine collection of prerevolutionary memorabilia. But there was no lack of others nearby: the Women's University Club (22 West 60th); the West-End Club (134 West 72nd); the West Side Republican, in a handsome brick building (still standing) on the Boulevard above 83rd Street; the Progress Club (1 West 88th, later home to the "progressive" Walden School); the Manhattanville; the Columbus (Columbus at 126th); the Riverside, Pontiac, and Hospital Graduates' (nos. 59, 70, and 161 West 104th); and, among those devoted to "special enjoyments," the New York Whist Club (235 West 72nd), the Riverside Whist (745 Amsterdam), the West Side Tennis Club (at 204 West 93rd before removing to Forest Hills in the 1920s), and a variety of boating and wheelmen's organizations.

The Colonial had the distinction of being the first important club in New York to admit women—strictly as guests. Its large clubhouse, still standing at this writing (mid-1988), had a separate ladies' porch on 72nd Street; an elevator lifted feminine visitors to the third floor, where they had their own reception and dining room for what the bachelor members called "dove luncheons." The Colonial also had an annual Ladies' Day and allowed women access to its basement bowling alleys, lectures, and art exhibits. "So liberal has been the patronage of the fair sex," the *Tribune* noted with some surprise in 1895, "that on one Sunday it was necessary to admit them to the big dining room and to confine the members who had brought no women to dinner to the smaller one."

By the turn of the century some West Enders already were nostalgic about their neighborhood. A group of pioneering developers organized Ye Olde Settlers Association to reminisce about times gone by. Charles Friedgen, who ran a pharmacy at 120th and Amsterdam Avenue, photographed some of the old wooden houses in his neighborhood and published the results as a series of nostalgic picture postcards. Hopper Striker Mott of West End Avenue, real estate man and scion of three fine old Bloomingdale families, devoted five-hundred-plus pages to his *Bloomingdale, The New York of Yesterday*, a shameless valentine to the Harsenville of his youth that opened with the magic words, "In the good old days . . . ." Charles Haswell, at ninety-seven the world's oldest practicing civil engineer, lived at 309 West 78th. Haswell was on the commission planning the great Hudson-Fulton Celebration of 1909 and had a clear memory of seeing Robert Fulton's original steamboat. Gazing back at his youth, he swore, "One day of life in those times was worth a week of today. The New Yorker now doesn't know what leisure and enjoyment mean."

There was still evidence of old times all around, on the blocks—and there were quite a few—that still had gardens and cold frames. One was the Welsh home, which was on a slope below Riverside Drive at 86th—87th,

reached by a wood stairway. James Welsh later recalled a long family tradition of the children and visiting cousins planting trees nearby, so that as adults "they could recognize the trees as they also grew up." Cherries, apples, peaches, and plums came from trees on the property. "A mess of fish," he remembered, "would be caught before breakfast by the younger boys for the morning meal before going to school." Luke Welsh, a Tammany stalwart, gave annual clambakes on the lawn for the judges and politicians, with the chef carefully adding a magnum of champagne to each ten-gallon copper pot of chowder.

Raoul Walsh, future Hollywood director and ladies' man, spent his boyhood at Riverside and 99th in the early 1900s. He, too, caught striped bass from the 86th Street wharf and played at being Long John Silver or a Pawnee chief in the orchard and woods nearby. In due course he took Dr.

SAN JUAN HILL

The lower West End was a tough Irish neighborhood in the 1880s and 1890s, an extension of the Hell's Kitchen district farther south; later it became a precursor of black Harlem known as San Juan Hill. Jacob Riis, the slum reformer, noted a degree of tension between older Irish settlers and the "intruding" blacks: "The local street nomenclature, in which the directory has no hand—Nigger Row, Mixed Ale Flats, etc.—indicates the hostile camps with unerring accuracy."

Some said San Juan Hill got its name from the many Negro Spanish-American war veterans who settled there. In another version, it was "so-called by an onlooker who saw the police charging up during one of the once common race fights." An all-too-typical incident took place one Sunday afternoon in 1900 in full view of over twenty witnesses, when a platoon from the 20th Precinct, apparently pursuing some neighborhood "bad boys," suddenly turned on several residents of West 60th Street, whose only fault was to be black and within reach of clubs and fists. Among the scores injured was a sick man, George Myers, just out of the hospital; a cop actually broke a billyclub over Myers's head.

One of the great San Juan Hill characters was Lillian Harris, or Pig Foot Mary, an enormous, deep-voiced woman who drifted up from the Mississippi delta in the fall of 1901. She used the stove at Rudolph's, a saloon on Amsterdam near 61st Street, to cook up a mess of pig's feet, and hawked them on the street from a remodeled baby carriage. For over sixteen years, until she moved north to Lenox Avenue, she ran a portable steam table that also dispensed hog-maws, chitterlings, and corn on the cob. They must have been good; she put her profits into real estate, and her holdings eventually came to $375,000.

William Lewis Bulkley, a former slave who had become a schoolteacher and principal after earning a Ph.D. from Syracuse University, moved to San Juan Hill and started a night school for adults, followed by a kindergarten for children of working mothers and the Hope Day Nursery for preschoolers. Mary White Ovington, a white social worker and journalist, devoted years to improving conditions on San Juan Hill, helping get the League for Political Education to provide a playground and the like. She and Dr. Bulkley were among the founders of the NAACP and the National Urban League. Her greatest achievement was persuading philanthropists Henry Phipps and Elizabeth S. Clark to finance model tenements in the area. The Phipps Houses on 63rd and 64th, the Tuskegee, the Hampton Apartments, and the Alfred Corning Clark Houses on 68th and 69th streets.

Riis was especially enthusiastic about the latter, which housed four hundred families. "The one tenant who left in disgust," he wrote, "was a young doctor who had settled on the estate, thinking he could pick up a practice among so many. But he couldn't. They were not often sick, those tenants. Last year only three died, and they were all killed while away from home. So he had good cause of complaint."

O'Hanlon's little girl Virginia there for private picnics and tried to work up the nerve to kiss her, "a prospect which filled me with dark misgiving."

Louise Homer, beloved Metropolitan Opera contralto, lived at 89th and West End with her husband Sidney, composer of "Sweet and Low" and other favorites. They overlooked a large vacant lot used for express wagons, with a large garden populated by dogs, pigs, hens, and a cow. "The horses and wagons trotted in and out from early morning till dusk," Sidney Homer recalled. "Our children loved to watch them. It was so quiet then that you could hear a cab turn into Eighty-ninth Street, or a trolley car stop on Broadway. At night all was as quiet as a country village."

"My daily walks with my grandfather in Central Park or along Riverside Drive," Lewis Mumford recalled, "left an ineffaceable impression of noble leisure." And photos taken early in the century preserve the impression with hallucinatory clarity: of spring mornings, when striped awnings snapped in a fresh breeze and sunlight glinted from gleaming carriages, dappling the ladies' white dresses and parasols as they strolled beneath the slender elms of the Boulevard or the Drive.

But the photos tell only half the story. Consider Riverside Drive, where residents' senses were assaulted by the horns and steam whistles of the passing river traffic, the clanging of trains passing below the park, and the stench from cattle cars that were sometimes parked for days on their way

to the abattoirs of the West 60s. The soft summer breeze off the river brought along clouds of mosquitoes, known as "Jersey songbirds," and winter, as journalist A. J. Liebling recalled, was worse: "The wind stung my face and made my eyes water, and sometimes made me clutch at area railings to keep my balance." The writer John Jay Chapman complained in 1892 that the wind blew right through his new brownstone off the drive on West 82nd. "Whether it comes in through the roof, or, as I think more probable, straight through the walls," he wrote to a friend, "being in it is like sleighing in a duster. Maggie had put all the blankets in the house on the bed and added—the lap rug, the red Italian blanket, the yellow counterpane, the eiderdown thing, besides leaving on the regulation embossed coverlet. I anchored these things down on the side opposite the window with a very heavy bolster. The cold, however, being frustrated on this side went round and came up through the mattress . . . ."

Then, the thrifty frame houses still scattered here and there might be quaint relics; the squatters' shacks on the empty stretches of Riverside Drive and even the Boulevard were not. Or, follow 70th or 71st Street all the way west, and you ended at a terrace overlooking, not the majestic Hudson, but the New York Central railroad yards. Downtown, west of Tenth Avenue, stretched one of the most crowded tenement districts in New York. "In these great barracks of houses," wrote an observer, "live Scandinavians, negroes, and a host of representatives of other nationalities. Most of the men of these tenements work in the New York Central Yards along the Hudson River shore. Sixtieth and Sixty-first Streets west from Tenth Avenue can boast of what are probably the steepest hills in all New York. The effect of the tenement roofs looking down these streets is novel in the extreme. The streets are poorly lighted, and the squalor is great." The area was also "a headquarters of gangs of roughs, selected because of its wildness and the hiding places among its rocks."

It was an age that abounded in railroad crashes, steamboat explosions, lynchings, strikes, riots (militia volunteers were instructed to "shoot to kill"), gas main explosions, factory workers scalped by machinery, children run down by trains. The *Times* used to carry fifteen or twenty items a day under the heading "Yesterday's Fires," and another busy column was the one headed "Business Troubles." Suicides were common, mostly prompted by money or health worries; the Medico-Legal Society was urging the state legislature to bring back the cat-o'-nine-tails for wife beaters.

Inevitably, some of these tragic tales concerned West Enders. There was Frederick Wagner, a violin player and a watchman at the Misses Ely's school, until it closed; he quarreled with his wife over drink and money, and ended up killing her and himself. There was Theodore Roosevelt's older brother Elliott, who had become a drug addict after treatment for a broken leg. He spent his last wretched year as "Mr. Elliott," living with a mistress in a house on West 102nd, and died at thirty-four, in T.R.'s words,

"like some stricken, hunted creature." Eddie Roebling, whose family built the Brooklyn Bridge, was another lame duck seemingly exiled to the West End. While his older brothers were conquering the worlds of engineering and manufacturing, Eddie was in and out of jail, ending as a recluse in an apartment on West 84th Street. Lovely Louise Nugent, patroness of the West Side Assembly's annual Charity Ball and wife of B. Altman & Co. partner Frank L. Nugent, was fatally burned in her kitchen when a pot of beeswax boiled over. Mrs. Charles Warren of West 89th came down with typhoid, and so did her daughters Susanne and Margaret; their cook turned out to be none other than "Typhoid Mary" Mallon, the first person identified as a carrier of typhoid bacilli in this country. The health authorities had previously forbidden Mary to work as a cook, but it was the only work she knew. After her stint with the Warrens, she was quarantined for life on an island in the East River.

A couple of other unfortunate West Siders—Henry H. Bliss of 235 West 75th Street, and Arthur Smith of 151 West 62nd—made history of sorts when Bliss alighted from a southbound Central Park West trolley in front of the Dakota the night of Wednesday, September 13, 1899. He had just turned to help the lady behind him—a Miss Lee—when he was struck by an electric cab. Smith was at the wheel.

Mr. Bliss was not unknown to newspaper readers. A few years earlier, his wife had been poisoned, and her daughter, Bliss's stepdaughter, was tried for the murder. (She got off.) Bliss himself proved a wildly uncooperative witness, responding with threats and curses when asked such simple things as his address. But what earned him a footnote in American history was getting in front of that cab, which happened to be carrying a Dr. Edson—son of the former mayor—back from a house call in Harlem. Of the two and a half million or so Americans killed in auto accidents to date, Henry Bliss was the first.

Isidor and Ida Straus met a nobler fate. They were on the *Titanic* when the "unsinkable" ship struck an iceberg the night of April 14, 1912. Urged by friends to get into a boat, Ida went to her husband instead, saying, "We have been living together for many years; where you go, I go." Isidor declined to accept a seat "before the other men," and they sat down side by side in deck chairs to wait for the end. The name of the little park by their home was later changed from Bloomingdale Square to Straus Park, and a memorial fountain placed there. With its reclining female figure gazing sorrowfully into the water, it remains a touching tribute from loving neighbors and friends; the date—1914, the last year of the long pre–World War I peace—makes it a memorial to an era as well.

It was an era that loved to erect monuments, and the West End was a terrific place to put them. The Grand Circle got two: at its hub, Gaetano Russo's *Columbus* on its Italianate eighty-foot column, and at the park

General Viele (possibly the figure on the steps) designed his own red brick villa at the southeast corner of Riverside Drive and West 88th Street.

Ninth Avenue Steam Elevated
Railway under construction,
1879. View is southwest, from
near 66th Street, looking toward
future Lincoln Center.

An 1886 view of Angels' Curve—also called Suicide Curve—the high point of the el, at West 110th Street. Morningside Heights and Leake & Watts orphanage in background.

88. EL. R.R. CURVE 110ᵀᴴ ST. N.Y. LOOKING W.

Top:
South from the Dakota in early
1880s: newly cut-and-filled
streets are leveling the rugged
topography, paving the way for
advance guard of row-house
developments.

Riverside Drive, 1903; the John
Matthews and Cyrus Clark
mansions flanked the foot of
West 90th Street.

Top:
"Bishop Potter's Residence" was actually built by the bishop's second wife, Dakota heiress Elizabeth S. Clark. Riverside Drive, northeast corner West 89th Street; Ernest Flagg, architect.

Charles Schwab mansion, Riverside Drive to West End Avenue, West 73rd–74th streets: "the largest and most lavish private home ever built on Manhattan Island."

A refined and elegant quarter:
private homes and St. Paul's
Methodist Episcopal Church
(now the Church of St. Paul and
St. Andrew) on West End
Avenue. View is to the north
from below West 86th in July
1900.

Right:
West End Avenue and West 97th,
1903.

The elm-lined Boulevard
(Broadway), north from West
79th–80th streets, c. 1896; block
opposite is now occupied by
Zabar's and the Shakespeare &
Co. bookstore.

Original home of Hellmann's
Mayonnaise was this delicatessen
on Columbus Avenue at West
84th Street, c. 1912.

Interior of Tax Commissioner
Theodore Sutro's limestone-
fronted home at 320 West 102nd
Street.

Lillian Russell.

Columbus Circle, 1907.

Left:
James Buchanan "Diamond Jim"
Brady.

Strollers near Grant's Tomb,
c. 1897.

Merry sightseers ride a
newfangled 1912 electric bus
past Soldiers and Sailors
Monument, Riverside Drive and
West 89th Street.

For an unidentified 1897
celebration, the Colonial Club
(left) and Hotel St. Andrew at
Boulevard and West 72nd are
decked with bunting. The
Ansonia Hotel will soon rise on
the vacant lot beyond Rutgers
Church at 73rd.

Climax of the 1909 Hudson-
Fulton celebrations: replicas of
the *Half-Moon* and the *Clermont*
approach temporary Water Gate
at the foot of West 110th Street.

Ambitious 1890s plans for the
Museum of Natural History
would have made it the largest
building on the continent.

An 1896 view of Broadway and
West 75th Street shows the house
built around 1857 by William
Kelly on the site now occupied by
the Astor Apartments. In Kelly's
day every July Fourth was celebrated with a lawn party and
dancing under lanterns, followed
by an 11 o'clock supper.

Looking northeast from near
West End Avenue and 89th
Street, 1902, with Broadway just
beyond the trees: "At night all
was as quiet as a country village."

Amsterdam Avenue and West
120th Street with typical wildlife,
c. 1900. This may be the same
goat that later stood in the
window of Friedgen's Drugstore
nearby.

Top:
Columbia alumni at 1909
commencement, not many years
after the university's move to
"Asylum Hill." Among
themselves, the maintenance
staff referred to the academic
folk as "the inmates."

West 70th Street and the
Boulevard, 1890, looking uptown
toward Christ Church and
Stanford White's Sherman Square
Hotel (at left).

The Boulevard at West 106th
Street, September 1900, with
Bloomingdale Square (later
renamed Straus Park) at the far
left. "One of the most beautiful
driveways in the world," said one
writer of the Boulevard, "with
two capital roadways, separated
by a central strip of lawns, trees,
and flowers."

entrance, H. Van Buren Magonigle's—or should we say William Randolph Hearst's?—*Maine* Memorial. As part of a circulation war with the rival New York *World*, Hearst's *Journal* started a fund drive for a *Maine* memorial to be built at Columbus Circle, where the newspaper tycoon owned half the nearby real estate. It was unveiled in 1913, with nine-year-old George Hearst, in a white Navy uniform, pulling the cord, while warships on the Hudson fired twenty-one-gun salutes.

Broadway also acquired a monument to Dante Alighieri by Ettore Ximenes in the triangle above 63rd Street, which was subsequently named Dante Park. And around 1902 a merchant named William H. Flattau privately added a thirty-foot-high replica of the Statue of Liberty—possibly one of sculptor Frédéric-Auguste Bartholdi's working models for the lady in the harbor—to the streetscape. He brought it from France and placed it where it still stands on what was then his warehouse at 43 West 64th, just east of Lincoln Square. Curiously, Lincoln Square never had a memorial to the Great Emancipator—but then, the square was not named for him, but for a local landowner.

Riverside Drive, to monument builders, was like a blank canvas to a painter. The Drive's first monument (1883) was a life-size bronze of George Washington, cast from the Houdon portrait in the Virginia state capitol and purchased but never mounted in the Tweed era. General Viele had found it in the basement of the Arsenal when he was parks commissioner and arranged to have it put up in Riverside Park at 89th Street on a knoll about halfway between his house and Cyrus Clark's. A simple unveiling was held on July Fourth, with speeches by the mayor and school commissioner. Five hundred schoolchildren sang "America" and were rewarded with lemonade and a rather seigneurial invitation from General Viele to "go to Riverside Park and play whenever they wanted to."

Ulysses Grant's funeral two years later was much more imposing. General Grant (as he was known by those who wanted to remember only his finest hour) was mourned as the savior of the nation, while to New Yorkers he had been a familiar, beloved figure, frequently driving his famous mare Maud S. among the fashionable turnouts in Central Park. A five-hour-long parade escorted his body to a small temporary tomb in Riverside Park, and a subscription drive was begun for a more grandiose national monument. John H. Duncan's design, a somber 150-foot-high variation on the tomb of Mausolus at Halicarnassus, was accepted in 1890, but it took another five years and three separate fund-raising drives to get it completed. It became "the Mecca of the American pilgrimage"; there were sometimes two thousand visitors a day, and passing steamers in the river blew whistles and tolled bells as they passed.

Ground was broken for the Soldiers and Sailors Monument in 1900—thirty-five years after Appomattox—with a stirring martial speech by Governor Theodore Roosevelt. The design by Charles and Arthur Stoughton

featured an eighty-foot marble shaft, capped with a massive dome and ringed with frothy Corinthian columns and fierce American eagles (provided by a French designer, Paul E. M. Duboy). It was to have been at 83rd Street, on Mount Tom, but when a nine-story apartment house went up there, "ruining" the site, it was hastily moved to a spot near the Washington statue at 89th, where (it was solemnly asserted) "there is no danger that the monument will ever be dwarfed by big apartment houses." The new monument was unveiled in 1902; it included a small granite-walled niche to accommodate the earlier statue, which was eventually removed to the Metropolitan Museum, and later to its present home, City Hall. (The empty niche remains, giving passers-by something to wonder about.)

The Drive got many smaller monuments as well: a bronze column at 72nd Street (now gone) dedicated to Henry Hudson; an equestrian statue of Joan of Arc at 93rd Street, dedicated in 1915 by the French foreign minister; another of soldier-publisher Franz Sigel at 106th; a bronze plaque in the park at 83rd honoring Cyrus Clark, the "Father of the West Side"; a marble Firemen's Memorial at 100th; and a stele and fountain at 116th honoring the Women's Health Protective Association. Perhaps the most curious (as well as the most graceful) is the elaborately carved, eagle-topped pink limestone fountain at the foot of West 76th Street, with its inscription, "Bequeathed to the people of New York by Robert Ray Hamilton." A descendant of Alexander Hamilton and General Philip Schuyler, Hamilton was a dashing sportsman who dabbled in state politics. He married unfortunately. Mrs. Hamilton, it developed, not only had another husband, but had attempted to fob off another woman's infant as her own, then stabbed the baby's nurse in a brawl. And just as what promised to be a most diverting divorce case was getting under way in 1890, Hamilton drowned on a hunting trip—leaving ten thousand dollars to be used to build this fountain in his memory. It was designed by Warren & Wetmore, the architects of Grand Central, and erected, over the Hamilton family's strenuous protests, in 1906.

The streets were filled with movement. On hot days the children liked to ride on the backs of ice wagons, and if they were lucky the iceman would give them a piece of ice to suck. There were hurdy-gurdies and organ-grinders, German bands, and hucksters and peddlers with "cowbell distractions." Horses went by in single and double teams, double teams with a tandem leader, and four-horse teams, harnessed to milk wagons, hacks, coupes, express wagons, streetcars, "omnibuses," drays, butcher carts, two-wheeled hansoms and "dog carts." (The city's eighty-five-thousand-odd horses generated some eleven hundred wagon-loads of manure a day, much of it stored near the Hudson wharves pending removal. When residents objected, contractors argued that "the odor of manure was the healthiest one could possibly breathe.")

"The Drive—Central Park—Four O'Clock"; from a pen-and-ink drawing by Gray-Parker published in *Harper's Weekly*, 1883.

Riding and coaching were still elegant recreations. Riverside Drive and West 72nd Street (the principal crosstown carriage drive) were unpaved as late as 1904, despite residents' complaints about mud and dust, because the driving public objected to any material that would make poor footing for horses. For a while in the early nineties a scheme for a four-million-dollar Hudson River Driveway was debated energetically. Leopold Eidlitz even drew up a plan, sort of a cross between the Bois de Boulogne and the future West Side Highway, to be built on landfill west of the railway tracks. Nothing came of it.

Parades were a great feature of life: parades every election day; the Columbian Parade of 1892; the Great Sound Money Parade of businessmen in 1897; the Dewey Parade in 1898 to honor the hero of Manila and the Great White Fleet, anchored offshore in the Hudson; Memorial Day parades, which from 1902 on all had the Soldiers and Sailors Monument as their goal. Greatest of all was the 1909 Hudson-Fulton Celebration, marking the

tricentennial of Henry Hudson's discovery of the river that bears his name, and the centennial of Robert Fulton's discovery that you could get rich running steamboats on it. The festivities included a gala procession, electric illumination of almost every major monument and public building in town, an airplane flight up the West Side by Wilbur Wright (the last public flight by either of the Wright brothers), and an unprecedented naval parade: a ten-mile column of warships, led by replicas of the *Clermont* and the *Half Moon*, which docked (after ramming each other slightly) at a huge white-columned Water Gate, constructed for the occasion at the foot of West 110th Street.

Even without naval parades, the riverfront was always lively: sail and steam vessels in constant motion, industrial wharves (mainly clustered around 79th and 96th streets), ferry slips, with here and there an elegant marina. At the foot of West 86th, the Columbia Yacht Club was the first and the classiest such establishment, founded in 1867. Its large shingled chalet-style clubhouse was designed by William B. Tuthill, architect of Carnegie Hall, and maintained handsomely with abundant oak furniture, handsome rugs on the floor, and portieres hung around the room. The hoisting of the pennant in mid-May was celebrated with a planked shad dinner, and the first regattas sailed about a month later. The club hosted the Prince of Wales twice, when he visited aboard the royal yacht *Renown*. James Gordon Bennett, playboy publisher of the New York *Herald*, anchored his yacht at the Columbia, worrying a good many wives with his wild floating parties. From the veranda, or from the walks in Riverside Park, you could see riding at anchor Commodore John G. Prague's sloop *Anaconda* (the architect had designed it himself) and J. P. Morgan's *Corsair* surrounded by a fleet of yachts, naphtha launches, and smaller sloops, yawls, and catboats, and, before long, gas-powered "automobile boats"—new and expensive toys that could set their owners back twenty-five thousand dollars and more. The more modest Hudson River Yacht Club, at 92nd, was also popular, and from year to year smaller, shorter-lived establishments would spring up at the water's edge: the Waverly Boat Club at the foot of West 75th, the Falcon Boat and Athletic Club at 77th, the Bloomingdale Boat Club at West 102nd.

After such efforts to give the West End an aura of "noble leisure," nothing would do, of course, New York being New York, but to tear the whole thing down and start over.

Suddenly, the already aging el no longer satisfied the hunger for fast transport. This time the answer was to go down, not up. For nearly three years starting in 1901, the Boulevard—renamed Broadway in 1899—was a wilderness of plank bridges and precariously balanced streetcar lines, as the crews of the Interborough Rapid Transit Company carried out the interminable cut-and-cover work of building the country's first large-scale

underground railway. They managed to tunnel beneath the Columbus monument without toppling it—a technical feat that is still cited in textbooks on geotechnical engineering. The elms along the Boulevard did not fare so well. The *Times* described Broadway's denuded condition upon the subway's completion in 1904: "As it stands, the cinder path through the middle of the little patch of anoemic grass which divides the Boulevard into the east and west drives is a ghastly parody of municipal ornamentation."

Heins & La Farge, the architects for the Cathedral of St. John the Divine, were hired to design the subway stations and buildings. Soon Broadway sprouted ornate control houses at 72nd, 103rd, and 116th streets: buff-colored Roman brick and limestone structures with skylights and copper-clad roofs. Colored mosaic tile and Grueby and Rookwood faience decorated the stations, each with its own colors and motifs: blue and white at 116th for Columbia University, bas-reliefs of a sailing ship at Columbus Circle. The main powerhouse, at 59th Street and West End Avenue, was designed by Stanford White and featured a Beaux Arts Renaissance facade with double cornice and parapet, and marble medallions above the window keystones. Inside were nine towering thirty-two-foot flywheel generators, each powered by a pair of giant angle-compound reciprocating steam engines—the largest stationary engines ever built, then or since.

The subway opened on October 27, 1904. The next day the *Tribune* announced "the birth of the subway crush." The complaints started immediately. Stations were overheated and underheated; the odors were almost as offensive as the rudeness. But the subway, impervious to the elements, cut the trip to Wall Street to a mere twenty minutes (a time, incidentally, that has never been improved). And it sparked a second and more intensive West End building boom.

This time around the builders focused on apartment houses, usually eleven to fourteen stories high, and since apartment-dwelling was still something of a novelty for the respectable middle class, many of them were lavish enough to win over the most reluctant tenant. When the Chatsworth at 346 West 72nd (facing north up Riverside Park) opened the same year as the subway, it offered an elaborately carved and decorated facade outside and a whole array of services within: café, billiard room, hairdresser, barber, valet, tailor, and private electric bus service to Broadway and Central Park West.

Of course, some New Yorkers still objected to the gregarious life of the large apartment houses. But it was apparent, as one writer noted, that "the time is coming when there will be comparatively few private dwellings on this island, except the palaces of the rich." And perhaps that would be just as well. After all, nearly everything that row-house life promised to a few, a first-class apartment building could deliver to the many: comfort, convenience, warmth, light, and air—plus terrific views. A properly staffed building might even solve the perennial servant problem. Over four

thousand apartment buildings went up between 1902 and 1910, many of them along Riverside Drive, Central Park West, and the major cross streets (72nd, 79th, 86th, 96th, 106th, 110th) and near Columbia University on Morningside Heights.

Even some of the long-held properties on Broadway were finally being developed—in some cases, after lying idle for over a generation. The Dorilton at 71st, designed by Janes & Leo, was opened in 1900. The thirteen-story Apthorp at 78th–79th was one of several large apartment houses built by William Waldorf Astor and his family (others were the Astor Apartments at 75th–76th and the Astor Court at 89th–90th); it featured high arched carriage entrances front and back with elaborate wrought-iron gates, a rooftop promenade, and a private 95-by-134-foot courtyard garden with two fountains.

The Apthorp, supposedly the world's largest apartment house when it opened in 1908, was beaten out within the year when the 231-by-94-foot Belnord Apartments opened at Broadway and 86th. Both were grandiose full-block buildings with large central courtyards, guaranteed to show the world that apartment life could be both convenient and elegant. Rents were pegged accordingly: at the Apthorp they ran up to sixty-five hundred dollars a year; at the Belnord, twenty-one hundred to seven thousand dollars.

It was the residential hotel, though, that remained the West End's specialty. Facing the Dakota across West 72nd was the Majestic, an eleven-story, three-winged hotel that opened in 1894 and was sometimes called "the Jewish place" by neighbors. The Marie Antoinette at Broadway and 66th was home to David Belasco and other theatrical folk, and was fashionable until the 1920s, when Leonard "Kip" Rhinelander, scion of an old New York family, brought his negro bride there. The place was never quite respectable afterwards. Other favorites included the Endicott Hotel on Columbus at 81st–82nd and the Bretton Hall at Broadway and 86th, both with palm courts where neighborhood families could drop in for tea and a Sunday afternoon concert. At the northwest corner of Columbus and 85th was the 100-by-155-foot Brockholst, with its Tiffany-decorated lobby and public and private dining rooms, designed and built by John G. Prague and T. E. D. Powers, who had built and/or sold more than two hundred residences nearby. Named for Brockholst Livingston, who had once owned the land (Powers had a distant family connection with the illustrious Livingstons), the Brockholst offered mostly two-, three-, and four-room family suites at relatively low cost: the largest suite (nine rooms) went for fifteen hundred dollars a year. The arched entrance, as usual, was around the corner, away from the el. On the Columbus Avenue side a window and a separate entrance opened into the public dining room, where the electric lights and chandeliers were in the form of lilies, each bulb enclosed in milky white glass "petals."

Plans more grandiose yet were afoot. In the Sunday *World* of October 24, 1897, Mr. Kirby, who built and managed the Marie Antoinette, discussed his plan to build the world's largest hotel, the Hendrick Hudson, on Riverside Drive. It would be nineteen stories high, constructed around a central courtyard, with rooms for 2,180 guests. Hothouses would provide all the hotel's flowers, and a private steam yacht would carry residents from the hotel's own dock to the business district downtown.

The Hendrick Hudson was finally completed in 1907, on a commanding site at 110th Street, a rambling, wonderfully pretentious block-long structure, with a pair of huge Tuscan villa-style towers. But for reasons never explained, it was only half its intended height: nine stories instead of nineteen. The honor of erecting the world's largest hotel would belong to another and quite different West End personality.

WHEN ALL NEW YORK WAS ON WHEELS

We claim a great utility that daily must increase;
We claim from inactivity a sensible release;
A constant mental, physical and moral help we feel,
That bids us turn enthusiasts, and cry "God bless the wheel!"

> —Will Carleton, quoted in Luther H. Porter,
> *Cycling for Health and Pleasure,* 1895

The League of American Wheelmen had 360 members in 1880, and every one of them seemed to be on hand for the annual meet that May. Once around Central Park they went (smashing up thirty of the high-wheeled mounts in the process) and then in a monster parade up "Riverside-avenue" to 83rd Street, where Parks Commissioner Viele joined them in posing for photographs atop Mount Tom.

Bicycling was still a dangerous, somewhat arcane art in the early eighties. Mark Twain, always a sucker for a new gadget, gave it a try, got eight days' instruction from "an Expert," and advised readers to "Get a bicycle. You will not regret it if you live." But the manufacturers soon brought out improved, lightweight "safety" machines that anyone could ride, and suddenly all New York was on wheels. "You cannot serve God and skylark on a bicycle!" the preachers thundered, but nobody cared. Ladies sallied forth in daring cycling costumes, schooner or Tyrolean hat, mutton-chop sleeves, tailored jacket—and *bloomers!*

The bicycle—*wheel* was the preferred term—offered heady thrills. To skim silently over street or lane at ten or fifteen miles an hour, *under your own power!*—this was a dream out of the Arabian Nights. "Flitting hither and thither," as one enthusiast put it, "our own powers are revealed to us, a new sense is seemingly created." The favored route was up the Boulevard from the Grand Circle, then across West 72nd and up Riverside to Claremont, for outdoor dining in a garden strung with Japanese lanterns. Central Park was off limits at first, except from midnight to 9:00 A.M., but the wheelmen turned nocturnal without complaint. Said *Harper's Weekly*

in 1886, "Silvery, noiseless apparitions may be seen moving like frightened ghosts along the leafy drive in the small hours of any pleasant July night." "Often have I asked a feminine boarder to don her divided skirt, so that she and I might slip away on our wheels in the summer night," added the poet Charles Hanson Towne, "going as far as the upper end of Central Park and back, feeling that we had taken quite a spin—as indeed we had. There might have been a pause at Macgowan's Pass Tavern, or even at the substantial and more aristocratic Casino, for a lemonade or a glass of Pilsener, and we might concoct a plan for a century run on the following Sunday."

A new menace appeared in the streets: the "scorcher" or bicycle speed fiend, "that idiot with head sunk between bent handle bars," body thrown forward and pedaling at the top of his speed. To protect the public, the police department obtained some "silent steeds" of its own and deployed a four-man bicycle squad, with only Officer Dennis Gleason assigned to cover the Boulevard from 59th to 106th. Every weekend he nabbed a few offenders, young lawyers and doctors among them as well as an occasional off-duty cop. Most, though, "scorched their way to freedom."

Wheelmen's clubs sprang up by the dozen. The Century Wheelmen, the Riverside Wheelmen, the New York Bicycle Club, the West End Cycle Club, and the Manhattan Bicycle Club, all on the West End, generally came in at or near the top in city and national competitions. They and the League of American Wheelmen were a formidable power: they forced the Ninth Avenue Elevated Railroad to run special bicycle cars to South Ferry and the end of the line in the Bronx, then known as the Annexed District; they prodded the city into finally opening Central Park to the wheel, and they got miles of streets paved with the new "noiseless" asphalt. When a bill came before the common council requiring cyclists to have brakes on their machines, the league declared that brakes were unnecessary, and the measure was voted down.

Bicycle races and pageants along the Boulevard and drive, sponsored by the *Journal*, the *Times*, and the *Evening Telegram*, were among the most spectacular displays of the era. General Horace Porter, hero of Chickamauga, served as a judge once and declared it left him with "the sensation following a ride in the merry-go-round of childhood." That particular extravaganza included a kaleidoscope of fancy-dress riders and a reenactment of Dr. Livingstone's discovery by seventy "explorers" and "Zulus" mounted on (what else?) Stanley brand bicycles. A big show might bring out tens of thousands of spectators to jam the sidewalks and central mall of the Boulevard from 59th to 116th streets, while the air rang with fireworks and "red fire" and the sound of band music.

The parade never seemed to end. "After dark Riverside Drive seemed alive with fireflies," wrote Lloyd Morris, "so numerous were the varicolored lamps flashing under the trees." While it lasted, it was one of the great

sights of the city, and on Sundays and holidays, men, women, and children would stand or stroll for hours along the Boulevard and Drive, entranced by the hypnotic, ceaseless display of "things on wheels."

For Diamond Jim Brady, the cycling craze was a made-to-order opportunity for gaudy self-display. Draped in a noisy plaid cycling suit, with white gaiters and deerstalker hat, he customarily rode at the head of a sparkling procession. He had a dozen extra machines for his friends (his own was of course custom-made, to bear his celebrated bulk), electroplated in gold and silver. Their progress through the park and up the Drive was meant to stop traffic—and generally did.

No less eye-catching was Brady's good friend Lillian Russell, her golden hair and gorgeous peaches-and-cream complexion set off by a white serge cycling outfit and a gold-plated wheel. Diamonds and emeralds set into the mother-of-pearl handlebars formed the monogram "L.R." Popular gossip assumed it was a gift from Brady; the more likely source was a publicity-wise wheel manufacturer.

According to her long-time friend Marie Dressler, Russell had taken up the wheel when she noticed her figure getting even more lush than usual. "Every morning, rain or shine," Dressler recalled, "we would climb on our wheels and, bending low over the handlebars, give an imitation of two plump girls going somewhere in a hurry." Their usual route included a turn or two around the Central Park reservoir and then a "pre-luncheon call" on their friend, the sporty Judge Smith, to smoke a couple of perfumed cigarettes.

When tandems came in, Diamond Jim upped the ante by ordering a *three*-seater, on which he would appear with Miss Russell or another beautiful showgirl. Behind them, a large jug of orange juice strapped to his back and doing most of the heavy work, was Dick Barton, a circus cyclist who had signed on as Jim's instructor. From time to time the party would halt for refreshment at a beer garden (which couldn't have done much for the "slenderizing" aspect of the program) or just to rest, and the classic tableau has Lillian leaning against a KEEP OFF THE GRASS sign in Central Park as she and a perspiring Jim swig their juice ("Beauty and the Beast," people called them) while the park police form a ring to keep the celebrity-watchers at a distance. As the party prepared to remount, Jim would press a five-dollar bill into each helpful constabular paw.

In the end, of course, the bicycle turned out to be merely the precursor of the auto. Diamond Jim also contributed to that development, by appearing on Fifth Avenue one spring day in 1895 in an ungainly, custom-built electric brougham—the first horseless carriage to be seen in New York. With a nattily uniformed chauffeur at the helm (and the press notified well ahead of time), he tore down the avenue at the lightning speed of eleven miles an hour, glorying in the stares of Saturday morning strollers. At least six horses bolted at the sight, Madison Square traffic was jammed for two

hours, and the police informed Mr. Brady that henceforth his new toy would be permitted on the streets only late at night, when no one else wanted to use them.

But other wealthy men also found the motorcar irresistible. In 1898 a group of them founded the Automobile Club of America, with headquarters at the Waldorf, later moved to the Ansonia. The following year a motorcade meandered through the streets and up to the Claremont, to the inevitable catcalls of unprogressive onlookers; a few years more, and Broadway from 57th Street north to 70th was Automobile Row, crowded with showrooms full of Duryeas, Daimlers, Cadillacs, Pierce-Arrows, Stanley Steamers, Hupmobiles, Studebakers, and a dozen now-forgotten brands.

Wheeled courtship on Riverside Drive in the 1880s.

A Miss Florence E. Woods, seventeen, who was staying with relatives on West 80th Street, became the first of her sex to obtain a permit to operate an automobile in Central Park. To qualify, she drove to the Arsenal and got Willis Holly of the park board to accompany her for a ride around the park in her "smart little electric knockabout built for two," and proved to his satisfaction that she was a very expert operator. Around the same time, an official in the district attorney's office was being quoted to the effect that automobiles fell under section 640 of the penal code with "wild and dangerous animals," but Miss Woods clearly disagreed. "Any girl can operate an automobile," she said, "as easily as she could drive a pony."

So, having twisted arms to get the streets paved, the wheelmen were now driven from them—literally—by the motorcar, and to add to the irony, America's very first recorded auto accident occurred on the Boulevard, and involved a New York cyclist and an out-of-town driver. It happened during the city's first "horseless-carriage race" on Decoration Day 1896. As reported in the *New-York Daily Tribune*:

> The wagon [automobile] operated by Henry Wells, of Springfield, Mass., wobbled furiously, going in a zig-zag fashion, until it seemed that the driver had lost control of it. Evylyn Thomas, of No. 459 West Ninetieth-st., was approaching on her bicycle, when suddenly the wheel and horseless carriage met, and there was a crash. A crowd gathered, and the woman was picked up unconscious, her leg fractured. An ambulance took her to the Manhattan Hospital, where last night it was reported that she would recover soon. Wells was taken to the West One-hundred-and-twenty-fifth-st. station, and held pending the result of the injuries to Miss Thomas. The wagon went on in charge of another operator.

A touching account and, if you think about it, eerily prophetic: the driver is in jail, the victim unconscious—but the horseless carriage, with God knows who at the wheel, rolls merrily on its way.

6

A PALACE FOR THE MUSES

*The Ansonia, the neighborhood's
great landmark, was built by
Stanford White. It looks like a
baroque palace from Prague or
Munich enlarged a hundred
times, with towers, domes, huge
swells and bubbles of metal gone
green from exposure, iron
fretwork and festoons. Black
television antennae are densely
planted on its round summits.
Under the changes of weather it
may look like marble or sea
water, black as slate in the fog,
white as tufa in sunlight.*

—Saul Bellow, *Seize the Day*, 1956

Toward the end of the 1890s, William Earle Dodge Stokes decided that he would build the world's grandest hotel on the Upper West Side. He would make it twenty stories high, with a great central tower going up another ten stories and with his own apartments, like an eagle's nest, on the topmost floor.

Stokes was just the fellow to do it. He had already put up dozens of brownstones and apartment houses nearby, including his own home at 262 West 72nd, he was one of the most ardent promoters of West End development, and—not least of his qualifications—he had recently inherited a hefty share of the eleven-million-dollar Phelps-Dodge copper and manufacturing fortune. He acquired the Broadway frontage of the old New York Orphan Asylum, from 73rd to 74th, brought over a French architect, Paul E. M. Duboy (*not* Stanford White), and work on the hotel began in 1899.

Five years later there it stood, looking like one of the great Beaux Arts

hostelries of Paris or the Riviera, only bigger: a rich, startling mass of scrolls, brackets, balconies and cornices, with leering satyrs over the doorways and domed corner towers topped with huge open lanterns. The apartments were sumptuous, many with oval or circular rooms giving panoramic views over the city. Standard furnishings included specially woven Persian carpets, ivy-patterned "art glass" windows, and domed chandeliers inset with mosaic. There was a Grand Ballroom and several cafés, tea rooms, and writing rooms, a lobby fountain with live seals, a palm court, a Turkish bath, and the world's largest indoor swimming pool. Enough, in short, to justify the label Stokes gave it: "The Most Superbly Equipped House in the World."

Only one thing was wrong. The building never got its central tower. *And* it rose to a mere seventeen, not twenty stories. Why? Well, it seemed Stokes liked the view from there. A few years ago I had the opportunity to ask his son, W. E. D. Stokes, Jr., about it. "They just put one floor on top of another," he said, "and they got up to the seventeenth floor, and they decided they wouldn't build any more."

If Stokes had built it east of Fifth Avenue, the Ansonia might have out-Waldorfed the Waldorf, but the Upper West Side location assured that it would remain relatively obscure — and that sooner or later it would decline into what can charitably be called seedy grandeur. In the early days, though, the Ansonia boasted a stellar clientele, heavily inclined toward the musical and sporting worlds. The oft-rehearsed roster generally begins with Enrico Caruso, who, as it happens, was one of the few who *didn't* stay there, and goes on to include such other operatic greats as Giulio Gatti-Casazza, Feodor Chaliapin, Lauritz Melchior, Ezio Pinza, Lily Pons, Bidu Sayao, and Tito Schipa, who did. Other celebrated guests have included Arturo Toscanini, Igor Stravinsky, Mischa Elman, Yehudi Menuhin, and impresarios Florenz Ziegfeld and Sol Hurok. (At one point Hurok, between successes, was locked out of his room for nonpayment and spent several nights "enjoying the fresh air and the peace of the city after midnight" on a bench in Central Park.) Authors Theodore Dreiser and Elmer Rice and editor Henry W. L. Stoddard were guests at different times, as were Jack Dempsey, Babe Ruth, most of the post–World War I New York Yankees, several *pre*–World War I German spies, a deposed Mexican dictator, and a tidy selection of other eccentrics, gamblers, geniuses, hustlers, and con men.

Florenz Ziegfeld, that relentless "glorifier of the American Girl," could top the list of Ansonia inmates under several of these headings. His ideas on deficit financing, especially, were decades ahead of their time. One *Follies* set-builder, for instance, claimed to own the most expensive wristwatch in America — said it cost him fifty thousand dollars: "It's what Ziegfeld gave me instead of what he owes me."

When he brought the celebrated French beauty Anna Held (the first Mrs. Ziegfeld) from Paris to Broadway in 1906, the event was celebrated with a degree of hoopla worthy of P. T. Barnum. His most inspired charade on the occasion was getting a Brooklyn dairyman named Wallace to sue the star, demanding payment for four hundred gallons of milk. The curious were duly informed that Miss Held, "like Cleopatra," actually bathed in the stuff to keep her skin soft. "The milk Meester Wallace sent was not fresh," she simpered to the reporters assembled at tubside. "Thees milk is *much* bettair."

The public adored her, but Ziegfeld seemed to regard his glorified wife coolly, as an investment. When she told him a second child was on the way, and she would have to bow out of their current production, he said nothing, but casually brought an abortionist around one afternoon, so the show—it happened to be called *Miss Innocence*—could go on. Furious, Held divorced him—but not till after the run of the show.

Ziegfeld's love life, and particularly his tempestuous affair with *Follies* lovely Lillian Lorraine, whom he installed at the Ansonia in a convenient tenth-floor suite, was as flamboyant as his stage productions. When Billie Burke, the British-trained comedienne, became the second Mrs. Ziegfeld in 1913, she had no sooner rid the apartment of Anna Held's gilt furniture than she began to learn, as she put it, "that I was destined to be jealous of the entire *Follies* chorus line as well as the *Follies* star list for the rest of my life." But, strange to say, they seem to have been a very happy couple. Ziegfeld, Burke said, never troubled to deny any accusations. His only comment, delivered in his dry, somewhat nasal voice, was, "The trouble with you, Billie, is that when you accuse me you always pick the wrong girl."

Ziegfeld also enjoyed practical jokes and, as Burke recalled, "would go to any amount of detailed trouble to fetch off a jape." Once he gave a special dinner at the Ansonia for his friend Diamond Jim Brady. Brady seated himself eagerly and looked about for the food, but grew suspicious when the waiters appeared dressed in rhinestone-studded copies of his own dinner clothes, and when the lids of their silver trays were raised, they contained only platters heaped with more costume jewelry. "Brady took it all right," said Burke, "but demanded his dinner."

Early in World War I, life at the Ansonia was as sunny as ever; below the surface, though, agents of the Austro-Hungarian Empire were at work on two fiendish plots. The first involved the Mexican general Victoriano Huerta, whose "government by assassination" Woodrow Wilson had refused to recognize in 1913. Huerta had fled his country soon after American marines landed at Vera Cruz in July 1914, and the following year found him at the Ansonia, plotting a return to power, this time with an assist from Kaiser Wilhelm II.

The idea was this. Huerta would go back to Mexico, regain power, and then declare war on the United States, backed by German funds, U-boats, and auxiliary cruisers. The German-Mexican alliance would undoubtedly defeat the United States, and Mexico would get back the territory she had lost seventy years earlier: California, Texas, and much of the Southwest.

After striking his bargain with two German "naval attachés," Captain Karl Boy-Ed and Captain Franz von Papen, Huerta hurried back to Mexico, assured of ten thousand rifles and a first credit of ten thousand dollars. Unfortunately for him, however, Allied counterespionage agents had bugged his rooms and had shared their findings with interested U.S. officials. He was apprehended in Texas, held for a time in an Army jail, and died in El Paso the following year.

The same two German agents, Boy-Ed and von Papen, decided to blow up the Ansonia in 1915. They had nothing against the hotel itself, but it so happened that the sixty-four vessels of the U.S. Atlantic Fleet were anchored in the Hudson, and a great international Naval Ball was planned at the hotel. Boy-Ed and von Papen knew the United States would enter the war sooner or later—the sinking of the *Lusitania* that May, with 128 Americans among the 1,195 lost, had probably made that inevitable. It was only good strategy to thin out the ranks of American senior officers before hostilities began. They arranged for a bomb to be brought to the hotel and planted during the festivities; the officers from the German ships would excuse themselves a little after midnight, and at 12:30 . . . .

But again, the plan was aborted. The U.S. Secret Service had taken the liberty of listening in on von Papen's telephone calls. A phalanx of uniformed police was posted outside the hotel, the ball ended cheerfully, and the fleet sailed on schedule—with all hands intact.

The Ansonia appeared as a backdrop in Saul Bellow's novella *Seize the Day*, but the building itself was not particularly popular with writers, aside from a few conspicuous exceptions. One was the acidulous playwright-novelist Elmer Rice (*The Adding Machine, Street Scene*), who lived there with his actress wife Betty Field. Cornell Woolrich (*Rear Window*) was another, and a third was Theodore Dreiser, who moved into a two-room apartment, suite 1454, a few weeks after his sixtieth birthday in 1931.

Like many another Ansonian, the aging author of *Sister Carrie* and *An American Tragedy* had a predilection for what he called woman troubles, and these could play havoc with his literary and political interests. When he undertook a Communist Party–sponsored trip in 1931 to investigate living conditions among Kentucky coal miners, he took along an unidentified but reportedly "very attractive" woman, and the result was that press coverage of the oppressed Harlan County wage slaves was almost totally obscured by front-page stories about their champion's indictment there for adultery. Back in New York, reporters crowded into Dreiser's Ansonia

rooms to get the facts. He was glad to oblige. He handed out a press release on the miners' plight, then attempted to refute the adultery charge with a lecture on his personal medical condition. "I told 'em I was impotent," he said later. "They can't prove that I'm not."

Another reporter, Gene Fowler of the *New York American*, went to the Ansonia late in 1918 to talk with Jack Dempsey, then just a few months away from beating Jess Willard for the world heavyweight title. What was the best way, Fowler asked, for a boxer to get out of a corner? "There are two ways, pardner," Dempsey answered. "One is to quit. The other is to fight your way out."

Just two years earlier Dempsey had arrived in New York as a hungry twenty-one-year-old with less than thirty dollars to his name. In later years he would be one of the city's great human landmarks, the kind, generous ex-champ and affable restaurateur, but in 1918 he was considered just a tough, mean kid—and worse: his draft exemption during the war just ended had earned him the detested epithet of "slacker." On the other hand, Willard wasn't much more popular. In fact, when their bout was announced for July 4, 1919, one California congressman introduced a resolution "to protect the Nation's birthday against desecration by a prize fight."

But the bout went on as planned. Willard (who hated boxing anyway) was huge but out of shape. He took a savage beating and failed to answer the bell for the fourth round. And the press, led by the *American* and the other Hearst papers, contrived a miraculous overnight rehabilitation of the Dempsey image. Nationwide, they carried almost six hundred thousand words on the affray, and when they were done the champ had become an exemplar of modest heroism and "a model of clean living."

The New York Yankees were Ansonia regulars, especially in the pre–Babe Ruth days, when the team shared the Polo Grounds with the Giants. So were many visiting teams. With nothing special to do in the morning, the players sat around in the spacious lobby and lingered in the huge, mirrored basement barber shop. A schoolboy resident of that era recalled his shock at seeing how many of them smoked.

Babe Ruth took a suite in the Ansonia when he joined the Yankees in 1920 and made it his home base, off and on, for ten years. It became a sort of imperial court, with the regal Babe, in a red dressing gown, puffing an expensive cigar as a parade of friends and strangers came to pay homage. He was already the most talked-about athlete in the country. Flamboyant on and off the field, he drove to the Polo Grounds in a sixty-seven-hundred-dollar Packard roadster that teammates claimed could reach ninety miles an hour on Riverside Drive (and with which he rammed another car at Eighty-sixth and Broadway on his way back from the 1922 Series). In 1929, someone complained that Ruth's salary was higher than President Hoover's, but he had a ready answer: "Why not? I had a better year than he did."

Ruth had only a single passion, baseball, but his pleasures included food, beer, women, and gambling, roughly in that order and usually in impressive quantities. In 1927, the year he hit sixty home runs (more

The Ansonia—in a 1907 postcard.

than most *teams* hit that year), he added the saxophone to his repertory. By Christmas he was boasting to reporters that he already knew two tunes. "By spring," he promised, "I'll be able to give you fellows a regular concert." The walls at the Ansonia are three feet thick and soundproof; the Babe's lusty tootling must have tested them mightily.

The quiet of its apartments had already made the Ansonia popular with musicians of a more serious ilk, and was the direct result of W. E. D. Stokes's sensible mistrust of the insurance companies soon to be indicted by his neighbor Charles Evans Hughes. He determined to make his building not just fire resistant, but fire*proof*, and the Ansonia, to the chagrin of the underwriters, has never had to carry a penny in fire insurance. The walls are so massive you could shoot yourself there, as one poor fellow did in 1910, and the sound wouldn't even reach your family in the other rooms.

The Ansonia's most illustrious musical guest was no doubt Toscanini, who took up residence in 1910 when he became conductor of the Metropolitan Opera. The Maestro could be almost demonic in his pursuit of musical perfection, but he also knew how to make his point with humor. To an erring orchestra he declared that when he died he intended to return to earth as doorkeeper of a brothel—"and I will not let a one of you in." One of his earliest and most quoted encounters was with a beloved prima donna, possibly his own future *inamorata* Geraldine Farrar. Whoever it was, the singer decided that day to disregard Toscanini's baton and sing at her own tempo. "Maestro," she declared, "you must conduct as I sing, for I am a star." Maestro regarded her coldly. "You a star? Just remember," he said, tapping his own chest with a forefinger, "when the sun shines, you don't see the stars!" Farrar, by the way, also made her occasional home at the Ansonia and later told her life story in a volume unique among autobiographies, printed in alternating chapters—half by Farrar, half, if the text is to be believed, by the ghost of her late mother.

Which recalls another grand Ansonia tradition: spiritualism. So many residents have dabbled in the occult that the hotel has been called "the heart of spiritualism in New York City," with more mediums and psychics per square foot than any other building in town. It's hard if not impossible to check such a claim, but it seems plausible. The earliest references to a "ghost of the Ansonia" date to 1903, when plaintive cries, thumps, and clawing sounds prompted grisly rumors of workmen buried in the massive walls. Eventually an expert was able to identify the precise nature of the cries. A two-foot section of wall was cut out and a saucer of cream set out as bait, and the ghost, a stray black cat, caught and sent to the Humane Society. The author's own ramblings and interviews have yielded up tales of seances, rappings, and sightings. Household ghosts reported as rumor include a family of Russian royalty killed in an apartment fire on the seventeenth floor. Reported as strict fact is the ghost of a child of about

four, either a girl or a boy in old-fashioned dresses, who appears from time to time in the turret room of W. E. D. Stokes's own apartment.

But it is music above all that characterizes the building. The roster of distinguished musicians who have been seen in the Ansonia would rival that of Carnegie Hall: Giulio Gatti-Casazza, general manager of the Metropolitan Opera, who came soon after Toscanini and often (in intervals between artistic feuds) joined him in walking the thirty-five blocks down Broadway to the opera house; Igor Stravinsky, draped in a tremendous astrakhan-collared traveling coat and cap made for him by Coco Chanel; Lauritz Melchior, who practiced archery in the 110-foot corridors; and (besides those mentioned earlier) Teresa Stratas, Leopold Auer, Karin Branzell, Bruno Castagna, Fausta Cleva, and literally dozens of others. By the mid-1960s, when a new owner threatened to raze the building, one resident estimated that at least three-quarters of the apartments were used by musicians, as homes, studios, classrooms, or all three. "The arts of New York would be destroyed if the Ansonia were demolished; it is really the only professional music building in New York. Where would we all go?"

Luckily, many have not had to go anywhere. The Ansonia is now listed on the National Register of Historic Places (largely thanks to the efforts of its musician residents) and enjoys permanent protection as a designated New York City landmark. Unhappily, these do nothing to protect the interior—which in the past decade has been "renovated" to the architectural standards of a Holiday Inn—nor did they come in time to protect the building or its residents from a series of predatory owners: one removed fifty tons of copper ornament, including the majestic rooftop lanterns; another was ultimately jailed for embezzling the tenants' rent money. Today, the Ansonia is also something of a legal landmark: two rival tenant groups are wrangling with three different partnerships that own the place and want to convert it to condominiums. Recent incidents of Ansonia history include nine years of intermittent rent strikes, several hundred housing-court lawsuits over everything from legal rent levels to exterior balconies allegedly held together with wire, and—most recently—the largest fine ever imposed by the city sanitation department (four hundred thousand dollars) for illegal removal and handling of asbestos.

But at least no one ever called the Ansonia a dull place. On the ground floor, rear, was a Keene's Chop House, where the opera singers used to go, and, out front, a Child's Restaurant, where legendary safecracker Willie Sutton was nabbed. In the early 1970s, the hotel's original steam room was converted by entrepreneur Steve Ostrow into a celebrated gay night club, the Continental Baths. Operatic soprano (and Ansonian) Eleanor Steber sang arias to an audience of towel-clad young men; but raunchy, campy Bette Midler, of West 75th Street, made them drop the towels to applaud. Indignant tenants forced Ostrow out, only to find the space reconverted to

Plato's Retreat, a *heterosexual* pleasure house where a twenty-five-dollar-per-couple fee secured entree to the seductively lit dance floor, the heated pools, the whirlpool baths, and (with their consent) the other guests. On a typical Friday night, in that innocent pre-AIDS era, a visitor could see—and join—hundreds of naked citizens performing every variety of sexual feat in the baths, on lounge chairs, in private cubicles, and in the large, thickly mattressed "swing room." The shy could visit another Ansonia tenant, an adults only magazine shop.

There are a host of other Ansonia stories. Some old-timers, for instance, will assure you that Stanford White not only designed the hotel, but also killed himself by leaping from its roof. Others will tell of ghosts, blighted romances, and the intrigues of exiled Balkan princes. All in all, though, it is the Ansonia's own builder who turns out to be perhaps its most colorful resident as well.

At Yale, W. E. D. Stokes had played on the school's first football team and was later a noted horseman, riding champion thoroughbreds from his own Kentucky stables. An enthusiastic ladies' man, he supposedly fell in love with his first wife, a noted Spanish beauty, when he saw her picture in the window of a Fifth Avenue photographer's shop. He had McKim, Mead & White design a marble-fronted house for her—still standing at 4 East 54th Street—but they were divorced before it was finished; he and W. E. D., Jr., remained on West 72nd until the Ansonia was built.

He sometimes said he "liked to shake people up." One way he did that was by turning part of his hotel's roof into a sort of stock farm, where—until the health department made him stop—he raised his own breeds of goats, ducks, and chickens. About five hundred chickens. "He had so many eggs he didn't know what to do with them," his son recalled, "so he gave the tenants all the eggs they wanted." The menagerie also included a small bear, for a while, and several weird, huge-clawed hybrid geese, the result of mating a snow goose and a Muscovy duck. The geese all took off one day and landed in the Central Park Lake, and Stokes capitalized on the chance to shake up some officials and scientists. He peppered City Hall and several prominent naturalists with queries, and soon the papers were running stories about the "snow geese" that had "flown all the way from the North Pole," while their owner was laughing up his sleeve.

Stokes was also a keen student of genealogy, who traced his own ancestry back to Charlemagne. This interest eventually combined with his own experience as a breeder to yield an unpleasant little tract on eugenics, called *The Right to Be Well Born*. In it, he bitterly denounced an immigration policy that invited "the diseased offscourings of Europe and the Orient" to "pollute and disease the standardized blood of the Plymouth Rock Colony." Sterilize the defectives, he argued, and there would be "no more 'sissies,' no more 'tom-boys,' and our vigor as a nation, in mental and physical

stamina, will be on the ascendancy." At the same time, he took pride in his benefactions to the Negro race, and for a time would employ only black help at the hotel.

A strain of violence seemed to run in the venerable Stokes family; Ned Stokes, who murdered the notorious broker Jim Fisk over a woman, was a first cousin, and the New York papers of the nineties and early 1900s often mentioned the middle-aged W. E. D. in headlines: STOKES INDICTMENT NOT DISMISSED, STOKES LIBEL DEMURRER OVERRULED, STOKES CONTEMPT CASE, ATTORNEYS SUE STOKES FOR FEES, STOKES IN BRAWL WITH CORONER HARBURGER. Active in the era's rough-and-tumble politics, Stokes also claimed to have a trunk of documents, including a bundle labeled "Blackguards, Blackmailers and Thieves," that held the darkest secrets of the Tweed Ring scandals of the 1870s. His own letterhead bore the cautious legend, "NO ORDERS, RECEIPTS, OR MATTERS INVOLVING PAYMENTS OF MONEY ARE VALID EXCEPT WHEN SIGNED BY W. E. D. STOKES."

So entertaining a character was he that it is easy to forget what he achieved for the future of the West Side. The Ansonia was virtually his one-man creation, designed largely with his own hand and built by his own Onward Construction Company, using terra-cotta fròm a company he established for the purpose in Perth Amboy, New Jersey. Besides the Ansonia, Stokes erected some forty fine row houses in the area, including at least one that still stands and is (at this writing) being considered for landmark status. In the 1890s he was urging improvements for the West Side that were forty years ahead of their time—a bridge uptown over the Hudson, enlarging Riverside Park with a two-hundred-foot-wide esplanade over the railroad tracks, and adding ballfields and gardens—and for several years he kept a model of the proposed improvements on view in the Ansonia's second floor.

His later years were filled with estrangements, lawsuits, and occasional violence. Guy Bolton, a young architect who worked with Stokes on the Ansonia, recalled that his employer would invite him to lunch "and take two guns out of his pockets and put them on the table. He was afraid someone was going to shoot him."

As it turned out, someone was.

In June 1911, a few months after his marriage to twenty-two-year-old Helen Elwood, Stokes paid a call on two chorus girls who had recently left the Ansonia for new lodgings in the Varuna Hotel, at Broadway and West 80th. Apparently his idea was to get back some compromising letters; instead, as the story was told later, both girls opened fire on him with pistols, and then three Japanese rushed in and attacked him with their feet and fists, jiu-jitsu style, sending him to the hospital.

Stokes eventually recovered, the girls were tried for blackmail and attempted murder, and acquitted, and that, you might think, would be the last you'd hear of them. But in the New York of 1911, a juicy scandal meant

good box office, and a great impresario of the day—not Ziegfeld, but the equally audacious Oscar Hammerstein—signed the chorines to a star turn at his New Amsterdam Theatre, where their show ran for weeks to a capacity house. They called themselves—what else?—"The Shooting Girls."

7

A PRIDE OF PLAYERS

This is the trio of musical fame,
Bolton and Wodehouse and Kern;
Better than anyone else you can name:
Bolton and Wodehouse and Kern.
Nobody knows what on earth they've been bitten by,
All that I know is I mean to get lit an' buy
Orchestra seats for the next one that's written by
Bolton and Wodehouse and Kern!

—Unidentified *New York Times* reviewer, 1917

I
f you love musical comedy (if not, feel free to skip this chapter), you may want to sign the author's petition to have several Upper West Side locations designated as historic sites. For instance: the boyhood homes of George and Ira Gershwin, Richard Rodgers, Lorenz Hart, Oscar Hammerstein II, Vincent Youmans, and Frank Loesser. Also for instance, the residences, at one time or another, of George M. Cohan, Victor Herbert, Irving Berlin, Guy Bolton, Jerome Kern, Edna Ferber, George S. Kaufman, George Abbott, Florenz Ziegfeld, and Moss Hart. If the Lower East Side was the cradle of vaudeville, you could also make a fair case that the modern Broadway musical was born just a little north of Columbus Circle. You could even pinpoint the moment of conception fairly precisely: the wee hours of December 24, 1915, when three Upper West Siders, author Guy Bolton (West 91st Street), lyricist P. G. Wodehouse (Central Park West), and composer Jerome Kern gathered in Kern's apartment at 226 West 70th Street and decided to work together.

The occasion was the opening-night party for the new Bolton-Kern musical, *Very Good Eddie*. It was Kern's third collaboration with Bolton, who had given up architecture after his stint on the Ansonia (he later showed an engaging tendency to take credit for the Soldiers and Sailors Monument). When the morning papers arrived, it was clear that *Very Good Eddie* was going to be a very big hit. The problem was, Bolton was really no great shakes as a lyricist. But Wodehouse was, and Bolton and Kern were delighted to add him to the team. Just how the subject came up isn't clear. Bolton's diary supposedly gave one version: "Talked with P. G.

Wodehouse apparently known as 'Plum.' Never heard of him, but Jerry says he writes lyrics, so being slightly tight, suggested we team up. Wodehouse, so overcome, couldn't answer for a minute, then grabbed my hand and stammered thanks." Wodehouse, on the other hand, claimed he only went along with the idea because of Bolton's "pathetic eagerness." Luckily, their mutual pity ripened into a warm sixty-year friendship, and their collaboration with Kern produced a string of sparkling theatrical gems (*Miss Springtime, Have a Heart, Leave It to Jane*, etc.) that inspired far-reaching changes in the musical theater.

These "Princess musicals" (most were produced at the tiny Princess Theatre on 39th Street) were lightweight concoctions with the approximate social significance of a Jeeves story. But in their own terms they were real art. Earlier musicals, like *Florodora*, were really revues; the action simply stopped now and then while somebody sang a song, then picked up again when it was over. The Princess shows had songs that defined a character or moved the action along, and fit into the plot like pieces in a jigsaw puzzle. They were also fresh and witty, elegantly staged, and charming ("When we agreed to do them, we decided to write the word 'charm' up above our desks," Bolton said), and they played to full and enthusiastic houses. Of their third offering, *Oh, Boy!*, in 1917, the *Times* ran the verse that appears at the head of this chapter, and added, "You might call this a musical comedy that is as good as they make them, if it were not palpably so much better." When their last team effort, *Oh, Lady, Lady!* opened in February 1918, Dorothy Parker wrote in *Vanity Fair* that the Princess was sold out "for months in advance" every time the triumvirate gathered together: "You can get a seat for 'Oh, Lady! Lady!!' somewhere around the middle of August for about the price of one on the stock exchange." By then they had changed forever the way American musicals were written and enjoyed.

New York's theater district had been leapfrogging uptown since the 1830s—from below Houston Street on Broadway, to East 14th Street, then to West 23rd, then to 42nd. By 1900 the smart money was betting the next move would be to Columbus Circle. A fair bit of that money came from the pockets of William R. Hearst, whose *New York Morning Journal* was at Broadway and 58th Street and who owned nearly half the property around the Circle. Several fancy theaters went up nearby, and a sprinkling of vaudeville emporia and smaller playhouses. By the twenties, more than two dozen of them were bringing legitimate theater, variety, and movies to the region between Columbus Circle and Cathedral Parkway—an abundance of entertainment unmatched since.

Hearst's Majestic Theatre, at the southern approach to Columbus Circle, opened in 1902 with a musical extravaganza version of *The Wizard of Oz*. Fred Stone, who played the Scarecrow, said, "That was way out in

the open spaces as the theatrical life of New York figured it then, and about the only way to get there was by four-wheeler, but we filled the house for a year." Victor Herbert's *Babes in Toyland* premiered there in 1903, beneath a sign saying, CAST OF 300, MOSTLY GIRLS. Later, as the Park Theatre, the same playhouse saw the American premiere of Shaw's *Pygmalion*, with Mrs. Patrick Campbell, and new productions by Booth Tarkington and others.

The Circle Theatre, at the southwest corner of Broadway and West 60th, opened in 1906 as a popularly priced vaudeville and burlesque house, with productions such as *Wine, Women, and Song* and *The Queen of the Moulin Rouge*. Later it became the Gus Edwards Music Hall. Edwards had the best of the "Skool Days" acts that were ubiquitous on the prewar vaudeville stage. Among the scruffy youngsters who capered their way through his act were Eddie Cantor, Mae Murray, Ray Bolger, Georgie Jessel, a nasal-voiced fellow called Walter Winchell, and a skinny wisecracker known as Julius—later Groucho—Marx.

Other West End vaudeville houses included the Colonial, at Broadway and 62nd, the Lincoln Square, between 65th and 66th, and Keith's 81st Street (still standing as the decorative front of a new apartment tower), this last being part of the famed Keith-Orpheum Circuit. In such a "refined vaudeville" house, young and old settled in the companionable darkness to enjoy an international cornucopia of drama, dance, song, and acrobatics. Lewis Mumford was an avid fan. "A single program," he recalled, "might offer, besides our American clog dancers and monologists, an Italian acrobatic team; a London music-hall performer; a French chanteuse, like Yvette Guilbert; a troupe of Japanese jugglers. How colorful, how suggestive of the world's own variety—and of its oneness, too—were these variety acts!"

Percy G. Williams ran the Colonial Theatre, considered "the smartest vaudeville theatre in town," and was always coming up with new ideas, like serving tea at the intermissions. He was the first producer to lure serious theatrical stars to the demimonde of the two-a-day, so his audiences got to enjoy an occasional bit of first-rate acting—Mrs. Patrick Campbell in a scene from *The Sword of Damocles* or John Barrymore in *His Wedding Morn*. But the Colonial held terror for artists who played the Monday matinee. "Among the first audience of the week," explained *Variety*, "is a crowd of young roughs, who are accompanied by young women, nearly as badly behaved." On the slightest provocation, the audience burst into hisses, catcalls, and a thundering CLAP! CLAP! CLAP-CLAP-CLAP! of hands—the notorious Colonial Clap—that unfailingly broke up whatever act was on stage. George Burns and Gracie Allen played the Colonial early in their careers and were a hit; so did Buster Keaton. Likewise Harry Houdini, who scored his first hometown triumph escaping from handcuffs and a strait-jacket on the Colonial's stage on October 2, 1905. Also an agile young Englishman named Charles Chaplin, who made his first U.S. appearance

there with Fred Karno's Komedians on Monday, October 3, 1910. (*Variety* observed dryly, "Chaplin will do all right for America"; five years later he was the world's highest paid entertainer.)

The Sixty-Third Street Theatre, east of Broadway, was touched by greatness when *Shuffle Along*, the first all-Negro musical to make it to Broadway, opened there on May 23, 1921, and ran for an astonishing 504 performances. With music and lyrics by Eubie Blake and Noble Sissle, *Shuffle Along* was welcomed by the *Evening Journal* as "a breeze of super-jazz blown up from Dixie." Langston Hughes said it "sounded the keynote" of the Harlem Renaissance. "It gave just the proper push—a pre-Charleston kick," he said, "to that Negro vogue of the '20s that spread to books, African sculpture, music, and dancing." But it was the songs, including "Bandanna Days" and "I'm Just Wild About Harry," that people remembered—the songs, and two of the chorus girls, later to be world-famous: Florence Mills and Josephine Baker.

Two years later, another all-black musical, *Runnin' Wild*, opened at the Colonial, written by and starring two *Shuffle Along* veterans, F. E. Miller and A. L. Lyles, with music and lyrics by James P. Johnson and Cecil Mack. Reviewers promised that *Runnin' Wild* would drive away the worst case of the blues. In the last scene of Act I, Miss Elizabeth Welsh, with chorus, came on to do the dance listed in the program as "Charston," destined to become, as the Charleston, the signature dance of the Jazz Age.

Sex, a torrid but otherwise undistinguished melodrama set in the underworlds of Montreal and Trinidad, opened at the Sixty-Third Street Theatre in April 1927. The author, listed as "Jane Mast" in the program, turned out to be the show's star, a little-known vaudevillian named Mae West. The *Tribune* critic noted the "stunned silence" of the audience at this "exhibition of complete frankness"; Walter Winchell assured the *Mirror*'s readers that "the stench that just arrived [in the West Sixties] is not the fault of the Street Cleaning Department." Mayor Walker had the show raided and the theater padlocked. And in exchange for a five-hundred-dollar fine and ten days in the workhouse, Miss West won the kind of renown that *good* reviews could never bring.

The Standard Theatre (at Broadway and 90th), the Riviera (later the Shubert-Riviera, at Broadway at 97th), and several others were basically "legitimate" theaters, though owners experimented fairly freely with various combinations of vaudeville, theatricals, and cinema—i.e., whatever would fill the house. These two were also part of what was called the "subway circuit," neighborhood playhouses where Broadway shows that had finished their downtown runs would appear briefly with the original cast and scenery, before touring the country or shutting down for good. Programs generally changed weekly and admission was a dollar, with matinees Tuesdays, Thursdays, and Saturdays.

Early in the century the *Times* carried an irate letter under the heading ACUTE PHONOGRAPHOMANIACS UPTOWN. The writer was deeply indignant at the "low songs" blaring from his neighbor's machine, especially one that referred to a "grand old rag"—"by which," the writer grumbled, "I presume he means our nation's flag." It was signed "West Sider," and its author probably wouldn't have been mollified to learn that his or her neighbors were not only playing those low songs, but writing them.

George M. Cohan, the guilty party in this instance, then lived at 47 West 86th. Charles K. Harris (196 Riverside Drive) also had much to answer for. "After the Ball," which he wrote and published in 1892, was popular music's first mega-hit, selling over five million copies. (Harris was also responsible for "Break the News to Mother" and "Hello Central, Give Me Heaven," among others.) Harry Armstrong ("Sweet Adeline") was on West 87th, George Evans ("In the Good Old Summertime") on West 86th, and Charles B. Lawlor ("Sidewalks of New York") on West 66th. Composer Albert von Tilzer, who wrote "Take Me Out to the Ball Game" in 1908 (and who, like his lyricist Jack Norworth, had never set foot in a ballpark) lived at the Majestic Hotel. Gus Edwards ("In My Merry Oldsmobile," "School Days") was on West 59th. On West 106th was Paul Dresser, composer of "My Gal Sal" and "Banks of the Wabash," the latter with lyrics by his brother, Theodore Dreiser. (When the still-youthful Dresser died a few years later, the novelist kept his brother's piano, removed the innards, and used it as his writing desk the rest of his life.) Irving Berlin brought his bride Dorothy to the Chatsworth apartments, at the foot of Riverside Drive, in 1912, but they'd hardly begun decorating when she died of typhoid, picked up on their honeymoon in Cuba. Berlin was inconsolable, but wise friends persuaded him to return to work, and he poured out his grief in a ballad, "When I Lost You." It sold a million copies within weeks, and George M. Cohan called it "the prettiest song I've ever heard in my life."

Vincent Youmans ("Sometimes I'm Happy," "Tea for Two") was born in 1898 at Central Park West and 61st Street. Composer-lyricist Frank Loesser (*Where's Charley?*, *Guys and Dolls*) was the son of a West 107th Street piano teacher who detested popular music; young Frank first distinguished himself musically by winning third prize in a city-wide harmonica contest. Composer Harold Arlen ("Blues in the Night," "Stormy Weather") lived at the San Remo. Composer Sigmund Romberg (*The Student Prince, The Desert Song*) lived just off Sherman Square on West 71st. Victor Herbert, who practically invented American operetta, lived for twenty years just off Riverside on West 108th, and his frequent collaborator Harry B. Smith was just around the corner in a town house with a famous wine cellar at 319 West 107th; the house is now the Nicholas Roerich Museum. (Smith, incidentally, published a newspaper column, "The Follies of the Day," that inspired the title for Ziegfeld's *Follies* shows. He also was the first Broadway lyricist to have his work published separately, as poetry—a

signal honor; Ira Gershwin was the second.) Smith wrote nearly a hundred shows, most (he cheerfully admitted) of minimal substance. When he wrote *Watch Your Step* with Irving Berlin in 1914 (starring Vernon and Irene Castle and a comic juggler named W. C. Fields), his credit in the program read, "Book (if any) by Harry B. Smith."

Writer-director George S. Kaufman, who worked with Irving Berlin on the Marx Brothers' first hit show, *The Cocoanuts*, grew up on West 101st Street and eventually honeymooned at the Majestic Hotel ("We were both virgins," Bea Kaufman recalled, "which shouldn't happen to anybody."). Though he had a hand in many a hit musical (*Animal Crackers, Strike Up the Band, The Band Wagon,* and *Guys and Dolls,* among others), Kaufman disliked music and often left the theater when the songs and dances were rehearsing. "George hated music so much," said Berlin after working with him on *The Cocoanuts,* "that if I'd written 'Rock of Ages' he'd have thrown it out."

Richard Rodgers saw his first Princess show—a 1916 revival of *Very Good Eddie*—at the Standard Theatre when he was fourteen. The effect, he said, was "shattering." He became a "Kern worshipper" and made up his mind that he would write for the musical stage.

He then lived at 161 West 86th, a recently erected apartment building where his father had a medical practice. A keyboard virtuoso at nine, he went to P.S. 166 on West 89th, where a perspicacious music teacher had him play all the music for the daily assemblies. In 1916 Richard's older brother Morty, a student at Columbia, introduced him to a couple of college chums: a recent graduate named Lorenz Hart and a skinny, blue-eyed pre-law student named Oscar Hammerstein II, who lived nearby on Columbus Avenue. Both were veterans of Columbia's famed varsity shows, and each, in turn, would join with Rodgers to create some of the most joyous and durable music ever to grace the American stage.

Rodgers decided early on that, above all, he would write songs people would want to sing. He eschewed Jerome Kern's intricate, complex melodies for sturdy, fresh tunes that often became instant classics. He also had the knack of turning them out almost as fast as he could write them down. Hammerstein once told of visiting Rodgers to drop off the lyrics for a new song. When he returned home, the phone was ringing. It was Rodgers, calling to sing the opening bars of "Oh, What a Beautiful Morning." Hammerstein, an agonizingly slow worker, had debated for a week whether or not to put the "Oh" in the first line, but no matter—it worked, and it was the first of some three hundred numbers they would do together.

But in 1916 that was far in the future. Meanwhile, Rodgers's twenty-four-year collaboration with Hart, which produced, among others, *A Connecticut Yankee, On Your Toes,* and *Babes in Arms,* had begun the day they met. At twenty-two, Larry Hart was gnomelike, dapper, and precociously

dissipated, but despite or because of his dissolute ways he managed to devise the freshest, cleverest lyrics of the Jazz Age. Within the year, Rodgers and Hart had their first hit song, "Any Old Place with You," and their first show, *Poor Little Ritz Girl*, but it took them eight more years to really click. Rodgers, in fact, was on the point of leaving show business for a secure position in babies' underwear when the phone called him away from dinner one night. The Theatre Guild wanted a composer for its first musical, a one-night Guild benefit. Did Rodgers want the job?

The result was the Rodgers–Hart *Garrick Gaieties*, an affectionate spoof of the *Follies* and its pulchritudinous kin. Robert Benchley, in the old humor weekly *Life*, called it "the most civilized show in town." Instead of closing after one night, it ran for twenty-six weeks, and the boys followed it up with another hit, *Dear Enemy*.

And did success change them? Not Rodgers. "I still lived at home with my parents," he wrote later, "and was still expected to let Mom know if I'd be late to dinner." As for Hart, "basically he was the same sweet, self-destructive kid I had always known."

George Gershwin was another West Side lad inspired by Kern's work. The Gershwin family was living at 316 West 103rd when he was hired as a thirty-five-dollar-a-week rehearsal pianist for the fifth Bolton-Wodehouse-Kern show, *Miss 1917*, at the Century Theatre on Central Park West. To relieve the monotony of playing the same tunes over and over, Gershwin ad-libbed his own subtle variations, which both helped keep the dancers awake and brought him favorable notice from the management. Soon after, he was hired as accompanist for the Century Sunday Concerts, which featured, among others, Fanny Brice, Eddie Cantor, and Bert Williams.

It wasn't long before he stopped playing other people's tunes, and they started playing his. With Irving Caesar, he wrote "Swanee," his first hit, in fifteen minutes, starting it on a Riverside Drive bus and finishing up at home while a noisy poker game went on in the next room. Other songs and scores followed in happy profusion, including dozens of tunes for George White's *Scandals* and shows with (among others and in various combinations) Bolton, Wodehouse, Hammerstein, George S. Kaufman, Morris Ryskind, and, above all, his brother Ira: *Primrose*; *Lady Be Good!*; *Tip-Toes*; *Song of the Flame*; *Rosalie*; *Oh, Kay!* In 1924 came "Rhapsody in Blue," composed on an old upright piano in the back room of another Gershwin apartment at 501 West 110th. The following year he finished his *Concerto in F* and *Tip-Toes* in a suite in the Whitehall Hotel at Broadway and 100th (home had gotten fairly noisy by then), and in 1927, the year of *Strike Up the Band* and *Funny Face*, George and Ira settled in adjoining penthouses at 33 Riverside Drive.

The Gershwins' famous parties, with their throngs of the wealthy and talented from all walks of life, helped make the notion of "penthouse

society" a byword for sophisticated glamor. In 1930 a Brooklyn-born stenographer (and self-taught singer) named Ethel Agnes Zimmerman visited the Gershwin apartment to audition for a part in *Girl Crazy*. She didn't know which was more thrilling—a shot at stardom or a glimpse of the fabulous Gershwin penthouse. She got both. When she opened in *Girl Crazy* as Ethel Merman, her clarion voice carried every syllable of "I Got Rhythm" and "Boy, What Love Has Done to Me!" to every seat in the house. George loved her, but offered a warning: "You'll be a star. But never, never take any singing lessons."

Theatrical folk had gravitated early to the West End. Lillian Russell, considered by many "the most beautiful creature since Helen of Troy," lived at 318 West 77th in the 1890s with the third of her four husbands, a handsome tenor known onstage as Don Giovanni Perugini and otherwise as John Chatterton. Soon, though, it was rumored that Russell—an outspoken suffragist who believed women should have the vote *instead* of men— would rather play poker all night with her cronies than bed down with her distinctly effete spouse. The public enjoyed reading the details of their spats in the daily press—especially when Perugini complained bitterly to reporters that his wife had used up his best handkerchief perfume and threatened to spank him with a hairbrush. But playgoers who paid to see the couple in their new comedy *Girofle-Girofla* were not amused when the show's musical gem had to be dropped because Perugini refused to sing a love duet with his wife. The show and the marriage both turned out to be limited engagements.

Playwright-director-producer David Belasco, who rejoiced in such effects as blood dripping from the ceiling in *The Girl of the Golden West*, lived on West 70th and, later, at the Hotel Marie Antoinette, at Broadway and 66th. Joe Weber and Lew Fields, the beloved vaudeville team, were both Upper West Siders, Weber in the Hendrick Hudson apartments and Fields on West 90th. Fields's daughter Dorothy was a prolific songwriter herself ("The Way You Look Tonight," "A Fine Romance," and about four hundred others). The Ansonia had another great vaudevillian, Al Shean (originally Schoenberg) of Gallagher & Shean—uncle and mentor of the Marx Brothers. It also had Ziegfeld, of course, with one or another of his wives and/or paramours, while Ziegfeld's partner Charles Dillingham lived on West 88th near Riverside Drive; Jacob J. Shubert, eternally feuding with critics and family as he and brother Lee built a theatrical empire upon what Brooks Atkinson dismissed as "familiar rubbish," lived at West End and 78th, and later at Riverside and 72nd. George Abbott, future dean of Broadway directors, lived at Riverside and 112th in the early twenties, when *The Fall Guy*, his first Broadway play, was produced. Promoter William A. Brady, whose properties ranged from Gentleman Jim Corbett to Elmer Rice's Pulitzer Prize-winning *Street Scene*, was at 316 Riverside. Brady's

wife Grace George was a star in her own right, and his daughter Alice (also an actress) got their young neighbor Humphrey Bogart his first acting job.

The actress-manager Amelia Bingham and her hot-tempered actor-husband Lloyd, a frequent brawler with the critics, had a house with stone lions out front at 103 Riverside Drive. (Comedians used to plead not to be buried when they died, but turned over to a taxidermist and placed among Miss Bingham's statues. It was a hoary jest even then.) Fanny Brice, the *Follies* comedy star, lived just off the drive on West 78th with her husband Nicky Arnstein, one of Broadway's most charming scoundrels; Barbra Streisand's *Funny Girl* was a sentimentalized version of their marriage. Brice stuck up for her husband, more or less, when he was arrested for masterminding a series of Wall Street holdups ("Mastermind!? Nick couldn't mastermind an electric light bulb into a socket."), but dropped him for fooling around with other women.

Farther up the drive were the great Shakespearean actor-manager Richard Mansfield and the theater operator (and whilom congressman) Henry Clay Miner, who rates a footnote for introducing the phenomenon of Amateur Night at his Bowery Theatre. One Friday night a particularly atrocious tenor refused to relinquish the stage, despite groans and catcalls from the audience. Miner's son Tom spotted a large crook-handled cane that another act used as a prop. He had the stage manager lash it to a long pole, stepped to the wings, deftly slipped the hook around the unsuspecting singer's neck and yanked him off. Since then the cry of "Get the Hook!" has been enough to drive the bravest performer from the stage.

Luminous, golden-haired Laurette Taylor, the most worshipped actress of her day, occupied a large town house at 50 Riverside in the twenties with her playwright husband Hartley Manners and their children, Dwight and Marguerite. The Mannerses' dinner parties were famous, peopled by the likes of Herbert Hoover, the Douglas Fairbankses, Alla Nazimova, John Barrymore, Herbert Bayard Swope, and Alexander Woollcott. This was all the more remarkable since, as theater historian Sheridan Morley put it, "they were by all accounts a highly strung family, deeply theatrical and prone to elaborate after-dinner charades and word games which always ended in hysteria while the entire family abandoned their guests to find their own coats and way home." One such guest was Noël Coward, then an unknown on his first visit to America, but he didn't mind; he used the experience as the basis of his wickedly hilarious "comedy of appalling manners," *Hay Fever*.

On the same trip, Coward visited the equally unknown Alfred Lunt and Lynn Fontanne, who lived at a theatrical boardinghouse at 130 West 70th, she in a third-floor suite, he in a basement front room. Over sandwiches and coffee from a Columbus Avenue delicatessen they planned future triumphs. "When all three of us had become stars of sufficient magnitude to be able to count upon an individual following irrespective of each other,"

Coward later recalled, "then, poised serenely upon that enviable plane of achievement, we would meet and act triumphantly together." And so they did. Ten or so years later, when all three were indeed first-magnitude luminaries, Coward wrote and all played in the deliciously immoral *Design for Living*, one of the few Broadway hits with *three* starring roles.

When silent films were coming of age, the Majestic Theatre experimented with an exhibition of "Kinemacolor"—colored moving pictures of George V's coronation ("Taken by Royal Command") and the Coronation Derby—and other smaller movie houses soon sprouted along upper Broadway: the Newsreel (later the Embassy) at 72nd, the Seventy-Seventh Street Theatre, Loew's 83rd Street, the Adelphi (later the New Yorker) at 89th, the Keystone at 100th, the Essex at 103rd, on up to the Nemo at 110th.

Hungarian-born William Fox of West 91st Street left the garment industry and opened the country's first "movie palace," the opulent Riverside Theatre, at 96th and Broadway. Eventually the 96th-to-97th street block on Broadway held *four* theaters. The Riverside had an open-air summer film theater on the sloping roof, and the Riviera next door had another full-sized theater upstairs, known as the Japanese Tea Garden, seating seventeen hundred; the boxes were pagoda-style tea houses, each elegantly draped with silk hangings.

You couldn't prove in court that Hollywood was also born on the Upper West Side, but D. W. Griffith was living on West 100th Street when he started in the film business. William Randolph Hearst of Riverside Drive created a film company, Cosmopolitan Productions, solely to glorify his showgirl sweetheart Marion Davies in lavish costume dramas. William Fox, having sold his Riverside Theatre to the vaudeville impresario B. F. Keith, formed the company that became 20th Century-Fox. Around the same time a West End Avenue glove merchant named Samuel Goldfish was talking his brother-in-law Jesse Lasky into going into movie production; they teamed up with neighbors Cecil B. DeMille and Adolph Zukor (both of West 114th) to form Lasky-Famous Players, with studios on West 23rd and West 56th. Goldfish, forced out in 1915, changed his named to Goldwyn and created the organization that became Metro-Goldwyn-Mayer. The original firm moved its headquarters to sunny California soon afterward, but still did business under a West Side name: Paramount Pictures, named for the Paramount apartment house (still standing) at 315 West 99th. (Speaking of trademarks, MGM's roaring lion was supposedly suggested by the *laughing* lion on the front of Columbia University's humor magazine, *The Jester*.)

Even as young men, it's pleasing to report, they showed the imagination that would make Hollywood great. Glove importer Goldfish had realized he could avoid customs duties by shipping crates of left and right gloves separately to, say, New York and New Orleans, leaving them unclaimed,

and later buying them for five dollars or so at the abandoned-property auction, where it was a good bet no one else would bid against him for a shipment of unmatched gloves. Fox had scored his first financial coup selling pretzels "with a souvenir of Admiral Dewey inside" to the crowds gathered on Riverside Drive for the great naval parade of 1899. There was nothing inside but more pretzel dough, but the buyers didn't learn that until Fox and his salesmen were long gone.

Meanwhile, the neighborhood was also furnishing the flickers with fairly impressive star talent. Richard Barthelmess, a leading man of the early silents, was raised and went to school in the West 90s. Francis X. Bushman, the handsomest (and highest paid) leading man of the early silent era, lived at Riverside Drive and 116th Street. The movies even attracted some well-established legitimate stage talent: Richard Mansfield starred in the first horror film, a 1908 one-reel version of *Dr. Jekyll and Mr. Hyde*, and Geraldine Farrar, the opera star, won a new following with such films as *Joan the Woman* and *Flame of the Desert*; her ecstatic fans were known in the twenties as Gerryflappers. Raoul Walsh, a uniform manufacturer's son from Riverside Drive, portrayed John Wilkes Booth in D. W. Griffith's *Birth of a Nation* and later directed a long list of gangster films and westerns. Humphrey Bogart, who starred in many of them, grew up in a town house three blocks from Walsh, and practiced for future roles by shooting out the construction lamps on Riverside Drive. (Some years later Bogie's future wife Lauren Bacall grew up in a considerably tougher part of the Upper West Side, under the el at Columbus and 86th.) Theda

Nine-year-old
West Ender
Humphrey Bogart,
already wearing the
expression he would later
make world-famous.

Bara, the dark-eyed, man-hungry vampire of the silents, was billed as The Wickedest Woman in the World when she opened in Fox's *Carmen* at the Riverside in 1915. A crowd of ten thousand showed up for the opening, and mounted police had to be called. Few would have guessed that the star was in fact a nice Jewish girl from Cincinnati, Theodosia Goodman, living at that moment with her mother in a sunny apartment a few blocks away on West End Avenue.

The glamorous Bennett sisters, Constance, Barbara, and Joan, lived at the Ansonia as children. Constance, the oldest and most precocious, caught the hereditary acting bug (their father was the matinee idol Richard Bennett) when she was only ten, and when Mrs. Bennett insisted she stay in school she sent herself a letter:

Dear Miss Bennett—
Won't you come over to the Liberty theater and try a new leading part, and I won't get any Body else. We have a Starr part for you called the Kidnaped Child it is a great part and just your tipe. Please come if your Mother will let you—

Yours verry truly
Douglas FairBanks

Mother was not convinced—possibly, sister Joan suspected, because Mr. FairBanks unaccountably seemed to have written on Ansonia Hotel stationery—and Constance's debut was delayed till the ripe age of eighteen.

Fairbanks and his first wife, Beth Sully, actually had been living just a few blocks up Broadway at the Apthorp a few years earlier in 1909, when their son Douglas, Jr., was born. As a bridegroom, Fairbanks had promised Mr. Sully he would quit acting and accept a partnership in the family soap company, but the frothier appeal of the stage and films won out. (Meanwhile, Mary Pickford, who would be Fairbanks's second wife, was living a few blocks up Broadway with *her* first husband, the Irish actor Owen Moore.) Another star of the silent era, Mae Murray of the languid eyes and bee-stung lips, had a magnificent duplex on an upper floor of the Hotel des Artistes on West 67th Street; down on her luck many years later, she would sometimes stay in a maid's room in the same building. Spencer Tracy and Pat O'Brien shared what they described as Dickensian lodgings—a twelve-by-twelve room with two iron bedsteads—in Mrs. Cornelius Muldowney's boardinghouse on West 96th. Movie tough guy James Cagney grew up across town in Yorkville, but also had an Upper West Side connection: his professional stage debut was at Keith's 81st Street Theatre, playing a chorus girl in a female impersonation act.

The Upper West Side *in* the movies could make a chapter of its own. It began in February 1902, when Durland's Riding Academy, an old Columbus Circle landmark, burned down and the Edison Company sent

cameraman Edwin S. Porter (future director of *The Great Train Robbery*) to film it. Their plan was actually fairly sneaky. Six days earlier, an Edison crew had rushed to a disastrous industrial fire in Paterson, New Jersey, but arrived too late. So, with the same strict regard for fact that would later characterize newsreel and TV coverage, they filmed sweeping panoramas of firefighters in action at Durland's, added footage of the smoldering ruins at Paterson, and released the result as *Firemen Fighting the Flames at Paterson*.

The movie industry would still be mainly New York-based for a few more years. Raoul Walsh shot a burning-ship sequence for *Regeneration*, the first feature-length gangster film, on the ferry route to Fort Lee; Douglas Fairbanks performed the fight scenes of *His Picture in the Papers*, the film that made him a star, at Sharkey's Athletic Club on Columbus Avenue. In the silents, Buster Keaton rode the el to the Polo Grounds in *The Cameraman*, the Terrace in Central Park became a Veronese piazza in *Romeo and Juliet*, and Bishop Potter's Riverside Drive mansion served as an English castle in Mary Pickford's 1921 *Little Lord Fauntleroy*.

The movies went west, and the Upper West Side was largely absent from the screen until 1948, when Jules Dassin arranged for a murder on West 83rd Street in *The Naked City*. Then in 1961 *West Side Story* was filmed among empty tenements that would soon be replaced by Lincoln Center. In 1970 *The Panic in Needle Park*, shot partly on location, showed the wrecked lives of the junkies, pimps, and hookers of Verdi Square—Broadway, Amsterdam, and 73rd Street—and featured Al Pacino in his first starring role. The seventies brought crews to the West Side to film scenes for *Shaft*, *Klute*, *The Sunshine Boys*, *The Odd Couple*, *John and Mary*, *The Eyes of Laura Mars*, *The Seven-Ups* (chase scenes only), *The First Deadly Sin*, *Paradise Alley*, *Three Days of the Condor* (assassination at the Ansonia), and *Rosemary's Baby* (demonism at the Dakota). At one time or another Art Carney has graced a bench on Broadway (in *Harry and Tonto*), George Segal has piled into a red Volkswagen to attend a funeral with Jack Warden, Joseph Wiseman, and Sorrell Booke (*Bye Bye Braverman*), Barbra Streisand has grappled with motherhood in Riverside Park (*Up the Sandbox*) and louts at Lincoln Center (*The Owl and the Pussycat*), and Kirk Douglas has tracked a killer from the old 68th Street station house (*A Lovely Way to Die*). Richard Benjamin (a real-life product of West End Avenue) and Carrie Snodgress shared a Riverside Drive apartment in *Diary of a Mad Housewife*, as did Jack Lemmon and Walter Matthau in *The Odd Couple*. Richard Dreyfuss shared a place on West 78th Street with Marsha Mason (*The Goodbye Girl*), who in turn lived with James Caan on 76th (*Chapter Two*). In the movies on the Upper West Side, Ron Liebman has sprinted across Central Park West twice, once naked and once in a gorilla suit (*Where's Poppa?*), Charles Bronson has set out from 33 Riverside Drive to avenge his wife's murder (*Death Wish*), Sylvester Stallone has climbed a fire escape

across from Zabar's (*Paradise Alley*), and a hundred-foot-high Marshmallow Man has terrorized Columbus Circle (*Ghostbusters*). Woody Allen has used the neighborhood often. In *Annie Hall*, whose closing scene is at Lincoln Center, Woody conjures up media guru Marshall McLuhan to settle an argument in the lobby of the now-vanished New Yorker Theater ("How you got to teach a course in *anything* is amazing," he tells Woody's film professor opponent). *Take the Money and Run, Manhattan, Broadway Danny Rose, Zelig,* and *Hannah and Her Sisters* (partly shot in the Central Park West apartment of Allen's partner Mia Farrow) all have Upper West Side scenes, and most of Allen's early movies were actually put together in film editor Ralph Rosenblum's apartment-*cum*-cutting room on West 84th Street.

For the dizziest chapter in local cinema history, however, you must go back to August 1926 and the days following Rudolph Valentino's sudden death of peritonitis at the Polyclinic Hospital on West 50th Street. The tragedy moved the heads of United Artists deeply. With two Valentino films in the can, they feared the public might be squeamish about a movie whose star happened to be dead, so they asked Frank Campbell, the brilliant funeral impresario, to take over.

Campbell did them proud. He laid out the Sheik on a catafalque in the Gold Room of the Frank Campbell Funeral Church at Broadway and 66th, where Caruso, Anna Held, Vernon Castle, Oscar Hammerstein, Olive Thomas, and Lillian Russell had preceded him. The studio's publicity department sent out invitations via print and radio, and the stage was set for the Great American Funeral. The room was banked with floral tributes. Joseph Schenk, the head of United Artists, was on hand, of course. Adolph Zukor, Marcus Loew, Doug Fairbanks, and Rex Ingraham were honorary pallbearers. Jack Dempsey came; so did Gentleman Jim Corbett, Mrs. Alfred E. Smith, Jr., Mrs. Richard Whittemore, whose husband had recently been hanged for murder, and four black-shirted *Fascisti* who came "on instructions from Rome" to stand guard over the body. Sultry Pola Negri, the screen star, knelt by the bier for fifteen minutes, collapsed, recovered long enough to say "It is true; we were engaged to be married," then swooned again. But for once the fans were the real show: a screaming mass of eighty thousand, mostly women and adolescent girls. They filled the streets; in fact, the first morning, they burst through Campbell's plate-glass window, surged into the Gold Room, and nearly knocked over the casket. The corpse was hastily transferred to a heavy silver-bronze casket (as Valentino's manager said, "This crowd is likely to do almost anything!") and order was more or less restored. And still the mourners, undeterred even by drenching rain, filled the streets far as north as 70th Street and tied up traffic in the neighborhood for days.

It was a scene to warm the hearts of the press agents who had, of

By 1902, subway excavation has
turned the Boulevard—renamed
Broadway—into a curb-to-curb
wilderness of scaffolding, planked
walkways, and exposed pipes and
sewers. View here is uptown
from the West 66th Street
station.

Top:
W.G. Spencer's bicycle shop at
the southeast corner of West
96th and the Boulevard. The
tower in the distance belongs to
St. Michael's Church, still
standing at Amsterdam and 99th.

The Majestic Theatre on
Columbus Circle introduced
American audiences to *The
Wizard of Oz, Babes in Toyland,
Pygmalion,* and (in the 1950s)
Your Show of Shows.

The Great Glorifier, Florenz
Ziegfeld.

Premiere production of *Babes in Toyland* at the Majestic, 1903.

Lillian Russell (center) and
embattled husband John
Chatterton in their final show,
Girofle-Girofla. After one
intramarital exchange, Russell's
friend Marie Dressler (at left in
long dress) promised Chatterton,
"If you ever say that again, I'll
throw you into the bass drum."

The Colonial Theatre introduced
Chaplin, Houdini, and Burns and
Allen to New York audiences.

Pouring rain couldn't keep fans
from Rudolph Valentino's
funeral—not after United Artists
and Frank Campbell's ballyhooed
it over the airwaves.

Walter Winchell of Broadway.

One of the semi-rural West End's less pretentious outing spots: William Schaaf's Bicycle Inn, a summer garden-hotel on the Boulevard at 112th Street.

Even in the rain, Columbus
Circle was a glittering place.

Gaiety under the el: Tom Healy's
Golden Glades cabaret,
Columbus Avenue and West 66th
Street.

The mammoth Reisenweber's
cafe on Columbus Circle
introduced New Yorkers to
afternoon dancing, Sophie
Tucker, and the delicious, sinful
strains of "Jass" music.

Arnold Rothstein, "The Brain."
"No matter how much dough is
around, The Brain sooner or
later gets hold of all of it."

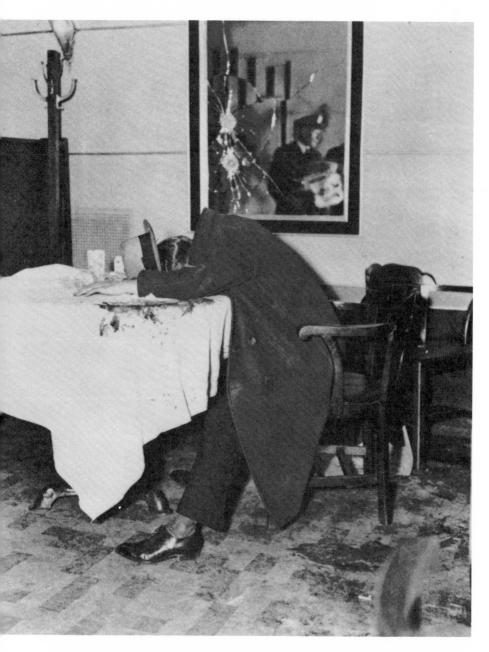

West Side beer baron Dutch
Schultz met his reckoning going
over accounts in the back room
of a bar.

Funeral of West 81st Street
mafioso "Joe the Boss" Masseria.
To avoid unseemly show, they
brought his coffin out through
the building's rear door.

Bank robber "Willie the Actor"
Sutton, characteristically adorned
with handcuffs.

course, carefully orchestrated the whole circus—except for one minor detail. Even as the mourners pushed in for a two-second glimpse of the Sheik, some of the reporters covering the circus got curious about the distinguished Dr. Sterling Wyman of Flower Hospital, who had been caring for Miss Negri ("Rudy would have wanted me to take care of you, my dear," he told her) and who had even set up a temporary infirmary at Campbell's for swooning fans. It turned out he was none other than Stephen Weinberg, a versatile imposter who on earlier occasions had successfully masqueraded as an army officer, a French naval lieutenant, lawyer, psychiatrist, sanitation expert, and aviator. But it worked out okay. Miss Negri not only declined to press charges, she kept "Dr. Wyman" on as her personal physician; said he was the best doctor she ever had.

"WHAT A GAY PLACE COLUMBUS CIRCLE USED TO BE!"

Reisenweber's started the Jazz Era and changed New York night life completely. The food was marvelous; and, if I do say it, the entertainment was the best the town had to offer. A lot of new songs were tried out at Reisenweber's. If the song went over there, we knew we had a hit on our hands. Inside of a week it was being sung all over America.

—Sophie Tucker,
Some of These Days, 1945

On the Boulevard and Riverside Drive, outdoor taverns still carried on the ancient tradition of Burnham's and Striker's Bay Tavern. Most were small beer gardens, like Dietrich's Columbia Casino on the Boulevard at 110th, William Schaaf's Bicycle Inn summer garden two blocks up, or The Widow's, a rambling old roadhouse at 112th and the Drive. The largest, Bernheimer & Schmid's Lion Palace, sprawled over two blocks from 107th to 109th streets on both sides of Columbus Avenue, with a saloon and picnic grounds, a target-shooting range, and a barnlike dancing pavilion; the huge Lion Brewery, "The Only Firm that Brews the celebrated Pilsner Bier," had been in business there since 1867.

Elm Park, on 91st Street east of Amsterdam Avenue, had an even longer history (it occupied what had once been Charles Ward Apthorpe's mansion and gardens) with one very grim chapter. On July 12, 1870, the 180th anniversary of the Battle of the Boyne, a thousand or so Protestant Irish families had marched up the Boulevard toward Elm Park for a day of speeches and band music. En route they were surrounded and attacked by a mob of Catholic Irish; the picnic became a seige, and several were killed and scores injured before the police broke up what became known as the Orange Riot of 1870.

The favorite family place was Henry Stillgebauer's Unter den Linden, on the Boulevard at 98th Street, planted with shade trees, with small tables for beer and sandwiches, and hung with colored lights. In May and June, when the lindens shed their sweet-scented white blossoms, you could drop in after dinner to enjoy waltzes or snatches of the classics from the German band in a setting that was still almost rural.

Claremont Inn, just north of Grant's Tomb, was larger and grander but never really popular—until it was taken over in the mid-nineties by a murderer. Edward S. Stokes, W. E. D.'s cousin, had been a friend and business associate of the flamboyant Wall Street buccaneer Jim Fisk, until Stokes moved in on Fisk's beautiful mistress, Josie Mansfield. Scandal and a sensational lawsuit followed, with charges and countercharges of blackmail, extortion, and libel—all of which became moot when Stokes shot his rival dead in the crowded lobby of the Grand Central Hotel. But the dead man was considered no great loss, and after two inconclusive trials and a short stay at Sing Sing, Ned Stokes turned restaurateur at Fifth Avenue's elegant, slightly raffish Hoffman House. When he took over the Claremont he outfitted the old Federalist house with sparkling plate and hung the garden with Japanese lanterns, stocked the cellar with fine vintages and the menu with canvasback and turtle soup. All were welcome, whether from Fifth Avenue or the Tenderloin. They came by bicycle, carriage, and on horseback, not the least put off by their host's lurid history, and they kept the place jammed.

By the 1900s the roof gardens atop the Ansonia, the Majestic, and dozens of other hotels around town had brought a new, vertical dimension to dining out. Some had fountains, waterfalls, landscaped gardens, and fuschia-draped arbors, and the entertainment ranged from string quartets to vaudeville. In September 1906, *Town and Country* informed readers that "Metropolitan Society, after holding aloof for years, has suddenly set its seal of approval upon these high-perched, airy Edens." They even drew patrons from out of town. "Thousands of New Yorkers who are summering in their nearby country homes or at resorts within easy access, have formed a habit of paying frequent nocturnal visits to the city by horseless carriage. Residents of Westchester or Long Island, spend an hour or two eating ices and sipping cooling drinks in such breezy bowers as are to be found on

hotel or club rooftop, and then are whisked away by motor car rapid transit to summer home or boarding place, pleased with having found a new means of breaking up the monotony of life."

And of course the hotels themselves were great resorts. On Lincoln Square, the Hotel Empire prided itself on catering to "polite, exclusive diners-out." The Daughters of the Confederacy welcomed the new century there with a dinner for Mrs. Jefferson Davis, and temperance reformer Frances Willard, founder of the Prohibition Party, had ended her days there in 1898. "Every trans-Atlantic steamer," boasted one guidebook, "brings guests to the Hotel Empire." The Marie Antoinette, nearby at 66th, was ornate and highly fashionable, and the St. Andrew, Broadway at 72nd, was "well spoken of." The Belleclaire, at Broadway and 76th, was designed by a Hungarian-born architect, Emery Roth, in rather daring Art Nouveau style, and was one of the most luxuriously appointed hotels in New York when it opened on January 12, 1903. Its roof garden commanded a view four or five miles up the Hudson. Crowded into the ground floor, embellished with cluster lights around the marble pillars, were a public restaurant, café, Palm Room, billiard room, and a Moorish library.

Most notable of all was "the Jewish place," the eleven-story Majestic Hotel, which looked across 72nd Street at the Dakota. A family hotel, it nevertheless boasted, besides the popular roof garden, a red-and-gold, slightly sinful-looking Pompeiian Room, where after-theater guests came to dance and marvel at the "electro-chromatic fountain," a futuristic-sounding device of which no description survives. In winter the management provided a series of modest concerts and balls for the guests, and Victor Sorlin, "the popular 'cello soloist," was considered a drawing card.

Then the Majestic got a press agent, a hypochondriacal Christian Scientist named Oscar Odd McIntyre, and stories about the place began to appear in the news columns. A fairly typical McIntyre squib claimed the manager had been arrested "for cruelty to animals"—on grounds that the goldfish in the hotel's aquarium were being kept up all night by revelry and bright lights. Soon a crowd of celebrities was helping to keep the fish awake. Lillian Russell and Sarah Bernhardt stopped by now and then; so did Pavlova, Nijinsky, Sigmund Romberg, William Gillette, and Enrico Caruso, who made the Majestic his first American home. When the newly fashionable hotel made a rule excluding pets, McIntyre, an ardent dog-lover, moved out the same day—and within a few years became one of the most widely read columnists in the country.

For a more robust brand of conviviality you went to Pabst's and Faust's beer halls on Columbus Circle, or perhaps to Tom Sharkey's at Columbus and 67th or the Pontiac at 81st, where there were bare-knuckle boxing matches of dubious legality but high entertainment value. The painter George Bellows had a studio nearby in the Lincoln Square Arcade; his *Stag at Sharkey's* became America's most popular boxing print. To stay within

the letter of the law, fighters and patrons would "join" the Sharkey or Pontiac "club" for the evening. Another Bellows painting, showing two pugilists in seemingly mortal combat, had as its sardonic title the phrase that appeared on every handbill: "Both Members of This Club."

Fred C. Dornheim's Café and Lunch Room at Columbus and 70th offered "Furnished Rooms for Gentlemen Only," with accommodations for stag and beefsteak parties. Clyde's, at Broadway and 75th, was a "high-class aristocratic Bohemia," where beefsteaks four inches thick were grilled by the proprietor and served by silent Japanese in a shadowy "dungeon" decorated with "freak paintings" by well-known artists. Ambrose Clark, sportsman and heir of the Dakota's builder, had a celebrated bachelor dinner at Clyde's; Admiral Dewey and his officers were fêted there, and so was Joseph Jefferson, beloved to generations for his stage portrayal of Rip Van Winkle. Summers, the roof was fitted up as a rustic garden with pagodas and cedar railings, and the whole restaurant moved topside.

Ivy League men were drawn to Healy's Golden Glades, a four-story restaurant at Columbus and 66th with *two* basement "dungeons," where the menu included Egyptian quail, French partridge, English grouse, and three kinds of duck. The Columbia freshmen gave a dinner there in 1903; the sophomores, true to tradition, planned to ambush them en route, but were foiled when huge furniture vans backed up to the curb in front of Healy's, "and like a flash, a hundred freshmen sprang out and dashed into the restaurant." There was also an uptown Healy's, a skating rink called the Crystal Palace at 95th and Broadway—the building survives today as the Symphony Space performance center—with a downstairs restaurant, the Sunken Gardens, where a good-looking nineteen-year-old from Hell's Kitchen named George Raft found his niche as a ballroom dancer before moving on to Hollywood.

At the Golden Glades you rubbed shoulders with the proprietor's innumerable cronies from the worlds of politics, sports, the theater, and the press. Tom Healy was one of the first to introduce cabaret to New York, and he also offered pugnacious, if good-humored, resistance to the meddling of bluenoses. In 1896 the state legislature set up a 1:00 A.M. drinks curfew for all except "bona fide hotel guests"; Healy installed four cots on his second floor and went right on serving. When Prohibition came in, Healy was hauled up before Prohibition Commissioner Hitchcock. The chief witness against him was the Reverend John Roach Straton, a humorless, passionate crusader who once accused the Museum of Natural History of "poisoning the minds and corrupting the morals of children" by teaching evolution. Straton made it his mission to hunt out vice in its lair, which led him to Healy's and thence to the witness stand.

"You say you were served with a Scotch highball?" he was asked. "Now, did you ever in your life taste Scotch whiskey?"

Straton was indignant. "No!" he answered. The commissioner there-

upon disqualified the preacher as an incompetent witness; case dismissed.

At Bustanoby's Domino Room, Broadway and 60th, the patronage was half Broadway, half Fifth Avenue. Bustanoby's was decorated in bold black and white, a theme carried into the furniture, draperies, and even the china, with what one regular called "a completely equipped turkey-trotting department in a ballroom at the rear of the main restaurant." For a time there were tables on the sidewalk, Parisian fashion, but New Yorkers were not yet ready for such Latinate innovations. The brothers Bustanoby had already created a revolution in New York nightlife when they offered dancing with dinner at their Café des Beaux Arts on 39th Street; at the Domino Room the dancing went on till dawn.

By night, Columbus Circle was brilliant with light. "On all the surrounding buildings are great electric signs," reported one habitué. "Long rows of steely electric arc-lights disappear in dwindling perspectives far down the intersecting streets. From six directions electric cars—moving clusters of light—dash across the center of the Circle, while from high up, at the top of its tall column, the statue of Columbus looks down, moody and dark."

At Reisenweber's, on the Circle's southern edge, people even went to dance at teatime, in the afternoon. Here was an establishment that spread out and up through three adjoining buildings and astonished with a stream of entertainment novelties. To Reisenweber's came Maurice Mouvet, the sleek, swivel-hipped original of a hundred silent-film gigolos, an international figure (actually born in Brooklyn, though he posed successfully as a romantic Latin) who had introduced the *danse des Apaches* to Paris and the tango to New York. "There is a rumor," it was reported, "that in the violence of the dance he had once (once is enough) broken his woman partner's neck."

Reisenweber's was the loudest, if not the gaudiest, of the lobster-palaces; from Reisenweber's, supposedly, came the period catchphrase "a warm bird and a cold bottle"—an ostensible allusion (with broad sexual overtones) to the lobster and magnum of champagne with which a gentleman would end the evening. In the vast, red-carpeted dining room—capacity 750—New York saw its first floor show, complete with dancing girls and a revue staged by Gus Edwards and climaxed by the Five Jansleys, who performed heart-stopping acrobatic feats atop a fifty-foot ladder. The turkey trot, most memorable step of the ragtime era, was introduced in Reisenweber's Hawaiian Room. In the rooftop dance hall, Sophie Tucker, the Red Hot Mama, would look around to see who had come that night, shake hands with the customers at some of the built-in settees, and launch into a program that ranged from the frankly suggestive to the sentimental and mawkishly patriotic—numbers like "I'm a Jazz Baby," "Everybody Shimmies Now," "Please Don't Take My Harem Away," "That's the Kind of June That Will Make a Rabbit Hug a Hound," "He Goes to Work in the Night-

Time and She Goes to Work Every Day," "I'm Glad My Daddy's in Uniform"—
and closing with her theme song, "Some of These Days"—songs, as the lady
said, that soon were being sung all over America.

Another high point for Reisenweber's came in January 1917, when cornetist Nick La Rocca opened there with a five-piece group he called The Original
Dixieland Jass Band. They were a phenomenal success. "Jass," or jazz,
replaced ragtime as the new popular fad despite, or maybe partly because of,
its suggestive name (in New Orleans, where it began, the verb "to jass" had a
fairly specific meaning in the city's red-light district). Within a month the
ODJB recorded "At the Darktown Strutters' Ball" and "Indiana" for the Victor
Talking Machine Company—the first jazz sides ever made—and when they
visited England soon afterward they were the sensation of London society.

Reisenweber's and the other cabarets broke down the barriers between
performer and audience, and the town was never the same afterward. For the
first time, socialites, well-heeled garment manufacturers and construction
men and their wives or girlfriends, musicians, artists, gamblers, politicians,
and what Sophie Tucker called "the boys of the underworld" met on common
ground in the search for action. Colonel William D'Alton Mann, the crusty,
blackmailing editor of *Town Topics*, complained that ragtime dances, those
"rotten and disgusting exhibitions of lewdness," should never have breached
"the barrier of the footlights." But from the distant vantage point of 1933, city
editor Stanley Walker of the *Herald* looked back at the century's early years.
"How innocent the old-time cabarets appear," he wrote, "viewed after the
years of the hot night clubs!"

Columnist George S. Chappell, a frequent *Vanity Fair* contributor and
author of the immortal *Through the Alimentary Canal with Gun and
Camera*, also had fond memories. "And what a gay place Columbus Circle
used to be!" he wrote. "There was the Domino Room, the first of our very
late dancing places, where no one thought of coming before midnight or
of leaving before blue-green dawn paled o'er the Park." He remembered
Reisenweber's too: "Its restaurant was crowded and the dance hall on the
roof produced one of the most genial evening hostesses, Joan Sawyer. Here
the Marimba Band first wafted my soul away on the buzzing of their
Guatemalan instruments, and Sophie Tucker later shouted her way into
my affections. Louis Fisher was the manager, I remember, who used to tell
me—oh, so gently—when it was time to go home.

"And then, among the more workaday restaurants, there was Pabst's,
foaming with customers and good beer, an excellent place to dine before
stopping in to see *Babes in Toyland* for the fifth time at the Majestic...."

On the circle, even the standardized, sanitized Child's Cafeteria had
glamor. F. Scott Fitzgerald described it at 4 A.M.: "Within its pale but sanitary
walls one finds a noisy medley of chorus girls, college boys, debutantes,
rakes, *filles de joie*—a not unrepresentative mixture of the gayest of
Broadway, and even of Fifth Avenue." And when night ended, "the great

plate-glass front turned to a deep creamy blue, the color of a Maxfield Parrish moonlight—a blue that seemed to press close upon the pane as if to crowd its way into the restaurant. Dawn had come up in Columbus Circle, magical, breathless dawn, silhouetting the great statue of the immortal Christopher, and mingling in a curious and uncanny manner with the fading yellow electric light inside."

8

SOCIETY'S PLAYHOUSE

*A gorgeous new theatre on the
West Side—more like a
Babylonian seraglio—completely
foiled every attempt at operatic
success. One could neither hear,
nor see. It was not the house for
opera comique—not even for
Ziegfeld's Follies. And when a
pretty girl can't entice the tired
businessman, it is a poor
showplace, indeed.*

—Geraldine Farrar,
Such Sweet Compulsion, 1938

Traditionally, Monday nights in Society were consecrated to the opera—
or more precisely, to the ritual of making oneself visible (and audible,
too, as a general thing) in a Diamond Horseshoe box at the Metropolitan Opera House at Broadway and 39th Street. But this November
night in 1909, the elegant coaches and automobiles were bound for
the West End.

Through Columbus Circle they rolled and then, in a seemingly endless
line, up Central Park West to 62nd Street, where light streamed out into
the cloudy night from the block-long, two-story limestone colonnade of a
lavish new theater that resembled a cross between La Scala and the Paris
Opera. Inside, the first-night audience was as brilliant as at any gala evening
at the Met, the men in black and white silk, ladies in blue chiffon, rose
satin, and sapphire velvet, all of which would be described meticulously in
the morning papers. The new theater had been christened with affecting
simplicity: The New Theatre. In every other respect it was the most
wonderfully pretentious playhouse ever built: a temple to Culture with a
plush, gilt-and-marble capital *C*.

If you knew the city's cultural scene you would have recognized in it

the hand of Otto H. Kahn, dapper financier and arts patron, chairman and chief stockholder of the Metropolitan Opera. (In the not-too-distant future, Kahn would be the first Jew to be offered a box at the Met; he would accept, but with characteristic tact he would reserve it mainly for the use of Gentile guests.) Other founders, unanimously upper-crust, included J. P. Morgan, John Jacob Astor IV, Harry Payne Whitney, James Hazen Hyde, William K. Vanderbilt, and August Belmont. The building, slightly larger than the White House at 200 by 225 feet, was designed by Carrère & Hastings, whose New York Public Library building on 42nd Street was nearing completion at the same time. It was a self-conscious essay in Beaux Arts civic architecture, intended to reflect the founders' vision of the New Theatre as the quasi-official home of the American Drama. There would be space as well for libraries, theatrical and musical collections, schoolrooms for theatrical and musical instruction, and even an endowment fund and pension funds for the staff.

But above all it would be an exemplary repertory company, sort of an American Old Vic, where the finest classical and modern plays would be mounted in the grandest possible style. Harvard-educated Winthrop Ames, the director, had already assembled a glittering company of American and British players, among them Annie Russell, who had created the title role in Shaw's *Major Barbara* a few years earlier; Rose Coughlan, formerly of the great Lester Wallack Company; Miss Jessie Busley; A. E. Anson; and Ferdinand Gottschalk. For the premiere offering of *Antony and Cleopatra* the stars would (of course) be the outstanding Shakespearean couple of the age, E. H. Sothern and his wife Julia Marlowe. As the *Evening Post* remarked cheerfully, there was not much doubt that the New Theatre had come "to stay and to prosper." Professor William Lyon Phelps of Yale declared, "The most important event in the history of the American drama was the laying of the cornerstone of the New Theatre," and even critic George Jean Nathan, normally vitriolic, had joined the ranks of the optimists. "The New Theatre," he wrote, "*is* going to champion the cause of the American playwright. It has a bank account; it can afford to take chances; it is going to take chances."

At nearly three million 1909 dollars, the New Theatre was also the costliest playhouse ever built. It was not true, as Guy Bolton and P. G. Wodehouse claimed, that the girders were made of gold, and thousand-dollar bills used in place of carpeting, but no other theater was so ornate or well equipped. There were a large revolving stage and pit, forty dressing rooms, three large rehearsal halls, and a lighting system so complex that a professional electrician had to be specially trained in its operation.

But it was the amenities on their side of the great velvet curtain that absorbed the glittering first-night audience: the thick-carpeted foyers and smoking rooms, the palm gardens on the roof and sweeping twin staircases of Connemara marble. The auditorium, where the grand tier boxes had

quickly sold out at twenty-five thousand dollars per, was bedecked with gilt ornaments and life-size sculptures and densely hung with red plush draperies and frosty chandeliers. Because the great room was elliptical in plan, every seat commanded a full view of the stage. And even with all 2,318 of them filled, the acoustics—so the builder claimed—were perfect.

They weren't. The next morning the *Tribune*'s critic complained that the New Theatre might have proved overnight what some had long argued: "that the art of speaking the lines of a classic drama in a spacious playhouse has disappeared"—though to be fair he might have added that the boxes had been filled with the sort of playgoers (Brooks Atkinson later called them "the kind of people who instinctively buy boxes") who visited the theater mainly to see one another and talk loudly during the performance.

The first season brought excellent and suitably uplifting productions of Maurice Maeterlinck's *The Blue Bird* and *Mary Magdalena*, first-rate revivals of the classic Shakespearean repertory, and a brilliant presentation of *The School for Scandal*. But Mr. Ames was not particularly adventurous in his material, and how could he be, answerable as he was to the elite of Wall Street? Would he consider (someone asked) putting on works by the more daring modernists—Shaw's *Mrs. Warren's Profession*, say, or Daudet's controversial *Sapho*? "Plays are either obviously salacious, and therefore untrue," Ames explained, "or obviously honest, and therefore true in their motives." He passed on both. The dream had been that the New Theatre would become, in Sothern's words, "a permanent and an honored institution," which would set a high standard of acting "and maintain it through the years like the Comédie Française." But Ames saw fit to stage only three dramas by American-born playwrights during the first two seasons.

Not only were the acoustics terrible, but the sheer immensity of the place sometimes seemed too much of a good thing. "I would make my entrance from Sixty-second Street," Julia Marlowe later recalled, "and then I would behold Mr. Sothern, coming in from Sixty-third." Within a month of the opening, wags had named it The Mausoleum.

Not too surprisingly, playgoers generally gave it a wide berth. By January even the private boxes were empty, unless the wealthy owners (themselves mostly out of town for the season) let their maids or butlers use them. One British critic dismissed the whole endeavor with a sneer: "The fact is New York, a little blasé with its riches and a little weary of its material magnificence, is bent just now on intellectualising itself." American producer Henry Miller was more down-to-earth: "You can't uplift the theatre in a gilded incubator." Running expenses were enormous, full houses rare, and when losses reached four hundred thousand dollars after two seasons, The Great Morgan experienced a change of heart. "Get rid of it," he said, and the backers pulled the plug. E. H. Sothern pronounced the epitaph, in terms a producer (if not a struggling playwright) would understand: "It was doomed to fail because it was built not for the masses but for the classes.

Well, the New Theatre catered to its fashionable clientele and it failed. No drama is worth anything that does not attract the mass of playgoers."

All of which, however, left the West End possessed of a truly magnificent playhouse, and under a new name—the Century Theatre—and a succession of new managements, it was put to a bewildering variety of uses over the next two decades. There were operas by the Metropolitan and by the short-lived Aborn Grand Opera Company. Walter Hampden played the Century as Caliban and Cyrano, and Eleanora Duse appeared in Ibsen's *Lady from the Sea*. Konstantin Stanislavsky and the Moscow Art Theatre did a season of Russian repertory. The Reverend John Roach Straton, on one of his periodic crusades to save New York from hellfire, went to see *Aphrodite* at the Century and reported, "It was a nightmare of nude men and women who were slobbering over each other and lolling on couches with each other, and dancing in feigned drunken revelry together. What possible art or entertainment can there be in the silly cavorting of harlots and degenerates?"

Spectacle plays, as they were called, became something of a house specialty. Max Reinhardt's extravagant staging of *The Miracle*, up till then the most costly production in theater history, called for hundreds of scene changes and required the virtual reconstruction of the auditorium into a replica of a Gothic cathedral. Robert Hichens's "claptrap drama" *The Garden of Allah* was done with real desert sand, real camels, and real Arabs, and with the beautiful Mary Mannering, lured out of retirement for the occasion, playing her sandstorm scene in patent-leather shoes and a tailored frock. And *Chu-Chin-Chow*, a "musical tale of the East," was billed simply as "The Most Gorgeous, Romantic, Colorful, Magnificent, Enthralling, Fascinating and Superb Spectacle Ever Known in the History of the Stage."

In the late twenties Texas Guinan opened a nightclub in the Century's basement, a sort of circus complete with calliope, shooting gallery, fish-pond, and dart boards. Cynical and wisecracking, covered with diamonds and sequins, Texas was one of the great public figures of the Speakeasy Era, the Queen of the Nightclubs. Her cheerful "Hello, sucker!" welcomed you to an establishment (she opened them nearly as fast as the police could shut them down) where millionaires could be found playing leapfrog on the dance floor and an evening out for a party of four or five could cost thirteen hundred dollars. But the floor show was lively, the showgirls pretty and scantily covered, the bootleg liquor never lethal, or almost never, and Texas always showed the suckers a good time.

The Century roof garden, with its multilevel promenade overlooking Broadway and Central Park, had also been transformed into a nightclub, the Cocoanut Grove, designed by Joseph Urban, of *Follies* fame. The exotic floor shows ranged from the all-Spanish revue *A Night in Spain*, with music by Quinito Valverde, to a revival of the legendary *Florodora*, whose sextette

("Are There Any More at Home Like You?") had created such a commotion in 1900. The merry *Chauve-Souris*—the "Bat Theatre of Moscow"—was a delightful Russian vaudeville imported for several seasons by the droll, unctuous impresario Nakita Balieff. The hit of the evening was the "Parade of the Wooden Soldiers," in which Balieff's girls, in astonishingly realistic

The Century Theatre, toward the end of its career.

makeup and costumes, went through a fascinating comic precision drill; for a time, the novelty shops could hardly keep up with the demand for

toy soldiers. "If you don't know where your husband is," one magazine advised, "you'll probably find him at this entertaining Russian revue."

The Century's main stage also hosted some innovative dance productions. In 1915 Isadora Duncan, a temporary refugee from war-torn Europe, appeared under Otto Kahn's auspices, playing for four weeks to painfully sparse audiences; she ended the engagement broke. The following January Sergei Diaghilev arrived with his Ballets Russes, which the *Times*, with cautious precision, called "the most elaborate and impressive offering that has yet been made in this country in the name of ballet as an art form." The audience caught its breath at the audacious Bakst sets, the daring rhythms and dissonances of Stravinsky's *Firebird*, the raw sensuality of the dance.

Within the week, the Catholic Theatre Movement was calling on Deputy Police Commissioner Lawrence Dunham to "edit" the Century's presentation of Debussy's *L'après-midi d'un faune*. In the first two performances the young satyr, having frightened away the Grecian maidens who came to bathe near his cave, picked up a filmy garment one of them had cast off and, placing it upon the rock where he had been reclining, lay down upon it caressingly as the music faded away. The *Times* described the third, sanitized performance: "Last night the faun placed the drapery gently on the rock and sat gazing at its silken folds. Then the curtain fell." Afterwards, Diaghilev stepped before the curtain to address the audience (in French) briefly and sardonically. "America," he declared, "is saved."

Two years earlier, in 1914, the Century had been the scene of a promising but, alas, premature experiment: one of the very first public demonstrations of talking pictures.

The heart of the apparatus was a projector and an extra-large synchronized phonograph, constructed in Germany and said to render theatrical scenes with "startling fidelity." There were no feature films yet, of course, only excerpts from vaudeville shows and opera, including the finale of *Mignon* and selections from others.

The tryout at the Century included the famous aria "Vesti la giubba" from *I Pagliacci*, with a German artist in the role of Canio. His singing in Italian was so beautiful that the audience was astounded—not only at the quality of the recording, but at the magnificent voice. Isidore Witmark, the music publisher who sponsored the demonstration, recalled the occasion with considerable merriment. "Little did they know," he said, "that the record of the German singer had been lost, and that to save the day, a Caruso record had been substituted!"

Another Century specialty was the spectacular musical revue, an art form pioneered by Florenz Ziegfeld in his annual *Follies* productions, with

extravagant costumes and staging and—above all—those fabulous *Follies* girls. The 1916 offering was *The Century Girl*, the venture that helped George Gershwin get his foot in the stage door. Produced by Ziegfeld and another West Sider, the genial Charles Dillingham, it boasted twenty songs by Victor Herbert and Irving Berlin and overflowed with stars: Elsie Janis, Sam Bernard, Frank Tinney, Leon Errol, Hazel Dawn, and the dancing duo of Maurice and Walton.

The Century Girl did fairly well, and the next year Dillingham and Ziegfeld brought in the firm of Bolton, Wodehouse, and Kern to follow it up with the even more extravagant *Miss 1917*. Among others, the cast included Lew Fields, Bessie McCoy Davis, Irene Castle, three classical dancers, three acrobatic dancers, two trained cows, a performing seal, and Harry Kelly and his dog Lizzie. Every time Ziegfeld added a new act to the company, Bolton was instructed to make the appropriate script revisions. In their memoir *Bring On the Girls*, Wodehouse and Bolton recalled *Miss 1917* as "a lamentable mishmash." Still, it had its light moments.

One came early in rehearsals, when an Italian tenor known as The Neapolitan Nightingale was in the middle of an audition. He had emitted only the opening notes (of "Vesti la giubba," naturally) when someone tripped a switch and the Century's vast revolving stage sprang into motion, carrying the impassioned singer off into the wings. Perhaps he thought it was part of the test. If so, he would let the management know he could be heard even from behind the lush draperies of a Joseph Urban set. Twice he was borne on, across, and off the stage, all the while carrying on with his fervent rendition, and reaching the sobbing climax as he completed the final circuit: "Ridi, Pagliaccio . . . e ognuno applaudira!" By then the authors, Dillingham, and Ziegfeld and his entourage of lovelies were not only applauding, but yelping and roaring with laughter. As they caught their breath, Wodehouse said, "a pity we can't keep it in."

"Yes," said Dillingham. "Tell Guy to fit it into that plot of his."

Which might have been a good idea. Large, lavish, and crammed with beautiful girls, *Miss 1917* nevertheless lost money and—perhaps obedient to the tradition that laughter at rehearsals is a bad omen—closed after thirty performances.

A year later, shortly after America entered the Great War, a skinny young man in army uniform and an oversized campaign hat stood on the Century stage and sang in a reedy, wavering voice. The show was *Yip! Yip! Yaphank*, the singer was Irving Berlin, and the song was "Oh, How I Hate to Get Up in the Morning." By the time the war began, Berlin had graduated from singing waiter in a Bowery saloon to a successful Broadway songwriter with a personal valet, but the War Department, no respecter of theatrical nobility, had whisked him into uniform and off to Camp Upton, near Yaphank, Long Island. There he had been set to writing an army fundraising show, with 250 enlisted men playing all the roles, including those

of the chorus girls, and another 90 in the band and orchestra. It opened August 20 at the Century for the first of eight planned performances and was pronounced "a rousing hit," from the pathos of "Poor Little Me—I'm on K.P." to the throat-catching finale, "We're On Our Way to France." (Another number, "God Bless America," was cut before opening night and saved for a later show; "It seemed a little like gilding the lily to have soldiers singing it," Berlin said.)

Instead of eight performances, *Yip! Yip! Yaphank* ran for six weeks and netted eighty-three thousand dollars ("and whatever became of all that dough," Berlin said thirty years later, "I don't happen to know—not even to this day"). The last performance was a uniquely moving theatrical moment. As they sang "We're On Our Way to France" for the last time, the entire cast and stage crew—soldiers all, remember—executed a smart "Brigade left and right," marched off the stage, rejoined, and continued up the center aisle to the exit. With a shock, the audience realized that this was the real thing, and the tears flowed copiously as Sergeant Berlin himself led the boys out of the theater and down Broadway to a waiting troop transport.

Ultimately, the West End did get a great national performing arts center, a few blocks and several decades away at Lincoln Square. Like the Century—though not under (or on) a single roof—Lincoln Center would offer a cornucopia of treats, from circus acts to musical comedy, dance, and the loftiest of high drama—and by one of those delicate ironies of history, Amyas Ames, the financier and arts patron who guided Lincoln Center through its early years, happened to be a second cousin (once removed) of the New Theatre's managing director, Winthrop Ames. It also happened that one of the first major problems confronting Lincoln Center was the mediocre acoustics at Philharmonic (now Avery Fisher) Hall. If the late Winthrop Ames had been able to make his actors heard in 1909, things might have worked out better for the New Theatre. He couldn't, but his cousin was luckier: one of his first acts was to gut Philharmonic Hall's interior and give it a five-million-dollar acoustic renovation.

By that time, the grand playhouse of Central Park West was long gone. The Century saw no major theatrical productions after the mid-1920s. The cost of upkeep, the impossibility of hearing any but the strongest-lunged performers, and the out-of-the way location all contributed to its demise. In 1930 the wreckers moved in, and the lavish, twin-towered Art Deco Century Apartments went up on the site. Marc Connelly, author of the Pulitzer Prize-winning *The Green Pastures*, lived there for over fifty years. Ethel Merman moved her parents and herself into a Century apartment in 1940, and when she married she and her husband took a ten-room duplex on the twenty-first and twenty-second floors. Other show-biz residents over the years included Ray Bolger, Jack Carter, theater tycoon

Lee Shubert, theatrical agent *extraordinaire* William Morris, Leo Lindy (of cheesecake fame), Fay Wray, Bill Cullen, Joey Heatherton, Nanette Fabray, Robert Goulet and his then-wife Carol Lawrence (who had achieved Broadway stardom, appropriately, in *West Side Story*) — not to mention the building's architect-builder, Irwin S. Chanin, who created some of the most beautiful playhouses in the Times Square district.

9

PARNASSUS ON THE HUDSON

Soon I was invited with other members of our company to visit the Rachmaninoffs at their hospitable home on Riverside Drive. We came on nights after the performance, and what memorable nights these were! There were lively theatrical and musical recollections, discussions of the day's events, stories . . . .

—Sergei Bertensson,
*Sergei Rachmaninoff:
A Life in Music*, 1956

"There never was such a street in town," recalled James Montgomery Flagg. "Fine modern apartment houses on the north side; and on the south, stables; brown, disreputable negro tenements; a garage that burnt up three different times; and on the corner, a notorious saloon which kept the night raucous with female yells, stabbings and bums hurtling out onto the icy pavements in wintertime."

Such, Flagg said, was West 67th Street between Central Park West and Columbus when he moved to a studio at no. 33 in 1903. But it was all about to change. Over the next fifteen or so years the one-time red-light district would become famous as a sort of high-class artists' colony: a block-long enclave of elegant high-rise studio buildings, densely populated with successful portraitists and illustrators.

Flagg himself was enormously popular as a magazine and book illustrator, and his World War I painting of Uncle Sam ("I Want YOU for U.S. Army") is still the most famous poster in the country. ("In the world," Flagg said.) Other artists of West 67th included painters Childe Hassam, Gifford

Beal, Leon Kroll, Stuart Davis; portraitists Emil Fuchs (rumored to be the natural son of Edward VII), Augustus John, and Neysa McMein; illustrators Howard Chandler Christy, Norman Rockwell, Ludwig Bemelmans, W. T. Benda, Walter Appleton Clark, Dean Cornwall, Paul Bransom, dean of animal artists, and Dada chieftan Marcel Duchamp, who had a bleak, untidy studio at no. 33, where the principal decoration was a bicycle with a mirror stuck in its front wheel. The artists shared the block with a rich intermingling of talent from the literary, intellectual, theatrical, and even scientific worlds. It is a clue to the Upper West Side's special appeal that, without ever being remotely an artistic or literary neighborhood (Upper West Siders traditionally leave that kind of thing to Greenwich Village), the block and neighborhood yet contrived to be a sort of metropolitan Parnassus, a home to the muses.

It seems to have started back in Colonial days. Charles Ward Apthorpe, like any self-respecting English gentleman, dabbled in the arts; he was a valued patron of John Singleton Copley, and his sister, Sarah Apthorpe Morton, was a lyric poet, pen name Philenia, known as the American Sappho. Gerrit Striker, Apthorpe's neighbor, was descended from a gifted "limner," Jacob Gerritsen Strijcker, who painted what is now the standard history-book portrait of Peter Stuyvesant. After the Revolution, Charles Willson Peale, the ebullient artist-entrepreneur now best remembered for his many portraits of George Washington, married Elizabeth De Peyster of Bloomingdale and lived in the late 1790s in a house near the De Peysters' that Peale called Art's Retreat. In the early nineteenth century, Edgar Allan Poe, George Pope Morris, Fitz-Greene Halleck, and others found reason to hang around the neighborhood, while John James Audubon had his country home—Minniesland, named for Mrs. Audubon—a short way up the Hudson shore on Harlem Heights. Even General Viele's son Herman, though trained as a civil engineer, soon switched to painting and writing plays and novels.

It was an artist-entrepreneur named Walter Russell who turned West 67th Street into an upper-class artists' colony. Sculptor, illustrator, and athlete as well (he claimed to have introduced figure skating to the United States), Russell approached the construction business with a heady combination of glib salesmanship, awesome self-confidence, and artistic vision. His friends believed he could sell anything, and for several years early in the century he had governors and bureaucrats seriously considering a landfill project he had dreamed up to create new real estate for lower Manhattan. At six square miles, it would have dwarfed a later age's Battery Park City.

His plans for West 67th were ambitious enough. With his friend the landscapist Henry Ward Ranger he organized a syndicate of artist-entrepreneurs and, more or less inventing the now-familiar scheme of cooperative building ownership along the way, erected six studio buildings on the block

between 1899 and 1918: splendid mock-Tudor edifices filled with luxurious duplex apartments and capacious studios—twenty-one-foot-high rooms adorned with balconies and fourteen-foot windows, where a prosperous portraitist or sculptor could carry out large-scale commissions and still have room to entertain his patrons. The emphasis here is on "prosperous." The studios of West 67th may look like a set for *La Bohème*, but Mimi and Rodolfo would never get past the doorman.

Though mostly forgotten today, the block's artistic denizens were well-established in their day. Troy and Margaret Kinney, illustrators and muralists, lived at no. 15, the Central Park Studios, as did Russell himself. At no. 27, the Sixty-seventh Street Studios, were Gifford Beal, a still-admired painter of city scenes, Paul Dougherty (brother of Walter Hampden, the Shakespearean actor), Lillian Genth, Charles Frederick Naegele, a portrait and figure painter, and the landscapist Henry Ward Ranger. With Flagg at no. 33, the Atelier Building, were Charles Bittinger, portraitist-stage designer Ben Ali Haggin (and his wife Bonnie Glass, Valentino's former dancing partner), Robert and Bessie Vonnoh, Guy Wiggins, Hugh Bolton Jones, Willard L. Metcalf, a painter of New England and arctic scenes, and Adolfo Muller-Ury, a Swiss-born portraitist of kings, popes, and presidents. And the Colonial Studios, at no. 39, had landscapists Charles C. Curran and Walter Griffin.

The Hotel des Artistes, 1 West 67th, was and is the showpiece of the block, built by Russell in 1917 and designed by George Mort Pollard. The picturesque facade is strung with tiny gargoyles and other Gothic and Tudor details. When first opened, the des Artistes had a large communal kitchen with a full-time chef. Electric dumbwaiters carried the orders upstairs. There were squash courts and a swimming pool, and at least one resident used to fence on the roof each morning before lunch with a private fencing master. The ground-floor ballroom helped set the hotel's tone in 1917, when a ball was held there for the opening of the spectacle play *Chu-Chin-Chow* and one of the lovely performers came as a latter-day Godiva, riding an elephant instead of a pony. The intimate Café des Artistes, also on the ground floor, still perpetuates the cheerful "bring on the girls" spirit of those years. Murals by Howard Chandler Christy, a long-time des Artistes resident, show thirty-six long-limbed beauties in a variety of sylvan settings, all of them delectable and all naked as a jaybird. Several of the models were well-known to the residents, which made the whole thing even more cozy.

Christy himself was a jovial, flamboyantly cheerful personality with a genius for getting the publicity he loved. Early in his career, he was known as what later would be called a pin-up artist. His saucy, elegant Christy Girls appeared in hundreds of magazine illustrations, and by 1921 he was so firmly established as an authority on feminine beauty that he was asked to judge the first Miss America contest. He later switched to portraiture,

in which his most ambitious project was a twenty-by-thirty-foot canvas for the U.S. Capitol Building, *The Signing of the Constitution*, which included thirty-nine full-length portraits and had to be executed, because of its size, in the sail loft of the D.C. Navy Yard. He was active into his eightieth year, and an unfinished canvas still rested on his easel when he died in 1952. His elegant studio was maintained for many years exactly as he left it.

DEATH, 67TH STREET STYLE

Two suicides at the Hotel des Artistes, both in 1929, helped define, in a perverse way, the spectrum of artistic glamor, West Side style.

On the afternoon of January 13, Renée Fuchs let herself into her brother's top-floor studio. Emil Fuchs had been court painter to Queen Victoria and Edward VII, and he gorgeously fulfilled the popular image of the "fine" artist: tall and gentle, with white hair and beard, a soft felt hat, and voluminous black bow tie. A bachelor, he maintained his sister in the Endicott Hotel on Columbus Avenue, whence she came daily to prepare his lunch. But when she arrived that Sunday she found him dead, seated in an armchair on the balcony overlooking the studio.

Aging, his work out of fashion, Fuchs had known for some time he was dying of cancer. That noon, he had dressed carefully, brushed his hair and beard, donned the silk sash with his medals on it, and arranged the portraits of his royal patrons in a semicircle facing the balcony. He ascended the steps, settled himself in a Sheraton armchair, and gazed at the faces of his former friends and patrons as he sipped a vintage port that had been given to him by Victoria. He spent a few minutes writing a short note to his sister. Then, using a small hand mirror to locate his heart, he shot himself. The weapon was a tiny pearl-handled revolver, inscribed "To Edward Fuchs from Edward, Prince of Wales."

A melancholy end, but rather stately. At the other extreme was the double suicide (if that's what it was) of poet-publisher Harry Crosby and his lover Josie Rotch in the ninth-floor studio of portraitist Stanley Mortimer.

Crosby, thirty-one, was a favorite nephew of J. P. Morgan and a scion of one of Boston's most patrician Back Bay families. He had been one of the more romantic literary figures of the twenties: poet, publisher (his Black Sun Press in Paris had published Hart Crane, James Joyce, and D. H. Lawrence), gambler, and opium devotee, he wore a black cloth flower in his buttonhole and liked to organize somewhat ritualistic orgies. On the afternoon of December 10, while Crosby's wife and mother were waiting for him to appear for tea at Uncle Jack's Madison Avenue town house, he and Josie had borrowed Mortimer's place for what their host assumed was a routine tryst. But when Mortimer forced his way

back into the apartment that night, after getting no answer to his knock, he found them in bed, barefoot but otherwise fully dressed, and innocently holding hands. Harry's right hand, draped around his lover's neck, gripped a .25-caliber revolver. Each had a bullet hole in the temple.

For a week or two the papers speculated wildly about the slaughter: Shell-shock? (Harry had been in the war.) Temporary insanity? A "thrill killing"? Crosby's own writings now seemed a sort of suicide note ("Death: the hand that opens the door to our cage, the home we instinctively fly to"), and one of his literary colleagues intimated that the suicide was Crosby's own best poem. Another and far better poet, on the other hand, e. e. cummings, saw fit to commemorate the occasion with a sardonic verse about "2 boston Dolls" who sought and found death "in the hoe tell days are/teased." His closing words would be called graphic, but hardly mournful: "BANG BANG." As for Harry, whatever had been in his brain, well, it sold newspapers. And the public, eagerly scanning the tabloids for the lurid details of sin and retribution among the Bohemians, couldn't but agree: there never was such a street as West 67th.

Less flamboyant, but arguably the best-loved painter in American history, was Norman Rockwell, who also spent a season at the des Artistes. Rockwell was born on the West Side in 1894, in what he called "the back bedroom of a shabby brownstone front at 103rd Street and Amsterdam Avenue." His only recollection of that first home was appropriately pictorial: "a blank sunlit wall suddenly obscured by slowly moving sheets, shirts, socks and brightly colored pink dresses." By the time he came to the des Artistes he was quite successful professionally, but his wife had just left him for another man, and he was finding enforced bachelorhood a dreary business. Even his art suffered. Many afternoons he would throw his brushes down and go for a walk in the park, until the pestering of drunks and panhandlers drove him back to work. (He said later that in one *Saturday Evening Post* cover from this period he "sort of put three legs" on the figure of a grocery boy. Luckily, no one seemed to notice.) In the end, a strange mischance drove him from the place for good. More or less out of the blue, an editor from *Good Housekeeping* claimed that Rockwell owed him a series of pictures. Panicky, the artist checked with the *Post's* lawyer, who said, "That's Hearst. He likes to sue," and warned the illustrator to lay low for awhile. Rockwell wasted no time. He returned to the hotel for his things (by the side door, to avoid process servers) and "sidled" onto the Twentieth Century Limited for a visit to California, which turned out unexpectedly well; he returned to New York the following April with a new wife. Unfortunately for the des Artistes, though, he soon left the hotel, and New York, for good.

Meanwhile, a lively group of young artists was nesting in the dank, echoing environment of the Lincoln Arcade Building, on the west side of Broadway at West 66th, now the site of the Juilliard School of Music. The first to arrive was George Bellows, a huge, gregarious, unkempt athlete (he had played semi-pro baseball in his native Ohio). In the summer of 1906, while still enrolled in Robert Henri's celebrated classes at the New York School of Art on 57th Street, Bellows moved his supplies and modest wardrobe into studio 616 of the Arcade Building. For the next four years he shared the space and the forty-dollar rent with a succession of roommates, among them a moody Princeton dropout and self-described "Broadway wise guy" named Eugene O'Neill.

Two of the canvases Bellows did there established him as a major painter. *Stag at Sharkey's* was inspired by the action at Tom Sharkey's Athletic Club on nearby Columbus Avenue and was hugely popular—particularly among devotees of the "sweet science." *The North River* was a boldly brushed scene showing the ice-green Hudson framed between a snowy Riverside Park and the red traprock of the Palisades; on its strength Bellows was elected the youngest member of the National Academy of Art.

Bellows's teacher Henri left the New York School of Art and followed his former student to the Lincoln Arcade early in 1909, where he set up his own portrait class in studio 606, a large room heated by a pot-bellied stove. His students included Edward Hopper, Rockwell Kent, Guy Pène du Bois, Glenn Coleman, Yasuo Kuniyoshi, and a high school sophomore named Stuart Davis. John Sloan, who had helped Henri get settled there, came by fairly often. After the first exhibit of student work at the Henri School, Sloan reported in his diary, he, his wife Dolly, and the Henris drifted down Broadway "to Pabst's at the Circle and had a couple of glasses of beer. Just to keep us from being in perfect health."

On the occasion of the famous 1913 Armory Show, which introduced the likes of Picasso, Braque, and Matisse to a scandalized America, the young artists who had organized it—Jerome Myers (at whose studio the sponsors first met), Gutzon Borglum (who would later sculpt Mount Rushmore), Walt Kuhn, Arthur B. Davies, and other radicals—decided to throw a beefsteak dinner for their "friends and enemies of the press." Healy's, on Columbus Avenue, was chosen as the perfect setting: sufficiently raucous, and midway between the Bohemian garrets of the Arcade Building and the swank studios of West 67th. There were speeches, bad jokes, and a high-kicking contest, the waitresses sang and danced, and so did the painters and critics, and the artists gallantly picked up the tab; budget-minded readers will note that dinner for forty-five or so—"all you can eat and drink," as it said on the menu—came to a whopping $234.

Other artists and institutions were stashed here and there around the neighborhood. Louis Vecchio, "formerly of Florence, Italy," had a studio at 140 West 81st, where he combined a portrait practice with personal

instruction in "dancing, grace, poise and stage arts." Thomas Shields Clarke, who designed the caryatids (representing the four seasons) on the Appellate Court building downtown at Madison and East 25th, lived at 50 Riverside Drive; Karl Bitter, whose stone figures of *Architecture*, *Sculpture*, *Painting*, and *Music* adorn the front of the Metropolitan Museum of Art, had a studio on the second-to-top floor of 44 West 77th, another "studio building" richly encrusted with Gothic traceries, which was also the home of Harrison Fisher, one of the "swank crowd" of prewar illustrators. Thure de Thulstrup, whose elegant city scenes enlivened the pages of *Harper's Weekly* in the 1880s and 1890s, was at 265 West 81st. His studio had a large collection of uniforms and military gear; his favorite souvenir (Thulstrup being a French veteran of the 1871 war) was the parade helmet of a Prussian officer. Cartoonists Rube Goldberg and George Herriman, creator of Krazy Kat, lived nearby. The National Academy of Design was located for over fifteen years in temporary quarters at Columbus and 109th, and the New York School of Fine and Applied Art, founded by Frank A. Parsons, offered the first U.S. course in interior decoration at the Studio Building, 2237 Broadway (80th Street), in a building (still standing) that also housed occasional shows by The Eight (a.k.a. the Ash Can School—Henri, Sloan, William Glackens, George Luks, Everett Shinn, Maurice Prendergast, Arthur B. Davies, and Ernest Lawson), and other young comers.

California-born Don Freeman, a sort of American Daumier, lived and worked in "a large, forsaken dentist's office" in the top of a three-story building on Columbus Circle, where "the entire city seemed to propel itself past my windows." He found endless delight and subject matter in the Circle's endless traffic, Hell's Kitchen urchins, soapbox haranguers, and "general pandemonium." From one wall hung a trumpet that also served as a brush holder. "But every so often when I felt like blowing off steam, the brushes would have to go." One evening he was serenading the neighborhood with an old tune, "My Wonderful One," when his friend and sometime collaborator, the playwright William Saroyan, wandered in. "Heard the music so I thought I'd come up," he said. "Go ahead, keep playing. It sounds great, especially from four blocks away!" ("That's New York for you," Freeman observed. "Leave your window open, and a playwright appears at your door.") Saroyan hung around for awhile, then added a part for Freeman to his new play, *The Beautiful People*: a long-lost brother who returns in the final act, playing "My Wonderful One" on a trumpet as he walks slowly homeward.

Paul Cadmus, born in a West 103rd Street tenement in 1904, also delighted in the city's pandemonium, favoring scenes of lust and/or violence for his highly detailed, dramatically sensational images. Cadmus leapt suddenly to fame in 1934 when his painting *The Fleet's In*, depicting several sailors and young ladies enjoying each other's company on Riverside Drive, was thrown out of the Public Works Art Project exhibition. Secretary of the

Navy Swanson explained why: "The painting represents the most disgraceful, sordid, disreputable, drunken brawl, wherein apparently a number of enlisted men are consorting with a party of streetwalkers and denizens of the red-light district." It is now, however, in the collection of the Naval Historical Center in Washington. (Cadmus's 1938 *Sailors and Floozies*, also set on the Drive, is in the Whitney Museum in New York.)

In 1944 the poetic Russian-French painter Marc Chagall, then in his mid-fifties and in deep mourning after his wife's sudden death, took a large apartment with a magnificent river view on the Drive at West 75th. He came to the right place. A friend of the artist arranged for a young lady from the neighborhood to come in and do his housework. She was Virginia Haggard MacNeill, daughter of an Irish lord and wife of an impecunious Scottish artist, and she became, in quick succession, Chagall's mistress, the mother of his son, and his wife. Chagall spent almost all his later life in France, but his stay in the neighborhood seems to have been in his thoughts twenty years later when he painted the huge allegorical panels that now grace the lobby of the Metropolitan Opera House at Lincoln Center. In the one called *The Sources of Music*, he shows the Tree of Life—floating in the air above the Hudson River.

At mid-century, the Lincoln Arcade Building still stood above Lincoln Square. (Actually, the original building had burned to the ground in 1931 in the first New York City fire in which every available piece of firefighting equipment was called to the scene; it was later rebuilt from the original plans.) Some, with wry affection, called it the Dog Kennel. With its bowling alley and theater, grimy offices, jewelers' and millinery shops downstairs, its echoing upper floors filled with everything from lawyers and detective agencies to artists and dance students, it was an uptown Bohemia unto itself. Raphael Soyer had a studio there in the forties and fifties, as did his close friend, the Viennese painter Joseph Floch, the futurist sculptor Alexander Archipenko, and the great Missouri-born muralist Thomas Hart Benton. Soyer made friends with the Arcade's dressmaker tenants. "I used to borrow their sewing machines and dummies and use them in my paintings," he said, "and I would ask the young girls who worked in the shops there to pose." Quite a few of those accommodating young ladies can now see their likenesses on the walls of the Whitney, the Hirshhorn, and other major American museums.

But it was 67th Street that caught the imagination—where life seemed to be about flashy artists, their brilliant friends, and their beautiful models. As Flagg liked to point out, it was a street of contrasts. The stables and garages survived into the forties, in piquant counterpoint to the proud facades across the way. The street even had its own "village blacksmith": Michael Cavanaugh, at no. 28. Flagg, who took such delight in the depravities of his neighbors, also found his home at no. 33 to be a perfect workplace.

On a spring day, with the window open, there would be no disturbing sounds except the musical ones from Maestro Buzzi-Peccia's vocal studio on the first floor—and the golden tones of Caruso, a frequent visitor, could hardly be called a nuisance.

On another quiet afternoon, in 1907, Gustav Mahler and his wife were in their eleventh-floor suite at the Majestic Hotel a few blocks up Central Park West at 72nd Street.

Mahler was in New York to conduct his first season at the Metropolitan Opera. The suite was large, with—of course—two grand pianos, and the composer was at work on a new symphony when a confused noise in the street drew him to the window. It was the funeral cortege of a fireman. A few days before, the Mahlers had read of his heroic death, and now as they watched, the mourners stopped almost directly below while someone delivered a short address. No words reached their window, only the murmur of the voice eleven floors below. There was a short pause, then a single stroke on a muffled drum, and the procession moved on in silence.

Alma Mahler looked anxiously across at her husband; she saw he was leaning out the window, his face streaming with tears. Later, she said, that muffled drumbeat would reemerge hauntingly in Mahler's Tenth Symphony—his unfinished final work.

Euterpe and Terpsichore, muses of music and dance, had been friendly to the Upper West Side since the 1790s, when Elizabeth De Peyster's singing first attracted the attentions of Charles Willson Peale: "So sweet a voice," he reasoned, "bespeaks an harmonious mind." Edward MacDowell, America's own great Romantic composer, was Columbia University's Professor of Music in the 1890s, but he didn't stay long. The notion that music might be worthy of serious study "had not yet penetrated the academic skull"— as one of his students (John Erskine) observed—and the music department was relegated to the second floor of a red brick building, a former unit of the Bloomingdale Lunatic Asylum, at 116th and Broadway.

In the early 1900s the composer Charles Ives ("our Washington, Lincoln and Jefferson of music," according to Leonard Bernstein) shared an apartment he and his friends called Poverty Flat at 65 Central Park West. When Enrico Caruso first came to New York in 1903 he, like Mahler, stayed at the Majestic. Toscanini, Stravinsky, and uncountable others graced the Ansonia with their presence. During the 1920s, Sergei Rachmaninoff lived at 33 Riverside Drive, which became a center for expatriate Russian performing artists, especially when Konstantin Stanislavsky and his Moscow Art Theatre came to town in 1922–23. (The house had been the home of Charles P. H. Gilbert, architect of this and many nearby mansions; the site is now occupied by the building that held the Gershwin penthouses.) Mischa Elman, the violin prodigy, lived at the Euclid Hall Hotel, 2345 Broadway; Frank and Walter Damrosch, major figures in the symphonic

and operatic worlds, lived on West 72nd, and their brother-in-law David Mannes, who later founded the Mannes School of Music, was on Amsterdam at West 75th.

Music, dance, and theater were fairly respectable by the time the Lincoln Center for the Performing Arts began to take shape in the 1960s. Philharmonic (now Avery Fisher) Hall was completed first, in 1962, and inaugurated with the *Fanfare for the Common Man*, composed for the occasion (or more accurately, adapted from his Third Symphony) by Aaron Copland. It was soon joined by the New York State Theater, the Metropolitan Opera, the Vivian Beaumont Theater, the new Juilliard School of Music across 65th Street (transplanted from Morningside Heights in 1968), and an open-air performing space, Walter Damrosch Park. In the next twenty-five years Lincoln Center would become a symbol of New York as recognizable as the Statue of Liberty, and a model for similar performing arts centers around the country and world. By now virtually every major conductor, soloist, dancer, choreographer, and singer in the world has performed there (not to mention the incomparable Big Apple Circus), while the innovative "Live from Lincoln Center" series on public television has brought cultural events to the widest audience in history and made world-class superstars of Luciano Pavarotti, Zubin Mehta, and George Balanchine.

Many Lincoln Center performers also are or have been neighborhood residents, including Beverly Sills, Isaac Stern, and Leonard Bernstein (long-time Central Park West residents), Itzhak Perlman, Jaime Laredo, Emanuel Ax, and Pinchas and Eugenia Zuckerman (Riverside Drive), Grace Bumbry, Marianne Krupsak, Kay Mazzo, and Duke Ellington (Lincoln Towers). By 1980, several years after Philharmonic Hall had been renamed Avery Fisher Hall in honor of the patron who paid for a complete interior and acoustical overhaul, one writer estimated that forty-six of the New York Philharmonic's one-hundred-six musicians were West Siders.

With less fanfare, the West Side also helped nourish what is arguably the only great, uniquely American music: jazz. The Original Dixieland Jass Band that enlivened the evenings at Reisenweber's may have been a fairly pallid imitation of the (originally) black music that came out of New Orleans and Chicago early in the century, but the jazzmen—and women—who came to (or from) the West Side later included some of the greatest. Thomas "Fats" Waller's family lived on West 63rd Street, shortly after the turn of the century. The legendary cornetist Bix Beiderbecke, whose all-too-brief life inspired the novel and movie *Young Man with a Horn*, stayed at 119 West 71st when he first came to New York. Bandleader Jimmy Dorsey had an apartment at the Hotel des Artistes, where he threw a party for Bette Davis the night before she left for Hollywood. Thelonious Sphere Monk, pioneer bop pianist-composer, also grew up on West 63rd, in the

Phipps houses, where the neighbors heard his playing and (one recalled) "used to holler at him to shut up." The trombonist-arranger Eddie Durham, who orchestrated "One O'Clock Jump" and other great Count Basie numbers, was also a child of the San Juan Hill area. By the 1940s and 1950s, Duke Ellington, John Coltrane, Paul Gonsalves, Doc Cheatham, Bill Evans, Teddy Wilson, Billy Strayhorn, and Don Ellis had settled on or near 106th Street. The legendary vocalist Billie Holiday spent her last, burned-out years in a room-and-a-half on West 87th Street. Benny Goodman lived briefly in the El Dorado on Central Park West (before settling permanently on the East Side) and elsewhere in the neighborhood were Miles Davis, Maynard Ferguson, Miff Mole, Nina Simone, Lena Horne, Roberta Flack, Herbie Mann, Les Elgart, Gerry Mulligan, Neal Hefti, and a good fifty other noted jazz musicians. It was two West Siders, appropriately, Orrin Keepnews and Bill Grauer, Jr., who founded Riverside Records, the first company devoted to reissuing classic jazz recordings, in 1952. Today Thelonious Sphere Monk Circle, a street within the Amsterdam Houses complex, honors Monk, and the full length of West 106th has been rechristened Duke Ellington Boulevard.

This last is a bit ironic. Musicians—especially jazzmen playing one-night stands—get around, like diplomats or gypsies, and none got around more than Duke Ellington. True, the Duke owned two houses on Riverside Drive (one for his sister and one for his son), and his only permanent address in his last decades was his and Evie Ellington's apartment at 140 West End Avenue, but he seemed truly at home only when he and his orchestra were on tour. "New York," he said, "is just where I keep my mailbox."

One day in 1974 Edward O. D. Downes, well-known musicologist, opera critic, and a Dakota resident off and on since the 1920s, got a call from a musical friend, who told him that a young English musician and his wife wanted to buy an apartment in the venerable building. The Dakota's rules required them to first be acquainted with someone in the building. Would Downes be willing to chat with them? "Sure," he answered. Since his guests were English, he invited them for tea, and asked his niece to come and pour. "Being totally ignorant about popular music, the name didn't ring a bell," says Downes. "I told her I'd agreed to meet with a young man named John Lemon, and he had something to do with popular music. There was a long silence, and finally she said, 'Uncle, that's John Lennon. He's one of the best-known musicians in the world.' "

Tea was quite pleasant. John mentioned that he had given up popular music, at least momentarily, for something more serious. "I think it consisted in taking a standard symphony, Beethoven or Brahms, and playing it out of doors, where there might be a breeze," Downes said, "and the musicians were to play what was in front of them, and if the breeze turned the page,

that's what they would perform. Not all that strange an idea, when you think of what some serious composers have done."

The upshot was to give the Upper West Side the most celebrated of all its popular stars. John Lennon and Yoko Ono bought the actor Robert Ryan's seventh-floor apartment (still occupied, the Lennons said, by the gentle ghost of Ryan's late wife, Jessie). The next year they bought some rooms on the ground floor for a studio, and by 1980 they owned twenty-eight rooms in the building. According to Stephen Birmingham in *Life at the Dakota*, John and Yoko were colorful but quiet neighbors, who would prepare sushi for the Dakota's annual courtyard party. When Yoko was pregnant, John would order in special brunches from the Silver Palate on Columbus Avenue, and when their son Sean grew to toddlerhood his father enjoyed long walks with him in Central Park.

Dakota resident John Lennon flashes the "V" sign after his successful contest with U.S. immigration authorities.

Other pop and rock musicians have also found the Upper West Side congenial, among them Harry Belafonte, Mitch Miller, Steve Lawrence and Edie Gorme, Eddie Fisher, Diahann Carroll, James Taylor, Paul Simon,

Mick Jagger, Billy Joel, Peter Allen, and Barry Manilow. Many settled into large old West Side apartments after they hit it big. Carly Simon, a native of Central Park West, was an exception. So was Bette Midler, who shared a cheap apartment on West 75th before fame struck at the Continental Baths.

But by the late seventies the Lennons weren't just Upper West Side residents; they were a local landmark. It was common to see a gaggle of paparazzi and fans waiting on West 72nd for a glimpse of John and Yoko, easily recognizable in bizarre dress and shades, as they stepped from the building into matching silver His and Hers limousines. The Dakota's switchboard got twenty or thirty calls a day from Lennon fans, and occasionally a group of girls would elude the doorman and prowl the halls hoping for a glimpse of the ex-Beatle. But that was the price of fame—and after all, it was just harmless fun.

10

L'AFFAIRE GORKY AND OTHER LITERARY EXCITEMENTS

*If New York has anything
approaching a literary center
today, it is the Upper West Side.*

—Susan Edmiston and Linda D.
  Cirino, *Literary New York:
  A History and Guide,* 1976

Maxim Gorky, the first of Russia's great proletarian novelists, was a hero to many Americans in 1906, both for his angry, realistic stories of lower-class life under the Romanovs and for his persecution at the hands of the tsar's police. When he and his wife came to New York to raise funds for a Marxist revolution in Russia, thousands came out in the rain to meet the boat. A few hours later the Gorkys were installed at the Belleclaire Hotel, where the socialist publisher H. Gaylord Wilshire, operating as a sort of one-man welcoming committee, had secured them a top-floor suite with a view of the Hudson that reminded the novelist of his beloved Volga.

At the Belleclaire, Gorky held court for hundreds of visitors, including Mark Twain and William Dean Howells. In the following days he was guest of honor at meetings, receptions, and gala dinners; at the Wilshire home on West 93rd Street, eminent thinkers such as H. G. Wells and Charles A. Beard listened intently to his observations on the Russo-Japanese War; he was even delighted by the obligatory jaunt to Grant's Tomb, and remarked appreciatively on how few policemen were to be seen in the streets.

For four days, in short, the Gorkys were the darlings of progressive literary New York. Then on the fifth day the *World* came out with shocking

news: "Mrs. Gorky" was in fact one Mme. Andreieva, a well-known actress; the real Mrs. Gorky, with three children, was back in Russia. Gorky's cordial relationship with America was over.

His friends protested that all was perfectly regular, that the writer and his wife, amicably separated, simply could not get a divorce in their backward country. To no avail. The Belleclaire's manager ordered them from the premises. "I'm running a family hotel," he told Wilshire, "and I can't afford to have these people in my house." Twain commented ruefully that "the man might just as well have appeared in public in his shirttail," and sadly withdrew his backing.

And from Boston, Gorky's erstwhile Brahmin comrades issued a statement that deliciously summed up the moral issues, 1906-style. They still approved of Gorky's plans for a proletarian revolution, they said, but "this horrid news" made it unthinkable to associate with the writer himself. "Consequently," they concluded, "we must make other plans for the liberation of Russia."

Few of the Upper West Side's hundred or so well-known litterateurs ever made so noisy a splash: Edgar Allan Poe was a well-behaved visitor in the summers of 1843 and 1844, when he wrote "The Raven." He and his wife were in the country for their health. A city doctor had suggested it might help Virginia Poe's consumption, so they took the upper floor of a cottage east of the Bloomingdale Road below 84th Street, convenient to the charms of the Hudson shore. Local tradition said the poet delighted in gazing out over the river from Mount Tom—the rocky knob in Riverside Park at the foot of 83rd Street—and gathered with Morris and other poets at Striker's Bay Tavern.

Mary Brennan, the landlady's daughter, remembered Poe reading aloud from his work while she played with the pages as they fell to the floor, entranced by the poet's copperplate handwriting. The mantelpiece from the parlor, by the way, with the initials E.A.P. carved in it (to Mrs. Brennan's considerable irritation), was rescued when the cottage was razed in 1888, and is said to be squirreled away somewhere in Columbia University. Today a portion of West 84th Street is officially named Edgar Allan Poe Boulevard, a plaque on the front no. 255 (the wrong address, unfortunately) commemorates his visit, and the poet is honored annually with one of the most lavish—and literate—of New York's many block parties.

After Poe, literary types were not conspicuous locally until the turn of the century—with a few exceptions. One was Delia Bacon, whose 1857 *Philosophy of the Plays of Shakespeare Unfolded* was one of the first books to deny Shakespeare's authorship of the plays attributed to him; she stayed in the neighborhood only briefly—in the asylum. Another was the inimitable William Furniss, financier-poet of "fair Bloomingdale," who versified nos-

talgically in the 1860s and 1870s on the old-time families and churches, "the quails we have shot on the old farm ground and the woodcocks in the corn." His work was privately published, and ran to such gems as:

> . . . these landmarks of the islands of Manhattan,
> Will sink in a short time from memory, to be quoted,
> And will be lost to all so much as a man without a hat on.

Edith Wharton's last New York home, strangely enough (since Fifth Avenue was more her natural habitat), was at 131 West 85th. Frances Hodgson Burnett, author of *Little Lord Fauntleroy*, made her home in the winter of 1902 at 44 West 87th, a place she found ornate and oppressive and which she avoided as much as possible. (However, a glimpse of a lone child playing near a boarded-up house across the street inspired an eerie, psychic tale, "In the Closed Room.") Elizabeth Cady Stanton, matriarch of the woman-suffrage movement, lived on West 61st when she published *The Women's Bible*, her last and most audacious work; a commemorative plaque (now gone) was placed at the site of her last residence, at Broadway and West 94th, on her 124th birthday, November 12, 1939. Ellen Glasgow, feminist, Pulitzer Prize winner, and one of the first great southern novelists, stayed at 1 West 85th off and on from 1911 to 1915, when she decided life in New York was "intolerably irksome." She returned home to Richmond, Virginia, where she was eventually buried beside her two favorite dogs, a Sealyham named Jeremy and a French poodle named Billy.

At 325 West 82nd from 1891 to his death in 1932 lived John Jay Chapman, a brilliant, now unjustly forgotten, man of letters. Edmund Wilson called him "much our best writer on literature of his generation," but also suggested he may have suffered "permanent psychological damage . . . by beating his head against the gilt of the Gilded Age." In youth Chapman had caned a man he mistakenly believed had toyed with his future wife's affections; in an agony of remorse he then thrust the offending hand into the coal fire, burning it to the bone. With the hand wrapped in a handkerchief, he took a street car to the hospital and underwent an amputation—a rather literal reading of the biblical injunction, "If thine hand offend thee . . . ." The same passion informed Chapman's political writings, which Jacques Barzun said "taught and inspired a whole generation." His son Victor, born in the house on West 82nd, was the first American aviator killed in World War I.

Zane Grey lived and practiced dentistry on West 74th Street before galloping to literary fame with *Riders of the Purple Sage* and other western sagas; Vaughan Kester wrote the stage version of *When Knighthood Was in Flower* around the turn of the century in the aging Furniss mansion— which by then had become a sort of artists' colony—at 100th Street and Riverside Drive. One colonist there was the young Gertrude Stein, then at

work on *Q.E.D.*, a novel of lesbian love that remained unpublished until after her death.

In 1899 Theodore Dreiser was living at 6 West 102nd and supporting himself as an editor and writer of pot-boiling magazine stories. This was long before his Ansonia days, and he never even thought of writing novels (he said) until his friend Arthur Henry pushed the idea on him. "I took out a piece of yellow paper and to please him wrote down a title at random—Sister Carrie." *Sister Carrie* was the grim chronicle of Carrie Meeber, an amoral Chicagoan transplanted to West 78th Street, who seeks glamor on the Broadway stage, destroys the man who loves her, and finds that success does not bring happiness. It was a revolutionary book, the first modern novel of city life, and it made its creator a literary hero—though Frank Doubleday, the original publisher, suppressed the book for a dozen years, the squeamish public bought only 456 copies of the first edition, and the author's net profit reached a grand total of $68.40.

F. Scott Fitzgerald lived in 1919 at 200 Claremont Avenue. He hated his advertising job (he was writing things like "We keep you clean in Muscatine," for an Iowa laundry; "It's plain there's a future for you in this business," his boss said), he hated 200 Claremont ("a high, horrible apartment-house in the middle of nowhere"), and at the first opportunity he quit both, went home to St. Paul, and wrote *This Side of Paradise*. Even so, glimpses of Morningside Heights appeared in his letters to Zelda ("the lights of many battleships drifting like water jewels upon the dark Hudson") and, possibly, in *The Great Gatsby*, where Tom Buchanan keeps an apartment for his mistress in a faceless block of flats, "one slice in a long white cake of apartment-houses."

The area also drew some of the century's most gifted mystery writers. Brilliant, goateed Willard Huntington Wright lived on Central Park West. He was literary critic for *Town Topics* and art critic for *The Forum* before he created (as S. S. Van Dine) the Philo Vance series—several of which were set on or near Riverside Drive. When he died in 1939 his ashes were scattered over the city. Rex Stout, creator of Nero Wolfe and Archie Goodwin, lived beside Morningside Park and later on West 116th, and set some of his scenes in the neighborhood ("My apologies to the residents [of West 83rd Street], but frankly the place was a slum.") Cornell Woolrich, the cult novelist whose bleak tales inspired the blackest of 1940s and 1950s film noir, spent his adolescence in his maternal grandfather's home on West 113th Street near Columbia University, where he studied briefly in the early twenties. Except for a very brief stab at marriage, he lived reclusively for most of his life with his mother at the Ansonia and other residential hotels (the St. Anselm Hotel, a gloomy pastiche of them, is the setting for his 1958 collection *Hotel Room*) and it's been suggested that the bleakness of such stories as *Rear Window* and *The Bride Wore Black* may reflect Woolrich's suppressed homosexuality. His will established a creative

writing scholarship at Columbia in his mother's name.

Most "New York" writers, of course, come to the city from out of town; that's why they find the place so exciting. Edna Ferber's first New York home, in 1912, was the Belleclaire Hotel. From her windows she saw, not the Hudson, but the typical city view of other people's windows. "I had never been confronted with this," she wrote, "and I hated it." Later she lived at the Majestic and, later still, when she was writing *So Big*, she had an apartment at 50 Central Park West with eight windows facing the park. (Even so, her view hardly rivaled the one Sinclair Lewis enjoyed from *his* Central Park West home in the El Dorado, at 90th Street; he chose it for its view of all the city's bridges.) George S. Kaufman's and Marc Connelly's sojourns on Central Park West were mentioned earlier, and the beloved *New Yorker* humorist Frank Sullivan (a Saratoga native) had a place at the upper end of the same avenue in the 1920s until he was forced to move out when the streets were torn up to build the subway. Eventually, he said, he began to grow lopsided from not walking on level pavements, and his tailor refused to fit his suits until he moved "to a less Alpine section of Manhattan."

Another successfully transplanted out-of-towner (Chicago to Morning-side Heights) was Franklin Pierce Adams, who as F.P.A. ran the most famous column of the old *New York World*, "The Conning Tower," filling it mainly with the diary of "Our Own Samuel Pepys" and readers' contributions. (Ira Gershwin, among many others, counted a "Conning Tower" sale as his first professional success.)

Heywood Broun, on the other hand, grew up on West 87th Street, and was living on Claremont Avenue in 1918, when he married Ruth Hale, an outspoken feminist (Women's Righter, in those days) and a founder of the Lucy Stone League; their wedding (at St. Agnes's Chapel, on West 91st) was nearly called off when Miss Hale balked at the word "obey" in the High Church Episcopal ceremony. In the twenties, when Broun was one of the country's most celebrated and controversial columnists, they lived happily — but on separate floors — in a house with a carved lion's head over the doorway at 333 West 85th. Their last home together was at the Hotel des Artistes.

F.P.A., Ferber, Broun, and their fellow Upper West Siders Dorothy Parker, George S. Kaufman, Alexander Woollcott, and Marc Connelly were the leading lights of the Algonquin Round Table, that coterie of glittering wits whose columns, light verse, plays—and well-publicized wisecracks— helped create the twenties vogue for the flippant and sophisticated. Though brilliant, the group seemed to some to produce relatively little work of lasting value, leading Frank O'Malley of the *Sun* to remark that if an explosion were to suddenly blow the group into eternity, American literature would stop dead—for twenty-four hours.

Robert Benchley, also of the Round Table crowd, may have taken that

remark to heart. He used to make a yearly pilgrimage to the top of Riverside Park, where young St. Clair Pollock still lay undisturbed in his grave. This would usually be in the sickly dawn light, following many nightcaps. Joseph Bryan III described the touching scene. "His companions read the inscription and commented on its pathos," Bryan wrote. "Benchley did not respond. He was in tears, they were astonished to find, and more astonished when they realized that his tears were not for the Amiable Child, but for his own 'wasted life,' his 'cowardice,' his 'weakness,' his 'failure.'" Benchley was then one of the nation's preeminent humorists, a radio and screen star and author of innumerable comic essays—"commotion recollected in tranquility," Bryan called them. Yet his tears, obviously sincere, convinced his friends that a sense of bitter failure did overcome him at these moments.

But some remained skeptical. "One year," Bryan explained, "they had hardly assuaged his sobs and straightened his tie before he was scribbling on the back of an envelope. Someone saw it as he slipped it under the door of Grant's Tomb, near by. The message read, 'Please leave 2 quarts Grade A and 1 pint whipping cream. U.S.G.'"

Will and Ariel Durant, authors of *The Story of Philosophy* and *The Story of Civilization*, lived at 5 West 69th in the late 1920s. Bertrand Russell visited them there when he came to New York for a public debate with Will over "Is Democracy a Failure?". During dinner he debated Napoleon's place in history with Will; afterward, on the way to his room on West 85th Street, he tried (without success) to seduce Ariel. "When I consider that Russell was soon to publish his view that a man compelled by his business to be absent from his wife for more than three weeks should be allowed a temporary moratorium on monogamy," Durant wrote later, "I tremble to think what might have happened in Central Park." He needn't have worried; Will and Ariel Durant's mutual devotion endured until their death, only hours apart, in 1981.

Fannie Hurst came to the West Side as a struggling newcomer just before World War I. She found pleasant lodgings in a rooming house at 340 West 85th that styled itself the Three Arts Club—for girls in "art, music and the drama"—but she was asked to leave the day she sold her first story to the *Saturday Evening Post* and was exposed as an author. "That disqualifies you, Miss Hurst," the manager said. "You evidently entered under false premises as a dramatic artist." Later, after best-selling melodramas such as *Back Street* and *Imitation of Life* had earned Hurst the title Sob Sister of American Literature, she had a baronial apartment at the Hotel des Artistes, where she took great pride in the living room, which had stained glass and thirty-foot ceilings, and which Edna Ferber (no fan of Miss Hurst's) called "a vast and lovely thing, if you like a room that looks like a Roman Catholic museum."

A. J. Liebling was attending P.S. 9 on West End Avenue when he discovered, to his delight, that his native city boasted no fewer than twenty-seven daily papers—a cornucopia that turned him into a lifelong newsprint addict. Later, as a *World-Telegram* feature writer and a war correspondent and columnist for the *New Yorker*, he wrote brilliantly and hilariously about the things he loved: the press, boxing, eccentric (and often criminal) characters of Broadway and elsewhere, and food; with commendable modesty, he described himself as "the best fast writer or the fastest good writer in the world."

Many of the wordsmiths who kept the New York press lively also lived in the area. The columnists and sportswriters were the best known: F.P.A., Woollcott, Damon Runyon, Runyon's Riverside Drive neighbor Grantland Rice (the man who dubbed Notre Dame's backfield the "Four Horsemen of the Apocalypse"), Gene Fowler, O. O. McIntyre, Walter Winchell. Frederick Lewis Allen, *Harper's* editor and author of *Only Yesterday*, was married in the West End Collegiate Church on West End Avenue in 1918; Robert Benchley was the best man, and the bride was Dorothy Cobb, the pastor's daughter.

The New Orleans–born playwright Lillian Hellman, who came to New York at age six, spent her adolescence in two West End settings: her parents' affectionate but "shabby poor" eighth-floor flat on West 95th, and the upper-middle-class West End Avenue home, with lovely oval rooms, of her maternal grandmother, a severe woman "given," Hellman recalled, "to breaking the spirit of people for the pleasure of the exercise. That New York apartment where we visited several times a week," Hellman added, "made me into an angry child and forever caused in me a wild extravagance mixed with respect for money and those who have it."

Anaïs Nin, author of *A Spy in the House of Love* and other erotic and poetic works, began her famous *Journal* at age twelve during World War I, when she and her mother lived on West 75th Street. In the mid-1920s Nathan Weinstein, a builder's son and a recent Brown University graduate, was staying with his parents on West 79th and cultivating the savage view of modern life that would later emerge, under the pen name of Nathanael West, in such tales as *Miss Lonelyhearts* and *Day of the Locust*. John Dos Passos lived briefly at 214 Riverside Drive while working on his monumental trilogy, *U.S.A.* Herman Wouk drew the characters and setting of *Marjorie Morningstar* from his boyhood experiences at various West Side addresses, mostly on or near the upper reaches of West End Avenue, while J. D. Salinger spent his early years at Riverside Drive and 111th Street in just the kind of large, ornate apartment house that forms the backdrop for his exquisitely crafted stories of troubled adolescence.

The West Side has also had a fair crop of publishers, a species essential (whatever authors may say) to the propagation of literature. Charles Scribner

lived at 258 Riverside Drive, the Peter Stuyvesant Apartments. Adolph S. Ochs of Tennessee, who built the *New York Times* into the country's leading daily, lived nearly half his life at 308 West 75th. The *Forum*, founded and edited by lawyer-industrialist Isaac L. Rice, offered space for almost anyone with something to say: Samuel Gompers, Theodore Dreiser, Henry Cabot Lodge, Brander Matthews, Louis Untermeyer, Ben Hecht. Professor Joel E. Spingarn of Columbia, a West 73rd Street resident, was a founder of the Harcourt, Brace publishing house, as well as head of the National Association for the Advancement of Colored People and founder of the Spingarn Medal; Alfred A. Knopf (15 West 95th) was a student of Spingarn's when he undertook an essay on "The Novels of John Galsworthy." With enviable directness, he struck up a correspondence with Galsworthy, visited him in England the next summer, and returned determined to be a publisher in the great eighteenth-century tradition—i.e., he would *read* books as well as merchandise them. Henry Luce was living with his missionary parents on West 122nd when he and his Harvard classmate Briton Hadden founded *Time* magazine in 1923. Bruce and Beatrice Gould, who built the *Ladies' Home Journal* into (for a time) the most widely read magazine in the world, started their New York careers on Morningside Heights—which they, like Fitzgerald, detested. Bennett Cerf, who would later join forces with Knopf at Random House, took a different route into the world of letters, having paused en route to accumulate a fortune on Wall Street. He went on to become not only a great and rather daring publisher (publishing *Ulysses* in this country when the customs department had declared the book obscene contraband) but also one of the great raconteurs of his age.

A publisher of somewhat darker stripe was Colonel William D'Alton Mann, a kindly-looking, patriarchal Civil War veteran who resided at 309 West 72nd and published a weekly journal of social gossip, *Town Topics*, that terrorized Society for decades. The colonel made a point of bringing to light "skeletons that have been accumulating dust in closets for years." His agents bribed Fifth Avenue servants and slipped into Newport mansions disguised as musicians to get the lowdown on upper-crust betrayals, divorces, and other scandals, which turned up as spicy paragraphs under the bland heading of "Saunterings." To no one's surprise, the crusty old moralist was eventually exposed as a blackmailer, who had routinely killed damaging items about various Morgans, Vanderbilts, and Whitneys *inter alia* in exchange for "loans" totaling several hundred thousand dollars. His office safe, he claimed, held the darkest secrets of the Four Hundred. Opened after his death, it proved to hold only a few bottles of brandy, but the brand of journalism he loosed upon a once-innocent public is still very much with us.

William Randolph Hearst, publisher of the New York *American* and *Morning Journal* (among a hundred or so others), occupied the top five,

treasure-filled floors of the Clarendon Apartments at 86th and Riverside Drive. A private elevator from the street brought editors, executives, and (rarely) writers from the *Cosmopolitan, Morning Journal,* and *American* staffs to Hearst's large bedroom-office, where he worked from noon till two or three in the morning, padding around in bare feet. A dreaded ordeal was being summoned to "wait for the Chief," in the adjacent anteroom, for a meeting that would often last well past midnight.

The New York *Evening Graphic,* known to its own staff as "the world's zaniest newspaper" and now mercifully forgotten by most, was at least partly a West Side product. The *Graphic* was the brainchild of Bernarr Macfadden, the millionaire publisher of *True Story* and *Physical Culture* magazines and self-proclaimed Father of Physical Culture. Its mission, he said, was to "publish nothing but the truth" and include as many pictures as possible, and throughout its brief career (1924–32) the *Graphic* (or *Porno-Graphic,* as many called it) rejoiced in such truth-filled headlines as THREE WOMEN LASHED IN NUDE ORGY, GIRL, 13, SOLD AS SLAVE TO CHINESE, and FIVE PRETTY GIRLS ATTACK LONE MAN IN TORTURE RIDE.

The *Graphic's* great contribution to journalism was the "Composo-graph"—Macfadden's term for a composite photo of shocking or revealing scenes that, for one reason or another, could not actually be photographed. It started when socialite Leonard "Kip" Rhinelander, scion of an old Knickerbocker family, married a "colored" girl, then caved in to family pressure and sued for divorce, claiming she had lied about her race. The dramatic high point in the case elicited a suitable *Graphic* headline: ALICE DISROBES IN COURT TO KEEP HER HUSBAND. Unfortunately, the disrobing took place in the privacy of the judge's chambers: no pictures. But that didn't stop the *Evening Graphic.* In the art studio in the Macfadden Building, 1926 Broadway—just up Broadway from the Hotel Marie Antoinette, where the couple had honeymooned—art director Harry Grogin wielded scissors and paste, and the next day's *Graphic* carried what seemed to be a photo of pathetic Alice Rhinelander, naked but for a slip over her thighs, confronted by the judge, the lawyers, and the dour Rhinelander clan. Other Composo-graphs, about as tasteful and truthful as the first, showed Rudolph Valentino's fatal operation, a pillow-fight between Daddy and Peaches Browning—whom we will meet in a later chapter—and the hanging of cop-killer Gerald Chapman.

Following the path Colonel Mann blazed came another long-time West Sider, Walter Winchell, who by no coincidence at all got his start writing squibs for the *Graphic.* As a young vaudeville hoofer, Winchell had performed in the "Newsboys' Sextette" at the Gus Edwards Music Hall on Columbus Circle. From the thirties on, when his "Walter Winchell on Broadway" was a daily feature in the New York *Mirror* and the other 165 Hearst dailies, and himself one of the country's most powerful columnists, he made his home at the Majestic Apartments.

Winchell's brash, irritating style helped elevate (if that is the word) gossip to a literary form. He also wreaked minor havoc on the American language, coining or popularizing such terms as *Reno-vated* (i.e., divorced), *whoopee, giggle water*, and *phooey*. It was typical of Winchell that he was on equally excellent terms with both J. Edgar Hoover and Mafia Godfather (and fellow Majestic resident) Frank Costello—and in fact, as he put it, with "every Gangster in town except Schultz." (Prohibition era gangster Owney Madden once sent Winchell, as a surprise, a Stutz roadster he had admired in a Columbus Circle showroom; the journalist briefly considered rejecting the gift, then decided it would be more tactful to accept.) By special police permission, Winchell had his car equipped with a police-band shortwave and siren. It was his delight to cruise the city streets at night, taking along a few celebrity friends. When an emergency call came in, they would rush to the scene, siren wailing. If the call took them up Central Park West, though, he would cut the siren as the car neared the corner of 72nd Street, where the Winchell children, both named for their father, lay sleeping. "I don't want to wake Walter and Waldra," he would explain, and the siren would stay off until the sedan was safely beyond earshot of the Winchell nursery. "Winchell," mused Stanley Walker of the *Herald-Tribune*, "is the perfect flower of Broadway, the product of his period as surely as prohibition and the night clubs and the tommy-guns."

And many more recent authors have been associated with the area. Albert Camus cannot be claimed as a local talent, but he *was* interviewed (by A. J. Liebling) in his West 72nd Street hotel room in 1946 for the *New Yorker*'s "Talk of the Town" section. William Styron wrote his first novel, *Lie Down in Darkness*, in a single room of a West 88th Street brownstone off West End Avenue; the place was so small that he and his roommate, a sculptor, had to use it in shifts. Joseph Heller wrote most of *Catch-22* in the foyer of a West End Avenue apartment. The hardboiled playwright-memoirist Ben Hecht lived many years at 39 West 67th, where he died in 1964 while reading a volume of e. e. cummings. (Hecht's collaborator on *The Front Page* and *Twentieth Century*, Charles MacArthur, was a Dakota resident in the first years after he and Helen Hayes married.) Playwright-screenwriter Murray Schisgal (*Luv, Tootsie*) is a Central Park West resident. James Baldwin, whose real home was Paris, kept an apartment at 470 West End Avenue. Tennessee Williams lived with a bisexual companion in separate rooms of an apartment on the thirty-third floor of 72nd Street's Mayfair Towers in the mid-sixties, a period when he was, in his own phrase, "a zombie except for his mornings at work." Mike Wallace came for a TV interview, but Williams's perennial struggle with drugs and booze was going so badly that the interview never materialized. Anthony Burgess, on the other hand, was "never happier or busier" than when he lived at 91st and West End, working on a musical called *Cyrano!* It might have been a hit,

but it had the bad luck to open during the Watergate hearings, when everybody stayed home to watch TV.

The pugnacious Norman Mailer ("I like a fight between friends," he confided to a correspondent) moved with his wife from Greenwich Village to a twelfth-floor sublet on West 94th after their daughter's birth. They stayed just about long enough to give a famous party there September 19, 1960; guests included publisher Barney Rosset of Grove Press, George Plimpton of the *Paris Review*, the socialist philosopher C. Wright Mills, poet Allen Ginsberg (who got into a brawl with Norman Podhoretz), and a couple of hundred others including "some guys off the street," and it ended when Mailer attacked his wife with a knife, an incident that, one guest observed, "shattered the literary scene in Manhattan."

Nobel laureate Saul Bellow wrote his novella *Seize The Day* in a cramped apartment at 333 Riverside Drive with a view (from the bathroom) of the Hudson. Like Wouk and Salinger, Bellow would eventually populate large stretches of the neighborhood with characters of his own creation, and bring the streets themselves to vivid, not to say horrifying life: upper Broadway, in all its sordid chaos, a symbol for "the soul of America at grips with historical problems." Bellow's fellow Nobelist Isaac Bashevis Singer has lived in the area longer (nearly fifty years) and sees it in a sunnier light in such tales as "The Cafeteria," "The Key," and "The Pigeons." Until a few years ago he enjoyed feeding the birds on the Broadway malls. He'd been doing it so long, he claimed, that they knew him by sight.

Boston-born poet Robert Lowell, celebrated for his crystalline imagery, manic-depressive episodes, and turbulent personal relationships, lived with his second wife, the novelist Elizabeth Hardwick, in an apartment on West 67th during the sixties. In early 1963 Hardwick, with neighbors Jason and Barbara Epstein, founded the *New York Review of Books*, laying out the first issue on their dining room table. A provocative intellectual journal (Lowell joked that it was meant "to fill in the gap left by the *New York Times* book section during the long newspaper strike"), it became one of the first major publications to oppose the Vietnam War and eventually was sold to a Mississippi publisher for over five million dollars. Lowell died in 1977, but Hardwick, now venerated among New York's women of letters, still lives on West 67th and has used images of the street and neighborhood in her autobiographical "so-called novel" *Sleepless Nights* (1980). Among current nonfiction writers, Isaac Asimov, with around a hundred-eighty titles to his credit at recent count, is a long-time denizen of West 66th Street; journalist-biographer Robert Caro (*The Power Broker, Lyndon Johnson and the Politics of Power*) is a Central Park West resident, while Riverside Drive boasts Jonathan Schell, whose chosen subject matter is no less than humankind's harrowing confrontation with nuclear destruction (*The Fate of the Earth*) and how to avoid it (*The Abolition*).

Viennese-born Frederic Morton, novelist, historian, and Upper West

Sider, did an article in 1980 on his neighborhood's social and literary life. Ten years earlier, Morton said, "the West Side was *yecch!*—cursed with the worst kind of respectability"—a neighborhood where Mr. and Mrs. Whole-sale Jeweler and Mr. and Mrs. Swimsuit Manufacturer watched "the colored people" drift over from Columbus Avenue and their own children drift away to the Village or the East Side. Now, he noted with some surprise, the area suddenly had experienced a "mass migration of intellectuals," mainly writers, mainly involved and political (left- and right-wing varieties), and mainly Jewish. He quoted a bemused Meyer Levin, author of the thriller *Compulsion*: "I was rehabilitating this brownstone—when was it? Six years ago? Suddenly it came to me. I'm an obsessive-compulsive! Back in the late twenties I worked in Palestine. And now I'm doing it all over again on the West Side—reclaiming ancient Jewish land."

Columbia University's literary contributions, from faculty and students, could make a separate book (and probably already has). Brander Matthews, critic and dramatist, was on hand when the college moved from its midtown campus to Morningside Heights in the late 1890s. Many of his students went on to careers in literature and the theater. The sprightly John Erskine studied at Columbia before the turn of the century and later became one of its greatest teachers of literature and writing; he was also a concert-rank pianist, president of Juilliard, and even committed a 1921 bestseller, *The Private Life of Helen of Troy*. ("He always gave you the feeling he'd just come in from lunching with Aristotle," said Helen Worden, who eventually married him.)

Carl Van Doren, editor, critic, and writer, was at Columbia from 1911 to 1930, fostering the study of American literature when most academics thought there was no such thing; his younger brother Mark, also a Columbia professor, was better known as a poet and biographer. And another Van Doren—Charles Lincoln, also a Columbia professor—won big on the TV game show "Twenty-One." In 1958 he admitted to a congressional com-mittee that the show had been rigged (as had several other game shows of the period), and television lost one of its few intellectual celebrities.

Columbia students who have made names for themselves with pen or typewriter include Langston Hughes, Federico Garcia Lorca, Herbert Gold, John Berryman, Bernard Malamud, and J. D. Salinger. Lloyd Morris, one of Erskine's most devoted students, later wrote *Curtain Time!* and *Incredible New York*, two of the most rewarding books you could hope to find about New York's theatrical and social history. Lionel Trilling, a student of Mark Van Doren, succeeded him as one of the school's key literary figures. Alfred Kazin, brilliant literary critic and memoirist, credited Carl Van Doren as the guiding force behind *On Native Ground*, Kazin's ground-breaking study of turn-of-the-century American writers. Kazin found the Upper West Side sunless and depressing, but in the 1940s he reluctantly "holed up in a

miserable hotel on West Ninety-fifth Street" in a linoleum-floored room lit by a naked overhead bulb. Later, while working on his memoir *A Walker in the City*, he lived near the top of Central Park West and roamed the nearby streets in search of "material." Like Bellow, he had strong, not entirely positive feelings. "Every day," he wrote in the autobiographical *New York Jew*, "I steered my way carefully, very carefully, between enclaves made up of blacks, the first Puerto Ricans, and Santo Domingans, poor whites from the South, squatters resisting removal 'necessary to urban renewal,' drunken supers and maddened tenants, belligerent pimps, addicts writhing like dervishes and staggering from one hydrant to another. The grimness of these bitterly ugly overcrowded streets was nothing to the anger of New York's untouchables forever slouching along the steps under the signs that said 'NO LOITERING.' "

It was Columbia, too, that gave the Upper West Side its only real *group* of writers, a counterpart to the literary cadres of Left Bank Paris or Greenwich Village: the writers of the so-called Beat Generation—meaning mainly poets Allen Ginsberg and Gregory Corso and novelists Jack Kerouac and William S. Burroughs, who met and became friends in or around the university in the 1940s.

Kerouac had come to the school in 1940 on a football scholarship, but managed to get his leg broken in one of his first games. He spent the time out reading Thomas Wolfe, who introduced him to "the city as Poem," and later earned an "A" in Mark Van Doren's Shakespeare course. Later still, as a Columbia dropout, he lived in his girlfriend's apartment on 118th Street near Amsterdam Avenue, which also quickly became a hangout for Ginsberg, who was then studying at the university, and Burroughs, who lived on Riverside Drive and, later, above a bar at Columbus and 64th.

With their literary ravings and impulsive hedonism, this tiny group of "junkies and geniuses" (the phrase is Ginsberg's) was laying the groundwork for some of the most interesting writing—not to mention the rebellions— of the 1960s. Not too surprisingly, their forties contemporaries were unimpressed; Kerouac's father, for one, raged at his son for hanging around with a bunch of "dope fiends and crooks." I like to think, though, that their antics won them a smile from the shade of Maxim Gorky. The old revolutionary would have deplored their politics, to be sure, but he would have loved their *chutzpah*.

11

A BOUQUET OF ROGUES

*Waldo Winchester says many
legitimate people are much
interested in the doings of tough
guys, and consider them very
romantic, and he says if I do not
believe it look at all the junk the
newspapers print making heroes
out of tough guys.*

—Damon Runyon,
"Social Error," 1930

I n the spring of 1938, an elderly and generally law-abiding widower
named Edward Mueller moved into a sunny twenty-five-dollar-a-month
flat on the top floor of a tenement at 204 West 96th Street, near
Amsterdam Avenue. He had been a building super nearby for many
years, while he brought up a family; now he thought he might make out
as a junkman. He was a better collector than a salesman, though, and his
small apartment soon filled to the ceiling with odds and ends picked up
from vacant lots and along the riverfront. His pockets stayed empty.

Mueller was a small, happy-looking man with a hawk nose, a wispy
white mustache, and a fringe of white hair. He usually dressed eccentrically
in layers of nondescript clothing. He had never bothered to give a name
to the mongrel terrier that accompanied him on his rounds. If anyone
asked why, Mueller would reply, "What good would a name do the dog?"
and reward the questioner with a merry, toothless grin.

He had another eccentricity, too. Having realized fairly soon that his
trade in second-hand goods would keep neither him nor his dog in food,
he had installed a small hand press in a corner of his kitchen, and for the
next ten years he used it to support his little household by printing small
batches of very bad counterfeit one-dollar bills, which he passed in shops

throughout the Upper West Side and other parts of town. For thousands of Mr. Mueller's fellow New Yorkers this practice resulted in slight economic annoyance. For the United States Secret Service, whose job it was to catch him, it resulted in intense and prolonged exasperation.

He wasn't greedy. He printed only two or three dollars of counterfeit a day, as the need arose, and he took care to spend only one of his handmade bills in any one place. That way, he said, "no one would lose more than the one dollar." He palmed off about five thousand of them altogether. The Secret Service, trying to trap him, interviewed hundreds of shopkeepers. They passed out tens of thousands of handbills, warning against the queer money. It did no good. Nobody, it seemed, troubled to look carefully at a one-dollar bill.

And a good thing, too. Mr. Mueller's handiwork was something really special: the worst, clumsiest forgeries the T-men had ever dealt with. They were printed on cheap bond paper, with inferior inks applied to zinc plates of embarrassingly poor quality. The lettering was crude and occasionally illegible, and George Washington's left eye was rendered as a blob of ink. The name under the portrait was spelled "WAHSINGTON."

But Mueller had no trouble getting people to accept them. And though he made no effort at all to cover his tracks, the Secret Service never came close to finding him, despite a search that exceeded in scope and intensity any previous manhunt in the annals of American counterfeiting. By early 1948 his case, file number 880, had become the oldest open one on the service's books. Most treasury agents regarded Old Mister Eight-Eighty as a "terrific headache"; some, more reflective, admitted that he was also, in terms of longevity at least, the most successful counterfeiter in American history.

It was luck, not sleuthing, that eventually delivered him into their hands. In 1948 a fire broke out in Mueller's kitchen, and the firemen threw his printing plates and some phony cash out the window with the ashes. The bills were found by some boys, who naturally thought they were some sort of inferior play money and swapped them around the neighborhood, whence they found their way into the hands of treasury agents. The trail led back to Mueller, and the genial paperhanger was indicted; in deference to his age and relatively innocent motives, he was required to serve only four months in New York's federal jail. His criminal career had made him one of the most sought-after felons of modern times, and his story was eventually told in a New Yorker profile and an MGM movie, but Mr. 880 never could see what the fuss was about. As he'd explained the day of his arrest, "It was my way of making a living."

If you had it in mind to find the likes of Mr. 880, the Upper West Side would be a fine place to start looking. Traditionally, the area has enjoyed, and often deserved, a reputation for barely skin-deep respectability—for

solid middle-class housefronts that concealed the most unrespectable goings-on, often involving illicit sex and gambling.

Appropriately, it was the death of a West Side gambler, "Whist Wizard" Joseph B. Elwell, that became the sensation of 1921. Elwell's bridge winnings, as high as thirty thousand dollars a night, had gone for five fancy cars, a yacht, and a stable of twenty thoroughbred racehorses. When he was found dying in his library at 244 West 70th, District Attorney Swann called it "the mystery of the generation," and the story made front-page news for a month. That reforming firebrand, Reverend John Roach Straton, preached eloquently on the dead man's evil ways, and the case was even recycled into fiction: in *The Benson Murder Case*, the first of the popular Philo Vance mysteries, the victim was found, like Elwell, seated in his study, *sans* bridgework and toupee, shot from the front.

The D.A.'s mystification may have been a bit disingenuous. Elwell had been an extremely successful playboy. (He had his locks changed in 1920 because so many different women had keys to his house.) Scores of witnesses were questioned after his murder: chauffeurs, cuckolds, a "Countess Szinawaska," and a mysterious "lady in gray," among others. The police even consulted a medium and a ouija-board expert, but it was no use. "There was every evidence," the *Times* sniffed fastidiously, "that Elwell was extremely discreet and rigidly observed the code of ethics of his class in ensuring against scandal the women who trusted him. His punctiliousness in this respect has proved to be one of the greatest drawbacks to the authorities in discovering a motive for his murder." Technically, the Elwell case is still open.

By the end of the decade, "punctiliousness" like Elwell's was on the way out, and by then the Upper West Side had long been noted for its high concentration of "kept women"; Cecil Beaton, that peerless snob and sophisticate, was not far off when he wrote of "the [West Side] houses given as parting presents by the Edwardian beaux to retired actresses and cocottes."

Occasionally there were misunderstandings. Early in the century Andrew Haswell Green, the elderly civic statesman known as The Father of Greater New York, often visited relatives at 235 Central Park West. Living next door with her Japanese servant, Kato, was a "little octoroon" named Hannah Elias, who had been kept by and was now blackmailing an elderly businessman named John R. Platt. Green did not know this, of course—or that the lady's cast-off lover, the somewhat dim-witted Cornelius Williams, had decided to kill Mr. Platt. To Williams, one white-whiskered octogenarian must have looked much like another, and the upshot was that Mr. Green received not only the fatal bullet, but a good deal of undeserved posthumous notoriety, while Platt enjoyed a ripe old age.

In the flush twenties the "kept woman" was a fairly open secret. Hearst's affair with Marion Davies, for instance, was common knowledge,

as was Mayor "Gentleman" Jimmie Walker's with actress Betty Compton, whom he kept in a grand West 72nd Street apartment. Actress Ruth Gordon, whose first New York home was the Three Arts Club, spoke of fellow "actresses" who were kept in elegant suites at the Belleclaire Hotel by young heirs who lived in the "castles" of Riverside Drive. A much-discussed 1924 murder victim was Louise Lawson, smothered in her bed at 22 West 77th. The dead girl was a twenty-five-year-old "music student" from Texas who had been known on Broadway as "a perfect blaze of jewels" and usually rode in her own chauffeured Pierce-Arrow. Her case, like Elwell's, led the police into areas that called for tact and delicacy, and like Elwell's her murder was never solved. She was buried, appropriately, on Valentine's Day.

By then the West End was frankly notorious. Memoirs (and police records) of the day mention "Sadie the Chink," who ran one of the city's best-known "parlor houses" at West End and 81st; "Cokey Flo" Brown, a small, steely woman whose testimony would later send vice king Lucky Luciano to prison, lived and operated a sleep-in house in a prim West End Avenue brownstone; "Dago Jean" kept an establishment on West 68th; and Babe Wagner had a high-class bagnio on Central Park West. Even *retired* madams, like the celebrated Everleigh sisters, found the West Side congenial. Driven from Chicago, where they had run the town's most opulent bordello (Prince Henry of Prussia, visiting America in 1902, had answered a reporter's question, "The sight in America I would most like to see? I would like to visit the Everleigh Club in Chicago."), they became the respectable Minna and Ada Lester, of 20 West 71st.

Above all, there was Polly Adler. Tiny, plump, gregarious, and pretty in a disarmingly old-fashioned way, Adler (*née* Pearl Vogel) was born in the White Russian *shtetl* of Yanow and found what she called her "golden land" on Riverside Drive. She was still in her teens when she took to procuring. She did make a stab at legitimate business—Polly's Apparel Shop, at 2719 Broadway, where Rosa Ponselle of the Metropolitan Opera was one of her best customers—but she soon returned to her true calling.

Her circle included some of the best-known figures of the era—Wallace Beery, George S. Kaufman (who kept a charge account), Dorothy Parker (a friend and admirer, not a customer), Robert Benchley, Arnold Rothstein, and Dutch Schultz. In the early thirties, investigations of the corrupt Walker administration brought Adler into the headlines—her and her "little black book," which allegedly listed her eminent clients' names, favorite drinks, and sexual preferences. By assisting in what she called "the determined squandering and guzzling and wenching of the newly rich," Polly Adler had become the country's best-known madam. In the 1931 edition of the Ziegfeld *Follies*, Helen Morgan portrayed a glamorous Russian ballerina, Mademoiselle Polly Adlervitch, and in *The Man Who Came to Dinner*, Kaufman and Hart had a character greet callers at a painfully respectable home with a cheery "Hello, this is Polly Adler's"—a sure-fire laugh line.

Eventually, Adler boasted, her clientele was "culled not only from *Who's Who* and the *Social Register*, but from Burke's Peerage and the Almanach de Gotha." Later, in retirement, she managed to live out yet another of the prostitute's classic fantasies: she moved to the West Coast, enrolled in college, and wrote her life story. Not too surprisingly, it was a best-seller, and Adler took special delight in the book's title: *A House Is Not a Home*.

The Dakota Apartments got their name from the gibe (plausible in the 1880s) that there was little to choose between the Upper West Side and Indian Territory. But some of the new West Side homemakers of that era did indeed find their situation unpleasantly similar to Custer's then-recent difficulty at the Little Big Horn. On one typical 63rd Street block (now part of Lincoln Center), the occupants of a new brownstone row found themselves beseiged among vacant lots and market gardens, with "impudent tramps and sneak-thieves, and ruffians of every stamp" on all sides. "Young girls are being continuously insulted," they complained. "Old women are attacked and beaten, and servant girls going to and from the groceries are waylaid and robbed." (A favorite trick was to kill the street lights, stretch a wire across the sidewalk to trip pedestrians, then run over and rob them under the pretext of lending assistance.) Some of the newcomers fled. Others held on, hoping for a quick influx of their own kind.

As far back as the 1840s, parts of the city had been conceded to "the gangs," loose organizations of thugs and murderers, many under the vague control of Tammany politicos, who delighted in such fragrant names as the Bowery Bums, the Plug Uglies, the Gophers, and the Dead Rabbits. By 1910 several were established on the West End: the Pearl Dusters laid claim to the area around 100th Street from Central Park to Broadway, and two others, the One-Armed Gang and the Parlor Mob, who had recently been chased out of Hell's Kitchen by the New York Central Railroad cops, ruled the San Juan Hill district.

In late 1911, Police Commissioner Waldo's Strong-arm Squad was making frequent trips to San Juan Hill, seriously damaging the prestige of several gang leaders. One who found this particularly irritating was John Painz, known in the Hill district as "the heaviest slugger of the One-armed Gang." He led twenty or so associates to the 68th Street station house, where he opened the discussion by bashing Policeman John J. Cullen with his own nightstick. Cullen drew his pistol, and the evening ended with Painz being taken downtown with a bullet in him, and the police reserves being called out to disperse a mob of a thousand or so that had surrounded the station house. None of which was considered unusual by the participants. But a police crackdown in 1914 put more than a hundred thugs in prison, and their heyday was over. During Mayor Mitchel's administration, Police Commissioner Arthur Woods went so far as to declare that "the gangster and the gunman are practically extinct."

Then came Prohibition, the "Noble Experiment" (as Irvin S. Cobb said, it "made the world safe for hypocrisy"). Overnight, small-time hoodlums rose to wealth and glory via bootlegging and its related professions: narcotics, prostitution, loan-sharking, hijacking (the Liberty Storage Warehouse on West 64th being one target), extortion, labor racketeering. And so it happened that Arnold Rothstein, Jack "Legs" Diamond, Irving ("Waxey Gordon") Wexler, Arthur ("Dutch Schultz") Flegenheimer, and Giuseppe ("Joe the Boss") Masseria came to have fancy homes on the West End.

If the reading public was soon on familiar terms with the exploits and language of these characters, it was due in no small part to yet another West Sider, Damon Runyon, star reporter and columnist for the Hearst chain. In the early twenties Runyon was living in a top-floor apartment at 251 West 95th, overlooking what he described as "one of the haunts of the bootleggers and gangsters of the period" at Broadway and 96th. He enjoyed the company of these colorful, gimlet-eyed "corner sharpies" and absorbed their stories. More than a few would later appear large as life, and considerably more appealing, in his hilarious, sentimental tales of Broadway's "guys and dolls."

Through most of the 1920s, Arnold Rothstein was undoubtedly the best-known West Side gangster. To all appearances just a remarkably lucky gambler, Rothstein was in fact the underworld's main banker and a powerful political fixer, and was said to have been the first to bring modern management methods to organized crime. He appears in Runyon's stories as Armand Rosenthal, The Brain: "Nobody knows how much dough The Brain has, except that he must have plenty, because no matter how much dough is around, The Brain sooner or later gets hold of all of it." Rothstein was credited with having fixed the crooked World Series of 1919; this he denied, but it remains the most durable part of his legend. He lived at (and owned) the Fairfield Apartments at 20 West 72nd when he was killed over a poker debt, in 1928.

That gave Legs Diamond, Rothstein's onetime bodyguard, a chance to take over his old boss's commanding position. But he blew it. Diamond (called "Legs" either for his speed in making a getaway or—more cynically— for a tendency to run out on his friends) had been set up as a professional bootlegger by Rothstein, but also dabbled in extortion, kidnapping, and torture. His headquarters, for a time, was the Monticello Hotel, on West 64th near Broadway. He appears in several Runyon tales as the dangerous but sentimental Dave the Dude, but a description by a less romantic writer seems more to the point: "He was one of the few genuinely pathological killers among the city gangs."

To his colleagues, Diamond's shiftiness made him less than ideal leadership material, and his love of drink and publicity made him a positive menace. By late 1931 there had been four attempts to kill him, including

one at the Monticello. By then Diamond had absorbed so much lead that *Times* writer Meyer Berger, a judicious observer of the lively gangland scene, described him as a "human ammunition dump for the underworld." The fifth try, in December in an upstate rooming house, was successful.

Also closely associated with The Brain was Waxey Gordon, a pudgy ex-pickpocket who, with Rothstein's backing, had made out very nicely in the beer racket. Gordon was a "streamlined," thirties-style gangster, fond of golf and horses, with a taste for two-hundred-dollar suits and silk underwear. He invested in real estate and Broadway shows; his ten-room apartment at West End and 88th was cared for by five servants and boasted a designer-built bookcase that cost two thousand dollars. It would be nice to know what he kept in it. What he kept in another apartment, on Riverside Drive, was his girlfriend, the classy stripper Gypsy Rose Lee. Gypsy's mother, the inimitable Rose of later Broadway fame, lived there, too, and was very taken with Waxey's "class." "In this world of stinkers," she said, "just give me a straightforward, true-blue gangster every time."

At the far end of the sartorial spectrum was Gordon's rival Dutch Schultz, who had ordered Diamond's killing and who looked, according to one detective, "like a small businessman ready to announce his bankruptcy." Nevertheless, and despite a weakness for blondes and a weak head for liquor, he lorded it over a fiefdom that covered the Bronx and extended down the West Side at least as far as 76th Street; in the Runyon canon he appears briefly as Heinie Schmitz, "a guy who has very large interests in beer and will just as soon blow your brains out as look at you."

The Schultz-Gordon rivalry reached a local climax on a May night in 1933, when machine-gun fire from a speeding car injured three in the after-theater crowd on Broadway near Schultz's Half Moon Cafe at 80th Street. By that time Gordon himself already had been arrested for tax fraud; he apparently deemed it imprudent to make bail, preferring to let Uncle Sam be his bodyguard until the fireworks were over. Schultz was also about to be tagged for a tax rap, but by early 1934, when a warrant went out for his arrest, he had vanished. The search for him began at the Hotel Endicott on Columbus Avenue, his last known address, and eventually covered several states. After more than a year, part of which was spent hiding at Polly Adler's, Schultz surrendered for trial in Albany and was acquitted of tax fraud by a well-greased jury of upstate farmers. For a very short time he remained preeminent among racketeers, only to be gunned down a few months later while counting policy receipts in a Newark bar.

Schultz was buried with little ceremony and no mourners—a definite sign of changing times. Why, just a few years earlier, "Joe the Boss" Masseria had enjoyed one of the finest gangland-style funerals ever, just around the corner from Schultz's old hangout. Masseria was a Mafia chief who figured in a Runyon tale as John the Boss, a liquor importer, and who in real life— until he was cornered by assassins in a Coney Island restaurant—occupied

a penthouse at 15 West 81st, across from the Museum of Natural History. He particularly gratified crime buffs by the manner of his death, a playing card—the ace of diamonds—clutched dramatically in his fist. The boys sent him to his reward with full honors: a solid silver coffin, the likeness of the departed framed in a six-foot wreath, a sixty-nine-car cortege, and sixteen cars filled with thousands of dollars' worth of floral tribute. And yet whoever was in charge of the obsequies apparently wanted it all within the bounds of good taste. According to the *Times*, they brought the casket down through a rear door—"in the vain hope of avoiding attention."

Another character who might have stepped from the pages of Damon Runyon was William Francis Sutton, also known as "Willie the Actor," a slight fellow with a pencil-line mustache who won fame in the twenties and early thirties as a daring and imaginative bank robber.

By any reasonable standard, Sutton's career should probably be regarded as a failure, considering that he spent about two-thirds of it behind bars. On the other hand, though, he did manage to escape from prison three times—once from "escape-proof" Sing Sing—and made at least a dozen other tries. In the end the public took him to its collective bosom as probably the most single-minded, dedicated jailbreaker of all time.

Born in Brooklyn, Sutton apprenticed himself in 1921 to a safecracker known as "Doc" Tate, a dandy with a tastefully furnished home on West 87th near Riverside Drive. Soon young Willie was wearing spats and silk gloves, the closets of his West 72nd Street apartment overflowed with custom-made suits, and his parties were favored by show people. He felt right at home in what he considered "the small town of the Upper West Side." "In those three-story brick apartment buildings," he recalled fondly, "you could find some of the wealthiest men in the city and some of the fanciest-kept women." Unfortunately, this idyll was interrupted in 1926 when he botched a safecracking job and was provided with more modest quarters, free of charge, by the State of New York; his later visits to the Upper West Side tended to be hurried, and one ended in his arrest at the Child's Restaurant in the Ansonia Hotel. Eventually Sutton decided banks were "where the money was," and that brought him to the Corn Exchange Bank near Broadway and West 110th early one morning in 1933.

Wearing a patrolman's uniform, Sutton got the bank porter to let him in just before opening time, then pulled a gun and corralled the staff as they entered. One attractive employee started to trade wisecracks as she came in. "Hey, look at the handsome policeman," she said. "Have you locked up any robbers lately?" To Sutton's surprise, the girl seemed genuinely hurt when she realized he *was* a robber. He offered a few comforting words, and soon they were deep in conversation.

When the bank manager finally arrived, in fact, Sutton's partner had to call to him to get his mind back on business. They cleaned the place

out, but the take was disappointingly low, less than thirty thousand dollars. Sutton was philosophical. "On the other hand," he mused, many years later, "it was one of the robberies I most enjoyed. You can't have everything."

After the mid-1930s, the Upper West Side began to lose its attraction for affluent mafiosi. The conspicuous exception was Frank Costello, "Prime Minister of the Underworld," who made his home at the Majestic Apartments, in the same building as the Broadway "colyumist" Walter Winchell. (All sorts of trails managed to cross near that spot. Bruno Hauptmann, who was executed in 1934 for the kidnap-murder of the Lindbergh baby, worked as a carpenter at the Majestic at the time of the crime; nearly half a century later and directly across the street, a demented rock fan shot John Lennon to death.) Operating behind the scenes, Costello became one of the most powerful men in the country, courted by gangsters and politicians alike. Winchell, in neighborly fashion, gave Costello a generally good press; in return the "godfather" provided reliable information for Winchell's column and radio program, and racing tips for the writer to share with another close friend, J. Edgar Hoover.

All was going smoothly for Costello until the Senate investigations of organized crime in 1950 put him in the spotlight and then (briefly) in prison. And worse was to come. On May 2, 1957, Costello, out of prison on appeal, strolled into the lobby of the Majestic a little after eleven at night. As he crossed to the elevator, a gunman shouted, "This is a message for you, Frank!" and fired a bullet into his head.

But this is a story without a corpse. Costello's wound was minor. His real danger, ironically, was from the police, who checked his pockets while he was at Roosevelt Hospital and found evidence to send him to prison for illegal links to a Las Vegas resort. After his release, he went into more or less complete retirement on Long Island and raised prize flowers until he died, in bed, at eighty-two. It may be just coincidence, but since Costello's day it seems most of our prominent mobsters have preferred the respectability of Fifth Avenue or the safety of the suburbs to the tumult of the Upper West Side.

To wind up this quick tour of Upper West Side rascality, I offer the tale of Dr. Arthur Waite, whose career was an eerie blend of ragtime-era charm, bland psychopathic malevolence, and sheer maladroitness perhaps unequaled in the annals of murder. But first, there's a prologue.

It begins in 1898 with the death of Mrs. Katherine Adams, widow. Mrs. Adams had shared an apartment at 86th and Columbus with her married daughter and a nephew named Harry Cornish, and the Friday before Christmas, Cornish received a small, anonymous package at the Knickerbocker Athletic Club on Madison Avenue, where he was the athletic director. In it were a small silver bottle holder from Tiffany's and a little brown bottle of Bromo-Seltzer. At dinner that night, Harry's aunt and

cousin teased him about the secret "female admirer" who, they suggested, wanted to save him from the effects of holiday drinking. To satisfy their curiosity, he brought the enigmatic gift home Saturday. Three days after Christmas, Aunt Katherine woke with a headache, drank a bromo from Harry's bottle, and died of cyanide poisoning.

The culprit appeared to be the dashing, socially brilliant Roland Molineux, a former club member who had recently quit after quarreling with Cornish. And not just Cornish, apparently; just six weeks earlier another club member, a rival in love, had perished in much the same way. (Which makes you wonder: did New Yorkers of that idyllic era literally not know the meaning of suspicion?) Molineux was tried and sentenced to death, but his father, a Civil War hero and eminent Brooklyn Republican, managed to win his son a new trial and eventually an acquittal. Meanwhile, Roland's lugubrious tales of his eighteen months in the Sing Sing death house, published as *The Room with the Little Door*, had won praise from literary critics, and a play, *The Man Inside*, was subsequently staged by David Belasco. After a few stormy years of freedom (he got into fistfights with Belasco, for instance, during performances of his play), he was placed in an insane asylum, where he died in 1917. All of which, as I said, is prologue.

Molineux was still in the State Hospital for the Insane at King's Park, Long Island, in 1915, when Dr. and Mrs. Arthur Warren Waite took a large second-floor apartment in the new Colosseum apartment house on Riverside Drive at 116th Street. They were a handsome couple: Clara tall, with high cheekbones and flashing eyes, the only daughter of a wealthy Michigan drug manufacturer; Arthur debonair, courtly, and athletic, a brilliant young surgeon and a noted amateur tennis champion. He often played at the nearby Columbia University courts, and won medals in tournaments at the 68th and 71st Regiment armories near Lincoln Square. Among his sporting companions were the leading columnist of the day, Franklin P. Adams of the *World*, and Mayor Mitchel's executive secretary, Samuel L. Martin. "Doc was always popular with us," Martin would say later. "He used to fill that little car of his full of fellows and drive us all in from the courts of an afternoon."

That winter, "Doc" poisoned his mother-in-law and—as the attending physician—had her cremated to get rid of the evidence. Then he invited his grieving father-in-law, John E. Peck, to stay with him and Clara until he was feeling better. The old man was dead by March. But before the son-in-law could get the second body burned, suspicion had been aroused, and Waite was arrested for murder. The trial got under way in May 1916, and it soon was clear that here was a killer of no mean ambition.

For openers, he was no doctor. Waite's only degree was from Edinburgh Dental College; he got it by passing off another student's exam results for his own. Later he worked for a South African medical organization until,

luckily for the patients, they fired him for theft. Nothing daunted, he had returned to Michigan in 1915, dazzled his childhood sweetheart and her well-heeled family with tales of international success, and carried her off triumphantly to the metropolis.

None of his New York associates had actually seen the good doctor at work, of course, but they did occasionally pile into Doc's little car and ride down with him to Bellevue Hospital. There he would vanish through the great front doors, to reemerge hours later, cheerful but visibly fatigued from his life-saving labors. If Clara or anyone else had followed him as he strode purposefully in, they might have been puzzled to see that his route led not to the operating theater but to a small hidden courtyard, where he would spend an hour or so shooting craps with the orderlies.

To get his hands on the Peck fortune, Arthur had started laying in an arsenal of deadly agents the previous December. Germ warfare was his specialty. When detectives searched his apartment, they found about a hundred test tubes and one-hundred-eighty glass slides on high shelves and in other out-of-the-way places. Most were neatly labeled: "Typhoid," "Diphtheria," "Pneumonia," "Influenza," "Tetanus," "Asiatic Cholera," "Tuberculosis," "Anthrax," and so on. Arthur had obtained them from such impeccable sources as the Rockefeller Institute and the Cornell Medical Center. Perhaps all that trafficking with hospitals had made him feel more like a real medic.

Mrs. Peck had popped off obligingly after Arthur dosed her soup with typhoid and pneumonia, and he expected the rest of the Peck clan to follow in short order. Clara's kindly Aunt Katherine, who had given Arthur the diamond for Clara's ring and then entrusted him with forty thousand dollars for investment, lived conveniently nearby on Claremont Avenue, so Arthur decided to dispatch her first. Father Peck and Clara's brother Percy would be next, then Clara herself, after which Arthur planned an extended visit to Paris where he and a lady friend—an entrancing brunette whom he had installed at the Plaza for the time being—would put the Peck millions to good use. (The lady's husband would have to be gotten rid of, too, but that was an afterthought.)

But disgustingly, Aunt Katherine refused to sicken. Arthur would go round to her home almost every day and empty a test tube of microbes into her milk or soup. He doctored a can of fish and presented it to her. But, as he testified, "They did not seem to have any effect." He dumped ground glass into her marmalade; she returned it to the grocer, who apologized and refunded her money.

So Arthur gave up on her for the time being. But when he directed his attentions to Clara's seventy-two-year-old father, what should have been swift, grim tragedy turned instead into a kind of extended grisly slapstick, for Mr. Peck turned out to be a most unreasonably robust subject.

Smiling, self-possessed, Waite took the stand and described how he

began dosing his father-in-law the first day of his visit.

"How many times did you administer germs to him?" he was asked.

"Oh, every day and as often as I got the chance."

"What germs did you give him?"

"Typhoid and all the others I had given Mrs. Peck, and then I got some new ones—some tubercular germs."

"Did Mr. Peck become ill?"

"No, the germs didn't seem to affect him as they had Mrs. Peck."

"What did you do then?"

"Then I tried to make him sick by giving him big doses of calomel. I gave him half a bottle at a time in his food. I gave him germs at the same time. I thought the germs would be helped along by the calomel or the condition it produced."

One of the jurymen laughed out loud.

"Then I tried some more things to kill him," Waite continued. "I gave him pneumonia germs and took him riding in the rain. I wet the sheets of his bed at night to give him a cold.

"Then one night I read in the papers how the soldiers were killed by chlorine gas. The paper said it was very effective, so I got some chlorate of potash and put hydrochloric acid on it and placed it inside his door. I fixed the electric heater with some stuff so it would smell as if varnish were burning if he waked up. But it didn't hurt him at all." (Do we begin to detect a plaintive note here?) Arthur also turned on the gas in the old man's room once, he said, "but it didn't work. A servant was blamed for that."

By this time Mr. Peck, surely one of the most uncomplaining house-guests known to history, must have had his host chewing the antimacassars in frustration. Abandoning finesse, Arthur got ninety grains of arsenic from a drug store, enough—in theory—to kill twenty men.

"How much arsenic did you give Mr. Peck?"

"All of it," Waite answered. "A little at first and then more until he had it all."

"How did you give it?"

"I put it in food, oatmeal, rice pudding, hot milk, soup and anything it seemed proper to put it in."

At last this most uncooperative of victims took to bed, and even so Arthur was finally obliged to dispatch him with chloroform and a pillow pressed over his face.

The jury was out for an hour (probably fifty-nine minutes too long), and Arthur Warren Waite, smiling and bland as ever, went to Sing Sing. He spent his time there reading (the prison librarian described Waite as his all-time best customer) and writing poetry. He became ill-tempered, legend has it, only when they interrupted his reading to lead him to the electric chair. The autopsy showed that he had an abnormally large heart.

But hold on. If the big-hearted doctor was so bland and charming,

what made him a suspect in the first place?

For that, the police (and the surviving Pecks) owed thanks to Miss Elizabeth Hardwick, a young New York City schoolteacher who happened to be distantly related to the Peck family. After Mr. Peck's death, Hardwick's brother had paid a condolence call at the Waite apartment. To his surprise, Arthur, usually so ingratiating and correct, had answered the door in his shirtsleeves and sent him away with a few brusque words. From this, Elizabeth had quite correctly deduced that Waite must be a murderer—an intuitive leap that makes her forever my heroine among armchair detectives. Acting on her conclusion, she decided to send a telegram to Percy Peck in Grand Rapids: "SUSPICION AROUSED. DEMAND AUTOPSY. KEEP TELEGRAM SECRET." But an unfounded charge would surely set off a scandal, maybe even a lawsuit. Better to sign a fake name. And that brings us back to our prologue.

Hardwick said later that she simply signed "a girlfriend's" name to the telegram. But if so, maybe a neighbor's long-departed shade was hovering nearby at the time. And Roland Molineux, if he was allowed to see the daily papers in his secluded quarters on Long Island, must surely have appreciated the irony of her choice. For the missive that trapped the poisoner turned out to be signed, most fittingly, with a name he should have known well: "K. ADAMS."

And that is the end of the story. Except that in all fairness the last word should go to that soul of patience, the long-suffering John E. Peck. On his last afternoon out, before he finally succumbed to Arthur's ministrations, Mr. Peck was chatting with Eli Williams, a tailor, in his shop at 2811 Broadway. Mr. Peck was not feeling too well. The night before, he had eaten pistachio ice cream at dinner. Now he had a stomach ache.

"My son-in-law gave me medicine," Mr. Peck said to the tailor, "but it didn't do me much good."

PART
——— III ———
THE UPPER WEST SIDE

12

"NO PART OF THE WEST SIDE IS REALLY SMART"

And the West Side I once knew is wholly dead, the tale of what has happened to it in thirty-five years a parable of decline, harshly tangible.

—Marya Mannes, *The New York I Know*, 1961

N ever had New York gotten so worked up over an athlete.

Gertrude Ederle was the unassuming daughter of an Amsterdam Avenue butcher, but when she swam the English Channel in August 1927—the first woman Channel swimmer, *and* faster than any of the men before her—the cheers from America couldn't have been louder if she'd walked it, and when she came home the morning of August 27th all New York turned out to give her a heroine's welcome. Airplanes circled overhead as her ship steamed up the Narrows, the harbor swarmed with the biggest fleet of small craft ever seen, and cheering admirers packed Broadway as she rode to City Hall in a blizzard of ticker tape, confetti, and flowers. The *Daily News* gave her seven full pages of coverage and a new red roadster, and after a stop at City Hall to accept the key to the city from Mayor Walker she rode home to a neighborhood that had become a sea of flags, bunting, and WELCOME, TRUDY signs. Every butcher's shop displayed her photo (and mentioned that this butcher's daughter ate meat three times a day). "Pop" Henry Ederle's own shop at 108 Amsterdam was nearly hidden in bunting except for one window, where a mechanized cardboard model showed his daughter swimming the Channel, at sixty strokes a minute. The crowd surrounded Trudy's home and wouldn't leave until she'd climbed onto the window sill and given them a little speech, and the next night, at a block party for five thousand on 65th Street, the nineteen-year-old was named Queen of Swimmers and presented with a huge purple-

and-gold crown suitable for a fairy-tale princess, which, in a way, is what she was.

Swimming was suddenly big business. In just one day Trudy got more than nine hundred thousand dollars in offers from stage and film producers, newspapers, and swimming pool interests, or so said her backer and attorney, Dudley Field Malone (who also represented Larry Fay, the gangster). For the neighborhood, it was a week of glory—only slightly tarnished a few weeks later, when word got out that the Ederles would soon be leaving for a new nine-room house in the Bronx. "Ma" Ederle's comment, though none too flattering to the Upper West Side, made perfect sense to her friends and neighbors: "We thought it was time we were getting some good out of our money."

The "Upper West Side," not "the West End." Gentility, alas, was in short supply locally. True, Lady Astor still kept a gorgeous apartment in the Apthorp; and Hattie Carnegie, future *couturiere* to the duchess of Windsor, lived on Riverside Drive and offered her exclusive line of "Originations and Importations" at 86th and Broadway. But the air of "noble leisure" was long gone.

The subway, for one thing, had changed the West End just as dramatically as the el had changed Bloomingdale. Miles of private homes had given way to enormous apartment houses, especially near the 72nd and 96th streets express stops. Central Park West, West End Avenue, and Riverside Drive were becoming avenues of apartment blocks, Broadway a commercial thoroughfare. In 1906 the Colonial Club building was renovated for offices; the churches around Sherman Square, in a kind of ecological succession, made way for stores, offices, and banks—while parts of Morningside Heights still had their wooden houses and resident goats well into the twenties.

The middle- and upper-class families still clung to Riverside Drive and Central Park West and, less securely, West End Avenue, as the working-class neighborhoods of Amsterdam and Columbus Avenues grew shabbier and more crowded. Children on Riverside Drive got to know the watchman at the Schwab mansion; on West End Avenue, at five or six in the evening, the police put away the ONE WAY signs and the street reverted to two-way traffic. Children would line the sidewalk then. Recalled one, "It was a show for us to watch the people in formal dress going out for dinner." The other side of Broadway, life was grimmer. On hot summer nights, families slept on fire escapes or carried their bedding over to the park to camp out for the night (where, in those relatively innocent days, they had no fear for their property or persons). To them, an apartment on West End was "like living on Park Avenue." Residents of the Dakota and other grand houses of Central Park West, on the other hand, were "never really aware of the Upper West Side," as one of them recalled. "Our friends were from out of

the neighborhood—in fact, it *wasn't* a neighborhood in the human sense, of knowing your neighbors."

The parks, though neglected, still defined the district—for children especially. In spring Central Park offered baseball, croquet, lawn tennis, pony- or goat-cart rides, and evening concerts by the Goldman Band. Riverside Park was a mess: rotting piers and rickety bridges where hissing clouds of steam rose from the freight trains below. At high tide, the Amsterdam Avenue boys would slide down the steep side of the railroad cut and climb over the parked trains to strip and swim. Broadway belonged to everybody. "Saturday and Sunday," said a child of the twenties, "you walked, you paraded up Broadway—up one side of the street and down the other, the boys and girls in their own groups. We went everywhere, but the Ansonia Hotel, with all those elegant theatrical people—that was the be-all and end-all."

When the Navy anchored in the Hudson, the sailors rowed ashore in launches to flirt with the "Riverside Drive girls." They skated at the St. Nicholas Rink, danced and dined at the Carlton Terrace on Broadway at 100th—or at what was left of Healy's at Columbus and 66th—finally reduced by Prohibition to a single dance hall, seventy-five cents for gentlemen, forty cents for ladies, open 'til one and still considered one of the liveliest places in the neighborhood. Notlek's miniature golf course at Riverside Drive and 120th was also open 'til one; 1929 was notable as the year miniature golf became a great national fad. At the Royal Chinese Grill (Hotel Alamac, Broadway at 71st) a jazz band played till 4 A.M., and Reuben's Pure Food Shop, birthplace of the Reuben sandwich, was on Amsterdam right across from the Ansonia; open all night, it was the final port of call for those returning from the Harlem jazz clubs or making the rounds of the uptown speakeasies.

One of the silliest spectacles of an already foolish era was provided by Edward West Browning of 29 West 81st Street, a twinkling, white-haired real estate man with a robin's-egg-blue Rolls Royce and a weakness for young girls and publicity. He first endeared himself to reporters when he ran this ad in the *Herald Tribune*:

> ADOPTION—Pretty refined girl, about fourteen years old, wanted by aristocratic family of large wealth and highest standing; will be brought up as own child among beautiful surroundings, with every desirable luxury . . . .

Browning was seeking a companion for his eleven-year-old daughter, he said. (The Society for the Prevention of Cruelty to Children had its own ideas, but couldn't prove them. Before his divorce, when he and Mrs. Browning were at 35 West 81st—one of his own buildings—Browning had built a spectacular twenty-one-room playhouse on the roof for their adopted

daughters, with colored lights, captive songbirds, and a lake big enough to float a small boat.) Applicants flocked to his office on West 72nd Street. All twelve thousand were dandled on his knee and interviewed, but nothing much came of it. To console himself, Browning became a "patron" of high-school sorority dances, and then he achieved his heart's desire: he married Frances Belle Heenan, a plump, pouty fifteen-year-old from Washington Heights. He called her "Peaches," she called him "Daddy," and for reasons hard to fathom at this distance, the public couldn't get enough of them.

An inspired journalist had labeled it The Era of Wonderful Nonsense, and Daddy and Peaches were true tabloid fare, right in there with flagpole sitters, goldfish swallowers, and nine-day bicycle racers. When they came back from their honeymoon a curious mob packed Grand Central Terminal; when the bride went on a shopping spree, mounted cops had to keep order and headlines screamed, CROWDS TRAMPLE PEACHES! When at length Peaches fled their love nest, trailing trunks, jewelry, and furs, she and Daddy both hired ghostwriters to plaster their "true" stories across the tabloids; and at their divorce trial (about six months after the wedding) an eager crowd literally burst the courtroom door to get in. Daddy gloried in these attentions. Every time he made headlines, he bought hundreds of newspapers, then sent his staff downstairs to fan out from his office at Broadway and 72nd and hand them out free to passers-by.

Daddy is pretty well forgotten, but there are still four tall, narrow apartment buildings in the West 70s—31 West 71st, 42 and 118 West 72nd, and 126 West 73rd, the latter three designed by Buchman & Fox—that still carry his crest and the initials EWB. Which is perhaps appropriate: the real legacy of the 1920s (apart from an enduring appetite for scandal) is its architecture. The era's best structures, and those who erected them, were a special breed, born of a time when ambition, technology, and fantasy were all woven together: Emery Roth from Galzecs, Hungary, patriarch of a New York architectural dynasty, whose buildings evoked Hapsburg castles and Mayan temples; Irwin S. Chanin, child of Brooklyn and tsarist Russia, whose streamlined towers glorified New York's power and brilliance; Italian-born Gaetan Ajello, who designed fifty-plus eclectic, richly detailed apartment houses from 71st Street to Morningside Heights before retiring, somewhat mysteriously, in his early forties. How much poorer the Upper West Side would be without their works, especially the romantic, soaring apartment skyscrapers—Roth's San Remo, Beresford, and El Dorado (the latter in association with Margon & Holder), Chanin's modernistic Deco Century and Majestic—that give Central Park West its distinctive, magniloquent skyline.

Ominously, though, builders of expansive, fashionable apartments were already looking eastward to a new residential boulevard, nearly twice as wide as West End Avenue, with a planted mall up the center (hence the name: Park Avenue) that the New York Central Railroad had just created

THE SAN REMO

Though he gave the avenue no fewer than eight apartment houses, the San Remo (1929) was the one Emery Roth called The Aristocrat of Central Park West—the city's first twin-towered building, facing—or rather, dominating—the park from a full-block site at 74th to 75th streets. Basically a twenty-seven-story skyscraper, the San Remo starts with a massive seventeen-story, full-block base, subtly set back to form broad terraces at the fourteenth, sixteenth, and seventeenth floors. The ten-story towers are almost stubby, but their mass is relieved with abundant Italian Renaissance details in terra-cotta, and especially the culminating classical monuments—patterned, like the Soldiers and Sailors Monument, on the Choragic Monument of Lysicrates in Athens, and topped with green copper lanterns.

New York's new Multiple Dwelling Act allowed an apartment building to rise as high as thirty stories, as long as it had at least a thirty-thousand-square-foot "footprint" and met certain setback rules. Roth's design was meant to capitalize on that; he also split the central tower in two, a notable innovation that made for efficient use of space (i.e., fewer interior corridors) and more windows with spectacular views—and gave the building a dramatic profile from as much as two miles away. He succeeded so brilliantly that by 1931 three more twin-towered buildings—the Chanin organization's

Century and Majestic and Margon & Holder's El Dorado (for which Roth was the associate architect)— had joined the San Remo to give Central Park West a dramatic new skyline.

A troop of appropriately prominent residents have enjoyed what the New York City Landmarks Preservation Commission termed the San Remo's "urbane amalgam of luxury and convenience, decorum and drama." There was David Nemerov, president of the posh Russek's department store in the thirties, who raised two talented children there, the poet Howard Nemerov and the photographer Diane Arbus, who as a girl would stand on a window ledge to taste the proximity of death; other residents have included Paul Goldberger, Robert Morgenthau, Mitch Miller, Dustin Hoffman, Diane Keaton, Harold Arlen, Tony Randall, Faye Dunaway, Mary Tyler Moore, Jack Dempsey (for over thirty years), Barry Manilow, Raquel Welch (a subtenant in Manilow's place), Eddie Cantor, Zero Mostel, and Steve Jobs, founder of Apple Computers, who bought the top two floors of the north tower and was reported in 1988 to be spending over fifteen million dollars on renovations—or roughly three times the original price of the entire building. There were also two well-known but fictional residents, Oscar Madison and Felix Unger, in several episodes of the "Odd Couple" TV series.

by roofing over its tracks on Fourth Avenue. Then came the 1929 crash, and Fashion pretty well fled the Upper West Side. After 1931 there would be little residential construction in the area for nearly fifty years.

But thanks to Roth, Chanin, Daddy Browning, and their ilk, there were plenty of apartments, and people moved from place to place in a way that seems astonishing now. The first month's rent was usually free, moving men, painters, paperhangers, and other laborers cost little, and moving day—traditionally May first or October first—saw the streets filled with vans. "We have no yesterdays," complained Alexander Woollcott, himself a temporary resident of West 67th Street. "We don't even know the names of the nice-looking people next door and it does not matter much, because before long the moving vans will back up callously for their furniture—or ours." The only unfailing sign of the typical New Yorker, said humorist Irvin S. Cobb, was that he either had just moved into a new neighborhood or was just getting ready to move out of the old one. "So far as I know," Cobb added, "General U.S. Grant is the only permanent resident of the Upper West Side."

The only fashionable one, perhaps. "Oddly enough," as a typical 1931 guidebook observed, "no part of the West Side is really smart—for which many without social ambitions give thanks since lack of a chic address sends down rents." Another guidebook, *All About New York*, listed no Upper West Side restaurants, no roof gardens; it did mention San Juan Hill, though: "All we can tell you about it is that here even the police go in twos!" *Dau's Blue Book* for 1934, a *Social Register*-type directory, still listed 190 "elite" households on the West Side above 97th Street; the 1937 *Dau's* had none.

Though West End Avenue, Riverside Drive, and Central Park West still looked aristocratic to Amsterdam Avenue, the once-prestigious brownstone and limestone rows had become, as one fastidious observer put it, "uninteresting side streets along which it is not pleasant to stroll." Writers on architecture had once compared the marble fronts and monuments of Central Park West and Riverside Drive to sugared cake decorations; in the thirties they might have likened the Upper West Side itself to a wedding cake—a stale one, whose ornate icing now concealed a hard, unappetizing interior. Like the Harsenville elders of ninety years before, the old West End families died out or moved away—or they stayed and pined for the days "before the foreigners came."

Private homes and large apartments became rooming houses, sheltering honest working-class families of all languages and colors, prizefighters, criminals, kept women, and the downwardly mobile "new poor" of the lean years. Novelist Laura Z. Hobson (*Gentleman's Agreement*) found herself pregnant and unmarried in an era when one still hid such things. She temporarily changed her name, sublet her East End Avenue flat, and with

part of the profits rented *two* apartments (one for the maid) at 128 West 77th until the baby came and she could openly "adopt" him. She told her East Side friends she was visiting friends in Grosse Point—and in social terms, at least, she wasn't far off.

George S. Kaufman had left the Upper West Side for East 94th Street by the thirties, but he kept an apartment near Central Park on West 73rd for recreational use. His usual playmates were girls from Polly Adler's establishment, but for a time he enjoyed an attachment to the glacially beautiful film star Mary Astor, who not only was a passionate lover but, as it unfortunately turned out, kept notes. A few years later Astor's husband subpoenaed her frank and amazingly detailed diary as evidence in a child-custody suit. For weeks the MARY ASTOR DIARY SCANDAL!!! pushed such trivia as the Spanish Civil War off the front pages, incidentally earning Kaufman the unwanted title of Public Lover No. 1 and confirming—in case anyone still doubted—that the Upper West Side was "that kind" of neighborhood.

It also did nothing for the tone of the place when the police captured Francis "Two-Gun" Crowley after a protracted exchange of bullets at 303 West 90th. Crowley was a five-foot-three, nineteen-year-old hoodlum from Queens, with a record for theft and bank robbery. In February 1931 he shot up an American Legion dance, escaped capture, and later killed a Long Island policeman. By the time he was cornered the tabloids had made him a celebrity, and ten thousand West Siders crowded around to watch him trade artillery fire with the police. After three hours he gave up (still wearing a pistol in each sock). He was quickly tried and executed. A rambling, melodramatic note, which he took time to scrawl during pauses in the gunplay, explained, "That's why I went around bumping off cops," he wrote. "It's the new sensation in films." In his case, apparently, life imitated art. (And vice versa; Crowley's finish supposedly inspired Warner Bros.' 1938 *Angels with Dirty Faces*.)

Still, many loved the neighborhood. Elmer Rice, the playwright, found this out soon after he wrote *Street Scene*, his Pulitzer Prize-winning drama of tenement life. For the set Rice planned to build an exact replica of a real lower-class tenement, and the one he selected was 25 West 65th Street, a "depressingly ugly" brownstone with "exactly the right arrangement of windows, stoop, vestibule and cellar steps." He brought Jo Mielziner, the stage designer, to look at it. "As we stood inspecting it," Rice said, "the janitress appeared, eying us suspiciously.

" 'We're planning a house,' said Jo, 'and we want to use this as a model.'

"She beamed and said, 'Yes, it *is* a beautiful house.' "

At the north edge of Columbus Circle, a huge Coca-Cola sign now towered above the auto showroom that had replaced Durland's riding academy. A gay place? Not any more. On his column, the Navigator was dwarfed by the General Motors building with its illuminated running sign advertising

the new-model Chevrolet; the old, low buildings around the circle seemed already asleep, save for the neon lights that drew an arrow alongside Child's Restaurant, pointing the way to a Chinese restaurant, FAR EAST CHOP SUEY AND CHOW MEIN. Soapbox orators lectured to a bored crowd of tired workingmen and ragged bums about the Second Coming, socialism, eugenics, and sin. As Damon Runyon explained, "Columbus Circle is a sort of public forum, and the coppers are not permitted to bother anybody with a message here, although they may run them bowlegged if they try to deliver any message anywhere else." Up in Central Park, the old reservoir had been removed to make way for the Great Lawn. Meanwhile its bed was occupied by unemployed men living in camps they called Hoovervilles ("In Hoover we trusted/Now we are busted"). Riverside Park had shantytowns, too, one known as Patchtown and another as Camp Thomas Paine. Among the men there, a Riverside Drive resident was startled one day to recognize the chef from Paris's Moulin Rouge.

Social decline meant that an eight-room apartment on the Drive now cost less than a two-room one on lower Fifth Avenue. "Old-fashioned apartments," one writer noted in 1931, "come as low as $75 for four rooms," and landlords offered three and four months' free rent to lure Depression-era tenants. At the Hotel des Artistes, twenty-two of the ninety-eight apartments were empty; in 1941 the Beresford and the San Remo *together* were sold for just twenty-five thousand dollars cash over existing mortgages. Aspiring authors and thespians, refugees from Ohio, Nebraska, and Mississippi, infested the rooming houses. The Three Arts Club at 340 West 85th, which had once ejected Fannie Hurst (but sheltered Ruth Gordon), still took in girl students in art, music, and the drama. An unsuccessful vaudeville aspirant, Lucille Ball, roomed at the Hotel Kimberly, Broadway and 74th, and found work as an artist's model at Columbus Circle (she posed as the Chesterfield Cigarette Girl) and later worked for Hattie Carnegie. Lauren Bacall, another fashion model who would go on to better things, was growing up under the el at Columbus and 86th, and a handsome Brooklyn boy named Issur Danielovich waited on tables at the Tip Toe Inn, 86th and Broadway, before Hollywood turned him into Kirk Douglas. Henry Fonda, James Stewart, and Joshua Logan shared a "small, smelly apartment" on West 64th Street, across from the YMCA and two doors down from a hotel run by Legs Diamond. (The odor came from a moldy shower curtain, which the boys couldn't discard for fear of offending the landlord). Fonda worked for a florist and painted sets in summer stock while waiting for his break. Stewart, more practical, contemplated a career in architecture (he had a degree from Princeton) or in the family hardware business.

Prizefighting had been more or less legitimate since Tom Sharkey's day, and the rooming houses near the St. Nicholas Arena on West 66th were also popular with aspiring pugilists, who did their roadwork in Central

Park. The Saint Nick had been built in 1896 as the country's first indoor ice rink; later it served interchangeably as a meeting hall, ballroom, and sports arena. Jack Johnson, Jess Willard, and other top-notch boxers fought there before and after World War I; Floyd Patterson had his professional debut there in 1952; the final event, in 1962, was a bout between two undefeated heavyweights, Billy Daniels and a young Olympic prizewinner, Cassius Clay, better known subsequently as Muhammad Ali. Clay won.

On Broadway, you couldn't walk three blocks without passing a movie house. Some, like the RKO 81st or the Riverside, still offered an abbreviated vaudeville bill; all offered serials, newsreels, at least two or three cartoons, *and* a double feature. At Broadway and 74th, Samuel "Roxy" Rothapfel, who lived on the Drive, completed the Beacon Theatre, last of the great movie palaces, modeled after his legendary Roxy Theatre. Oddly, it never made money. But most did; at Columbus and 84th, one building owner even lopped off the upper floors of an apartment house to meet building code requirements and turned the lower floors into a movie house, the New Schuyler. You couldn't give apartments away, but you could always sell movie tickets.

From time to time a new manager would even try to breathe life into the aging Majestic Theatre, also known variously as the Cosmopolitan, the Park, the Columbus Circle, and the International. For a time Billy Minsky offered his special combination of "low gags and tall gals," but even burlesque couldn't wake the place up—until 1949, when it was reopened as the International, the first playhouse specifically designed for television. The show that premiered there January 28, 1949 was the *Admiral Broadway Revue*, starring Sid Caesar and Imogene Coca; rechristened *Your Show of Shows*, it became the most esteemed variety show in television history—which was not entirely surprising, since the writing staff included (among others) Mel Brooks, Milt Kamen, Neil Simon, Larry Gelbart, and Woody Allen.

General Viele had correctly prophesied that the West End would be attractive to "the great and prosperous class of our Hebrew fellow-citizens." By the 1930s, according to one estimate, a third of those living in the new Broadway and West End Avenue apartment houses between 79th and 110th streets were Jews, mostly transplanted to the West Side's "gilded Ghetto" from the Lower East Side, the Bronx, or Harlem. Seven new synagogues appeared in the area, joining Shearith Israel, the city's oldest congregation (1654), which had relocated to Central Park West and 70th Street in 1897. Rabbi Stephen Wise, leading American Zionist of his day, founded the Free Synagogue on West 68th Street (1907), the flagship institution of the Reform Jewish movement, and Felix Adler's Society for Ethical Culture moved to new quarters on Central Park West, where Professor Adler lectured on everything from war to marriage and woman suffrage (he was against it). The older,

mostly native-born, German-Jewish families enjoyed the relative grandeur of Central Park West; more recent arrivals from Eastern Europe gravitated toward the upper reaches of West End Avenue.

Not a block in this well-to-do Jewish neighborhood was without its bake shop, candy store, or fancy delicatessen, according to the real estate tycoon William Zeckendorf, who moved into the Dorilton Apartments on West 71st Street as a boy of twelve in 1917. "An amazing number of people knew each other," he added. "On the Jewish New Year it was the custom for the gentlemen and their ladies, in their furs, to walk up and down that part of Broadway greeting their friends." In *Marjorie Morningstar*, the novelist Herman Wouk, a slightly later child of the Upper West Side, would write of Marjorie Morgenstern, whose Jewish immigrant father made the classic trek from the humble Lower East Side via the Bronx to the grandeur of a seventeenth-story apartment in the El Dorado: "By moving to the El Dorado on Central Park West her parents had done much, Marjorie believed, to make up for their immigrant origin. She was grateful to them for this, and proud of them."

The 1930s brought a fresh wave of Jewish refugees from Hitler's Europe, who were soon right at home. Their refugee paper, *Die Aufbau*, became one of the most thoughtful news dailies in the United States. At Steinberg's Famous Dairy Restaurant, the Tip Toe Inn, and the Eclair pastry shop (still in business on West 72nd) they argued politics over glasses of tea and addressed the refugee waiters—quite correctly—as *Herr Professor*. Some also brought with them an incongruous Teutonic arrogance. Jimmy Ernst, son of the German-Jewish surrealist painter Max Ernst and then a nineteen-year-old refugee with a seven-dollar-a-week furnished room at Broadway and 81st, was unfavorably impressed with some of his better-heeled *landsmen*. "Fastidiously dressed and with an air of superiority, they took their after-dinner strolls on Broadway with ill-concealed disdain on their faces, and in their voices, for the fact that this was a far cry from being Berlin's Kurfurstendamm or Cologne's Hohe Strasse. They could be clearly heard complaining in their native language about unswept sidewalks, the discourtesy of janitors, surly waiters, incompetent household help, all-too-casual postal service, noisy subways, badly sprung buses, insulting cab drivers, too many street beggars, LaGuardia's love of Negroes, the unpleasant sound of Yiddish and the slovenly *Ost-Juden* (East-European Jews) who had made the 'respectable ones' look bad in Germany and presented the same problem here."

All of which might have made the West Side a "Jewish" neighborhood, except for the continuous arrival of blacks from North and South, Russians, Ukrainians, Haitians, Dominicans, Puerto Ricans, and others. A small colony of Filipinos settled among the Irish of the West 60s. Italian grocery and meat shops lined parts of Columbus Avenue; on West 99th Street was what the *WPA Guide* called in 1939 "a Negro colony, an outpost of Harlem."

A handful of Puerto Rican families had settled near 104th and Broadway and even had the city's first Spanish-language cinema, the Nuevo Edison. Meanwhile Amsterdam Avenue was still lined with Irish homes, Columbus with Irish pubs, and there was plenty of tension between the Irish and the Jews, especially in the late thirties, when Father Coughlin spread the anti-Semitic poison of his so-called Christian Front over the radio airwaves. It was all part of the ferment, the piling on of nationalities and accents, that made the area part of what the social historian (and Columbia graduate) Lloyd Morris called "Cosmopolis under the El."

The Ninth Avenue Elevated had nourished the Upper West Side like an iron umbilicus; by the thirties it had degenerated into an obstructive, deafening eyesore. Passing trains raised havoc with radio broadcasts, and if you had the el for a neighbor you learned the trick of pausing halfway through a sentence while the train roared by, picking up your thought when it was gone. Drunks brawled in front of the bars and emptied their bladders against the el's pylons, and mothers warned their daughters to find a safer route home. It was pulled down in 1940, and the scrap steel sold to Japan to be used, as old-timers will still tell you without prompting, at Pearl Harbor.

If World War II caught Americans by surprise, it shouldn't have. Many had tried to warn us about the Nazis—including such otherwise antithetical Upper West Siders as theologian Reinhold Niehbur and gossip columnist Walter Winchell. Pierre van Paassen, the crusading Dutch-born clergyman-journalist, came to the Upper West Side as a refugee in 1939, and exposed Der Fuhrer's detailed plans for world conquest in a small, urgent book called *The Time Is Now* (the title was suggested by an electric time signal flashing from across the Hudson into his room at 90 Riverside Drive)—and for his pains was branded a war-mongering sensationalist.

All through the war New York was America's main harbor (as it was in 1776) and the prime port of embarkation for Europe-bound G.I.s. The Upper West Side's single Japanese restaurant, on Columbus Avenue, closed down right after Pearl Harbor; so did the local office of the Japanese Army, which had been on Columbus Circle. There were anti-aircraft batteries in Central Park, and war games complete with tanks; a neighborhood Victory Garden was planted in the landscaped grounds of the empty Schwab mansion. (Charlie Schwab had died in 1939, bequeathing his lavish home to the city for the mayor's residence, but a proletarian Mayor LaGuardia indignantly rejected it: "What, *me* in *that*?!") The Air Force took over the Manhattan Towers Hotel at Broadway and 76th for a training center; draft and rationing boards set up shop in local schools, and windows were hung with flags and blackout curtains. Well-bred young ladies pulled their weight arranging U.S.O. and officers' club dances, while the mediums and spirit-ualists who plied their racket along Central Park West and 72nd Street did

a brisk trade among the mothers and widows of dead soldiers, and the unruly gangs of Columbus Avenue tormented the blackout wardens by throwing lighted matches from the windows. Manhattan's most conspicuous wartime disaster occurred in February 1942, when the opulent French liner *Normandie* caught fire at North River Pier 88 while undergoing conversion to a troop ship. One of the few men who might have saved her was living at the time at 99th Street and Riverside Drive: Vladimir I. Yourkevitch, the *Normandie*'s architect. But crowds and police lines kept Yourkevitch from the pier; he finally left the scene in tears, rushed home, and watched from his apartment window as his ship burned and sank. The most significant local war effort was conducted in great secrecy at Columbia University: the Manhattan Project, which produced the first atom bomb, began there, under the direction of the brilliant physicist J. Robert Oppenheimer, an Upper West Side native from Riverside Drive and 87th. Meanwhile, even the war didn't stop groups of conscientious objectors from picketing at Columbia to protest the draft—perhaps as elegant a demonstration of political freedom as the world ever offered.

Soon after the war, an American memorial to the six million Jews killed in Europe was planned for Riverside Park. The sculptor, Jo Davidson, made a model showing the last survivors of the Warsaw Ghetto, which the parks department rejected on the grounds that the sculpture was "a pretty bloody and terrifying business." All that finally came of it was a granite slab near the park's 83rd Street entrance, reading:

THIS IS THE SITE FOR THE AMERICAN MEMORIAL TO THE HEROES OF THE WARSAW GHETTO BATTLE APRIL–MAY 1943 AND TO THE SIX MILLION JEWS OF EUROPE MARTYRED IN THE CAUSE OF HUMAN LIBERTY.

But by the fifties, few were interested in memories of war or holocaust. General Dwight D. Eisenhower, recently sworn in as president of Columbia University, was living on Morningside Drive and trying to get the university to offer courses in good citizenship. The issue of the day was youth gangs and juvenile delinquency, and on sultry evenings the parks and street corners were overrun with young hoodlums in motorcycle boots and leather jackets.

Some of the embryonic mobsters may have been inspired to higher things in 1964 when three Florida beach bums, one of them known as Murph the Surf, scaled the facade of the Museum of Natural History one October night, let themselves into the Morgan Memorial Hall of Minerals and Gems (then on the top floor), and made away with twenty-two prize items, including the Edith Haggin DeLong Star Ruby (the "most perfect" ruby in the world), the Midnight Star Sapphire, and the Star of India Sapphire, the latter two gifts from J. P. Morgan. Most of the loot was recovered (the DeLong Ruby was ransomed for twenty-five thousand dollars), and the culprits were quickly caught. The Great Jewel Robbery,

they revealed, might never have been brought off without the unwitting help of the museum staff. The windows in the gem hall had been left open two inches (for ventilation), and the Star of India burglar alarm left out of whack with a dead battery: further evidence, if any were needed, that things were really going to hell on the West Side.

By mid-decade, switchblades and zip guns were cherished status symbols; when a sixteen-year-old was stabbed near the 81st Street IND station there was talk of a 10:30 P.M. curfew for teenagers, but nothing came of it. Booker T. Washington Junior High, at Columbus and 107th, was known as the worst in the city after a spate of stabbing and zip-gun affrays. On one not-too-unusual Friday night in June 1956, police broke up a mob of two hundred teenagers massed on the Drive to do battle for the "exclusive rights" to Riverside Park; they arrested thirty-eight and found a bayonet, iron pipes, and dozens of other weapons secreted under parked cars in the vicinity. Warner Brothers would soon glamorize such troubled

Lobby card advertising *West Side Story*, 1961. Condemned San Juan Hill tenements served as background for the movie.

adolescents in *Rebel Without a Cause;* the film's star was a young actor named James Dean, who had been living in a fifth-floor walk-up on West 68th Street. The teenage gangs also inspired Arthur Laurents and Leonard Bernstein to write a musical update of *Romeo and Juliet.* In its first version, it recounted the hopeless love of an Italian boy and a Jewish girl in the slums of Delancey Street; they called it *East Side Story.* But by the time the show opened in 1957 Maria had become Puerto Rican, and the show was called *West Side Story.*

Before the war, Manhattan's Hispanics had settled mainly in the East Harlem *barrio;* now, suddenly, block after block of the Upper West Side was being taken over by these exotic newcomers from the Caribbean, with their noisy *charanga* music at night and, in the mornings, the crowing of roosters raised in the courtyards for cockfights. The sudden influx tested the neighborhood's liberalism, not always to its credit. ("It was like an invasion of red ants," said one frankly hostile resident.) By the mid-fifties Puerto Ricans made up 14 percent of the population east of Amsterdam Avenue above 86th Street, and as urban renewal pushed them out some moved south into the tenements of the 80s. On West 84th Street one hot July night in 1961, a black woman and a Puerto Rican woman started swapping insults, then blows. It grew into a general melee. The papers labeled it a riot, and the *Post* and the *Herald-Tribune* ran a series on the block and neighborhood they called "the worst in the city"—a judgment seemingly confirmed the following year when a second, larger riot broke out on West 94th.

Columbia University public-spiritedly built a two-hundred-thousand-dollar ballfield and field house in Morningside Park and ran a summer sports program that pulled in six hundred boys of all nationalities. "One team," said a news account, "can send out an infield composed of a white boy at first base, a Puerto Rican at second, a Negro at shortstop and a Chinese at third—and they can make the double play." (The program director did complain that to prevent fights, he had to keep *parents* off the field.) Only cynics pointed out that the university also got the use of a field house and track in a city park, maintained by the parks department at taxpayer expense.

An aspiring actor named Dick Cavett was living on West 89th at the start of the sixties. More or less fresh from Yale, he had come to New York to break into show business. By day he trudged the usual rounds of agents' offices, he said, then came home to his fifty-dollar-a-month, roach-infested fifth-floor walk-up: "At night I watched TV, read, went to the New Yorker movie theater, or watched my Puerto Rican neighbors make love in the apartment directly across the air shaft. The nights were hot, the windows were open, and by getting on the roof I could simultaneously arouse, educate, and frustrate myself by taking in the erotic circus that took place almost nightly on the queen-size bed just below. When either they or I

tired, I would sit by the chimney and, like Gatsby looking at the light on Daisy's dock, gaze at the East Side skyline, resolving that someday I would live over there, by hook or some other means."

For the most wretched, the poorest, the Upper West Side was what Joseph Lyford, paraphrasing Martin Luther King, Jr., called an "airtight cage." In 1966 Lyford gave the horrifying population figure of 152,000 people, or over 1,000 a block, just between 82nd and 106th streets. (Reckoned in terms of standard 200-by-600-foot city blocks, the density was actually worse: 1,650 per block.) They were about 70 percent white—Jews (the largest single group), Irish, Italian, WASP—plus about 26,000 Puerto Ricans, Mexicans, Cubans, Dominicans, and other Latin Americans; 18,000 American Negroes; and 2,500 "others," mainly from Japan or China but also from Korea, the Philippines, Russia, Lebanon, the Ukraine, and Africa. The poor of all races suffered spectacular levels of cardiorespiratory diseases, tuberculosis, venereal disease, mental illness, trichinosis, amoebiasis, hepatitis, and schistosomiasis. Prostitution, murder, drunkenness, and drug addiction were epidemic; Lyford reckoned that as many as 25 percent of the *national* total of registered addicts may have been living on the Upper West Side. A white householder in the West 90s complained that her street was littered with "a thousand beer bottles every Monday morning," then paused and added, using a favorite racist euphemism of the era, "the Element, you know." Another complained of a flood of, "I'm sorry to say it, you know, the wrong types—'muddy water' from the north." She retreated downtown, from 96th Street to 86th, 79th, and finally 72nd.

Social critic Marya Mannes described her neighborhood around the Dakota in 1961. " 'Nice' people still live in these brownstones," she wrote, "many of them refugees of the late 1930s, German and Austrian Jews who are psychiatrists, scholars, musicians, teachers, artisans, unable to afford living elsewhere; together with a number of American professionals, they form islands of decency in a brown sea of squalor." Rising around them, Mannes saw a tide of black and Puerto Rican poverty and violence: "the sullen boys with pomaded ducktails and the tough girls with scornful eyes, hanging around the stoops, chattering roughly." Not that she blamed them. "Their only sin," Mannes went on, "lies in their majority: they outnumber their white neighbors-in-squalor—the perverts, addicts, delinquents, criminals and failures who infest the city."

Others, though, saw a new age of integration and tolerance dawning on the Upper West Side. In *Beyond the Melting Pot* (1963) Nathan Glazer and Daniel Patrick Moynihan pointed to Father James Gusweller's Church of St. Matthew and St. Timothy on West 84th near Central Park West— successfully integrated for years, the black and white parishioners reaching out together to the growing Puerto Rican community; and to the new West Side housing co-ops like Morningside Gardens, which had replaced several

blocks of slum tenements at 123rd to 125th streets: "Here Negroes and whites do begin to form an interracial community that is rapidly being taken for granted, and one in which a mixed couple (the West Side is the area where they are most numerous) no longer leads to the turning of heads."

Upper West Siders elected outspoken liberals (William F. Ryan, Bella Abzug) to Congress, marched for peace and disarmament, picketed the board of education for local control of schools, went south on Freedom Rides. In June 1964 Andrew Goodman, a twenty-year-old student from West 86th Street, and Michael Schwerner, twenty-four, a Columbia social work graduate, vanished a day after arriving in rural Mississippi for the Congress of Racial Equality's "Freedom Summer." When the local police refused to investigate, the FBI stepped in and eventually found their bodies and that of James Earl Chaney, a local activist, in an earth dam by a cattle pond. Widespread revulsion against the crime and its aftermath—no one was tried for it until more than three years later—helped to secure passage in 1965 of the first national Voting Rights Act.

Upper West Siders championed their neighbor Joseph Papp when he started his free productions of Shakespeare in Central Park; they petitioned for the Equal Rights Amendment (which some of them helped draft), and in following years would circulate petitions to secure the blessings of liberty to blacks, Hispanics, draft resisters, whales, gays, striped bass, Soviet Jews, Palestinians, and women, in roughly that order; and they flocked to Central Park for antiwar rallies, hippie festivals of peace and love, and the first Earth Day in 1971. Marjorie Morningstar was being supplanted by Allison Portchnik, the over-educated, liberal Upper West Sider described by Woody Allen and Marshall Brickman in *Annie Hall*: "like, New York Jewish Left-Wing Liberal Intellectual Central Park West Brandeis University . . . uh, the Socialist Summer Camps and the . . . the father with the Ben Shahn drawings and really, you know, strike-oriented."

Staid Columbia University was suddenly radicalized in 1968 when students protesting a planned university sports building (remember that playing field in Morningside Park?) took over the administration offices and classrooms. Suddenly the protests were also about civil rights and the hated Vietnam War, and students all over America and Europe were following Columbia's example. Ike and Nicholas Murray Butler would have been horrified, but revolutionaries were also an old Upper West Side tradition, from Victoria Woodhull and Elizabeth Cady Stanton to Lolita Lebrón of West 94th Street, leader of the Puerto Rican nationalists who sprayed the United States House of Representatives with rifle fire in 1954. Upper West Sider J. Robert Oppenheimer, having helped beget the A-bomb, labored for nuclear disarmament in the Cold War-ridden 1950s, and was promptly labeled a "security risk." Alan Max of West 113th Street was managing editor of the Communist *Daily Worker* (until drummed out of

Heedless of flying lead,
thousands gathered at West End
and 90th Street to enjoy the
police shoot-out with cop-killer
Francis "Two-Gun" Crowley in
May 1931.

Balloon-seller, daddies, and
strollers in Straus Park, c. 1920.

Street scene, Broadway and West
86th Street, 1930s; Belnord
Apartments in background at
right.

Daddy Browning and Peaches.
The darlings of the tabloid set
pause to enjoy their own
publicity.

November 7. 1934.

Building the Hayden
Planetarium, November 1934.

Top:
The 79th Street Yacht Basin and
the Henry Hudson Parkway were
just part of Robert Moses's West
Side Improvement, built 1934–
37.

By 1961, Commissioner Moses
was still at it, with (south to
north) Fordham University,
Lincoln Center, and the Lincoln
Towers housing project all under
way simultaneously.

The gala twenty-fifth birthday
party for Lincoln Center, 1984.

A street vendor on West 64th
and Broadway does a brisk
business in T-shirts.

Zabar's, the General Motors of
delicatessens, now fills half a
block of Broadway above West
80th Street.

the Party for opening the *Worker's* pages to dissenting opinions) and his son Steve Max was instrumental in building the Students for a Democratic Society, or SDS, into a national movement in the sixties. (For that matter, the first student strike of the thirties—also a decade of vigorous civil rights and antiwar activism—had been at Columbia in 1933.) Interestingly, the most successful revolutionary to come out of the West Side was probably a soft-spoken 1949 graduate of West 79th Street's Notre Dame High School, Corazon Cojuangco, later to be President Cory Aquino of the Philippines. That is, unless you count Fidel Castro, who honeymooned for a few weeks in 1948 at his brother-in-law's apartment on West 82nd Street. Castro drove around the city in a rented white Cadillac and supposedly toyed with the idea of enrolling at Columbia; instead, he got hold of a copy of Marx's *Das Kapital*, which seems to have served his purposes just as well.

In the turbulent seventies, the Union Theological Seminary and the Cathedral of St. John the Divine also became centers of war resistance; so did Riverside Church, where the Reverend William Sloane Coffin fanned the flames of protest (and courted prison for himself) by helping nearly a thousand war protestors return their draft cards. Antidraft militants David Eberhardt and Philip Berrigan sought sanctuary from the FBI in the Church of St. Gregory the Great on West 90th; the G-men hauled them off to jail anyway. In the mid-seventies Patricia Hearst—heiress, kidnap victim, armed revolutionary, and subject of a nationwide manhunt—hid out briefly on West 90th Street, just four blocks from her grandfather's old home on West 86th. The race riots of the sixties were not repeated in the seventies, but H. Rap Brown, a black militant on the FBI's most wanted list, was captured in a gun battle at the Red Carpet Lounge on West 85th.

It was the nonpolitical, business-as-usual gunplay that bothered most people—that, and the Upper West Side's now-endemic drunkenness, addiction, burglaries, muggings, rapes, and worse. "I've never been afraid before," one elderly Upper West Side woman told *New York Times* writer Joan Cook in 1971, "but now I'm scared of the people I see on the streets, especially the young people. Isn't that awful? I don't know why, I have the feeling that they wouldn't stop at anything." Another, seventy-three-year-old Mrs. Rothschild, had lived on West End Avenue for forty-five years and used to think nothing of going out at three in the morning to walk her pet bulldog in the park. "Now I'm afraid to go to the corner to buy a newspaper at 7 P.M.," she said with disgust. "A friend of mine got sick the other night and the doctor wouldn't come. He said he was afraid of the neighborhood." By now, East Siders invited to dinner by West Side friends or colleagues would decline awkwardly or suggest some safe neutral ground—or find new friends. And anyway, there was "nowhere to eat" on the West Side. Jules Feiffer wove a terrifying black comedy, *Little Murders*, around the everyday events of Upper West Side life—sporadic gunfire outside the triple-locked

door, a "breather" who phoned daily at the same hour. The play flopped on Broadway, did well in a Village revival (and later as a movie), and to many West Siders it didn't seem far-fetched at all.

One Christmas season in the early seventies Roseann Quinn, a twenty-eight-year-old teacher of deaf children, was killed in her West 72nd Street apartment by a man she had picked up at a bar. The murderer killed himself in jail, and a West Side novelist, Judith Rossner, fictionalized the case in *Looking for Mr. Goodbar.* (The murder investigation—police had traced the murderer to Indiana—also became a TV movie, *Trackdown.*) For many, the Goodbar case spoke all too eloquently of the emptiness and danger of life in this degraded neighborhood.

The financial crisis of the mid-1970s, when the city was threatened with imminent bankruptcy, helped make things even worse, if possible, for the Upper West Side. The state released thousands of long-term patients from mental hospitals, and many instinctively found their way to one of the neighborhood's sixty-two single-room occupancy welfare hotels—SROs— which drastically changed many blocks. They did offer shelter to the old and infirm, but they also harbored criminals, junkies, prostitutes, and drunks. Formerly proud hotels, the Endicott, the Belleclaire, the Marseilles, became sinks of vice and crime; in one, the Park Plaza on West 77th, six elderly women were strangled or suffocated for their Social Security checks before the authorities noticed anything amiss.

Squatters reappeared in numbers for the first time since the 1880s, especially along West 87th and Columbus Avenue, and in the Manhattan Valley area, where many buildings had been emptied of their mainly poor and working-class tenants to make way for redevelopment that never happened. To poor tenants seeking housing in an extremely tight market, the sight of so many vacant, basically solid homes awaiting demolition was an affront and a challenge. A few families, mostly black and Puerto Rican, pried open the boarded-up buildings at night, took possession, did what fixing up they could, and fortified them. By the spring of 1970 local radicals had organized this into a quasi-formal movement, which they dubbed Operation Move-In.

In some buildings—*nice* buildings—a month didn't go by without a burglary or an armed robbery. Back apartments in converted brownstones were especially vulnerable, as burglars worked their way through entire blocks, using auto jacks to rip out the heavy iron grills. Only good humor and a liberal outlook kept life tolerable. A police drive to clean up other parts of town drove scores of streetwalkers to the West 70s and 80s. At one block association meeting the discussion turned to the hookers who had taken up permanent positions nearby on Broadway, five or six to the block, and called, "Goin' out, honey?" to every passing male—with the result that neighborhood women couldn't walk home without being subjected to coarse invitations from cruising motorists. Still, one young schoolteacher

was appalled when her neighbors wanted to get the cops. She looked at them wide-eyed and asked, "Why don't we get them help from a social worker?" One newcomer to the neighborhood in the early seventies was greeted his second day by two knife-wielding assailants who forced their way into his apartment and relieved him of a new stereo and color TV. He considered leaving, then decided he might as well stay. "Armed robbery," he reasoned, "is just the Upper West Side's version of the Welcome Wagon."

And yet it was a kind of golden age for the Upper West Side, though (as always with golden ages) hardly anyone noticed at the time. Amid the danger and occasional squalor, writers, artists, musicians, social reformers, and political activists nourished an atmosphere of courage and experiment— of what Frederic Morton affectionately called "Bohemia, such as it is, on the Upper West Side." Most West Siders had no intention of giving up on a neighborhood where you could browse till midnight in the New Yorker Book Shop at 89th and Broadway, whose owner, Pete Martin, had started San Francisco's legendary City Lights Bookstore with Lawrence Ferlinghetti back in 1952. For them, it was an involved, exciting community, flourishing despite, and partly because of, the nastiest facts of urban life. If you couldn't go out at night and the kids had to go to private schools and judo class, if you had to accept a modicum of mugging, purse-snatching, burglary and bicycle thefts, and so on, that was still an acceptable price to pay for the libraries, the museums, the theaters, the stores, the parks, the sheer variety of activities. "Four years ago," another woman told Joan Cook, "we rented a house in the country so the children could dig in the earth and play with the squirrels and watch the flowers grow. After the second day, they were saying, 'Mommy, where's the library?' Even the maid was bored to death."

One wonderful reason to stay was a trio of revival movie houses: the once-elegant Regency, the snug, seedy Thalia—where the linked double bill (*Potemkin* always shown with *Alexander Nevsky, The Maltese Falcon* with *The Thin Man*) changed daily, and especially the New Yorker, at Broadway and 88th. The latter started in the late fifties, when Dan Talbot, a Warner Bros. story editor, decided that the only way he would get to see the films he liked was to open his own theater. He bought the old Yorktown theater on Broadway above 88th, reopened it as the New Yorker, and put together the most remarkable collection of features ever shown commer-cially, from D. W. Griffith's *Intolerance* to Allen Ginsburg and Jack Kerouac's *Pull My Daisy;* monster films, underground films, commercial and critical failures, Nazi propaganda, rarely seen movies by Hitchcock, Godard, Ozu, and dozens of others. A three-hundred-page guest book was kept open for comments and requests; program notes were contributed by, among Talbot's other friends, Pauline Kael, Kerouac, and Jules Feiffer. Director Peter Bogdanovich and film critic Roger Greenspun (among others) confessed that they more or less grew up at the New Yorker, and theater historian

Miles Kreuger considered Talbot "totally responsible" for launching the worldwide cults for Bogart, W. C. Fields, and Bette Davis in the sixties. Even after it was sold in 1973 to the Walter Reade chain, the New Yorker's reputation for the offbeat was sustained with two bizarre, long-running midnight features, *Pink Flamingos* and *The Rocky Horror Picture Show*. The line of weirdly costumed and made-up enthusiasts waiting to get in usually stretched halfway to West End Avenue.

At Stryker's Pub, a small, attractive bar in a West 86th Street brownstone with a historic name and a less-than-ideal piano, guitarists Chuck Wayne and Joe Puma were the regulars, and sometimes a twelve-piece band squeezed into the nook that served as a bandstand. Up at Columbus and 97th was Mikell's, an easygoing jazz-and-soul place in an urban-renewal building, a regular stopping place for Chico Hamilton and his quartet, Roy Haynes and the Hip Ensemble, and for local groups, aspiring and established. The West End Bar, once a hangout for beatniks and Columbia students, grew into a bricked-and-boarded club for the likes of Eddie Durham and Ruby Braff, the music sometimes broadcast live, as in the old radio days, over the college station WKCR.

In 1971 John Corry, a *Times* writer from West End Avenue, wrote a series of articles exploring the variety of life in New York City as manifested in a single block, West 85th between Central Park West and Columbus. People generally felt safe, Corry found. There had been a few addicts (mostly regarded as mindless nuisances) and a few murders in the 1960s— one man killed in a knife fight, a girl raped and strangled in a rooming house, a man choked to death with a telephone cord—but nothing really out of the ordinary. The middle class, especially its younger representatives, was beginning to move back. The prostitutes in their crotch-length hot pants, leather suits, and Dynel wigs, pimps in their big cars were considered entertainment rather than criminals. "We sit on the stoop at night and watch for girls going off to work," said a young woman who'd moved to the block from Queens. "It's kicky." The prostitute, for her part, regarded herself as a member of the local business scene and mistrusted the "new girls" who were into dope and carried knives.

Corry found Erich and Liselotte Drucker, eighty-seven and eighty, who still held hands when they went out walking; he found a mildly bewildered girl living happily with three homosexuals, one of them her former lover; he found an elderly woman, once the cook for a wealthy family, now living alone with no radio or telephone and convinced the tenant downstairs was pumping poison gas into her room; and he found fashion model Shere Hite, who said she didn't like Christmas or New Year's Eve—nobody did, she said—and to ward off year-end melancholia she gave West 85th Street's biggest Christmas party, with two turkeys, a borrowed Christmas tree, and a hundred guests. (Hite's social insights later found their way into print, and onto the best-seller list, with the publication of *The Hite Report*, the

---

first of her none-too-scientific but highly readable studies in sexuality.)

And the holiday season, Corry found, brought distinctly urban pleasures to the neighborhood between the parks. Henry and Alison Stolzman were going to Bethesda Fountain in Central Park on New Year's Eve. "It is the most marvelous thing that you can do in New York," Mr. Stolzman said, "Last year we turned down invitations to parties, and we went to Central Park. Just after midnight it started to snow. There were crowds of people around and everyone got excited. Can you imagine anything like that somewhere else?"

MOSES AND THE PROMISED LAND

In Lincoln Square did John D. III
 A stately palace of the arts decree,
Where architects and artists ran
 Through budgets measureless to man . . .
Culture doesn't come for free.

—Martin Mayer,
in *Horizon* magazine, 1962

The revolution that would change the Upper West Side started formally in 1956, when Robert Moses, head of the Mayor's Committee on Slum Clearance, announced plans to demolish the old San Juan Hill district and build in its place the Lincoln Center for the Performing Arts.

Moses had already done more than anyone since Peter Minuit to change the map of New York. As a recent Yale graduate in 1913, he had walked daily from his home at West End and 95th to Chambers Street, where he labored over reforms—never enacted—of the city's charter and civil service structure. In the twenties, still nowhere near the levers of power, he spent hours walking the city and envisioning it as he thought it should be. When Mayor LaGuardia named him parks commissioner in 1934, Moses had already spent two decades conceiving an amazingly ambitious program of civic improvements, and over the next thirty-odd years he amassed and wielded—sometimes ruthlessly—the power to build them. Holding as many as a dozen city and state posts at once, he directed virtually all public construction in New York, carving vast tracts into immense housing developments, linking them with great bridges and highways, and sprinkling the five boroughs with parks, playgrounds, swimming pools, and cultural amenities.

An earlier Moses project, the West Side Improvement of 1937, had remade the Hudson shoreline, covering over the riverside railroad tracks, creating the Henry Hudson Parkway on landfill, and adding 132 acres and

dozens of playgrounds and ballfields to a revitalized Riverside Park. Since then, Moses had completed (among a score of other projects) a new exhibition hall and convention center, the New York Coliseum, at Columbus Circle, and had begun implementing a vast citywide program of slum clearance and housing construction, carried out under Title I of the Federal Housing Act of 1948—which, by no coincidence, he had helped to draft. On the Upper West Side, the targeted slum areas included a large area east of Amsterdam Avenue between 86th and 105th streets, another west of Amsterdam from 83rd to 86th—and the area destined to become what Moses considered his "greatest achievement," Lincoln Center.

What really happened to get the project started will probably remain a matter for conjecture. In one widely repeated version, Rockefeller and William Zeckendorf were looking for ways to get some profit out of the San Juan Hill area; one of their wives looked up from a canasta game and said, "Build a cultural center." What is clear is that everything about it got somebody mad. Social critic Paul Goodman contemptuously tagged Lincoln Center an "emporium of the arts." Jane Jacobs, a leading urban critic, added that this cultural shopping center would be a sterile island, cut off from the life of the city. There were constitutional objections to using public moneys to benefit Catholic Fordham University (which got a new Manhattan campus out of the deal); ethical objections to the sale of land to favored developers at cut-rate prices; policy objections by the federal housing administrator to Moses's method of selecting housing developers.

Critics also pointed out that urban renewal would uproot eight hundred businesses and seven thousand low-income families, mainly Puerto Rican and black. Moses, they argued, was motivated by arrogance, racism, and worse; surely there must be a more equitable solution to the city's housing problems. Protesting residents picketed City Hall and blitzed federal officials with telegrams. Raphael Soyer, still working in the doomed Lincoln Arcade building, painted his protest: the canvas, titled *Farewell to Lincoln Square*, now in Washington's Hirshhorn Museum. "It shows a crowd of people walking aimlessly," Soyer explained, "dispossessed people. Joseph Floch is there, and a couple of young women. I even painted the demolition man, very small, in the back, and I'm there too, waving goodbye to the building."

But Moses knew only one remedy for urban blight: "uncompromising surgical removal." ("It was the worst slum in New York," he told an interviewer long afterward, "and you call it a 'neighborhood'? *Christ*, you never could have *been* there!") San Juan Hill was emptied and sealed off (the vacant streets and tenements became, briefly, a plein air set for the movie version of *West Side Story*); in 1959, on schedule, President Eisenhower came to Lincoln Square for the groundbreaking, and by 1966 three vaguely classical boxes of glass and chalky travertine surrounded the central plaza: Philharmonic Hall, the New York State Theater, and the Metropolitan Opera House—three undistinguished works by three distinguished archi-

tects (Max Abramovitz, Philip Johnson, and Wallace K. Harrison). To the south were Fordham University and its law school; behind and north of them were Eero Saarinen's Vivian Beaumont Theater, and Skidmore, Owings & Merrill's Library and Museum of the Performing Arts. By the end of the decade they were joined by the new Juilliard School of Music at 65th Street (transplanted from 122nd Street) and, in the corner between the Met and the State Theater, Walter Damrosch Park with its Guggenheim Bandshell.

Eventually the eighteen-block Lincoln Square Urban Renewal Area also included the Martin Luther King, Jr., Junior High School at Amsterdam and West 65th, the Fiorello LaGuardia High School of the Performing Arts and the American Red Cross headquarters at 66th, the Lincoln Square Synagogue at 69th, and one of the first public schools since the start of the century (P.S. 199, on West 70th Street) to be designed by a major firm, Edward Durell Stone & Associates—and behind them, to the west, the great gray mass of Lincoln Towers, apartment mega-blocks on a scale immense enough to satisfy a Mussolini. Acres of new architecture, the best of it in a style that might charitably be called Late County Seat Moderne, but no matter; the sheer volume of cultural activity at Lincoln Center soon made the place world famous, and more than justified its sponsors' hopes to make it a world-class showcase for the arts.

Does Lincoln Center also get credit for the eventual revival of the Upper West Side? Many have said so—especially the Center's official and unofficial spokesmen. Others retort that the neighborhood's resurgence took place in spite of, not because of, Lincoln Center: that New York already had a Philharmonic Hall, a Metropolitan Opera, and so on, and Lincoln Center only, well, centralized them (and incidentally took them away from other parts of town); that culture doesn't come for free, but neither (as Martin Mayer slyly hinted) need it bear a billion-dollar price tag. But on the Upper West Side, issues like these are *never* really settled. The fun is in the continuing argument.

And ironically it was a group of Upper West Siders, living just a few steps from Lincoln Center, who handed the seemingly invincible Robert Moses his first serious setback in over twenty years. It started when several young mothers learned that a parks department crew was about to bulldoze their favorite glen to make additional parking spaces for the elegant Tavern-on-the-Green restaurant in the park at 66th Street. Measured on the gigantic scale of Moses's achievements, a one-acre parking lot was barely visible. But the West 67th Street mothers who fought it were educated, well-to-do, *angry* West Siders. They picketed the site with a baby-carriage brigade and, spearheaded by such articulate neighbors as Fannie Hurst, they made the "mothers' war in Central Park" into front-page news. Unwisely, Moses refused to give an inch, and instead sent police and a work crew into the park after midnight to get the fences and bulldozers into place. The public and the press, long used to admiring the "man who gets things done,"

howled at what was variously called "a sneak attack under cover of darkness" and "a dirty, lousy stab in the back." The *Journal-American* ran a touching five-column photo of a four-year-old boy defending his playground with a toy gun. (It was the canny West 67th Street photographer Arnold Newman who took that shot, posing his son in the role of the brave little soldier.) In the end, Moses was forced to compromise; the glen became not a parking lot but a playground, and the Battle of Central Park became, in effect, Robert Moses's political Waterloo.

For decades he had directed a succession of stupendous public works programs, as he put it, "without the suggestion of scandal or criticism"; after the Battle of Central Park (such is fickle public opinion) he was criticized loudly and often. A few months later came sensational revelations of lucrative insider deals and supposed mob connections at the Manhattantown slum clearance area north of 97th on Central Park West—preceded by widespread protests against the plan, which was accused of destroying "one of the oldest Negro communities in New York outside of Harlem." There never was any proof of malfeasance on Moses's part, but that wasn't really what mattered; the upshot was that slum clearance on the Upper West Side ground to a halt. In the end, parts of the Manhattantown area would remain vacant for over thirty years.

Robert Moses completed other major projects after Lincoln Center, most notably the Verrazano-Narrows Bridge and the New York World's Fair of 1964–65. But his plans now faced ever more vocal criticism and skilled, organized community opposition, and his once-illustrious reputation began to crumble. (Later, another Upper West Sider, journalist Robert Caro, would reduce it, at least temporarily, to rubble: Caro's voluminous, Pulitzer Prize-winning 1975 biography, *The Power Broker*, portrayed Moses as a passionate, brilliant idealist who fell from grace even as he rose to power, and whose wrongheaded policies were almost single-handedly responsible for "the fall of New York.") By the early sixties Moses's long-time rival, Governor Nelson Rockefeller, was able to ease him out of most of his official posts, including a Lincoln Center directorship, and large-scale slum clearance became a thing of the past.

For the neighborhood around Lincoln Center, the reprieve was just in time. Moses had envisioned "a reborn West Side, marching north from Columbus Circle, and eventually spreading over the entire dismal and decayed West Side." He wrote those words in 1961, when bulldozers were poised to obliterate what he and many others saw as nothing but dumping grounds for prostitutes, addicts, and transients. Suddenly, though, a relatively young population, hopeful if not yet affluent, "discovered" the area. Artists—singers, dancers, actors—found working quarters in nearby lofts and basic, affordable housing in the spacious apartment houses and brownstones. WABC-TV began to expand its broadcasting operations on West 67th, and new shops and restaurants appeared to serve the new,

sophisticated clientele—the Ginger Man, O'Neal's Baloon (*saloon* still being a taboo word), and, in the ground floor of the Liberty Storage and Warehouse building on West 64th, the—what else?—Liberty Café.

Nearby, Rebekah Harkness, the Standard Oil heiress and ballet patron, also took a whack at theatrical angeling. She bought the old Colonial Theatre (which in the interim had been the Walter Hampden's Theatre and an NBC television studio) and gave it a five-million-dollar facelift, with powder-blue velvet walls (just the color of Mrs. Harkness's Rolls Royce) and an enormous, immoderately distracting mural, *Homage to Terpsichore*, in which a dozen or so nudes, mostly male, soared in ecstasy about the lightly draped figure of the Muse, who bore a more-than-passing resemblance to Mrs. Harkness. First Lady Betty Ford, Martha Graham, George Balanchine, and Agnes de Mille were on hand for the opening in 1974, but after losing another three million or so in three seasons the patrons called it quits. "It's this damn stock market," she said. "Dancers never have any money."

Whether Lincoln Center gets the credit or not, the neighborhood was beginning the long climb back. Upper West Siders of the sixties and seventies began organizing into block associations and local groups for protection, parties, tree planting, community gardens, block beautification, and peace marches. In this part of town you never heard that chestnut about the city's "coldness." Elsewhere, tenants might still "live in a building for twenty years and never know who your neighbors are"; on the West Side you heard newcomers to the area talking delightedly about "the wonderful sense of *community*" you got in New York.

As prosperity slowly returned in the late seventies, the contrasts in income and "life-style"—a self-conscious, academic term that suited the era—were as sharp as ever, but people were beginning to enjoy as well as resent them. Up at Columbia University, President McGill described his neighbors with mingled apprehension and hope: "an astonishing collection of artists, writers, middle-class professionals, reform politicians, students, revolutionary political agitators, prostitutes, welfare families, and a remarkable little group of stark-raving lunatics attracted to our district by its colorful ethos."

Then on July 4, 1976, the rest of the world suddenly rediscovered the Upper West Side.

13

THE NEW GILDED AGE

*In recent years the Upper West
Side has been transformed into
one of Manhattan's most
fashionable neighborhoods. This
renaissance is most apparent on
Columbus Avenue, a once shabby
thoroughfare now crowded with
trendy shops, ice cream parlors,
and countless restaurants.*

> —New York Yellow Pages,
> 1987–88 edition

*I think I've had about all I can
take of this Upper West Side
Renaissance.*

> —Woman at West 79th Street
> block party, 1978

Bicentennial Day! The Henry Hudson Parkway was closed to make a pedestrian promenade, and revelers crowded into Riverside Park and the empty highway for a grandstand view of the greatest parade of sailing vessels in modern times, or maybe ever: Operation Sail '76. Against the backdrop of a twenty-two-nation flotilla of gray warships, anchored across the river below the Palisades, the Coast Guard training bark *Eagle* led the parade, brilliant white in the watery sunshine, golden-eagle figurehead at her prow, the crewmen on her yardarms leaning into the wind. Behind her, their sails seeming to fill the river, came the *Danmark* from Copenhagen, Italy's elegant four-master *Amerigo Vespucci*, Japan's *Nippon Maru*, Norway's *Christian Radich*, the Soviet Union's *Tovaritsch* and *Kreuzenstern*—more than 225 sailing ships under thirty-one flags, with thousands of smaller craft darting beside them like dragonflies as the crowd cheered and waved.

Hordes of guests descended on anyone with a river view. Selma Weiser, owner of the Charivari boutique on upper Broadway, had an outdoor

barbecue for seventy-five or so at her Riverside Drive penthouse. Film critic Judith Crist and her husband, at Riverside and 90th, gave an all-night party Saturday, July third, with old movies and dancing to 1940s tunes ("Who wants to get up early on Sunday anyway?" she asked), and radio personality Barry Farber gave a legendary penthouse bash for several hundred at the Normandy, complete (so rumor said) with champagne, caviar, and dancing girls.

Riverside Park became a vast, international picnic ground. Thousands stretched out on blankets, chatted with neighbors, read books and newspapers, played guitars, listened to transistor radios, and strolled over to gawk at the Russian four-masters when they anchored at the 79th Street Boat Basin. A few even visited Grant's Tomb. A spontaneous outpouring? Not exactly. Ogilvy & Mather, the ad firm, was doing a lot of image-polishing for the Democratic National Convention in New York that summer. But New Yorkers were rediscovering that they lived in a place where great things still happened. As their kids tumbled happily about, a Cuban mother from 105th Street spent the afternoon in the park sharing histories and recipes with a Jewish colleague from 79th. "I never really *talked* to anyone like her before," Mrs. Ortiz said with surprise. A white grandmother who had fled the "muddy water" at 96th Street nervously joined the riverside crush and was amazed when "nothing happened": "We were pressed all together, white, black, Puerto Rican, and everybody was so polite, it was a pleasure." On assignment for the *Times*, Richard F. Shepard had spent the Fourth near his youthful West Side haunts, and wound up his front-page Bicentennial piece quoting a California woman who was selling T-shirts on West 79th Street. "She said," he wrote, "what older New Yorkers would rarely confess: 'New York must be the most wonderful city in the world. I've never seen anything like it.'" The Upper West Side, like the rest of New York, had decided to start feeling good about itself again.

The restaurants were the first sign. A year before the Bicentennial, West Sider Michael Weinstein and some partners had braved the odds and opened the Museum Café at the corner of 77th and Columbus Avenue—the first stylish new restaurant to open on Columbus in decades. In the next half-dozen years they watched one restaurant or café after another spring up nearby: Dazzel's, the Red Baron, Mrs. J's Sacred Cow, the Rockinghorse Café, Pershing's, the Café Central, La Tablita, Genghiz Khan's Bicycle, and a good twenty more. On and off Columbus were wine bars (Stephen's, Vintages), gay bars (Boot Hill, The Works), and "intellectual" hangouts (The Library, The Public House); J. G. Melon's, on Amsterdam Avenue, was a favorite with actors, dancers, and writers; Ruskay's, at Columbus and 75th, was the avenue's raucous showpiece, open twenty-four hours, with overblown Art Deco decor and a noisy, expensively dressed crowd every night. But this first flush of prosperity was largely confined to

the West 60s and 70s—Columbus Avenue's "strip." Venture any farther north, and you came to the block-long Endicott Hotel at 81st–82nd, now reduced to a welfare hotel, standing like a dam against the tide of prosperity, its sidewalk littered with the bottles (and persons) of junkies and drunks: Welcome back to the old Upper West Side.

Over on Broadway, meanwhile, Zabar's became possibly the world's first delicatessen to hang up a MasterCharge sign. The shop at Broadway and 80th had been purveying lox and whitefish, bagels, and "appetizing" since Louis and Lillian Zabar started it in 1934, but in the sixties and seventies it grew into what novelist Nora Ephron, a neighbor and five-times-a-week customer, called "the ultimate West Side institution," messy and middle class, giving the impression of disorganization without being disorganized and "the appearance of warmth without being truly friendly." Other neighborhood establishments—Murray's Sturgeon Shop, Barney Greengrass the "Sturgeon King"—had similar menus and genealogies, but Zabar's was the one they called "the General Motors of specialty foods." By 1980 the erstwhile family deli had grown into a multimillion-dollar business with extensive real estate interests, capable of successful price wars and lawsuits against giants such as Macy's and Cuisinart.

And it was food above all that continued to draw the "bridge-and-tunnel crowd" to what *New York* magazine called the Yupper West Side. By 1983 even the Endicott Hotel had been emptied, fumigated, and converted to expensive co-ops, and movie mogul Dino De Laurentiis turned the restored Palm Court into what he called DDL Foodshow, a specialty shop where improbably handsome waiters (probably from Central Casting) served pheasant and roast suckling pig under theatrical lighting. One legendary summer, nineteen brazenly overpriced ice cream parlors sprouted suddenly between 70th and 89th, driving out the neighborhood's long-established but plebeian Carvel and Baskin-Robbins shops. During another, the famed Cajun chef Paul Prudhomme opened a temporary restaurant, a road-show version of his New Orleans establishment, at Columbus and 77th; epicures stood on line for four hours to try K-Paul's blackened redfish at sixty dollars a plate, and when the health department briefly shut him down for lack of an inspection certificate, Mayor Koch came in person and brought along the health and building commissioners to set matters right.

Hot on the restaurateurs' heels were the boutiques. Candy stores, cleaners, shoe-repair shops vanished, to be replaced by shops with ingenious concepts and, whenever possible, cutesy names: Only Hearts (romance-oriented bubble bath, jewelry, lingerie), To Boot (a "gallery" of cowboy footwear), R. G. Crumbsnatcher's (kiddie clothes), Akitas of Distinction (animals), Looking Too (lingerie), the Erotic Baker, Inc. (breast- and buttock-shaped pastries—actually an uptown branch of a Greenwich Village establishment), Le Bear Boutique (an emporium devoted to teddy bears), The Last Wound-Up ("the world's largest collection of wind-up toys and music

boxes"). Henry Galiano, a former museum curator, filled a shop around the corner from the Museum of Natural History with skulls, bones, antlers, and assorted fossils, named it Maxilla and Mandible, and did a thriving business with med students, Satanists, and horror-movie set decorators. On Amsterdam Avenue, Fred Terman opened a pet salon and called it Groomingdale's, then got a stiff note from a department store with a somewhat similar name, and changed it to the less euphonious Amsterdog. (There's irony here. When the department-store family came to New York, they probably took the name "Bloomingdale" from the once-fashionable West Side district; at least, New York City directories show no Bloomingdale family before the 1850s.) To the locals' amazement, West Side itself was suddenly a trendy name, as in Westside Zoo (clothing and accessories), West Side Kids (children's wear), West Side Story (an uptown restaurant), West Side Yarns (knitting supplies; formerly the Ladies' Hobby Shop). West Sox Story sold socks. West Side Stripper refinished antiques, and West Side Express offered home deliveries of escargot and Cajun-style fried shrimp. A laundromat opened that called itself Soap 'n' Suds; so did a restaurant called Pasta and Dreams, and it was rumored that the venerable Riverside funeral home would soon be called Coffins 'n' Stuff. In 1985 Mohan Murjani, the designer-jeans mogul, attained some sort of marketing milestone at Fizzazz, the Columbus Avenue outlet for his line of Coca-Cola brand sportswear: for the benefit of hardcore shopping junkies, Murjani installed the world's first sidewalk vending machine for designer clothes.

The performing arts blossomed in lofts, churches, storefronts—and real theaters. John Michael Tebelak and Stephen Schwartz had blazed the theatrical trail in 1971 with *Godspell* at the Promenade Theatre, a former church-in-a-hotel at Broadway and 76th; in 1979, Beresford resident Phyllis Newman opened a funny, touching one-woman show, *The Madwoman of Central Park West*, at the Grand Finale night club on West 70th (and later took it to Broadway). In between, Meridee Stein produced and directed the First All-Children's Theatre (First ACT) in a loft on West 65th Street; the Lincoln Square Arts Guild took over the cavernous police headquarters on 68th for a performance center; the 78th Street Theatre Lab opened in the former quarters of the Psychodrama Institute; the Equity Library Theatre set up shop in the old Master Institute Theatre on Riverside at 103rd; and the Second Stage Theatre, a highly praised venture founded to "give a second chance" to neglected works by Lanford Wilson, J. R. Gurney, Tina Howe, and others, moved in upstairs from the Promenade. There were drama and dance at the Theatre of Riverside Church, the Riverside Shakespeare Company at the West Park Presbyterian Church, and the Potter's Field Shakespearean company in the Synod House of the Cathedral Church of St. John the Divine, where Dean Charles Parkes Morton nurtured dreams of the cathedral as a center for the community's life and culture. Even Bloomsday, a bookstore (later renamed Shakespeare & Co.) up the

block from Zabar's, got into the act with an annual cover-to-cover reading of *Ulysses* by distinguished West Side personalities as close as possible to June 16, the date in 1904 on which Joyce placed the novel's action. The production began at 8:00 A.M. Saturday and ran until Molly Bloom finally said "Yes . . . " sometime late Sunday afternoon.

Two of the neighborhood's oldest, shabbiest movie houses suddenly took on new life. The opulent, gilded interior of the Beacon Theatre became an official New York City landmark, and programs under the new management ranged from Ray Charles and Japan's Grand Kabuki to a spirited debate between LSD guru Timothy Leary and Watergate conspirator G. Gordon Liddy. Meanwhile, two local impresarios, Allan Miller and Isaiah Sheffer, took over the empty Symphony Theatre at Broadway and 95th, got a ten-thousand-dollar start-up grant from the Ford Foundation and a lot of elbow grease from neighbors, and started Symphony Space, a community-oriented performance center that became a sort of artistic town square for the neighborhood. Admission was minimal or free for most events, which might be anything from a day-long Wall-to-Wall Bach or Mozart concert (audience participation emphatically encouraged) to *H.M.S. Pinafore*, O'Casey's *The Plough and the Stars*, the annual Christmas Revels, or birthday celebrations for the likes of Leonard Bernstein, Aaron Copland, Virgil Thompson, and John Cage.

By 1980 no less an authority than *Town & Country* urged readers to "explore the city's newest boutique- and restaurant-crammed street, Columbus Avenue from 67th Street to 79th Street." By 1982 *New York* magazine was calling it New York's Left Bank ("Forget St. Germain—Columbus Avenue has it all") and wondering, "Has Columbus Avenue peaked?" It hadn't. A 1979 entertainment guide listed 99 restaurants, a new high, between 59th and 125th streets; a 1987 guide listed 244, including 74 on Columbus, plus 29 pizza places and a half-dozen fast-food joints. At brunchtime on warm weekends in the mid-eighties, a river of locals and tourists spilled onto the sidewalks of Columbus Avenue and was beginning to lap at Amsterdam. Evenings brought the crowd to flood volume; they gathered early around the tables in front of every café, accumulated in long lines for designer ice cream confections at Haagen Dazs and Steve's, and drifted past a kaleidoscope of sidewalk vendors and entertainers: rap singers, tap dancers, string quartets, fire-eating jugglers, conjurers. And as they sat or strolled, they discussed movies, menus, the latest municipal scandals, and above all the commodity that made billionaires of the Astors: Manhattan real estate.

The West Side real estate revival started as a grassroots affair: individuals, couples, families sprucing up isolated buildings or blocks. On West 76th between Central Park West and Columbus in the early seventies, on West 88th between Columbus and Amsterdam, West 105th near Riverside Drive,

you began to detect freshly puttied windows, refurbished doorways, swept sidewalks: unmistakable field marks of the returning middle classes. "Brownstoning" became a recognized way of life. You scraped up the down payment for a run-down row house (total price: twenty-five thousand to forty thousand dollars maximum), did most of the repairs yourself, and ended up with a comfortable home—maybe even a few dollars left over. You could take a floor or two for yourself, rent out the others, and live rent free; and there were tax-incentive and tax-abatement programs (J-51, 421a, and others) to ease your entry into the real estate game. The main thing was to get in early and believe in the West Side's future. One brownstoner on West 83rd was Blake Fleetwood, a free-lance writer. In the late seventies it occurred to him to do an article in the Sunday *Times* magazine about social change in his neighborhood, and in the process he put a new British-derived term into circulation. It was "a gradual process," he explained, "known by the curious name of 'gentrification.' "

One developer, H. R. Shapiro, cannily sensed the coming revival as early as 1974 and began work on two new apartment buildings, the twenty-six-story Toulaine, at 130 West 67th, and the thirty-story Nevada Towers, in its own triangular plaza, bounded by Amsterdam, Broadway, and 69th Street. To his sorrow, Shapiro had arrived before the party started; he went bankrupt halfway through construction, and both buildings stood unfinished for years.

They made an apt symbol for a West Side that still seemed unable to shake off its decades-long economic decline—especially when the national recession and malaise of the late seventies were amplified locally by New York City's near-bankruptcy. That period was also punctuated by the blackout of 1977—a brief, cautionary incident that has perhaps been too easily forgotten. When the lights went out at 9:34 on a mild July evening, a gleeful mob raced down Broadway, smashing shop windows and merrily carrying off radios, clothing, shoes, anything they could grab. Meanwhile, just out of earshot near Riverside Drive, people were sitting quietly on their stoops, sipping wine, playing guitars, chatting with neighbors, and watching the lights of New Jersey across the river. When morning came, they learned that many neighborhood businesses, and the neighbors that ran them, had been wiped out. The blackout and looting hit all New York, of course, but for Upper West Siders, with their long tradition of liberalism, it seem particularly depressing. The shops that survived all put up steel security shutters—something almost never before seen in the neighbor-hood—and the streets became just that much grimmer.

But by the early eighties that kind of problem seemed far in the past. Manhattan was entering the greatest building boom since the Bronze Age, the weekly real estate section of the *Times* had swollen to the size of a normal Sunday paper, and the Upper West Side was *the* place to be. Bankers who had recently redlined the area were suddenly proud to serve "the

Upper West Side, where personality is a way of life." You couldn't stand on Broadway or Columbus without seeing a tower crane or two at work. Broadway above Columbus Circle changed—overnight, it seemed—to a typical high-rise-lined canyon, and new buildings of thirty and forty stories began to sprout, though more sparsely, in the 70s, 80s, and 90s. As scores of old rental buildings headed for conversion, even one-time Marxist revolutionaries and Earth Day veterans could be overheard earnestly discussing mortgage points and the odds of getting Scott or Jennifer onto Grandma's lease before the old lady's building went co-op.

The numbers involved sounded like Monopoly money. On Bicentennial Day a four-bedroom, park-view apartment at the Beresford was being offered for "$85,000 (negotiable)." In 1988 a new *one*-bedroom condo on West 79th with a view of a wall cost $185,000; a two-bedroom apartment in a new Broadway building was going for $235–245,000, but the developer was slightly apologetic about "these seemingly low prices" and assured buyers that they didn't imply cut-rate work.

There were incredible bonanzas to be found in older buildings: rambling old apartments that could be purchased for $25,000 and resold for ten times the price. One Dakota tenant bought an apartment for $5,000, divided it, and sold off half for $55,000; another bought an apartment for $10,000 and sold the antique mahogany and marble mantlepiece for $35,000. A dancer living at Lincoln Towers noted that she could buy her studio apartment for $78,000 and sell it the next day for $130,000. There was just one catch. "It's great for those who don't care about where they live," she said. "They can take the money and run. But where do you go if you love this place?"

On Columbus Avenue not long ago, two young men double-parked a stretch Lincoln Town Car and a Coupe de Ville behind the American Museum and started handing out flyers. In two hours they'd gotten five new accounts for their fledgling company, aptly named the American Dream Machine Limousine Corp.

The Upper West Side in the early eighties was a good place to pursue the American dream, i.e., to get rich. Zabar's branched out octopus-fashion to take over several adjacent stores and was written up on page one of the *Wall Street Journal*. Selma Weiser built up her original Charivari boutique, originally opened in 1967 on the ground floor of the run-down Euclid Hall Hotel at 85th and Broadway, into five shops, at choice locations on Broadway, Amsterdam, and Columbus avenues. Harlem-born John Catsimatidis, working out of a cramped second-floor office above West 87th Street, built the Red Apple superette into a hundred-million-dollar supermarket empire by age thirty. Bill Zanker was told by his father in 1980 that it was time to get a job, but the twenty-six-year-old film major "didn't know how to do anything but go to school." He got his New School professors to give classes,

put up five thousand dollars of bar mitzvah money to print a catalog, and distributed it from his Central Park West studio. Today his Learning Annex is the largest for-profit adult education company in the United States, with operations in fifteen cities across the country, and offers 120 courses a month in everything from hot-air ballooning to "101 Ways to Moonlight with your Personal Computer" and "How to Have a Successful Extramarital Affair."

The Riverside funeral home didn't change its name, but it was acquired by Texas-based Service Corp. International, whereupon its former president opened a rival operation, Plaza Memorial Chapel, prompting a local rabbi to comment, "Even in death, competition is good." Then St. Luke's Hospital broke new marketing ground using the radio to tout its referral service, the New York Doctor Hot Line. Columbia University, one of the city's biggest landowners, got a real estate consultant on board to help the school capitalize on its Morningside Heights retail space. (Columbia did, however, find it "inappropriate" when an adjunct business school professor, corporate raider Asher Edelman, offered students a hundred-thousand-dollar finder's fee for targeting companies for him to take over.) Others found success in the arts. Jens Nygaard, once an unemployed former prodigy who slept on the benches at Richard Tucker Park, organized the Jupiter Symphony, now considered one of the city's finest orchestras. At the same time, TV commercials were making two West Side celebrities almost unbearably familiar to New York-area viewers: disk jockey Jerry Carroll as the maniacal barker for the Crazy Eddie electronics chain, and theatrical *grande dame* and long-time Dakota resident Lauren Bacall, who parodied her own gold-digging *How to Marry a Millionaire* persona in campy ads for Fortunoff's jewelry store.

Thirty-two-year-old Sydney Biddle Barrows went Bacall one better when she was arrested on Columbus Day, 1984, for running a call-girl operation out of a town house at 304 West 74th Street. It was a very high-class operation, as befitted the young lady's education (Stoneleigh) and heritage (two *Mayflower* ancestors), and it quite diverted the public from such dreary fare as the current presidential election. Her story was basically a reprise of the Polly Adler saga, but the differences were significant. Adler was driven out of town by the cops and it took her a decade and a half to resurface and publish her memoirs; Barrows was interviewed within weeks in the *Wall Street Journal* and on TV, and *Mayflower Madam*, the story of her "secret life," appeared a little more than a year after her arrest. (It was also made into a TV movie. Candice Bergen, Barrows's real-life neighbor, played Barrows, while Barrows herself, in a bit part, turned up in the last scene as a reproachful former friend. Go figure *that* out.) Adler said she had stumbled into pandering, and she boasted of entertaining the most colorful celebrities, wits, and gangsters of her era; Barrows stressed the preponderance of tired businessmen and "financially successful nerds"

among her clientele, and her memoir was a virtual treatise on recruitment, training, employee motivation, and quality control that would have done credit to the *Harvard Business Review*. The best epitaph for the 1980s may be that it was the decade when it took management tips to sell a sex book.

It was the decade, after all, that opened with John Lennon's murder. Lennon said he loved New York "because I can walk around feeling so free," but in December 1980 he was gunned down on the sidewalk in front of his home. Tearful pilgrims came by the thousands to hang flowers and messages outside the Dakota, and a nearby patch of Central Park, where Lennon used to ramble with his son Sean, was landscaped and named Strawberry Fields as a living memorial.

Sensational Upper West Side crimes still titillated the public from time to time—though the neighborhood was finally beginning to lag behind the rest of the city in that department. Tabloids and TV thought they had something hot five months before Lennon's death, when thirty-year-old violinist Helen Hagnes Mintiks of West 75th Street was abducted and murdered during a performance at the Metropolitan Opera House. They promptly dubbed the killer the Phantom of the Opera, but he turned out to be only a baby-faced stagehand of twenty-one. (He later shared a prison hospital room with Lennon's killer on Riker's Island.) The most entertaining criminals, like Sydney Barrows, were illicit but not bloodthirsty. Hardly in her class, but fun anyway, was John Papanastassiou of Riverside Drive, a graduate student in economics who financed his education at Columbia by stealing hundreds of rare volumes from libraries in New York and London; they nabbed him at the Princeton Club trying to peddle a purloined first edition of Galileo's *Discorsi* to a book dealer from West End Avenue who had agreed to double as an undercover customs agent for the night. Also fun was John Chin, a board of education employee arrested for firing a gun into a neighbor's apartment on West 95th Street; investigators soon learned that Chin had loaned fifteen or twenty thousand dollars to another West Sider, the city's dynamic new schools chancellor Anthony J. Alvarado. Alvarado then quit *his* job when it came out that he had been taking such "loans" from quite a few board of education employees indeed. Geoffrey Lindenauer, another city employee, was caught accepting bribes in the bathroom at Hisae's, a noisy Japanese restaurant on West 72nd, and ended up with a two-year federal prison sentence for his part in New York City's Parking Violations Bureau scandal. A more eminent white-collar felon, Wall Street inside-trader Ivan Boesky, though much too wealthy to be a West Sider (his *fine* came to a hundred million dollars), was a figure frequently seen on Morningside Heights in the months before his sentencing in 1988, doing charitable work at the Cathedral of St. John the Divine *and* pursuing Talmudic studies at the Jewish Theological Seminary. He got three years anyway.

Drugs and gambling remain ineradicable on the West Side, as they are everywhere. One betting parlor at Amsterdam and West 94th was raided twenty-seven times in twenty-seven months. Needle Park is still considered the "real" name of Verdi Square at 73rd–74th and Broadway, where dealing still goes on in plain sight and junkies nod beside Falstaff's statue. Especially near upper Central Park, some streets are virtual war zones given over to drug markets and crack factories; new drug-financed gangs ruled the area, including two Dominican organizations, Willie's Gang and The Gumbs Brothers—more disaffected, and much more violent and ruthless, than the youth gangs that ruled the same area in the fifties. In 1987, hundreds of armed officers, with military-style helicopter support, made a sweep of West 107th Street, the scene of 621 drug-related arrests that year, but the dealers only shifted their operations slightly. "Go three blocks north or three blocks south," said a policeman a year later, "you can't walk the street at night."

The real crime, many believe, is the displacement of the poor and aged to make way for prosperous newcomers. In the 1880s, developer John Crimmins had the police haul the West End's squatters from their shacks. Only the technique had changed a century later, when—to name just a few—landlord Tony Postiglione was convicted of hiring thugs to scare tenants out of his rent-controlled building on West 85th, and Zenek Podolsky and George Roitman of installing junkies and prostitutes in their West 77th Street properties for the same purpose. A painting shown at the Goddard-Riverside Community Center on Columbus Avenue gave a graphic, underside view of neighborhood redevelopment, 1987-style: it showed a black child dumped in a garbage can; above loomed a building labeled "Opulence Towers Condominiums" and an inverted American flag—the traditional distress signal—with dollar signs for stars. Militants used the terms *gentrification* and *atrocity* interchangeably and seemed to blame all or most of the problems of the poor on greedy landlords and overprivileged yuppies.

It's hardly so simple, of course. Until recently, New York boasted the greatest public housing program and the most generous welfare system in the country. Even the detested yuppie invader usually turns out, on closer inspection, to be merely the traditional American professional or businessman trying to climb the traditional economic ladder. The new homeless of the Upper West Side, like anywhere else, range from dignified widows forced to live in doorways to the old-fashioned Bowery-style bums and junkies and formerly certifiable crazies who would be on the street whatever the housing and economic situation. Rapacious landlords haven't helped, but the most basic causes involve New York's loss of manufacturing industries, Reagan-era budget cuts, and—at a more fundamental level—American attitudes toward work, money, education, birth control, and mental illness. One highly publicized local case involved Joseph Mauri, who was written up in *New York* magazine in 1985, when he was about to

be evicted from his ninety-eight-dollar-a-month room in a 70th Street brownstone because his landlady wanted it for a sewing room. "Why couldn't she have had some compassion?" pleaded Mauri, who said he was jobless and would have to live on the streets; "most of my life's over." Many readers were touched, even indignant (though it was never made clear why his landlady *shouldn't* have her sewing room), but in follow-up stories it developed that Mauri—a man in his mid-fifties—had had no trouble finding a room in a residential hotel in the West 80s, and that he had a job worth about $35,000 a year, when he cared to work at it. But by then he had starred in a documentary about New York's heartlessness and was touring the Soviet Union to crusade for the city's dispossessed. Moral: If you do it right, even homelessness can be marketed profitably.

A Second Gilded Age. That's the 1980s on the Upper West Side, according to one endearingly fatuous real estate ad—penned, apparently, by someone who didn't know that gilt and gold are not the same—and to some extent the Upper West Side indeed has come full circle. When fashion designer Perry Ellis bought a town house near Central Park on West 70th (almost next door to Mauri's old digs, as it happened) he spent three years and three and a half or four million dollars renovating it with, among other things, replicas of bathrooms from London's Savoy Hotel and a wine cellar paved with Japanese river stones. Steve Jobs, founder of Apple Computers, bought the top two floors of the San Remo's north tower and hired architect I. M. Pei for a reported *fifteen*-million-dollar renovation that included twelve-foot-high nickel-bronze doors and bedroom windows said to cost seventy-nine thousand dollars apiece. Extreme examples, to be sure, but the point is, today's newcomers don't want funky atmosphere: they want a parking space for the BMW and—even if they're being funded by Mom and Dad back in Scarsdale—they want the same gracious homes and amenities as their predecessors of fifty or a hundred years ago.

Will rampant gentrification destroy the diversity that made the neighborhood attractive in the first place? With aspirations closer to those of the 1890s than the 1960s or 1970s, it's no longer the liberal-intellectual, artistic neighborhood of ten or even five years ago; the evidence is in the xeroxed flyer in Central Park that recently offered a thousand-dollar reward for return of a Siamese cat, in the soft rustling of *Wall Street Journals* on the downtown no. 1 Broadway local in the morning, and in the shuffling of tenders and prospectuses in the evening, the eighty-dollar running shoes of joggers in Riverside Park, in the half-million-dollar conversion of New York's oldest Spanish-language movie house, the Nuevo Edison at 103rd and Broadway, to the Columbia Cinema (where, ironically, the first offering was *La Bamba*—in English). A neighborhood psychoanalyst notes wryly that patients once came to her to get in touch with their feelings about love affairs and marriages: "Now it's all 'My damned marketing v.p. grabs

the credit for all my work' and 'I need you to help me be a tougher negotiator.' I sometimes miss the old-fashioned neurotics."

If you listen to some old stalwarts, the newcomers are soulless and shallow, completely obsessed with money and status symbols. "The landlord reads *People* magazine and he triples the rent," says Warren Thomas, an antique dealer who pioneered lower Columbus in the early seventies and has since relocated. "The place is overrun with idiots who come up there just because it's 'Columbus Avenue.' When you go out for a walk, it's not your neighbors you meet—it's not a *neighborhood* anymore." Mothers who want their children to live to voting age see it differently—like the one on West 92nd who says, "Twelve years ago my oldest had to fight every day. If he had money, he hid it in his shoe. Now even my young daughters can play down the street and nobody bothers them." For everyone who misses the warmth and diversity of the old West Side, there is another who remembers the nights punctuated with breaking glass and screams, the ubiquitous drunks and muggers, the triple-locked doors, and welcomes gentrification gladly.

In fact, the gilt may already be wearing off. On lower Columbus Avenue, skyrocketing rents quickly pushed out the pioneer shops and restaurants. But by 1988 the skyrocketing rents ($135–$200 per square foot for prime locations at the start of the year) were driving out even the ritzy shops that replaced them. Empty shops had become a rarity; now you began to see two or three on a block. The smart money now is betting that upper Amsterdam will be the new Columbus Avenue, and even though it is still more *barrio* than boulevard, rents per square foot have already jumped from fifteen to sixty-five dollars and up. Barney Greengrass, the "Sturgeon King" at 86th, is a sort of historic anchor—the shop where Irving Berlin used to send for his weekly order of nova, sturgeon, and homemade borscht, and where Moe Greengrass, the founder's son, still likes to dazzle the customers with card tricks. Further uptown, a scattering of new restaurants and shops—Paris–Milano, the Blue Pelican, the Erotic Baker (forced uptown by rising rent)—share the avenue with Ana's Beauty Salon, El Caribe restaurant, La Negra Pola (*Comidas Criollas, Especialidad en Mariscos*), and *bodegas* where men sit out front on upturned milk crates and play dominoes ferociously. At 95th and Amsterdam Joe Adinaro opened a new restaurant with a mahogany bar and lighting redolent of the gaslight era; he gave it a name that was both a literary allusion and "a little bit of a dig": Goodbye Columbus. Warren Thomas and his shop, As Time Goes By, are now at 98th and Amsterdam, and he likes it there—it's quiet, not dangerous, has the advantages of his old neighborhood and "it's not overrun with Yuppies. Yet."

Also surprisingly changed, and very pleasantly, is the half-mile or so of Columbus Avenue above West 87th. This was where Moses's West Side Urban Renewal Plan fizzled out in the late 1950s, and all through the

sixties and seventies it was a patchwork of run-down and abandoned tenements and brownstones, interspersed with chunky high-rises and vacant lots, while arguments raged over the area's ultimate fate. In the late seventies ad hoc groups took over several rubble-strewn blocks for gardens, and for a few years a profusion of grapes, corn, tomatoes, peppers, and flowers anachronistically evoked the market gardens of the 1870s. Finally, in 1983, the board of estimate gave its blessing to a complicated, community-initiated arrangement that included both market-rate and subsidized housing. Construction resumed and was largely complete by 1987–88. Instead of the uniform high-rise blocks originally planned, there are town houses and low- to high-rise apartment buildings, varied in style and color; a few rehabbed tenements; a mix of (fairly) reasonably priced shops; and new housing for the elderly. Also included were a home for a neighborhood dance company, the Ballet Hispanico (in two renovated carriage houses), preservation of the landmarked Claremont Stables on West 89th Street (the last livery stable in Manhattan)—and a community garden. The master plan was fulfilled—albeit twenty or thirty years late—and the result is a real rarity: a new, functional, traditional neighborhood, economically and racially integrated, and with the kinds of shops and businesses that make for a stable community: in a word, the old Upper West Side.

So the Upper West Side remains after all a great ethnic area, enclave piled on enclave, the sounds of *salsa* and joyous Pentecostalism drifting down Columbus or Amsterdam Avenue, the Korean greengrocer busily sorting snow peas outside his family shop—some of which will find their way to the Vietnamese and Szechuan restaurants next door. Elderly socialists still watch the world go by (and comment ponderously on where it went wrong) from the benches on Broadway, dignified couples in their seventies and eighties take a weekend stroll in white gloves and Panama hats. True, the three great revival houses—the Regency, the New Yorker, and the Thalia—are gone. True, a real estate brokerage, J. I. Sopher, now occupies the premises once inhabited by the Plato's Retreat sex club. But the backpacks and sneakers still hold their own against the attaché cases and Reeboks. There is still a liberal sprinkling of artists, writers, playwrights, composers, producers, performers of every stripe, and enough mental, spiritual, and New Age cults to repopulate California, if the need were to arise. The graffiti on Broadway still tend toward the immoderate ("JAIL BUSH! IRAN-CONTRA DRUG PEDDLER!" is fairly typical in *anno domini* 1989) and bus kiosks are still festooned with flyers for movers, piano tuners, concerts, apartment sales, book fairs, personal computer services—and for Zen massage, the Reiki Usui System of Natural Healing, trance readings, and classes in psychic awareness and astral travel.

There are also signs of a more traditional spiritual revival. A few years ago the congregation at St. Michael's Church was down to thirty; in 1987 it was up to three hundred; All Angels' grew from fifty to four hundred

even though its original building was torn down. Riverside Church had an all-time high of thirty-three hundred members in 1988, mostly under forty-five, while the number of orthodox Jews had grown so that there is talk of a "Jewish Revival" on the Upper West Side. Family life is on the way back. While national pundits worry about a "birth dearth," the strollers and tricycles are gridlocked on Broadway and Columbus Avenue, the newest condominiums are listing "baby centers" among the advertised amenities, and toddlers and parents are lined up at the baby swings in the Central Park playgrounds. Love Generation alumni seem to be particularly well represented among the new crop of moms and dads—at least, Fay Leeper, who has a kiddie boutique on upper Broadway, swears she can't keep up with the demand for tie-dyed rompers.

Social consciousness is still very much alive, thank you. Most neighborhood churches operate shelters and soup kitchens; Goddard-Riverside Community Center runs a camp in upstate Rifton, New York, where children from welfare hotels can get a much-needed two weeks in the country. Project Reachout was begun in 1979 in the carriage room of a West 90s housing project to aid SRO occupants; now it tackles the more arduous challenge of bringing some nutrition and comfort to the homeless on park benches and in doorways. "God's Love—We Deliver," headquartered in a Presbyterian church, brings free meals to over a hundred homebound AIDS victims daily. Locally, Alzheimer's disease has found a formidable opponent in San Remo resident Princess Yasmin Aly Khan, daughter of Rita Hayworth and the Iranian playboy Aga Khan; she brought her mother home in 1986 to nurse her through the final phases of the disease and has dedicated herself ever since to raising funds for a cure. Activists still set up tables in front of Zabar's to collect funds for the Action Committee to Help the Homeless Now and People for the Ethical Treatment of Animals. Early one school year, two hundred demonstrators—parents, children, educators, and politicians—blocked morning rush-hour traffic on the West Side Highway to protest budget cuts in the local schools. At one "enlightened" day-care center called B. J.'s Kids a few years back, the three- and four-year-old children (actually, the staff prefers the "non-ageist" term "new people") pressured a Columbus Avenue toy shop to remove a feathered headdress from a teddy bear because it was disrespectful to Native Americans. (Their class activities also included a miniature sit-in at the United Nations.) When baker Louis Lichtman closed his forty-year-old shop at 86th and Amsterdam, blaming a 400 percent rent rise, his neighbors responded with protest rallies and petitions, and when the Beacon Theatre was about to be converted to a disco, West Siders organized a Save the Beacon committee, collected twenty thousand neighborhood signatures on a petition, and organized an all-star concert and a three-block-long summer festival to preserve the historic theater. Developers dread Community Boards 7 and 9, which represent the Upper West Side and are said to be

the most tenacious and effective in all New York's five boroughs. Block and parent associations, tenant coalitions, and other neighborhood groups are also alive and well—at least seventy and probably twice that number or more, from the Manhattan Valley Spanish Civic Organization and the Japanese Association for Help to the Aging, Inc., to the Far West 77th Street Block Association and the West Side Seniors for Action. They tackle issues from AIDS and evictions to crime control, tree plantings, and broken playground equipment, and they prove what West Siders have known for a long time, that you damn well *can* fight city hall.

In the closing years of the twentieth century, the Hudson shore between 59th and 72nd Streets is a scene of weird beauty: a moonscape of cinder mounds, weeds, and litter, traversed by the elevated portion of the West Side Highway, bordered by twisted, fire-blackened industrial wharves, their rusting derricks like dinosaur skeletons, with the sweep of the Hudson and the Palisades as a backdrop. The George Washington Bridge looks close enough to touch.

This is the abandoned Penn Central rail yard, Manhattan's last frontier, seventy-seven acres (including fourteen under water) of undeveloped commercial land, nearly the size of lower Manhattan's Battery Park City. In the rail era it served the meat packers, printers, and manufacturers of the Lower West Side; later, only the Barnum & Bailey trains parked here when the circus came to town.

It's really a nursery for dreams. Once, W. E. D. Stokes hoped to build a tunnel from there to midtown and construct vaults and markets under Riverside Park. In the 1960s the Amalgamated Lithographers Union made plans to put fifteen thousand people there—along with shopping, a park, piers, a new headquarters for the *New York Times*, and an international complex called the United World Center—in a riverfront housing project they dubbed Litho City. Community opposition and disputes between the union and the railroad killed it. In the mid-seventies Donald Trump, a sort of latter-day W. E. D. Stokes, took an option on the property and proposed a development with a riverfront park that would be (*pace* Trump's spokeswoman, Louise Sunshine) "like a cross between San Francisco's Ghirardelli Square and Copenhagen's Tivoli Gardens." Again, no dice. Abraham Hirschfeld, a real estate tycoon with political ambitions, took a crack at it after that, with Argentine developer Francisco Macri; their Lincoln West project (designed by Litho City architect Jordan Gruzen) was only days from groundbreaking in 1985 when it failed through lack of financing.

By 1985 Trump was back, with the most grandiose plan yet. Television City would be an 18.5-million-square-foot residential-commercial development, with the world's tallest building—150 stories, 1,675 feet—and six smaller buildings of "only" 76 stories each, with huge new spaces for

television and movie studios (for WNBC-TV, whose lease at Rockefeller Center is due to run out in 1997) and 7,600 luxury apartments: the ultimate in Upper West Side gentrification.

Meanwhile, an even more conspicuous project, because it seemed to stand on the toes of beloved Central Park, was being put together by publisher-developer Mortimer Zuckerman: Columbus Center. With the opening of the Javits Convention Center, the thirty-year-old New York Coliseum at Columbus Circle was ready to be decommissioned. The land— a 3.4-acre plot originally assembled by Robert Moses—belonged to the city's Metropolitan Transportation Authority, and Zuckerman arranged to buy it from the city for $455.1 million, making it the most expensive land in the United States. (At that price, the twenty-four dollars Peter Minuit supposedly paid for all of Manhattan in 1626 would buy just 1.124 square inches of land on Columbus Circle.) On it, Zuckerman would build two prismatic, glass-clad towers by the Israeli architect Moshe Safdie, sixty-eight and fifty-eight stories high, with a hotel, offices (for, among others, Zuckerman's partner in the venture, the Salomon Brothers investment house), a shopping mall, and luxury apartments.

Trump and Zuckerman were hardly alone. The Zeckendorf Company, Peter Kalikow, Bruce Jay Eichner, Lewis Futterman, the Glick Organization, and the communications giant Capital Cities/ABC, Inc.—not to mention Lincoln Center, Columbia University, the New-York Historical Society, and even the West Side YMCA—all had substantial building projects in the works by early 1988. (Not the largest, but probably the weirdest scheme was the one to erect a ten-story corrugated-steel-clad apartment house on steel columns *over* a landmarked Clarence True town house at West End and West 85th. The architect, an *East* Sider, insisted it was an idea whose time had come, adding that "there is something unbourgeois about it.") Would the old neighborhood soon vanish into the shadows of the new high-rises?

At Television City, Donald Trump's Midas touch seemed to be in working order. At first. (When he hired environmental consultants to check the soil, they told him yes, the site was polluted—but he could probably make money drilling for oil.) But the opposition mobilized quickly, organizing around every issue from transportation and utilities infrastructure to parks, damage to Broadway's merchants, community involvement, and local *versus* City Hall's interests—and above all the plan's unheard-of scale. At one point in the delicate negotiations, Trump offered to share the profits on Television City for forty years in return for a twenty-year tax abatement. When the idea was turned down, Trump called Mayor Koch's advisors "jerks"; His Honor responded that "if Donald Trump is squealing like a stuck pig, I must have done something right," and the discussion continued on this high plane even after NBC arranged for quarters elsewhere.

Opposition to Columbus Center was even more vociferous. Architecture

critic (and Central Park West resident) Paul Goldberger called Safdie's design a "grotesque intrusion" and accused the city of selling its architectural birthright for a mess of pottage. The Municipal Art Society, ordinarily the most mild-mannered of civic groups, sent out a letter signed by Goldberger's neighbor, TV pundit Bill Moyers. It started, "Dear New Yorker: I got mad the other day"—and went on to tell how "a rich developer from out of town and one of the wealthiest companies in the city" had conspired with City Hall to "gang up" on Central Park. "Mayor Koch, Zuckerman, and Salomon Brothers would not only rob the Park of sunlight and sky," Moyers charged, "they have already robbed the democratic process of fairness and openness." With supporters ranging from Jacqueline Onassis to Lauren Bacall, Christopher Reeve, and James Stewart Polshek, head of Columbia's architecture school, the M.A.S. then sued to invalidate Zuckerman's purchase of the site, alleging that the environmental review process had been glossed over. One telling point was that the "architectural competition" that preceded the sale was a farce, since the city had clearly been interested only in selling to the highest bidder. A few months later Salomon Brothers pulled out of the project. The price of the land dropped to a mere $357 million, while Zuckerman quietly replaced Safdie with David Childs of Skidmore, Owings & Merrill, who reconceived the project as a smaller, stepped cluster of three towers, sensitively designed to harmonize with the Circle and with Central Park West's landmark twin-towered buildings. Ironically, as of mid-1988, work was going full blast on two nearby towers just to the south, not much lower than anything Zuckerman had in mind; while on the Circle itself, it isn't construction crews that gather, but groups of vagrants, waiting for the free bus to the city's homeless shelters.

Will these megaprojects ever get off the drawing board? Not a shovel of earth has been turned on either one—but given the still-frenzied pace of New York construction, both may be up and occupied before this book is printed. (Construction men work faster than publishers.) On the other hand the 1987 stock market crash made investors understandably nervous; in mid-1988 it's easy to suspect that what once looked like an irresistible wave of real estate development has swept northward up Manhattan, only to spend its force on the shoals of the Upper West Side. That is precisely what happened after the 1929 crash; for proof, just look at the many choice corners along Broadway still occupied by the "temporary" taxpayer buildings someone put up during the building boom of the 1920s. Nevertheless, at this writing (September 1988) the Trump Organization recently announced that Trump City (the latest name) "is moving ahead" and will complete the required six-month public review process by mid-1989; around the same time, Mortimer Zuckerman was predicting that Columbus Center would come on the market "sometime around 1993." Optimism is, after all, a developer's most important resource.

"In Manhattan's West Eighties, where I live, there is nothing to write about but people," said that dour, disenchanted West Sider Alfred Kazin. " 'Nature' hardly exists, and the architecture, when it is not simply eccentric, can be seen from the street as representing nothing but the calculation of how much money can be squeezed each month out of these cubicles."

Kazin's neighbors, on the other hand, love their neighborhood's brownstone blocks and gargoyle-encrusted apartment houses. They are grateful for the dowdiness and economic stagnation that turned developers away from their area for half a century, leaving it a peerless preserve for vanishing architectural species. (Recently, the Friends of Terracotta, a preservationist group, published a "Field Guide to Apartment Building Architecture"; no fewer than eleven of the sixteen representative buildings mentioned by the author—not a West Sider, by the way—were located on Riverside Drive, Central Park West, or points nearby.) Upper West Siders get very aggravated when demolition and redevelopment seem to be getting out of hand, and lately some of them, spearheaded by the M.A.S., Community Board 7, and several recently formed ad hoc groups—Landmark West!, CONTINUE (Committee of Neighbors to Insure a Normal Urban Environment), and Westpride, a watchdog group formed mainly to keep an eye on Trump's doings—have been fighting hard and ingeniously to save the buildings Kazin thought not worth writing about. Besides delaying and/or stopping a number of major projects, they also helped convince the City Planning Commission in 1984 to rewrite the Upper West Side's zoning code: new buildings are now broader and lower than the typical sixties or seventies high-rises, and must be compatible in general outline and quality of materials with their older neighbors.

Inevitably, some interesting old structures fell as the land under them rose in value. Up at 110th Street the last el station, a Tuscan-style orange-brick building that still had a sign over the door reading ELEVATOR TO TRAIN, went in 1979. All Angels' Church, which had begun its career inside what is now Central Park, went the following year. The Harkness (originally the Colonial) Theatre at 63rd and Broadway was demolished to make way for Harkness Towers. Campbell's (latterly Gutterman's) Funeral Home, of Valentino fame, was demolished; the site is still empty. The last portion of what had been Reisenweber's lobster palace served as an SRO hotel for years and was finally pulled down in 1987; so were the St. Nicholas arena, whose site is part of WABC-TV's 2.5-million-square-foot office-and-studio "campus" near Lincoln Center, and the marble-fronted Progress Club (later the Walden School) on Central Park West. The 81st Street Theatre on Broadway was gutted in 1987, having served (since Mae West stopped doing vaudeville in it) as home to the Muppets, when "Sesame Street" was filmed there, and to "Love, Sidney," a short-lived sitcom that was set on the Upper West Side and starred two long-time West Siders, Tony Randall and Swoozie Kurtz. In this case, though, the ornate 1914 building designed by Thomas

Lamb was preserved; it is now occupied by a suitably theatrical branch of the Conran's home-furnishings chain and serves as the portal to The Broadway, a new twenty-one-story condominium building.

Perhaps the villain in the piece—if villain there must be—is the city itself. "The present in New York is so powerful that the past is lost," John Jay Chapman wrote in 1909, and that, at least, hasn't changed. As *Harper's Monthly* complained a hundred and thirty-two years ago, New York "is never the same city for a dozen years altogether. A man born in New York forty years ago finds nothing, absolutely nothing, of the New York he knew." Today's New Yorker at least has quite a few hundred-year-old-plus buildings to look at, so maybe we aren't doing so badly at that.

Since 1965, when the Landmarks Preservation Commission set up shop, thirty-five major Upper West Side structures have become official New York City Landmarks, among them the Central Savings Bank, the Ansonia, the Apthorp, Belnord, Century, and El Dorado apartment buildings, the American Museum of Natural History, the Isaac Rice mansion, several notable turn-of-the-century churches, and all of Riverside Drive and Park, as well as others that fall within five designated historic districts between 73rd and 105th–106th streets. None can be demolished or altered (outside) without permission from the Landmarks Commission. At this writing the commission was being asked to designate another half-dozen major buildings and seven additional historic districts, ranging from the sixty-two-block-long Central Park West Historic District, with some 2,100 buildings, down to two tiny districts on West 82nd and West 101st with fifteen buildings each. Critics of landmarking include some developers, some building owners large and small, Capital Cities/ABC, Inc., which has opposed almost every landmark designation, whether or not their property was involved, and a number of clerics who see themselves doomed to perpetual upkeep of architectural white elephants. (One of the latter frequently rises at hearings to denounce his preservationist opponents' "satanic" machinations.) They accuse the Landmarks Commission of indifference to owners' rights and call the whole business elitist and retrograde. Others (your author, for one) would like to see every brick and stone preserved as is—a position admittedly hard to justify on any but sentimental grounds. Perhaps the main point about landmarking is that while it may occasionally be capricious or even unfair, it is giving New York, for the first time, some of the continuity that the great European capitals have always taken for granted. This is probably a healthy thing. New Yorkers of the nineteenth and early twentieth centuries had a tremendous gift for accomplishment and an enviable belief in themselves and their future, and their buildings are a physical embodiment of that energy and optimism. Maybe preserving them will help keep *us* optimistic and energetic.

Luckily, there are still plenty of landmarks, of all types. Look at Broadway when the asphalt paving is wearing thin, and at the bottom of

the potholes you may see the tracks where the red streetcars ran in the World War I era. In the sidewalks in front of old brownstones, coal-hole covers still carry the imprints of pre-1900 iron foundries: "Jos. Reinagel Ironworks, 588 Amsterdam Av. N.Y.C."; "Abbott Hardware Co. and Ironworks, 636–638 Columbus Ave." There are street signs, carved into the masonry of corner buildings, that predate the naming of the West End's avenues, and say "Tenth Ave." and "Ninth Avenue" instead of "Amsterdam" or "Columbus." Keep an eye peeled, too, for the occasional building or alley that deviates from the rectangular grid: like the rectory of St. Michael's Church on West 99th, it may indicate the route of the Bloomingdale Road; or it may (like the odd-shaped tenements at Columbus and 109th) indicate the one-time presence of the el; or even (like the angled alleyway at 71–73 West 83rd and the raked wall of 2871 Broadway) mark the boundary of a colonial-era farm.

Better yet, look for spots where the land itself—if you can still speak of "the land" in Manhattan—evokes the past: the steep hill at 123rd Street and Amsterdam Avenue, where the gallant Colonel Knowlton fell in 1776; the broad knoll at 79th and Broadway, where Burnham's inn and summer house stood above the river; the once-steep rise near Columbus and 91st that was the center of Charles Ward Apthorpe's demesne, "like Rome with seven hills."

The best place to exercise the imagination is the viaduct at 96th and Riverside Drive. Below you, traffic churns on and off the Henry Hudson Parkway. But mentally peel away the covering of landfill and concrete, and you can still make out the ancient contours of Striker's Bay. There shooting parties played on the lawn in the 1840s; there James Striker set out in 1777 to join General Washington in New Jersey; and there, another hundred years before that, a Dutch farmer from Greenwich Village nearly drove himself crazy trying to build a home in the forest.

Columbus Day, 1943: a patriotic rally at Columbus Circle.

EPILOGUE

I n *The Fate of the Earth*, Upper West Side writer Jonathan Schell imagined the scene that would present itself to a fireproof, blastproof observer looking west across Central Park toward the Dakota while a one-megaton atom bomb exploded a mile or so above the Empire State Building. The light and heat from the fireball would begin to ignite everything flammable and melt almost everything else. The blast wave would arrive about five seconds after the light. "Some buildings might be crushed, as though a giant fist had squeezed them on all sides, and others might be picked up off their foundations and whirled uptown with the other debris. On the far side of Central Park, the West Side skyline would fall from south to north. The four-hundred-mile-an-hour wind would blow from south to north, die down after a few seconds, and then blow in the reverse direction with diminished intensity . . . ."

Schell's point, of course, was to drive home the easily forgotten reality of the nuclear threat; singling out the Upper West Side, the Bomb's spiritual birthplace, may have been poetic justice. Short of holocaust, though, those who know the neighborhood suspect it will survive the latest influx of newcomers and new construction, and go on into the twenty-first century as diverse and rambunctious as ever—and with the same precarious harmony among its warring elements, and still bearing traces of "noble leisure" in whatever remains of its boulevards and grand buildings. They have noticed that people who move to the Upper West Side tend to go native. They learn to sit on park benches and stoops, and join block associations. They crowd into West 77th Street the night before the Thanksgiving Day Parade to watch Kermit the Frog and Woody Woodpecker fill with helium, they play volleyball in the parks, and, as one recent arrival put it, "find things to do with people from the neighborhood. I never thought of doing that on Third Avenue."

The parks may be the key. You can see one from just about any streetcorner, and if there really is such a thing as a melting pot, it must be something like Central, Riverside, or Morningside Park: a place to sunbathe, picnic, ride a bike, or play ball with little thought (for the moment, at least) of race or class. A patrimony from Andrew Haswell Green, Calvert Vaux, Frederick Law Olmsted—and Robert Moses—the parks make landed gentry of all comers, and while they last the Upper West Side will be, in some measure, a protected enclave.

And yes, the people: the accordion player with his tin cup, the nursing-home patient taking the afternoon sun on a Broadway bench, the radiant young dancer waiting in fourth position for the light to change, the gourmets at Zabar's, the Westchester tourists in their colorful native garb, the trendy singles at the café tables, the derelict snoring on the stoop next door, young

families wheeling brand-new infants, Holocaust survivors with fading numbers on their forearms, the actors, attorneys, swimsuit manufacturers, bag ladies, junkies, hookers, students, musicians, therapists, brokers, and writers. Most neighborhoods are rich or poor, artistic or commercial, Latino or black, Jewish, Irish, Italian, or Haitian, small-town or cosmopolitan; the West Side contrives to be all of them at once. Raphael Soyer, at eighty-nine, was still painting in a studio at Columbus and 74th. "Whenever I walk along Columbus Avenue," he said shortly before his death in 1988, "I always look at the people. I rarely go to the zoo or theater; the streets of New York, the parks of New York—these are my theater."

If the characters in that theater have any single quality in common, I suspect humor is somewhere near the heart of it—that, and a kind of wry optimism. This was displayed rather well a few years back when NASA's seventy-five-ton orbiting space laboratory suddenly decided to fall back to earth. No one knew where it would come down, people the world over peered fearfully at the sky—and on West 85th Street someone hung out a banner proclaiming, WELCOME SKYLAB. The idea seems to be that, whatever you throw at it, the West Side will cope somehow, so you may as well spare yourself worrying about it ahead of time.

Perhaps no one put it better than Isaac Rice. I like to think of Rice as a quintessential Upper West Sider; lawyer, capitalist, musician, chess patron, and publisher, he built and lost and rebuilt a fortune in railroads and electric boats and in the process founded what is now the General Dynamics Corporation. His daughter Dorothy came to him one day, in a stew over some possible disaster. Rice liked to deal in parables.

"An old man on his deathbed," he told her, "gathered his family to his side.

" 'My sons,' he said, 'I have had many troubles in this world. But most of them never happened.' "

That's optimism . . . and *that's* the spirit of the Upper West Side.

ANNEXES

ANNEX A

WHO WAS WHERE

ADDRESSES (MOSTLY FORMER) OF NOTABLE WESTSIDERS

The items in this "directory" represent all eras and varying degrees of reliability. (For convenience, a few of the principal architectural and other landmarks are also listed.) Multiple listings are generally in chronological order; addresses indicate *locations*, and do not necessarily refer to the building now on the site; an asterisk indicates a site marked with a plaque. Current addresses are provided for reference/amusement only; please respect the residents' right to privacy and keep your distance.

Abdul-Jabbar, Kareem (Lew Alcindor, 7'2" basketball great), graduated from Power Memorial H.S., 161 W 61

Adams, Brooke (bright-eyed leading lady; former child actress), 43 W 61

Adams, Franklin Pierce (columnist: "The Conning Tower"), 612 W 112; 329 W 82

Adler, Felix (founder, Ethical Culture school/church), 152 W 77

Adler, Polly (*née* Pearl Vogel; celebrated Jazz Age madam), 63 W 70

Ajello, Gaetan (architect of numerous West End apartment houses), 418 CPW; 315 W 106

Akeley, Carl (naturalist, big-game hunter), 1 W 89; 35 W 67

Akiyoshi, Toshiko (Tokyo-born jazz pianist-bandleader), 38 W 94

Albee, Edward (playwright), Manhattan Towers Hotel, 2166 Bway (as luncheonette counterman)

Ansonia Hotel, 2109 Bway (WS, W 73-74)

Apthorp Apts, 2207 Bway (WS, W 78-79)

Apthorpe, Charles Ward (merchant; member, Royal Governor's Council), Elmwood, near future Columbus Ave & W 91

Aquino, Cory (President, Republic of Philippines), student at Notre Dame Convent School, 168 W 79

Arbus, Diane (photographer of the bizarre & unfortunate), San Remo Apts

Archipenko, Alexander (futurist sculptor), Lincoln Arcade

Arendt, Hannah (historian, political scientist), 317 W 95; 130 MSD; 370 RSD

Arlen, Harold (composer: "Stormy Weather," "Blues in the Night"), San Remo Apts

Armstrong, Harry (songwriter: "Sweet Adeline"), 251 W 87

Arnaz, Lucie (actress), 271 CPW

Asimov, Isaac (author), 10 W 66

Astor, Sir William Waldorf and Lady Mary (moneyed Anglo-Gothamite landowner-developer; nephew & rival to "the Mrs. Astor"), Apthorp Apts (occasionally)

Bacall, Lauren (smoky-voiced stage and screen star), W 86 & Columbus (childhood home); Dakota Apts

Baker, Carroll (actress; star of *Baby Doll*, fifties sensation), Langham Apts

Balanchine, George (choreographer, impresario), 27 W 67

Baldwin, James (impassioned, groundbreaking black/gay novelist), 470 WEA (occasionally)

Ball, Lucille (model, aspiring vaudevillian), Hotel Kimberly, Bway & W 74

Balsam, Martin (durable film character actor), the El Dorado

Bara, Theda (Theodosia Goodman; silent-film "vamp"), 500 WEA

Barnet, Will (artist), 43 W 90

Barrows, Sydney Biddle. *See* Devin, Sheila

Baruch, Dr. Simon (made first successful diagnosis of appendicitis) and son Bernard (financier, advisor of presidents), 51 W 70; 345 WEA

Bayne, Samuel Gamble (oilman; founder, Seaboard National Bank), 355 RSD

Beach, Rex (novelist), the El Dorado

Beal, Gifford (painter), 27 W 67

Beard, Charles and Mary (husband-and-wife historian team: *An Economic Interpretation of the Constitution*), 400 W 118

Beebe, Dr. William (naturalist and underwater explorer), 33 W 67

Beiderbecke, Leon Bismarck "Bix" (pioneering jazz cornetist, piano player), 119 W 71

Belafonte, Harry (singer, producer), 300 WEA

Belasco, David (playwright, director, producer), 247 W 70; 1961 Bway; Hotel Marie Antoinette; Belleclaire Hotel, Bway & W 77

Bellow, Saul (Nobel Prize–winning novelist), 333 RSD

Bellows, George (artist), Lincoln Arcade

Belnord Apts, 209 W 86

Bemelmans, Ludwig (illustrator, author: *Madeline*), Colonial Studios, 39 W 67

Bennett, Richard (dapper stage leading man), and daughters Barbara, Constance, and Joan (actresses), Ansonia Hotel

Beresford Apts, 1–7 W 81, 211 CPW (W 81-82)

Bergen, Candice (actress), and husband Louis Malle (director), 222 CPW

Berlin, Irving (songwriter: "He *is* American music!"—Jerome Kern), Chatsworth Apts, 346 W 72; 235 W 71; 30 W 70

Bernstein, Leonard (child prodigy, composer, conductor), Dakota Apts

Bickmore, Professor Albert S. (creator & first director of American Museum

of Natural History), 264 W 71; 130 W 80

Bingham, Amelia (much-married actress-manager), 103 RSD

Bitter, Karl (monumental sculptor), 44 W 77

Blaine, Nell (artist), 210 RSD

Bliss, Henry H. (real estate man; first American killed by a car, 1899), 235 W 75. *See* Smith, Arthur

Bliven, Bruce (longtime editor *New Republic*), 450 RSD

Bliven, Bruce, Jr., and Naomi (historians, writers), 451 WEA

Boas, Franz (founder of American cultural anthropology), 123 W 82

Bogart, Dr. & Mrs. Belmont De Forest (society doctor, illustrator; Humphrey's dad and mom), 245 W 103

Bolton, Guy (playwright), 253 W 91; 348 CPW; 50 W 67

Bonaparte, Joseph (former king of Spain), Claremont, Hudson River near W 123

Boothe, Clare. *See* Luce, Clare Boothe

Borglum, Gutzon (heroic sculptor of Mount Rushmore), 126 W 104

Brady, William A. (producer), and Grace George (Mrs. Brady, actress), 316 RSD

Brady, James Buchanan "Diamond Jim" (legendary gourmand and first-nighter), 7 W 86

Brickman, Marshall (screenwriter, often with Woody Allen), San Remo Apts

Brill, Abraham (pioneer U.S. psychoanalyst), 100 W 78; 98 CPW; 150 W 70

Broun, Heywood (unkempt columnist), 140 W 87 (boyhood home); and Ruth Hale (feminist writer, founder Lucy Stone League), 333 W 85; Hotel des Artistes

Brown, Helen Gurley (writer, editor: *Sex and the Single Girl, Cosmopolitan*), Beresford Apts

Browning, Edward West "Daddy" (real estate man, noted pedophile), 35 W 81; 153 W 72 (office)

Burden, Carter & Amanda ("New York's perfect young married couple"—*Vogue*, 1965), Dakota Apts

Burgess, Anthony (author: *A Clockwork Orange*), W 91 at WEA

Burke, Billie (fluttery stage and screen star), Ansonia Hotel

Burnett, Frances Hodgson (children's author: *Little Lord Fauntleroy, The Secret Garden*), 44 W 87

Burnham, William (innkeeper: Burnham's Mansion House), Bloomingdale Rd, SW corner W 79

Bushman, Francis X. (top star of silent screen), Colosseum Apts, 435 RSD

Cadmus, Paul (scathing "superrealist" painter), 150 W 103 (birthplace); 148 W 95

Cady, Josiah Cleveland (architect, American Museum of Natural History), 315 W 89

Caesar, Irving (songwriter, lyricist: "Swanee," "Tea for Two"), 269 W 72

Campbell, Frank E. (funerary impresario: The Funeral Church), 1970 Bway (home and business)

Cantor, Eddie (saucer-eyed singer-comedian), San Remo Apts

Carey, Hugh (ex-governor, New York State), Hotel des Artistes

Carnegie, Hattie (couturiere), 251 W 86 (business); 180 RSD (home)

Carroll, Diahann (singer, actress), 173 RSD

Carroll, Madeleine (British-born actress), Pomander Walk

Caruso, Enrico (immortal operatic tenor), first U.S. domicile was Majestic Hotel, 2 W 72 (*plaque on Ansonia Hotel)

Castro, Fidel (Cuban dictator, 1959–), 155 W 82 (on honeymoon in brother-in-law Rafael Diaz Balart's apartment, 1948)

Century Apts, 25 CPW (W 62-63)

Cerf, Bennett (publisher, anthologist, TV personality), 790 RSD (boyhood home)

Chagall, Marc (artist), 42 RSD

Chaliapin, Feodor (gigantic Russian basso), Ansonia Hotel*

Chanin, Irwin S. (architect-builder of Century Apts, Majestic Apts, numerous theaters), Century Apts

Chapman, John Jay (crusading man of letters), 325 W 82

Cheatham, Adolphus "Doc" (long-lived jazz trumpeter), 50 W 106

Christy, Howard Chandler (artist, illustrator; first Miss America judge, 1921), Hotel des Artistes

Clark, Cyrus (capitalist, developer; "Father of the West Side"), RSD and W 90; 327 W 76

Clarke, Thomas Shields (sculptor), 50 RSD

Clayburgh, Jill (actress), and husband David Rabe (playwright), 440 WEA

Cohan, George M. ("Give My Regards to Broadway!"), 47 W 86; 151 CPW

Cojuangco, Corazon. See Aquino, Cory

Collyer, Dr. Herman L. (father of the terminally untidy Collyer brothers), 153 W 76

Coltrane, John "Trane" (immortal jazz saxophonist), 203 W 103

Columbo, Joe (crime "family" head), fatally shot at Columbus Circle rally, 1971

Comden, Betty (librettist, lyricist, usually with Adolph Green: *Singin' in the Rain, The Band Wagon*), 145 W 67

Connelly, Marc (playwright: *The Green Pastures*), Century Apts

Copland, Aaron (composer), Century Apts

Cortissoz, Royal (influential N.Y. *Tribune* art critic), 169 W 83

Cosmos Club (intellectual: "Members must have read Humboldt's *Cosmos*"), 323 W 77

Costello, Frank (long-lived Mafia "Godfather"), Majestic Apts

Coward, Noël (debonair actor, playwright, composer, novelist), Hotel des Artistes (sublet, 1924)

Crosby, Harry (ill-fated poet, publisher), suicide at Hotel des Artistes, 1929

Crouse, Lindsay (actress), and David Mamet (playwright, director), 127 W 79

Crowley, Francis "Two-Gun" (outlaw), captured at 303 W 90 (1931)

Dakota Apts, 1 W 72

Damrosch, Frank (conductor, director Carnegie Hall), 47 W 72

Damrosch, Leopold (conductor, father of Frank and Walter D.), 181 W 75

d'Auliffe, Mme. (exiled *dame d'honneur* to Marie Antoinette), Bloomingdale Rd near W 72

Davenport, Marcia (novelist, biographer), 315 W 100

Davies, Marion (comedienne; consort of W. R. Hearst), 331 RSD

Davis, Miles (jazz trumpeter), 312 W 78

Davis, Stuart (artist), 15 W 67

Dean, James Byron (actor; posthumous teen idol), 19 W 68

De Lancey, Oliver (senior Loyalist officer in New York during Revolution), Hudson River near W 87

DeMille, Cecil B. (epic Hollywood director), 622 W 114

DeMille, William C. (playwright), and daughter Agnes (choreographer), 357 W 118

Dempsey, Jack (beloved heavyweight champ, restaurateur), Ansonia Hotel; Century Apts; San Remo Apts

Dennis, Sandy (actress), and Gerry Mulligan (jazz saxophonist), 411 WEA

de Thulstrup, Thure (elegant *Harper's Weekly* artist of 1890s), 265 W 81

Devin, Sheila (a.k.a. Sydney Biddle Barrows, the "Mayflower Madam"), 112 W 80

De Vinne, Theodore L. (printer; huge plant building now a city landmark at 12 Lafayette Pl), 300 W 76

Dewey, John (philosopher, educator), 2880 Bway; 1 W 89

Diamond, Jack "Legs" (sadistic Prohibition era gangster), Dorilton Apts, 171 W 71; Monticello Hotel, 35 W 64

Dillingham, Charles B. (Broadway impresario, frequent Ziegfeld collaborator), 322 W 88

Doelger, Peter (brewer), 339 W 100

Donahue, Phil (emotive talk-show host), and wife Marlo Thomas (actress), El Dorado Apts

Dos Passos, John (novelist), 214 RSD

Downs, Hugh (amiable TV host), Beresford Apts

Drake, Alfred (star of *Oklahoma!*), 2 W 67

Dreiser, Theodore (novelist), 6 W 102; 429 W 123; 3609 Bway; 608 RSD; 225 CPW; 605 W 111; Ansonia Hotel; Park Plaza Hotel, 50 W 77

Dresser, Paul (songwriter; Theodore Dreiser's brother), 203 W 106

Dreyfuss, Richard (Canadian-born actor), El Dorado Apts

Duchamp, Marcel (pioneer Dada painter: *Nude Descending a Staircase*), Atelier Bldg, 33 W 67

Dunaway, Faye (actress), El Dorado Apts

Duncan, Isadora (self-dramatizing rebel-*danceuse*), Hotel des Artistes

Durant, Will and Ariel (authors: *The Story of Civilization*), 5 W 69

Durland, William (proprietor, Durland's Riding Academy, Columbus Circle & 3 W 66), 246 W 76

Duvall, Robert (actor), 257 W 86

Ederle, Gertrude (swimmer, conqueror of English Channel), 108 Amsterdam

Edwards, Gus (vaudevillian, songwriter: "In My Merry Oldsmobile"), Cumberland Hotel; 22 W 59

Eidlitz, Cyrus L. W. (architect: Times Tower), 347 W 86

Eidlitz, Leopold (major Gothic Revival architect), Hudson River near W 87; 309 W 89

Eisenhower, General Dwight D. (president, Columbia University), president's residence, 60 Morningside Dr

The El Dorado, 300 CPW (W 90-91)

Elgart, Les (jazz trumpeter, bandleader), 295 CPW

Ellington, Edward Kennedy "Duke" (svelte jazz composer, bandleader), 140 WEA: also, office-studio at 333 RSD

Ellington, Mercer (Duke's son and successor), 331 RSD; 20 W 64

"Mr. Elliott." *See* Roosevelt, Elliott

Ellis, Perry (fashion designer), 57 W 69; 39 W 70

Elman, Mischa (violin prodigy), Euclid Hall Hotel, 2345 Bway

Elwell, Joseph B. (renowned early-twenties bridge whiz, ladies' man, & murder victim), 244 W 70

Ephron, Nora (humorist, novelist), Apthorp Apts

Ephron, Phoebe and Henry (screenwriters: *Daddy Long Legs, Desk Set*), 527 W 110

Epstein, Jason and Barbara (writers, publishers), 33 W 67

Erlanger, Abraham L. (theatrical mogul), 232 WEA

Erskine, John (virtuoso Columbia University literature professor), 415 W 115; 609 W 113; 39 Claremont; 130 Claremont

Estes, Eleanor (children's author: *The Moffatts*), 344 W 72

Evans, George (songwriter: "In the Good Old Summer Time"), 101 W 86

Everleigh, Minna and Ada (celebrated Chicago madams, retired to West End respectability), 20 W 71

Explorers Club; in Majestic Apts

Faber, J. Eberhard (pencil manufacturer), 335 RSD; 307 W 88

Farrar, Geraldine (famed Met soprano, later star of twenties silents), Ansonia Hotel; 18 W 74

Farrow, Mia (actress), Langham Apts

Feliciano, José (musician), 382 CPW

Ferber, Edna (novelist, playwright: *So Big, Dinner at Eight*), Belleclaire Hotel; Majestic Hotel; the Prasada, 50 CPW

Ferguson, Maynard (virtuoso jazz brassman, bandleader), 530 WEA

Ferrer, José (actor), and Rosemary Clooney (singer), Dakota Apts

Fields, Lew M. (vaudevillian, with Joe Weber), son Herbert (librettist), and daughter Dorothy (songwriter: "On the Sunny Side of the Street"), 307 W 90

Fisher, Carrie (actress), El Dorado Apts

Fisher, Harrison ("swank" turn-of-the-century illustrator), 44 W 77

Fitzgerald, F. Scott (novelist of "flaming youth"), 200 Claremont

Flack, Roberta (jazz singer), Dakota Apts

Flagg, James Montgomery (illustrator: "Uncle Sam Wants *You*"), Atelier Bldg, 33 W 67

Fontanne, Lynn, and Alfred Lunt (Broadway immortals), 130 W 70

Foster, William (inventor, glove manufacturer), 300 RSD

Fox, Michael J. (boyish TV and film actor), 194 RSD

Fox, William (film producer: 20th Century-Fox), 316 W 91

Francis, Joseph (pioneering 19th-century lifeboat designer), "Striker's Bay, foot of W 96"

Friml, Rudolf (frothy operetta composer), 869 RSD

Friedlander, Isac (Russian-American graphic artist), 905 WEA

Fuchs, Emil (portraitist of royalty), Hotel des Artistes

Furniss, William P. (lawyer; homespun poet of post-Civil War Bloomingdale), W 100 near Hudson River

Garland, Judy (actress; America's favorite torch singer), Dakota Apts

Garth, David (political public relations genius), Hotel des Artistes

Gershwin, George and Ira (immortal songwriting team), 316 W 103; 501 W 110; 108 W 111; and adjoining penthouses at 33 RSD

Gest, Morris (theatrical producer), 200 W 79

Gilbreth, Frank and Lillian (*Cheaper by the Dozen* management engineers), 310 W 94; 380 RSD

Gish, Dorothy and Lillian (silent-screen luminaries), Pomander Walk

Glasgow, Ellen (novelist), 1 W 85

Glazer, Milton (graphic artist), 27 W 67

Gluck, Alma (operatic soprano), 315 W 100

Goldberg, Reuben L. (cartoonist, *Evening Mail*: creator of improbable "Rube Goldberg" machinery), 309 W 99; 420 RSD

Goldfish, Samuel. *See* Goldwyn, Sam

Goldin, Harrison (long-time NYC comptroller), the El Dorado

Goldman, Edwin Franko (composer, band conductor; long-time Central Park concert impresario), 194 RSD

Goldman, Henry (financier), 26 W 76

Goldwyn, Sam (Hollywood producer, original partner in Metro-Goldwyn-Mayer), 601 WEA (with brother-in-law Jesse Lasky); 10 W 61

Gonsalves, Paul (tenor saxophonist, long with Duke Ellington), 50 W 106

Goodman, Andrew (1964 civil rights martyr, with Michael Schwerner and James E. Cheney), 161 W 86

Gordon, Ruth (actress, screenwriter), Three Arts Club, 340 W 85

Gordon, "Waxey" (gun-shy Prohibition era mobster), 590 WEA

Gorky, Maxim (Russian revolutionary novelist), Belleclaire Hotel, Bway & W 77, briefly

Gorme, Edie, and Steve Lawrence (singers), Beresford Apts

Gould, Elliott (curly-haired film leading man), Park Royal Hotel, 23 W 73

Grant, Lee (actress), 300 WEA

Green, Adolph (librettist, lyricist, often in collaboration with Betty Comden), and Phyllis Newman (singer-actress), Beresford Apts

Green, Henrietta Robinson "Hetty" (miserly "Witch of Wall Street"), died 1916 at son's home 7 W 90

Grey, Zane (dentist, western novelist), 100 W 74

Griffin, Merv (durable TV talk-show host), Langham Apts

Griffith, David Wark (pioneer movie director), unknown address on W 100

Guggenheim, Meyer (patriarch of mining, financial dynasty), 36 W 77 (1888–1905); other neighborhood Guggenheims included Meyer's son and successor Murry, 29 W 76, daughter Rose (Mrs. Albert Loeb), 123 W 75, black-sheep son William, 1 RSD, and grandson Alfred F., Belnord Apts

Hamlisch, Marvin (Broadway and film songwriter), 171 W 81

Hammer, Armand (billionaire industrialist), 168 W 77 (as medical student); Ansonia Hotel

Hammerstein, Oscar (impresario; grandfather of Oscar II), 947 WEA

Hammerstein, Oscar II (lyricist), 106 CPW; 320 CPW; Endicott Hotel; 60 W 76; 509 W 121

Harbach, Otto (librettist: *No, No, Nanette!!*), Kenilworth, 151 CPW

Hardenbergh, Henry J. (architect: Dakota, Art Students League, Plaza Hotel), 121 W 73

Hardwick, Elizabeth (novelist & critic), and Robert Lowell (poet), 15 W 67

Harnick, Sheldon (lyricist: *Fiorello!, Fiddler on the Roof*), Beresford Apts

Harris, Charles K. (songwriter-publisher: "After the Ball"), 196 RSD

Harrison, Rex, and Lilli Palmer (stage, screen greats), Beresford Apts

Harsen, Jacob (patriarch of early nineteenth-century Harsenville), near W 71 St W of Bloomingdale Rd

Hart, Moss (playwright), Ansonia Hotel

Hassam, Childe (leading American Impressionist), 25 W 67

Haswell, Charles H. (nonagenarian civil engineer & memoirist), 324 W 78

Hauptmann, Bruno Richard (convicted Lindbergh baby kidnapper-killer), was carpenter at Majestic Apts at time of ransom payment

Hayton, Lennie (jazz composer-pianist), 300 WEA

Hayworth, Rita (b. Margarita Carmen Cansino; forties screen goddess), San Remo Apts

Healy, Tom (restaurateur: Healy's Golden Glades; real estate man: Pomander Walk), 119 W 69

Hearst, Patricia (much-sought heiress-hostage and/or revolutionary), hid out briefly in 1974 at 317 W 90

Hearst, William Randolph (newspaper magnate), Clarendon Apts, 137 RSD

Hecht, Ben (novelist, playwright: *The Front Page*), 39 W 67

Hefti, Neal (composer, bandleader), 161 W 75

Held, Miss Anna (wasp-waisted French songstress), Ansonia Hotel

Heliker, John (landscape and portrait artist), 865 WEA

Heller, Joseph (novelist: *Catch-22, Good as Gold*), 390 WEA

Hellman, Mrs. Richard (mayonnaise maker *extraordinaire*), 490 Columbus

Henri, Robert, School of Art, Lincoln Arcade

Herbert, Victor (composer), 321 W 108

Herriman, George (cartoonist: "Krazy Kat"), 330 W 95

Hershey, Barbara (actress), 55 W 90

Hite, Shere (model, freehand sociologist of sex), 1 W 85

Hobson, Laura Z. (novelist: *Gentleman's Agreement*), while pregnant and unmarried, laid low at 128 W 78

Hoffman, Dustin (diffident, versatile screen actor), San Remo Apts

Holder, Geoffrey (dancer, actor), and Carmen de Lavallade (danceuse), 215 W 92

Holiday, Billie (b. Eleanora Fagan; tragic jazz vocalist), 26 W 87

Holliday, Judy (short-lived comedienne: *Born Yesterday, Bells Are Ringing*), Dakota Apts

Holm, Celeste (actress—the original Ado Annie—and pro-parks activist), 88 CPW

Homer, Louise (operatic soprano) and Sidney (composer), 40 W 92; 266 W 89

Hooglandt, Adrian (eighteenth-century farmer and schoolteacher), terminus of Bloomingdale Rd, Hudson River near 116

Horne, Lena (classy jazz singer), 300 WEA (when married to Lennie Hayton); 140 WEA

Horton, Chauncey E. (ice cream manufacturer), in business at 302 Columbus—which still bears company name on cornice

Hotel des Artistes, 1 W 67

Houdini, Harry (magician, escape artist), 278 W 113

Howe, Charles Francis (of Howe & Hummel law firm, "the men who robbed the robber barons"), 3135 Bway

Hudson, Rock (movie heartthrob and early AIDS victim), Beresford Apts

Huerta, General Victoriano (exiled Mexican ruler), Ansonia Hotel

Hughes, Barnard, and Frances Sternhagen (actors), Pomander Court

Hughes, Charles Evans (N.Y. Governor; U.S. Chief Justice), 320 W 88; 329 WEA*

Hurok, Sol (theater & dance impresario), Ansonia Hotel

Hurst, Fannie (author: Back Street), Three Arts Club, 340 W 85; 27 W 67; Hotel des Artistes

Hurt, John (serious-faced film actor), 348 WEA

Huxtable, Ada Louise (architecture critic), St. Urban Apts, 285 CPW (childhood home)

van Huyse, Theunis Idens (Dutch-born farmer), farmhouse was above Hudson River near foot of W 97

Inge, William (playwright: Come Back Little Sheba, Picnic), Dakota Apts

Ives, Charles (home-grown atonal composer), 65 CPW

Jackson, Anne, and Eli Wallach (stage and screen actors), 90 RSD

Jacobs, Mike (ticket broker, fight promoter), 200 W 95

Jagger, Mick (rock idol), 304 W 81

Jennings, Peter (newscaster), Beresford Apts

Jobs, Steve (cofounder, Apple Computers), San Remo Apts

Jones, James Earl (larger-than-life dramatic actor), 263 WEA

Jones, Thad (trumpet soloist long with Basie orchestra) 161 W 105

Jong, Erica (novelist: Fear of Flying), 20 W 77

Karloff, Boris (b. William Pratt; British-born character actor: Frankenstein), Dakota Apts

Kaufman, George S. (playwright, director: Dinner at Eight, The Man Who Came to Dinner), 241 W 101 (boyhood home); Majestic Hotel (honeymoon)

Kazin, Alfred (critic, novelist), 440 WEA; 110 RSD

Keaton, Diane (actress: Annie Hall), San Remo Apts

Keefe, Edward (artist), Lincoln Arcade

Kern, Jerome (composer), 107 W 68; 206 W 92; 226 W 70

Kerouac, Jack (Beat novelist; with future wife Edie Parker and, at times, William S. Burroughs and Allen Ginsberg), 421 W 118

King, Billie Jean (tennis champ; Bobby Riggs's 1973 nemesis), 101 W 79

King, Moses (publisher: King's

Handbook of NY, King's Notable New Yorkers, King's New York Views), 2 W 88

Kingsley, Sidney (actor-playwright: *Dead End*), Dakota Apts

Klein, Calvin (fashion designer), 55 CPW; Beresford Apts

Kline, Kevin (actor), 117 W 87

Knopf, Alfred A. (publisher), 15 W 95 (boyhood home)

Knowlton, Lieutenant Colonel Thomas (military hero of Bunker Hill and Harlem Heights), fell in battle near Amsterdam & W 123, 1776

Kober, Arthur (author), 241 CPW

Koch, John (American Realist painter), El Dorado Apts

Kopman, Benjamin, and Yuli Blumberg (Russian-American Expressionist artists), 77 W 104

Kroll, Leon (painter), Hotel des Artistes

Kronenberger, Louis (literary critic), 16 W 77

Kunz, George F. (mineralogist & Columbia professor; Tiffany's first gem expert), Hendrick Hudson Apts, 380 RSD

Landowska, Dame Wanda (harpsichordist), Prasada Apts, 50 CPW

Lane, Burton (composer: *Finian's Rainbow*), Majestic Apts

Lang, George (restaurateur: Café des Artistes), Atelier Building, 33 W 67

Langham Apts, 135 CPW (W 73-74)

Lansky, Meyer (long-lived underworld banker), Majestic Apts

Laredo, Jaime (Bolivian-born classical pianist), 685 WEA

Lasky, Jesse L. (theatrical and burlesque promoter), 601 WEA; 150 W 79

Lawlor, Charles B. (songwriter: "Sidewalks of New York"), 157 W 66

Leach, Robin (host of TV's "Rich & Famous" shows), Dorilton, 171 W 71

Lebron, Lolita (Puerto Rican nationalist; shot up U.S. House of Representatives, 1954), 315 W 94

Lennon, John (ex-Beatle, rock idol, peace activist), and Yoko Ono (conceptual artist), Dakota Apts

Lerner, Alan Jay (lyricist: *My Fair Lady, Gigi*) Beresford Apts

Lester, Minna & Ada. *See* Everleigh sisters

Levin, Meyer (author: *Compulsion*), 62 W 91

Lewis, Sinclair (author; Nobel Prize winner, 1930), 2469 Bway; the El Dorado

Lewis, Ted (jazz clarinetist-bandleader), Majestic Apts

Lichtenstein, Rabbi Morris (founder, Society for Jewish Science, head-quartered at 100 W 72), 166 W 73

Liebling, A. J. (journalist, author, fight and food lover), 307 W 79 (boyhood home)

Lincoln Arcade building, 1947 Bway (WS, W 63-64)

Lindsay, John (New York City mayor), Hotel des Artistes

Lindy, Leo (restaurateur and cheesecake impresario), Century Apts

Livermore, Jesse L. (stock market plunger and suicide), 194 RSD; 8 W 76

Livingston, Henry Brockholst (Revolutionary War soldier and U.S. Supreme Court Justice), Oak Villa, W 91 near Hudson River

Loesser, Frank (composer, lyricist), 14 W 107 (boyhood home)

Loew, Marcus (movie producer), 210 RSD

Loudon, Dorothy (Broadway leading lady & comedienne), 101 CPW

Louis-Philippe, duc d'Orléans (future "Citizen King" of France), said to have lived and taught at approx Bway and W 75 while in exile, 1796–98

Lowell, Robert. *See* Hardwick, Elizabeth

Luce, Clare Boothe (*Time*wife, playwright: *The Women*), born in "family hotel" on Riverside Drive; early childhood in "dingy flat on Columbus Avenue"

Luce, Henry (founder-publisher *Time, Life, Fortune*), 514 W 122

Luciano, Charles "Lucky" (mafia boss; reputed vice king), Majestic Apts

Luciano, Felipe (singer, songwriter), 382 CPW

Luckinbill, Laurence (actor), 271 CPW

Lukeman, H. Augustus (sculptor: *Memory* (Straus memorial at 106 & many civic works), 160 W 86

Lunt, Alfred. *See* Fontanne, Lynn

Lyons, Leonard (Broadway columnist), Beresford Apts

McDowall, Roddy (British-born actor and photographer), the El Dorado

MacDowell, Edward A. (American Romantic composer), 381 CPW

McEnroe, John (temperamental tennis star), and wife Tatum O'Neal (actress), Beresford Apts

Macfadden, Bernarr (naturist, health nut, publisher *New York Graphic*), 17 W 64; Macfadden Publications Building, 1926 Bway

McGraw, John (NY Giants manager, 1902–32), 76 W 85

McIntyre, Oscar Odd (columnist: "New York Day by Day"), Majestic Hotel

MacLaglen, Victor (rugged movie leading man), Pomander Walk

McMein, Neysa (*née* Marjorie; illustrator beloved of Algonquin crowd), Lincoln Arcade; Hotel des Artistes; 2 W 67

Madison, Oscar, and Felix Unger (Neil Simon's "Odd Couple"), the San Remo (in occasional TV episodes); Dorchester Apts, 131 RSD (in stage and screen versions)

Madonna (Marianne Louise Ciccone, flamboyant rock star), and Sean Penn (actor), 65 CPW (having been rejected first by San Remo)

Maeterlinck, Maurice (Belgian dramatist-poet; Nobel Prize, 1911), Hotel des Artistes

Mahler, Gustav (neurasthenic Romantic composer), Majestic Hotel

Mailer, Norman (pugnacious novelist), 250 W 94

Majestic Apts, 115 CPW (W 71–72; former site of Majestic Hotel)

Mallon, Mary ("Typhoid Mary"), apprehended while cooking for Charles Warren family, 326 W 89

Malone, Dudley Field (legal champion of radical and underworld characters), 270 RSD

Mamet, David. *See* Crouse, Lindsay

Manilow, Barry (songwriter, singer), San Remo Apts

Mann, Herbie (Herbert Jay Solomon; jazz flutist, bandleader), 105 W 73

Mann, Colonel William D'Alton (blackmailing publisher of *Town Topics*), 309 W 72

Manners, J. Hartley (playwright), and Laurette Taylor (actress), 50 RSD

Mannes, David (violinist) and Clara (pianist, daughter of Leopold Damrosch), 325 Amsterdam (Mannes College of Music, which they founded, is now at 150 W 85)

Mannes, Marya (writer, social critic; daughter of David & Clara Mannes), Dakota Apts

Mansfield, Richard (Shakespearean actor-manager), 316 RSD

Masseria, Giuseppe "Joe the Boss" (Mafia executive), 15 W 81

Masterson, William Barclay "Bat" (sportswriter, *Morning Telegram*; former sheriff), 257 W 43

Mathewson, Christy (legendary NY Giants pitcher), 76 W 85

Matthews, Brander (professor, author), 681 WEA

Matthews, John (19th-century soda-water "king"), RSD NE corner W 90

May, Elaine (brilliant comedic actress-director), San Remo Apts

Mead, Margaret (anthropologist, social guru), Beresford Apts

Meara, Anne, and Jerry Stiller (actors, sometimes as topical Irish-Jewish comedy team), 118 RSD

Mehta, Ved (Indian-born writer-journalist), 544 W 113 (first U.S. home, 1949)

Meier, Caspar (19th-century shipping magnate), Willow Bank, Hudson River near W 118

Melchior, Lauritz (operatic tenor), Ansonia Hotel

Menuhin, Yehudi (violin prodigy), Ansonia Hotel

Merman, Ethel (clarion-voiced Broadway songstress), Century Apts

Midler, Bette (singer, "The Divine Miss M"), 102 W 75; won fame at

Continental Baths, in Ansonia Hotel basement

Mielziner, Jo (stage designer), Dakota Apts

Miner, Henry Clay (turn-of-the-century burlesque proprietor), 323 W 90

Mintiks, Helen H. (1980 "murder at the Met" victim), 102 W 75

Mole, Irving Milfred "Miff" (jazz trombonist), 250 W 88

Monk, Thelonious (jazz pianist, composer), Phipps Houses, 243 W 63

Moore, Mary Tyler (perky actress-producer), San Remo Apts

Morehouse, Ward (theater critic), Pomander Walk

Morgenthau, Robert (NYC District Attorney), San Remo Apts

Morningstar, Marjorie (Morgenstern— teenage heroine of popular Herman Wouk novel), the El Dorado

Morris, William (leading theatrical agent of 1930s to 1950s), Century Apts

Mosel, Tad (novelist), El Dorado Apts

Moses, Robert ("master builder" of New York City; parks commissioner; director of Triborough Commission, about 20 other posts), 1 W 70; 261 W 70

Mostel, Zero (heavyweight, uninhibited actor, singer, artist), Belnord Apts

Mott, Hopper Striker (real estate man of old Bloomingdale family; turn-of-the-century Upper West Side historian), 288 WEA

Mott, Valentine (famed early nineteenth-century surgeon), Bloomingdale Rd at W 93

Mueller, Edward (dollar-bill counterfeiter), 204 W 96

Mumford, Lewis (writer, social and architectural critic), b. W 97 and Amst; 230 W 65 (boyhood home); 200 W 105; 59 W 93; 66 W 84; 66 W 93; 100 W 94; 153 W 82

Murray, Mae (silent-screen star of the "bee-stung" lips), Hotel des Artistes (as star, in opulent duplex; subsequently in garret)

Neel, Alice (twentieth-century portraitist), 300 W 107

Nemerov, David (president, Russek's department store) and children Howard (poet), and Diane (see Arbus, Diane), San Remo Apts

Newman, Arnold (portrait photographer), 39 W 67

Nichols, Mike (innovative actor-director), Beresford Apts

Nin, Anaïs (diarist-novelist: *Delta of Venus*), 158 W 75 (childhood home)

Nugent, Frank L. (silent partner, B. Altman & Co.), 343 W 88

Nureyev, Rudolph (fiery, athletic ballet dancer; defector from Kirov, 1961), Dakota Apts

Nygaard, Jens (founder & conductor, Jupiter Symphony), 155 W 68

O'Brien, Pat (gentle, tough-looking actor), roomed at 153 W 96

Ochs, Adolph S. (publisher: *The New York Times*), 308 W 75

O'Hanlon, Dr. Philip F. (City Coroner's physician; editorial in New York *Sun*, 21 December 1897, "Yes, Virginia, there is a Santa Claus," addressed to his daughter), 115 W 95

Olmsted, Frederick Law (landscape architect, codesigner of West Side parks), lived in former Mount St. Vincent convent, Central Park during Park's original construction

O'Neill, Eugene (playwright; Nobel Prize, 1936), Lincoln Arcade (as George Bellows's roommate)

Oppenheimer, J. Robert (physicist; "Father of the Atomic Bomb"), 155 RSD (boyhood home)

Orkin, Ruth (photographer), 65 CPW

O'Sullivan, Maureen (gentle Irish-born actress; mother of Mia Farrow), Langham Apts

Paine, William H. (original impresario of Italian opera in New York City, 1850), Striker's Bay, foot of W 96

Palance, Jack (menacing screen actor), Dakota Apts

Papanastassiou, John M. (ambitious rare-book thief), 549 RSD

Papp, Joe (producer; founder Shakespeare-in-the-Park, Public Theater), 420 CPW

Parker, Dorothy (poet, writer, Algonquin wit), 57 W 68 (childhood home); early in career, roomed at Bway at W 103

Parkhurst, Reverend Charles H. (reforming pastor of Madison Square Presbyterian Church, president Society for Prevention of Crime), Ansonia Hotel

Patinkin, Mandy (actor-singer; Broadway's original Sweeney Todd), 200 W 90

Pauley, Jane (NBC-TV newscaster) and husband Garry Trudeau (Doonesbury cartoonist), 271 CPW

Peale, Charles Willson (18th-century portraitist), "Art's Delight," former schoolhouse near Bloomingdale Rd

Pearlstein, Philip (evocative figure painter, teacher), 163 W 88

Penn, Arthur (director: *Bonnie and Clyde*), 2 W 67

Perlman, Itzhak (virtuoso violinist), 173 RSD

Pickford, Mary (b. Gladys Mary Smith; "America's Sweetheart"), 270 RSD

Pinza, Ezio (operatic baritone), Ansonia Hotel

Pitts, Zasu (spunky, often tearful actress), Ansonia Hotel

Poe, Edgar Allan (eerie poet: "The Raven"), summer visitor at Brennan cottage, near Amsterdam & W 84 (*plaques on 215 and 255 W 84—on E and W sides of Bway—both claim the honor)

Pollock, George (Federalist era linen merchant), Claremont, Hudson River at W 124; Pollock's 4-yr-old son St. Clair ("An Amiable Child") d. 1797 and is buried today in Riverside Park; nearby St. Clair Place is named for him

Pomander Walk, 261-67 W 94/260-66 W 95

Pons, Lily (French operatic soprano); Ansonia Hotel; Prasada Apts, 50 CPW

Post, George B. (architect, City College, N.Y. Stock Exchange), Claremont, RSD & W 124 (childhood home)

Potter, Bishop Henry Codman ("The Workingman's Bishop"; founder, Cathedral Church of St. John the Divine), corner RSD & W 89

Quinn, Roseann (victim of "Mr. Goodbar" murder, 1973), 253 W 72

Rachmaninoff, Sergei (Russian pianist-composer), 33 RSD

Randall, Tony (fastidious comic actor, opera lover & Upper West Side patriot), San Remo Apts; Beresford Apts

Rathbone, Basil (hawk-nosed movie leading man), Kenilworth Apts, 151 CPW

Reed, Rex (once-outrageous star-watcher and film critic), Dakota Apts

Reeve, Christopher (youthful film star: *Superman*), 100 W 81

Resicka, Paul (artist), Broadway Studio Building, 246 W 80

Reuben, Arnold and Edith, 300 W 70; Reuben's Pure Food Shop (home of the Reuben sandwich), 2270 Bway (W 81–82)

Rice, Elmer (misanthropic Pulitzer-winning playwright & novelist), Ansonia Hotel

Rice, Grantland (sports columnist), 616 W 116 (with Rube Goldberg, 1910); 450 RSD

Rice, Professor Isaac L. (lawyer, chess enthusiast, industrialist; founder of General Dynamics Corp.) and Dr. Julia Barnett (anti-noise reformer), Villa Julia, W 89 at RSD; Ansonia Hotel

Ripley, Robert (journalist: "Ripley's Believe It Or Not"), 65 CPW

Ritchard, Cyril (actor, director), Langham Apts

Roach, Max (jazz drummer), 69 W 105

Robinson, Boardman (socialist illustrator-muralist), 140 W 105

Rockwell, Norman (beloved *Saturday Evening Post* illustrator), 854 Amst (birthplace, 1894); Hotel des Artistes

Rodgers, Richard (composer), 161 W 86 (childhood home)

Roebling, Edmund (ne'er-do-well son of Brooklyn Bridge's designer), 156 W 84

Romberg, Sigmund (Hungarian-born composer: *Student Prince, Desert Song*), 115 W 71

Roosevelt, Elliott (Theodore's drug-addicted older brother), died at 313 W 102 in 1894

Rosenblum, Ralph (film editor—including "local" films *The Pawnbroker, Annie Hall*), 344 W 84

Roth, Emery (architect: San Remo, Beresford, Normandy), 210 W 101; Alden Apts (which he also designed; latter was his final home)

Rothapfel, Samuel L. "Roxy" (movie-palace impresario), 420 RSD

Rothstein, Arnold (gambler, underworld financier), 355 W 84 (boyhood home); 20 W 72

Runyon, Damon (newsman, writer; *Guys and Dolls*) 251 W 95; 440 RSD; 320 W 102; 330 W 113

Russell, Lillian (reigning stage beauty of 1890s), 318 W 77; 1732 Bway

Russell, Rosalind (wisecracking, leggy actress), Pomander Walk

Russell, Walter B. (sculptor; developer of W 67 St studio bldgs), Central Park Studios, 15 W 67

Ruth, George Herman "Babe" (baseball immortal), Ansonia Hotel; 110 RSD

Saks, Isidore (department store tycoon), Langham Apts

Salinger, J. D. (reclusive author: *Catcher in the Rye*), 3681 Bway; 390 RSD; 221 W 82

Salk, Jonas (physician, creator of first polio vaccine, 1954); born at 7 W 92

San Remo Apts, 145–146 CPW (W 74–75)

Sayao, Bidu (operatic soprano), Ansonia Hotel

Schell, Jonathan (author: *The Fate of the Earth*), 410 RSD

Schuller, Gunther (musicologist-conductor; led Scott Joplin revival of 1970s), 610 WEA

Schwab, Charles (youthful "Steel King"; founder U.S. Steel), Riverside, RSD to WEA, W 73-74

Scribner, Mr. & Mrs. Charles A. (publisher), Peter Stuyvesant Apts, 258 RSD

Selznick, David O. (producer: *Gone With the Wind*), 449 RSD (boyhood home)

Sharkey's Athletic Club (setting for George Bellows's *Stag at Sharkey's*, 1907), 120 Columbus

Shattuck, Frank (head of Schraffts's restaurant chain), 137 RSD

Shean, Al (b. Albert Schoenberg; vaudevillian: Gallagher & Shean), Ansonia Hotel

Sheedy, Allie (actress), 145 W 86 (childhood home)

Sherman, General William T. (U.S. Army, ret.), 75 W 71 (final home)

Shikler, Aaron (artist; official portraitist of JFK), 44 W 77

Shubert, Jacob J. (founder, with brothers Lee and Sam, of U.S. theatrical empire), 375 WEA

Shubert, Lee (see above), Century Apts

Silkworth, Dr. William D. (patient in his clinic at 293 CPW founded Alcoholics Anonymous), 304 W 75

Sills, Beverly (beloved operatic star-director), Beresford Apts

Silvers, Phil (actor-comedian; TV's Sergeant Bilko), Beresford Apts

Simon, Carly (singer-songwriter), Langham Apts

Simon, Paul (singer-songwriter), San Remo Apts

Simone, Nina (b. Eunice Waymon; jazz vocalist), 336 RSD

Singer, Isaac Bashevis (sometimes mystical Yiddish author; Nobel Prize, 1978), Belnord Apts, 209 W 86

Smith, Arthur (cab driver: caused first U.S. auto fatality; *see* H. H. Bliss), 151 W 62

Smith, Harry B. (songwriter, librettist), 319 W 107

Snyder, C. B. J. (influential New York City school architect), 230 W 97

Soule, George H. (author, economist), 2469 Bway

Sousa, John Philip, Jr. (bandleader), 2610 Bway

Soyer, Raphael (painter, portraitist), Lincoln Arcade (studio, 1950s); 88 CPW & 54 W 74 (studio)

Spingarn, Professor Joel E. (author, publisher; founder Harcourt Brace Jovanovich and NAACP), 9 W 73

Stanton, Elizabeth Cady (pioneering suffragist, women's rights leader), 26 W 61; Stewart Apts, 250 W 94 *(plaque removed)

Stapleton, Maureen (actress), 15 W 70

Stefansson, Vilhjalmur (arctic explorer—the "Blonde Eskimo"), 1 W 89

Stein, Gertrude (author, long-time roommate of Alice B. Toklas), Furniss house, RSD & W 100

Stern, Isaac (violinist, impresario; credited with saving Carnegie Hall from demolition), Beresford Apts

Stoddard, Henry L. (editor, New York Mail), Ansonia Hotel

Stokes, W. E. D. (West Side developer; builder of Ansonia Hotel), 228 W 75; Ansonia Hotel

Stone, Harlan Fiske (Columbia Law School dean; U.S. Chief Justice), Colosseum Apts, 435 RSD*

Stout, Rex (novelist, creator of Nero Wolfe), 8 Morningside; 364 W 116

Strasberg, Lee (founder of The Actors' Studio), Langham Apts

Straus, Isidor (Macy's owner) and Ida; Boulevard, corner W 105

Straus, Nathan (department store owner and civic leader), 1 W 81

Straus, Oscar (Cabinet officer, diplomat), 5 W 76

Stravinsky, Igor (Russian-born composer), Ansonia Hotel*

Streep, Meryl (solemn-faced film leading lady), Beresford Apts

Strayhorn, Billy (composer-arranger long with Duke Ellington), 15 W 106

Street, Julian (writer, playwright), 151 W 86

Streisand, Barbra (earthy, golden-voiced singer-actress), and husband Elliott Gould (actor), Ardsley Apts, 320 CPW

Striker, James (Revolutionary soldier, Harsenville village elder), Striker's Bay, foot of W 96

Styron, William (novelist: Lie Down in Darkness), 314 W 88

Sullivan, Frank (beloved humorist; "Sage of Saratoga"), 8 W 105

Sutherland, Donald (Canadian-born actor), San Remo Apts

Sutton, William Francis, Jr. "Willie the Actor" (bank robber and convict), W 72 near WEA

Swanson, Gloria (durable film star), Pomander Walk

Talleyrand-Périgord, Prince Charles-Maurice de (French statesman), guest at "Major Thompson's," Bloomingdale Rd near W 75

Taylor, Elizabeth (glamorous British-born star), Bereford Apts (in apartment borrowed from Rock Hudson)

Taylor, Laurette. See Manners, J. Hartley

Teasdale, Sara (poet), old Beresford Hotel; old San Remo Hotel

Tharp, Twyla (innovative dancer-choreographer), 336 CPW

Thomas, Evylyn (first American injured by an auto, 1896), 459 W 90

Thompson, Dorothy (outspoken journalist, political columnist), 88 CPW; Alden Hotel, 225 CPW

Thompson, J. Walter (pioneering adman), 14 W 76

Three Arts Club (the forbidding Lillian Archer's rooming house for girl students in art, music, and the drama), 340 W 85

Tiemann, Daniel (paint manufacturer, reform mayor of New York City, 1850), RSD corner of W 127

von Tilzer, Albert (composer: "Take Me Out to the Ball Game"), 98 Morningside; Majestic Hotel; Belnord Apts

von Tilzer, Harry (songwriter), 203 W 54; Belnord Apts

Toscanini, Arturo (preeminent 20th-century conductor), Ansonia Hotel*

Townsend, Ralph (architect of numerous UWS apartment buildings), 194 RSD

Tracy, Spencer (tough, humorous actor), roomed at 153 W 96

Trilling, Lionel (literary critic, Columbia professor), 35 Claremont

True, Clarence (leading Upper West Side town house architect), 330 W 83; office 102 W 82

Trumbull, Walter (sports editor, NY *Herald*), 450 RSD

Untermeyer, Louis (poet, anthologist), 310 W 100

Valentino, Rudolph (original film Sheik of silent era), Hotel des Artistes (and funeral was at nearby Campbell Funeral Church)

van den Heuvel, Baron John Cornelius and Charlotte (Apthorpe), Bloomingdale Rd near W 79

Van Dine, S. S. (author: Philo Vance detective novels) 241 CPW; his ashes also were scattered over the city

Van Paassen, Pierre (crusading Dutch-born journalist), 90 RSD

Van Vechten, Carl (white chronicler of Harlem Renaissance), 101 CPW; San Remo Apts

Verdon, Gwen (dynamic, dancing Broadway leading lady), Dakota Apts

Viele, Brigadier General Egbert L. (sanitary engineer, founder of modern Upper West Side), RSD southeast corner of W 88

Vishniac, Roman (Russian-born biologist, photographer, linguist, antiquarian, philosopher), 219 W 81

Vogel, Polly (Polly's Apparel Shop, 2719 Bway). *See also* Adler, Polly

Waite, "Dr." Arthur W. (evil-minded but inept poisoner), Colosseum Apts, 435 RSD

Waller, Thomas "Fats" (jazz pianist & composer), parents moved from San Juan Hill area just before his birth, 1904

Walsh, Raoul (director: *White Heat, High Sierra,* many others), RSD & W 100 (boyhood home)

Weaver, Sigourney (actress), Oliver Cromwell Apts, 12 W 72

Weber, Joe (vaudeville star: Weber & Fields), Hendrick Hudson, 380 RSD

Weil, Simone (short-lived, saintly activist-philosopher), 549 RSD

Weld, Tuesday (*née* Susan Ker Weld; lustrous-eyed film actress), the El Dorado

West, Mae (long-lived, splendidly vulgar sex symbol; "Goodness had nothing to do with it, dearie!"), 266 WEA

West End Café (major area jazz club;

erstwhile Beatnik hangout), 2911 Bway, W 114–115

Westinghouse, Herman H. (chairman, Westinghouse Air Brake Co., Westinghouse Lamp Co., Westinghouse Electric & Manufacturing), Belnord Apts

Weston, Jack (heavyset character actor), 101 CPW

Wexler, Irving. *See* Gordon, "Waxey"

Wharton, Edith (novelist), 131 W 85 (last N.Y. home)

Williams, Tennessee (playwright), Mayfair Towers, 15 W 72

Wilshire, H. Gaylord (socialist publisher-promoter; later major Los Angeles real estate developer), Belleclaire Hotel; 301 W 106

Wilson, Teddy (legendary jazz pianist), 415 CPW

Wilson, William ("Bill W."; founder of Alcoholics Anonymous), was patient at Silkworth Clinic, 293 CPW

Winchell, Walter (language-fracturing Broadway gossip "colyumist"), Majestic Apts

Winters, Shelley (b. Shirley Schrift; outspoken, sometimes raunchy Brooklyn-born actress), Mayfair Towers, 15 W 72

Wise, Rabbi Stephen (Zionist; founder Free Synagogue), the El Dorado

Wodehouse, Sir Pelham Grenville (novelist, lyricist), 375 CPW

Wood, Fernando (pre–Civil War Tammany mayor), Boulevard at W 76-77

Woodhull, Victoria (nineteenth-century feminist, free-love advocate), 302 W 79

Woollcott, Alexander (Algonquin wit, critic, raconteur), Hotel des Artistes

Woolrich, Cornell (novelist: *Double Indemnity*), Ansonia Hotel

Wouk, Herman (novelist: *Marjorie Morningstar*), 845 WEA; Regent Hotel, Bway and W 104; Normandy Apts, 875 WEA

Wray, Fay (early film star, beloved of King Kong) Century Apts

Wright, Willard Huntington. *See* Van Dine, S. S.

Youmans, Vincent (ill-starred Broadway composer), 13 CPW* (birthplace, 1898)

Yourkevitch, Vladimir Ivanovitch (naval architect: *Normandie*), 317 W 99

Zeckendorf, William, Sr. (real estate developer), Dorilton Apts, 171 W 71

Ziegfeld, Florenz (*Follies* impresario) and Mrs. (*See* Anna Held, Billie Burke), Ansonia Hotel

Zimbalist, Ephraim, Sr. (violinist-composer), 315 W 100

Zukor, Adolph (long-lived—102 years—Hollywood producer; founder of Paramount Pictures), 611 W 114

ANNEX B

WEST SIDE WALKING TOURS

RIVERSIDE DRIVE:
"THE MOST BEAUTIFUL AVENUE IN THE WORLD"

First proposed in 1865 by William R. Martin, the Drive was to have been the city's most elegant equestrian boulevard—and a spur to West Side development. Fifteen years passed—a considerable delay by the standards of those energetic years—before the first 72nd-to-125th-Street section was opened, and at that the citizens had to do it themselves, by force (see chap. 4).

Today you can use the Drive without breaking in. There are no scheduled carriage rides, unfortunately, but the M-5 bus covers the route. If you walk the distance, allow about three hours plus.

1. In the 1890s, West 72nd Street was still a fine residential avenue, and the main route from Central Park to the "Riverside-avenue," as it was first called. Our tour makes a handsome start here with two limestone-fronted turn-of-the-century chateaux (311 West 72nd and no. 1 Riverside Drive), positioned where West 72nd Street curves uptown to form

the Drive's beginning; both are by Charles P. H. Gilbert, a prolific town house architect whose own home, long since demolished, was nearby at no. 33 Riverside Drive. (At the highway entrance, you also can still find the plinth of a now-vanished monument to Henry Hudson.)

2. Riverside Park (original design by Frederick Law Olmsted and others, 1873–1910; reconstructed 1937). A flawed gem of urban park design. A gem because Olmsted allowed the Drive to wind along the West Side's rocky spine in harmonious counterpoint to the steep, narrow park below, then filled the park with glades, groves, promenades, playing fields, and bridle paths. (An earlier plan would have cut a ruler-straight Twelfth Avenue through the park's midline.) Flawed by erosion, neglect, and "autos-first" planning: squeezed between the Drive and the six-lane Henry Hudson Parkway, most of this "riverside" park stops far short of the water.

3. The Chatsworth, 346 West 72nd, corner of Henry Hudson Parkway. An early, expansive version of the pre–World War I apartment tower, its brick facade voluptuous with limestone cherubs and caryatids. Original apartments ran to fifteen rooms; a sun parlor occupied the whole top floor, and the management provided a café, billiard room, hairdresser, barber, valet, tailor, and private electric bus service to Central Park West and the Columbus Avenue el. (1904; John E. Scharsmith, architect.)

4. Schwab House, West 73rd to 74th streets. A full-block apartment complex, typical of its era (1948). Only the name recalls the six-million-dollar mansion erected here in 1902–6 by Andrew Carnegie's protégé, "Steel King" Charles M. Schwab. With formal gardens, Schwab's home took up the whole block; it was patterned after *three* French Renaissance chateaux and was probably the largest and most lavish private home ever seen in Manhattan. During the Depression it was offered to the city as the mayor's official residence, but Fiorello LaGuardia turned it down flat. Schwab died broke in 1939 and Victory gardens flourished on the grounds during World War II; the bulldozers moved in soon afterward.

5. No. 33 Riverside Drive (northeast corner of West 75th) was a glamorous address in the Jazz Age, when George and Ira Gershwin's adjoining penthouses were a legendary meeting place for luminaries from the worlds of music, literature, and the theater.

6. Nos. 35–36 Riverside Drive (West 75th to 76th) were the earliest row houses (1888–89) to be erected on the Drive. Originally the south half of a row of four, these were designed by Lamb & Rich, architects of Barnard College, for George and Clarence Lowther, whose nearby coal yards were well-known local eyesores in the Drive's early years.

7. At West 76th Street, detour uphill to West End Avenue: the West 76th to 77th Street block is the last survivor to show how West End Avenue looked when lined with chateauesque private homes. The group on the west side was designed by Lamb & Rich (1891) with tiled roofs, brick and stone in varying shades of tawny buff, orange, red, and brown, bell-roofed and copper-framed dormers, and intricate terra-cotta crests. Architectural historian Sarah Bradford Landau called this "one of the most colorful and unrestrained rows anywhere, a personalized miniature of Fifth Avenue on the West Side."

At the corner of West End Avenue and West 77th Street, the West End Collegiate Church and School was designed (1893) by Robert W. Gibson in an ebullient Dutch-derived style (high pitched roof, warm ochre brick with contrasting stringcourses, ornate crow-stepped gables) that would look fine on an Amsterdam guildhall. Church and school date from 1628, making them possibly the oldest of any surviving New York City institutions. The school suspended classes only once—during the Revolution—and is considered the oldest in North America.

8. Back on the Drive, the pink limestone fountain that adorns the park wall at the foot of West 76th Street was bequeathed to the city by Robert Ray Hamilton, wealthy sportsman-politician who drowned on a hunting trip in 1890. A descendant of Alexander Hamilton, he went out in a blaze of scandal, with a divorce pending and his wife—by all accounts a bigamist as well as a "bold adventuress"—in prison for "atrocious assault." Hamilton's eminent family wanted him forgotten, but the monument was put up despite their opposition.

9. True houses, 40–46 Riverside Drive (West 76th to 77th streets). Grandiose but playful row-house architecture as practiced by Clarence True, an archi-

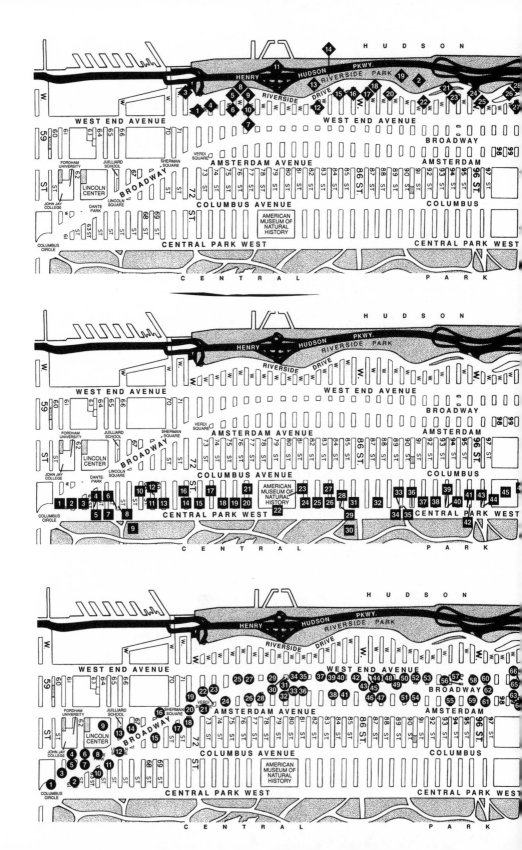

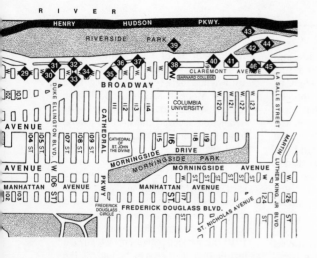

WEST SIDE
WALKING TOUR
MAPS _____

RIVERSIDE DRIVE

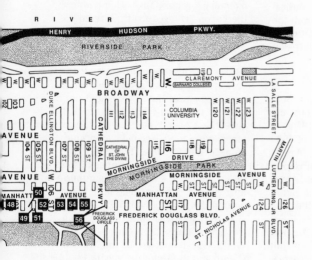

CENTRAL PARK WEST

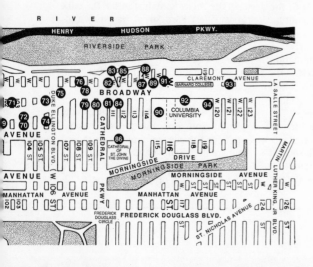

BROADWAY

tect-developer who claimed to have single-handedly "insured a most promising future for the Drive" back when its beauties were not thoroughly appreciated. (And see this block under fleecy clouds and a blue sky to understand why the Drive was once called "the most beautiful avenue in the world.") In 1945, artist Marc Chagall lived and worked at no. 42. Other nearby row-house mansions by True include nos. 74–77 Riverside Drive (below West 80th Street) and nos. 81–89 (below West 81st).

10. Lillian Russell's home, 318 West 77th. In the 1890s, when "Airy Fairy" Lillian Russell reigned on the musical stage, she dwelled a few steps from the Drive in a "cosey nest" lined with embroidered silk and enormous tiger-skin rugs.

The West Side Improvement, a 107-million dollar, long-overdue reconstruction, got under way in the 1930s. A McKim, Mead & White design of 1920 was greatly revised by Robert Moses's talented designers and builders, who in only 31 months covered the shore-hugging railroad tracks, created the Henry Hudson Parkway on new landfill, and added 132 acres and 140,000 lineal feet of footpaths to the park. The new four-level design included eight full playgrounds, tennis courts, baseball diamonds, and handball/basketball courts that ingeniously shared a wall with the newly enclosed railroad. Not to mention the centerpiece . . .

11. The 79th Street Grade Elimination Structure (in the park at West 79th Street). Public Works Administration money was available in 1934 for "elimination of highway grade crossings." The result here: a three-layer marvel that is to a normal "grade elimination structure" as a wedding cake is to a slice of toast: traffic circle on top, two-hundred-car garage at the bottom for users of the

70th Street Yacht Basin (built at the same time), with a circular fountain sandwiched between and ringed by a vaguely Moorish arcade. And all atop the old Penn Central freight tracks—the detail that secured the needed federal funding. (Clinton Lloyd, chief architectural engineer.)

12. 101–5 Riverside Drive (below West 83rd Street). More Clarence True houses. These were originally garnished with rounded bays and towers, which unfortunately jutted out onto public land. In 1910 the parks department, which had jurisdiction, threatened to lop off the offending projections. Homeowners thereupon arranged for the alterations that now give these buildings a somewhat truncated look.

13. The path leading south into Riverside Park at West 83rd winds past two little-noticed features: first, a splendid outcrop of the mica-schist bedrock that gives the Upper West Side its rugged topography; and second, a plaque, embedded in the stone, honoring Cyrus Clark (1830–1909), the "Father of the West Side" (see chap. 4). A half-mile-long river-view promenade begins just beyond the playground here; a tiny enclosure marks what was to have been the site of the U.S. memorial to the World War II martyrs of the Warsaw Ghetto and the Holocaust (chap. 12).

14. The rocky knob just inside the park above West 83rd Street was known locally as Mount Tom, and was the site originally chosen for the Soldiers and Sailors Monument. Earlier, it had been a favored haunt of Edgar Allan Poe, who summered nearby in the 1840s.

15. No. 120 Riverside Drive (originally Mount Tom Apartments) was responsible for the change in plan that moved the Soldiers and Sailors Monument six blocks uptown. When it opened in 1898 its height (then only 9 stories—the 12-

story addition at No. 125 came later) was considered so overwhelming as to ruin the site for the planned monument.

16. The Clarendon (apartments), at the southeast corner of West 86th Street, was owned for many years by William Randolph Hearst, who filled the upper five floors with his growing family and burgeoning hoard of art and antiquities—the nucleus of the fabulous trove now at San Simeon. (1907; Charles E. Birge, architect.)

17. The Normandy, the full-block building at West 86th to 87th streets, is a coveted address, and the last major design (1939) by Hungarian-born architect Emery Roth (1870–1947), whose skyscraper–apartment houses enliven the Central Park West skyline (see tour 2, nos. 2, 18, 24, 35, 36, and 37). Traditionalist Roth here gives us twelve stories of tentative Art Moderne, then tops it off with a reassuring pair of Renaissance towers. Delightful touch of class: a basement workshop kept just to maintain the venetian blinds in those rounded corner windows. Site of Oliver De Lancey house, burned by rebels in 1777 (see chap. 2).

18. 87th Street viaduct. A concealed iron bridge here carries the Drive over an ancient gap in the bedrock.

19. Soldiers and Sailors Monument, Riverside Park at West 89th Street. A monument to New York City's Civil War dead—and to civic procrastination. Governor Theodore Roosevelt laid the cornerstone of this pompous memorial in 1899—34 years (!) after Appomattox. (Dedicated 1902; Stoughton & Stoughton, architects, with sculptures by Paul E. M. Duboy.)

20. Yeshiva Chofetz Chaim, at the southeast corner of West 89th Street, was originally Villa Julia, the mansion home of Isaac L. and Julia Barnett Rice (1903,

Herts & Tallant, architects). The Rice children, depicted with their mother in bas-relief above the side porte cochere entrance, liked to pose for passers-by before the great front door. A precious relic: one of only two freestanding mansions to survive from the Drive's golden years, and the only one still with grounds and a garden.

21. Joan of Arc Park, West 92nd to 95th streets between the upper and lower Drives (1.578 acres), including Joan of Arc statue at West 93rd. In 1915, his country at war, French Ambassador Jean Jusserand came here to dedicate this equestrian monument to France's national heroine. The statue, widely copied in France, earned sculptress Anna Hyatt Huntington (1876–1973) the *Légion d'Honneur*—a doubly signal honor for a non-French woman. Set into the pedestal (John V. Van Pelt, architect) are stones from Rheims Cathedral, where Joan gave a crown to Charles VII, and from the dungeon at Rouen, where he left her to be tried and burned.

22. Architect Ralph Townsend designed and, for a time, lived at 194 Riverside Drive, an expansive seven-story building with ruggedly ornate corner towers. Local folklore has it that Townsend lived on a boat offshore while the building (his first major project) was going up.

23. The first new apartment residence on the Drive in thirty-five years, no. 222, a 1988–89 condominium development at the northeast corner of West 94th (Fox & Fowle, architects), harkens back to the styles of earlier years with a limestone base, Norman brick facade, terraced setbacks, and an ironwork entrance canopy.

24. From 95th to 98th streets a second viaduct, originally adorned with massive bronze lanterns (1902), carries the Drive over what was once a little cove in the Hudson shore. Theunis Idens had a

farmhouse nearby in the 1680s, and later residents, the Striker family, gave their name to the vicinity: Striker's Bay (see chaps. 1–3).

25. The ochre brickwork and the limestone frieze of rattlesnakes, buffalo skulls, and mountain lions on the Cliff Dwellers' Apartments (at the northeast corner of West 96th Street) suggest the architect's fascination with the U.S. Southwest. Could this have inspired Rodgers and Hart's "Way Out West on West End Avenue"? (1914; Herman Lee Meader, architect.)

26. The Upper Drive. An undulating, fitfully green island separates the drive's upper and lower roadways from 97th to 113th streets. This stretch was intended for magnificent private homes; the island would have provided a sort of communal lawn—and privacy: "These dwellings have a roadway of their own, so deftly hidden among the shadows that it can hardly be discovered from the park carriages" (Martha J. Lamb, 1884).

27. Digress uphill briefly for a look at the Paramount, 315 West 99th, an eight-story, white brick apartment house of circa 1900, from which Hollywood's Paramount Pictures took its name. (1911; George F. Pelham, architect.)

28. The Firemen's Memorial at 100th Street, a stolid composition of pink marble figures and bronze bas-relief, was erected on this pink-granite plaza in 1913 to honor fallen "soldiers in a war that never ends." Later (1927) the ASPCA added a second tablet in memory of the fire*horses* of an already-bygone era. (Attilio Piccirilli, sculptor, and H. Van Buren Magonigle, architect, the duo whose *Maine* Memorial—also unveiled in 1913—stands at Columbus Circle.)

29. Master Apartments, 310 Riverside Drive (at the northeast corner of 103rd Street). An ebullient Art Deco monolith,

and the first building in this area to use stepped setbacks; now a residential hotel and home of the Equity Library Theater (call 663–2028 for program information). The first three floors originally housed an educational center: Nicholas Roerich's Master Institute of United Arts (see no. 33, below), two libraries, an auditorium, and the Riverside Museum (modern art). (1929; Helmle, Corbett & Harrison and Sugarman & Berger, architects.)

30. Riverside Drive–West 105th Street Historic District. A grandly Parisian enclave of Beaux Arts marble town houses created (1899–1902) by four leading architectural firms under a covenant that restricted them to "such houses as are a benefit to the neighborhood." Of special interest:

■ No. 331 was bought by W. R. Hearst, who spent a million dollars remodeling it (fountains, statuary) for his sweetheart Marion Davies. (1902; Janes & Leo, architects.)

■ No. 332, where a heroic statue of twelfth-century Buddhist theologian Shinran-Shonin now stands guard, was the home of Dr. Jokichi Takamine, the Japanese chemist who first (1901) isolated adrenalin.

■ No. 333 had become a rooming house by the 1950s when Nobel Laureate-to-be Saul Bellow lived there; later Duke Ellington bought it for his sister Ruth, and maintained his studio, office, and trophy room there. (He also bought no. 331 for his son and musical heir, Mercer Ellington.)

31. Equestrian Monument to Major-General Franz Sigel (upper Drive at West 106th Street). German-born Sigel (1824–1902) came to the United States in his twenties. In the Civil War he served in the Union Army and played a major role at the Second Battle of Bull Run, later edited and published several important

English- and German-language newspapers in New York City. (1907; Karl Bitter, sculptor.)

32. Children's Mansion, 351 Riverside Drive (at the northeast corner of West 107th Street); built in 1909 for cigarette tycoon Morris Schinasi, whose brother had bought the Isaac Rice mansion (no. 20) the year before. It housed a girls' finishing school in the 1930s, later was owned by Columbia University and operated as a day-care center. The architect, William B. Tuthill, is better known as the designer of Carnegie Hall.

33. Once the home of librettist-lyricist Harry B. Smith, the Nicholas Roerich Museum, 319 West 107th Street now has permanent displays devoted to the work and collections of this remarkable Russian expatriate (1874–1947): artist, writer, scenarist (*The Rite of Spring*, with Stravinsky), explorer, and mystic. (A rare glimpse, too, into an 1898 Clarence True town house.) Call 864-7752 for hours and special events.

34. Below West 108th Street, look at the bucolic side yard and scrap of lawn between the town houses at nos. 352–53 Riverside Drive, with the side wall of the town house at 330 West 108th forming an elegant, ornate backdrop. Digress to the east onto West 108th Street for an unusual low-rise block recently proposed as a new landmark district: architectural touches include freestanding columns, terra-cotta angels, the lushly carved limestone overhanging porches at 324–28 West 108th, and the unique third-story window alcove at no. 316, with diamond-paned windows facing the sunset over the Hudson. Eastward, the block is framed by the orange brick walls and slate roof of the Manhasset apartments (tour 3, no. 78).

Riverside Drive, 110th to 120th streets: the West Side's grand, leafy esplanade,

lined with spacious holdovers from the golden era of New York City apartment-house construction. Leading off . . .

35. The Hendrick Hudson at 380 Riverside Drive (at the northwest corner of West 110th Street), where rooftop water tanks were originally concealed in a pair of wonderfully pretentious, Tuscan villa-style towers. Erected in 1907 by the builders of the Chatsworth (no. 3, above) the Hendrick Hudson offered similar amenities, including a river-view roof garden. (William L. Rouse, architect.) Watch, too, for the soaring iron canopy at no. 404 Riverside Drive and inviting porte cochere at no. 410 (both at 113th Street).

36. The Samuel J. Tilden statue stands at West 112th Street in a small elm-shaded plaza beside the upper Drive. Tilden (1814–86) was the reformer who led the attack on the Tweed Ring. He parlayed that into the governorship of New York (1875-76), then ran for the White House in 1876, winning the popular vote but losing the office to Hayes in the only officially contested presidential election (and one of the dirtiest) in U.S. history. Tilden's permanent legacy to New York City: the bequest that established what is now the New York Public Library. (1926; William O. Partridge, sculptor.)

37. The Lajos Kossuth statue at West 113th Street, erected in 1928 "by a liberty loving race of Americans of Magyar descent," honors the fiery Hungarian patriot (1802–94) who led the short-lived insurrection of 1848. (John Horvay, sculptor.)

38. The 116th Street approach to Columbia University is framed by a complementary pair of curved apartment houses: the Colosseum (435 Riverside Drive, south corner) and the Paterno (440 Riverside Drive, north corner); note the Paterno's porte cochere, evincing its

aristocratic leanings. Well-known Colosseum residents have included silent-film star Francis X. Bushman, Columbia Law Dean (and later Supreme Court Justice) Harlan Stone, and the notorious poisoner "Dr." Arthur Waite (chap. 11). (1910; Schwartz & Gross, architects.)

39. Drinking fountain, in Riverside Park at West 116th Street. The stele and fountain just inside the park were erected in 1910 by the Women's Health Protective Association of New York to celebrate the group's twenty-fifth anniversary—*and* to symbolize their long-delayed success in a drive to introduce purification of the city's water supply. (WHPA founder/president Mary Elizabeth Trautman lived at 333 Riverside Drive.)

40. The Interchurch Center, 475 Riverside Drive (119th to 120th streets) is the ecumenically vigorous, architecturally bland headquarters of the National Council of Churches and other major clerical organizations. (Call 870–2200 for information on tours and exhibits.) The cornerstone includes a fragment from the agora in Corinth "where many hearing Paul believed." It was laid with great ceremony in 1957 by Dwight Eisenhower, whose health was then uncertain. Since Ike's death would have meant a quick change in casting, the words on the stone cautiously identify him only as "the President of the United States."

41. The Drive's most striking architectural landmark, at West 120th to 122nd streets, is Riverside Church (Baptist-interdenominational), built with material aid from John D. Rockefeller, Jr. The steel-framed tower, modeled after Chartres Cathedral, houses a twenty-two-story office tower, crowned by the Laura Spelman Rockefeller Memorial Carillon, the world's largest (seventy-four bells, including the twenty-two-ton Bourdon, the largest tuned bell ever cast). The view from the belfry (admis-

sion 25 cents) is magnificent and highly recommended; for hours, call 749–7000. A catholic selection of portraits is carved into the arches of the west portal: here you'll find Confucius, Buddha, Mohammed, Pasteur, Darwin, and Einstein—the last of whom once made a special trip here just to see his likeness adorning a church. (1930; Charles Collens and Henry C. Pelton, architects.)

42. General Grant National Memorial/Grant's Tomb. Who is buried in Grant's Tomb? Ulysses S. Grant, of course—*and* his widow, by his side. Julia Grant vetoed the site originally suggested, in Central Park, because park regulations would have barred her interment beside her husband. This massive neoclassical pile, modeled on the tomb of Mausolus at Halicarnassus, occupies a site once proposed by George Washington for the U.S. Capitol. By all means visit the solemn interior, white marble in dim light from amber stained glass; but don't miss the playful, colorful mosaic benches outside, designed by Pedro Silva, constructed by neighborhood kids in the early 1970s, and subsequently the target of conservative 1980s ire. For hours, call MOnument 6–1640. (1897; John H. Duncan, architect.)

43. An "Amiable Child" is buried in Riverside Park, slightly north of Grant's Tomb and a few steps down (west) from the Drive. Four-year-old St. Clair Pollock, favorite son of linen merchant George Pollock, died in 1797 and was buried in what was meant to be the family cemetery. Soon afterward, Pollock had to sell out. He thereupon gave the tiny plot with the boy's grave to a kindly neighbor with the request that it be kept "always inclosed and sacred"—a wish that has, astonishingly, been honored down the years.

44. Claremont, the Federalist mansion occupied by Pollock, was situated on the knoll north of Grant's Tomb; it survived

as Claremont Inn until 1953, when the parks department demolished it; a playground is there now. To the north a mile-long viaduct extends to West 135th Street, crossing the geological fault valley where the village of Manhattanville flourished in the mid-nineteenth century. The original 1901 viaduct, a designated city landmark, was declared unsafe in 1983, dismantled, and replaced in 1986–88 with an exact replica.

45. International House, 500 Riverside Drive, faces Grant's Tomb from the east. Built with Rockefeller money in 1924 as a "world home" for students, "given over to the idea of promoting peace through a fellowship of students." Abutting International House to the south . . .

46. Sakura Park, its formal plantings now gone somewhat to seed, offers an invitation to stroll along tree-shaded alleys. An appropriate place to end our tour,

as this delightful setting, like Riverside Drive itself, was built (1932) to designs by Frederick Law Olmsted's firm. At the garden's West 122nd Street corner is a bronze figure (erected 1918) by Gutzon Borglum—a onetime West Side resident best known for his Mount Rushmore presidential carvings. This portrait shows the uniformed figure of Daniel Butterfield (1831–1901), who was General Meade's chief of staff at Gettysburg. It would be fitting to reach this spot near sundown: Butterfield was the composer of *Taps*.

- - - - - - - - -

The tour ends here. To return to its starting point, recross Riverside Drive for the downtown M-5 bus, or take the IRT subway (stops on Broadway at 125th and 116th streets). The area is also well supplied with buses: the M-4 line (on Riverside Drive), M-104 (Broadway), and M-11 (Amsterdam Avenue).

CENTRAL PARK WEST: MANHATTAN'S OTHER SKYLINE

New York Times architecture critic Paul Goldberger, who lives there, has called Central Park West "plain and simple, New York's finest street at large scale." Its glory is a unique collection of early twentieth-century apartment buildings and apartment hotels from the era (1880–1930) when New Yorkers reluctantly accepted, then fervently embraced, the apartment style of life. These are the buildings that made it happen: the Dakota, Kenilworth, El Dorado, Century, Majestic, with just the right sprinkling of churches, synagogues, museums, and other public institutions to give you a reason—besides the architecture—to pay a visit. They're still imposing—though new and taller neighbors are beginning

to crowd them from the west.

Start from the north end of Columbus Circle, where the last of the old-fashioned subway-side newsstands makes an appropriately picturesque starting point. Calvert Vaux's recently renovated Ladies Pavilion in Central Park, with its cast-iron gingerbread decorations, formerly stood here as a shelter for trolley passengers.

1. The forty-five-story shaft of the Gulf + Western Plaza (1967; Thomas E. Stanley) was the first of the Upper West Side's crop of new towers, and is home to, among other things, Paramount Pictures, now a G + W holding. Close up, its bland bulk does nothing for what might

have been a dramatic triangular parkside site, but visit the forty-third-floor restaurant, Top of the Park, for dramatic views of the neighborhood.

2. The Mayflower Hotel at West 61st to 62nd streets (1926; Emery Roth) was long popular with the theater crowd. It is now scalped of its original neo-Italian Renaissance balconies and other ornaments. A plaque honors the composer Vincent Youmans ("Tea for Two," "Sometimes I'm Happy"), born on this site in 1898.

3. Century Apartments, 25 Central Park West (1931; office of Irwin Chanin; Jacques Delamarre, architectural director). Overhanging sixteenth- to eighteenth-floor terraces and boldly streamlined thirty-story towers are suitably theatrical touches. The Chanins had built many Times Square theaters before erecting this twin-towered, full-block apartment house whose multilevel and duplex apartments have been home to Marc Connelly, Ethel Merman, Ray Bolger, and other leading lights of Broadway. (Also Irwin Chanin.) Understated Moderne design still looks fresh after nearly sixty years. The name commemorates the ill-fated Century (originally the New) Theatre (chap. 8).

4. The West Side YMCA at 5 West 63rd Street (1930; Dwight James Baum, architect), capped with an octagonal red-roofed tower and tall bronze lantern, has playful Lombardi Romanesque arches and tiles inside and out.

5. The Society for Ethical Culture (1902; Carrère & Hastings, architects, with Robert D. Cohn) and the Ethical Culture School (1910; Robert D. Cohn) share the West 63rd to 64th street block. Both were founded in 1876 by Felix Adler, who emphasized nonsectarian moral teachings, and advanced educational methods. The older building was once considered a prize specimen of Art Nou-veau architecture; architect Cohn was a close friend of Adler and was the society's president from 1921 to 1944.

6. Holy Trinity Lutheran Church, at the northwest corner of West 65th Street (Schickel & Ditmars, architects, 1904), is particularly inviting on winter evenings, during the free "An Evening with Johann S." Bach concerts. The colorful rose window and slender copper-clad spire are attractive features.

7. The massive, exuberantly decorated Prasada, at 50 Central Park West (1904; Charles W. Romeyn, architect), has been home to Wanda Landowska, Ezio Pinza, and other musical greats. The original mansard roof is gone, but the Italian Baroque portico of rusticated columns and iron bow windows remain as appropriately florid touches.

8. No. 55 Central Park West, southwest corner of West 66th Street (1929; Schwartz & Gross, architects). Basically a stolid apartment block enlivened with Art Deco: polychromed and graded brick brightens to skyward; abundant ziggurat motifs in awning, terra-cotta brackets and finials. The film *Ghostbusters* alleged that Ivo Shandor, a mad doctor, designed the building, using "cold-riveted girders with cores of pure selenium." Supposedly this made the whole building "a huge superconductive antenna that was designed and built expressly for the purpose of pulling in and concentrating spiritual turbulence. In other words, it's spook central!"

9. Central Park's Tavern-on-the-Green restaurant at West 67th Street, with its flamboyant colored chandeliers and light-frosted trees, incorporates Calvert Vaux's polychrome 1870 sheepfold. Livestock that gave the nearby Sheep Meadow its name lived here until ousted by Parks Commissioner Moses in 1938. The playground on the hill to the north was the site of the "Battle of Central Park."

10. At West 67th Street, the double-height studio windows of 2 West 67th across the street (1919; Charles A. Rich and F. Mathesius, architects) signal the entry into what once was artists' territory. The Hotel des Artistes, with its restrained neo-Gothic facade at 1 West 67th (between Central Park West and Columbus), is the block's showpiece, and has been home, briefly or otherwise, to celebrities ranging from Noel Coward and Isadora Duncan to Fannie Hurst, Norman Rockwell, and Howard Chandler Christy (1918; George M. Pollard, architect). The building was erected by a syndicate of artists (see chap. 9), and the tiny gargoyles above the second floor appropriately represent painters, writers, musicians, and artists. The ground-floor Café des Artistes, with Howard Chandler Christy's murals of frolicsome nymphs, is a favorite area dining spot.

11. Second Church of Christ, Scientist, at the southwest corner of West 68th Street (1900; Frederick R. Comstock, architect). A handsome Beaux Arts design with a high arched entrance and triangular pediment, the building was recently the subject of a hard-fought landmarking dispute.

12. Free Synagogue, 40 West 68th (1923; S. B. Eisendrath and B. Horowitz, architects), was founded by Zionist and religious leader Rabbi Stephen S. Wise as a public forum and as the flagship institution of Reform Judaism in the United States; it is now home to Hebrew Union College. It and the West Side Senior Center next door are constructed of the same native Manhattan schist that forms outcrops in Central Park.

13. Shearith Israel Synagogue, at the southwest corner of West 70th Street, is the fifth home of the oldest Jewish congregation in America, established secretly, probably in a loft or borrowed room, in 1654 by Sephardic (Spanish-Portuguese) Jews who fled the Inquisi-

tion for the relative hospitality of New Amsterdam. The building (1897; Brunner and Tryon) is a New York City landmark; a separate wing replicates the interior of the congregation's first building.

14. The Majestic Apartments, West 71st to 72nd streets (1930; office of Irwin Chanin, Jacques Delamarre). The other full-block, streamlined, twin-towered apartment from the Chanins. Planned as a monster fifty-three-story monolith, but cut down by revised zoning.

15. The Dakota, 1 West 72nd (Henry Janeway Hardenbergh, 1884). The first and, to many, still the finest New York apartment house, built by pioneer West Side developer Edward Clark. The richly carved freestone trim, steep peaked roofs, arched windows, cupolas, and bay windows give the feel of a country manse and probably helped sell proper New Yorkers on the (then) somewhat risqué notion of apartment dwelling. (But note the building's blank brick west wall—as though no one who counted was expected to live where they could see it.) Chapter 4 explains the Dakota Indian high above the 72nd Street entrance.

16. Egomaniac-developer "Daddy" Browning (chap. 12) built the white brick studio-apartment buildings at 31 West 71st (Robert L. Lyons, 1916) and 42 West 72nd (Buchman & Fox, 1915). Look for the EWB monogram.

17. The West 73rd to 74th Street Historic District includes a fine collection of row houses built by Clark and his heirs. Hardenbergh houses on the north side of West 73rd were among the neighborhood's first; the long neo-Georgian row on West 74th, by Percy Griffith, are the last (1904–7).

18. The San Remo, 145–46 Central Park West, West 74th to 75th streets (Emery Roth, 1930). A twentieth-century apartment-skyscraper with classical Italian

Baroque details, and the most spectacular member of the Central Park West skyline—at least from a distance—and with an appropriately stellar group of residents. Rusticated limestone base, with slender twin towers topped by miniature choragic monuments (compare the Soldiers and Sailors Monument on Riverside Drive).

19. A nearly intact turn-of-the-century neighborhood, the Central Park West–76th Street Historic District begins with the neo-English Gothic Universalist Church at 76th Street (originally church of the Divine Paternity; William A. Potter, architect, 1898). West 76th—one of the city's earliest (1973) designated historic districts–offers varied 1890s row houses in varied styles by several noted architects, including (at nos. 8–10) John H. Duncan, designer of Grant's Tomb. Pioneer ad man J. Walter Thompson once owned the English basement house at no. 14, diplomat-statesman Oscar Straus had no. 5, and mining millionaire-philanthropist Murry Guggenheim lived at no. 29.

20. The Roman Eclectic-style New-York Historical Society (West 76th to 77th streets) was designed by two sets of architects at widely different times. The columned 1903 central facade is by York & Sawyer (best known for their banks); the simpler northern and southern wings were added in 1937–38 by Walker & Gillette. Within are exhibits and collections on U.S. and especially New York history, art, design, and crafts, not to mention the peerless library and print and photo collections, and a program of historic-architectural walking tours (information: 873–3400).

21. Digress onto the "Park block" of West 77th Street, one of the grandest and least-known boulevards in town:

■ The Studio Building at 44 West 77th, a 1909 artists' building (notice the dou-ble-height studio windows) by Harde & Short, is thickly encrusted with Gothic limestone traceries inside and out (an equal amount of decoration was removed for safety reasons in 1944).

■ The American Museum of Natural History occupies the land from here to 81st Street, originally known as Manhattan Square, but renamed Margaret Mead Green to honor the great cultural anthropologist who lived across the street at the Beresford. The 77th Street facade by J. C. Cady & Co., in granite ranging from light brown to pink, is one of the finest Romanesque Revival works in the country. Behind it is the original 1876 museum building by Calvert Vaux, now hidden among a score of later exhibition, research, office, and utility buildings. (Part of it can be seen from Columbus and 79th.) Continue up Central Park West to . . .

22. The Theodore Roosevelt Memorial at Central Park West and West 79th Street, with its broad stairs, triumphal arch, and bronze doors: designed by John Russell Pope, architect of the Jefferson Memorial in Washington, in neo-American Classic style. It also serves as the principal (or at least, best known) entrance to the American Museum of Natural History. Roosevelt's young cousin FDR laid the memorial's cornerstone in 1931 as New York's governor, then, as president, opened it in 1936. The equestrian statue of TR with a grateful American Indian and an African tribesman is by James E. Fraser; atop the great Ionic columns are heroic figures of Lewis and Clark, Daniel Boone, and John James Audubon.

23. Attached to the museum on the south side of West 81st Street is the eighty-foot dome of the Hayden Planetarium (Trowbridge & Livingstone, architects), which introduced thin-shell reinforced concrete roof construction

to the United States in 1933. The planetarium is a separate institution within the American Museum (Sky Show information: 769–5920). Inset in the pavement by the planetarium entrance is an array of three hundred bronze stars and galaxies, a recent addition by New York artist Michelle Oka Doner.

24. The Beresford, 211 Central Park West and 1 West 81st, another full-block apartment building by architect Emery Roth (1929)—this time with *three* towers, to dominate the view from downtown as well from Central Park and the East Side. Also by Roth (and his home at the time of his death in 1947) is the sixteen-story, neo-Renaissance Alden Hotel (1926) above West 82nd Street.

25. The six-story apartment building at 227 Central Park West (at the southwest corner of West 83rd Street; Thomas & Wilson, architects) is a century-old survivor, built in 1888. The top four floors are extremely well preserved, with a heavy projecting cornice, brick pilasters at every bay, and elaborate terra-cotta panels at every window.

26. The red brick building at the northwest corner of West 83rd is the Bolivar Hotel (circa 1926). The name seems to honor Simon Bolivar, the great South American liberator; in fact, it commemorates an equestrian statue of Bolivar that was unveiled atop Summit Rock, the nearby hill in Central Park, by President Harding in 1921. The statue, by Sally James Farnham, is now with those of other South American heroes at Central Park South and Sixth Avenue (Avenue of the Americas).

27. No. 73 West 83rd Street, a circa-1895 tenement, has a rhomboidal, not rectangular "footprint." Its east wall (and that of no. 71 next door) follows an eighteenth-century boundary line, between William W. Woolsey's estate on the east and John E. Le Conte's on the west.

28. The yellow brick Art Deco facade of 241 Central Park West (at the northwest corner of West 84th Street) would have occupied the whole block, but nearby row-house owners wouldn't sell their property (see no. 29). The 1930 building is distinguished by the handsome buff brickwork and the vaguely floral motif (tulips? cornstalks?) of the buttresses. (Compare 55 Central Park West, no. 8 on this tour, completed the year before by the same architects, Schwartz & Gross.)

29. The three row houses at 247–49 Central Park West (below West 85th; Edward L. Angell, architect, 1889) are the last of a row of nine private homes that filled the 84th–85th Street block in 1889. In the 1920s, no. 249 belonged to the widowed Rebecca Wendel Swope, whose family began buying Manhattan real estate around 1800 and followed a unique policy of *never* selling. (In the 1930s, her sister Ella Wendel was a famous recluse, living alone in an empty mansion at Fifth and 39th, and reportedly turning down stupendous sums for the vacant lot next door where her dog exercised.) Mrs. Swope died at eighty-seven in 1930, but her unoccupied home stayed as she left it until World War II, with a caretaker on the premises, still furnished with antiques, rare tapestries, and priceless books.

30. At the northeast corner of West 85th Street, enter the park and follow the uphill path to lamppost no. 8505 (all park lampposts are numbered, the first two digits indicating the nearest cross street). Face south and you are looking at the site of Seneca Village, a shantytown of the 1850s that may have been a village of free New York blacks in the 1820s and 1830s. An unidentified stone foundation beside the beech tree marks the onetime location of the village's African Methodist Episcopal Zion Church.

Now look at the rock outcrop to

your left. In 1842 the Croton Aqueduct paralleled Ninth Avenue down to 85th Street, then crossed here into the Yorkville Reservoir, which, with a receiving reservoir at 42nd and Fifth, was the heart of the city's first large-scale water system. Today the city water supply flows underground, and Central Park's Great Lawn replaces the original reservoir (the reservoir in the park today is a later addition, from 1865); the rough cut in the outcrop ahead of you shows the old aqueduct line. (Fragments of the old reservoir wall still stand east and west of the police station and workshops along the 86th Street transverse road, and some of the stone from the dismantled aqueduct was used to construct the Church of the Paulist Fathers at Columbus Avenue and 59th Street.)

31. Back at Central Park West, the block from West 85th to 86th streets is filled with two matching apartment buildings: Rossleigh Court (1905) and Orwell House, originally the Hotel Peter Stuyvesant (1906; both by Mulliken & Moeller).

32. St. Urban Apartments, 285 Central Park West (at the southwest corner of West 88th Street; Robert T. Lyons, 1906) was one of the avenue's first large-scale apartment houses. The recessed, arched carriage entrance, massive mansard roof, and domed, circular corner tower were opulent Beaux Arts touches, intended to evoke the atmosphere of a Parisian *hôtel particulier*.

33. No. 1 West 89th Street, recently restored, has a striking polychrome facade combining Dutch and so-called Queen Anne details (Clarence True, architect, 1899). Alternating courses of limestone and red brick give a pleasing zebra effect, and elaborate Georgian "Gibbs" surrounds set off the entrance and the two central bays facing the park.

34. No. 293 Central Park West, between West 89th and 90th streets, was a typical small turn-of-the-century apartment in Italianate style, originally intended for one family per floor (1899; Neville & Bagge; alterations by Clarence True). It became an office building in 1907, later housed Dr. Silkworth's well-known drying-out clinic, the spiritual birthplace of Alcoholics Anonymous.

35. No. 295 Central Park West, on the south side of West 90th Street. Emery Roth again, this time at the tail end of his career (1940) and working in a fairly sleek, modern style: white granite facade; simple, severe lines; and deep setbacks at the sixteenth and eighteenth floors.

36. The twin Art Deco towers of the El Dorado at 300 Central Park West, 90th to 91st streets (1931; Margon & Holder with Emery Roth) are the northernmost and newest in Central Park West's skyline. Stepped-back terraces are adorned with modernistic railings, and geometric interlocking gratings adorn the ziggurat-like crowning towers. It was home to the fictional Marjorie Morningstar and the real-life Sinclair Lewis, who had a huge twenty-ninth-floor apartment and referred to the building as Intolerable Towers.

37. The Ardsley, 320 Central Park West at 92nd Street (Emery Roth, architect, 1931). Roth's Art Deco design this time incorporates Mayan motifs in the upper floors and the multicolored street-level reliefs. Contrasting bands of dark brickwork grow more playful toward the top.

38. Surprisingly well preserved is 325 Central Park West (between West 92nd to 93rd streets), a modest building with white limestone detailing and marble loggias at the fourth and fifth stories; the architect, George F. Pelham, designed numerous Upper West Side apartment buildings.

39. The Turin, 333 Central Park West,

at the northwest corner of West 93rd Street (1909; Albert Joseph Bodker) has four towers that were originally crowned with heavy cornices; the vertically continuous window shafts and the arches at the fifth and ninth floors still give distinction. A recent renovation luckily emphasizes, rather than hides, the original decorations.

40. No. 336 Central Park West, southwest corner of West 94th Street (1929; Schwartz & Gross), was Central Park West's earliest Art Deco building, with variegated "tapestry" brickwork and vaguely Egyptian motifs (possibly stylized papyrus plants) in the flared terracotta trim and crowning water tower. (Compare nos. 55 and 241 Central Park West.)

41. The five 1893 neo-Renaissance row houses at 351–55 Central Park West (northwest corner of 95th Street; Gilbert Schellenger, architect) became the focus of a fierce landmarking dispute when they were slated for demolition in 1987. More interesting is their neighbor to the north . . .

42. No. 360 Central Park West, a 1928 high rise (sixteen stories) by Rosario Candela, built on the site of the Scotch Presbyterian Church, which had moved here from West 14th Street in 1893. This was one of several churches that experimented in the late twenties with various combinations of "church-hotel" (compare Broadway tour, no. 26) and "church-apartment house." Most didn't pan out financially; this did. The limestone base facing West 96th Street is still distinctly ecclesiastical, and contains the church and its associated Alexander Robertson School.

43. The First Church of Christ, Scientist, one of the largest church buildings in the city (1903; Carrère & Hastings), was erected at the northwest corner of West 96th Street by Mary Baker Eddy's leading New York City disciple, Augusta F. Stetson, in the style of London's great Baroque churches, with a marvelously decorated, curved auditorium (capacity, 2,000) and seven types of rare marble. When Mrs. Stetson ultimately fell out with her leader and was excommunicated, she sued the Mother Church—and pointedly erected a high fence between the church and her home next door at 7 West 96th.

44. No. 370 Central Park West, at the southwest corner of West 97th Street is a rare neo-Tudor, low-rise apartment house (1917; Fred F. French & Co.) complete with half-timbering and gables. The style, then popular in suburbs such as Garden City, was favored for tenement renovations (see Broadway tour, no. 34); French also used it conspicuously at his Tudor City development, flanking the east end of 42nd Street.

45. Park West Village, 97th to 100th streets, Central Park West to Columbus, was the first housing development completed after the Manhattantown scandals of 1957. The four eighteen-story buildings are bland, pink-brick boxes arranged around a central courtyard and parking lot—the slum clearance/urban renewal "superblock" approach that later came in for severe criticism. On the other hand, the quality here makes most recent "luxury" buildings seem shabby by comparison; co-oped in 1986, they have been pretentiously rechristened The Vaux and The Olmsted.

––––––––––

Pause at West 100th Street to sense the contrasts. Well-heeled Central Park West is (mostly) behind you; the section of park to the east and north is the most rugged and in some ways most beautiful area of the park, including Harlem Meer, the lake immediately below. Visible to the west on West 100th is the green copper spire of Trinity Evangelical Lutheran Church (George W. Conable,

architect, 1909). The ornate, five-story red brick building on the northwest corner, no. 405–6 Central Park West, was designed by Charles Stegmayer in 1899 for the brewer–real estate operator Peter Doelger, whose large house was at 100th and Riverside Drive. Best features: the Second Empire limestone window framings, and the prominent roof pavilion facing 100th Street, with its large pressed-metal anthemion.

46. No. 409 Central Park West (above West 100th Street) is the avenue's only surviving two-and-a-half-story building. It was converted from a dry cleaning establishment to Kingdom Hall of Jehovah's Witnesses (A. L. Seiden, conversion architect).

47. Philip Braender, a tire manufacturer and construction man, erected the ten-story Braender, 418 Central Park West (at the southwest corner of West 102nd), in 1903 to vaguely French Second Empire-style designs by Frederick C. Browne. Paired gryphons with spread wings support the balconies below the ninth floor; other touches include the "buttress" arch between the round corner towers, marble-and-onyx trimmed lobby, and a courtyard fountain, now converted to a planter.

48. The block West 102nd to 103rd was built up with two low-rise (six- and seven-story) apartment houses just before World War II. The shorter, no. 420, was designed and built by Horace Ginsburn; no. 425 (H. J. Feldman, architect) has neo-Colonial terra-cotta decorations at the doorways.

49. Seen from the south, the eighteen-story 444 Central Park West, at the northwest corner of West 104th Street, is a commanding presence, and must have been even more so when built in 1929: not terribly large, but considerably taller than anything nearby, with dramatically stepped-back terraces and fine neo-Romanesque detailing. Architects were Boak & Paris, who also designed the Metro (originally the Midtown) Cinema (Broadway no. 64).

50. At 104th, turn left to see the Manhattan Valley Townhouses (Rosenblum/Harb, architects, 1987)—seventy-six partially subsidized condo units in twenty-two new, four-story town houses occupying parts of West 104th and 105th streets and both sides of Manhattan Avenue. Sponsor for the project was the Manhattan Valley Development Corporation with assistance from The Urban Concern, Inc. In the 1890s this was a secluded row-house neighborhood dominated by the rich red brick of the New York Cancer Hospital and the thirty-foot cliff in Central Park at 104th to 106th streets that inspired circa-1900 developers to label the area Undercliff— a catchy name that never caught on.

51. Nos. 446–47 Central Park West (1900; Neville & Bagge, architects) has a fairly exuberant facade, with rounded projecting bays and lively color contrasts between the dark red brick and the freely applied limestone detailing. Reconverted to apartments from an SRO hotel in 1966.

52. The Towers, originally the New York Cancer Hospital (Charles C. Haight, architect) was built 1883–90, the first institution in the United States devoted to the study and treatment of cancer, predecessor of today's Memorial Sloan-Kettering Institute. Originally funded by John Jacob Astor, it had five round towers, the theory being that microbes (a recent discovery in the 1880s) accumulated in corners; no corners, no germs. The building was operated by the notorious Bernard Bergman as a nursing home in the 1960s; in 1974, he was indicted for Medicare fraud and the institution closed. Recent plans—stalled (at least temporarily) by community opposition—called for an attached thirty-

nine-story condo tower, by architects Victor Caliandro and John Harding, to rise behind it.

53. No. 465 Central Park West (between West 106th and 107th streets) is a modest mid-block building (seven stories) by G. F. Pelham, circa 1900, with limestone quoins, window surrounds, and elaborate central entablatures setting off the dark red brick. The larger (fifteen-story) 467 Central Park West, with touches of neo-Romanesque detailing, dates from 1928 (Gronenberg & Lauchtag, architects).

54. The full block of five-story apartment buildings at 471–77 Central Park West (West 107th to 108th streets; Neville & Bagge, architects, 1896) is nicely restored, although original materials are hidden—pale yellow paint and brown trim hides the original yellow Roman brick and limestone detailing.

55. Nos. 478–79 and 485 Central Park West (West 108th to 109th streets) were built as a unit in 1898. Like many on nearby blocks, these buildings were abandoned in the seventies after decades of hard use; unlike most, they have been well restored (Edward L. Angell and William Higginson, architects).

- - - - - - - - - -

West 110th Street (Cathedral Parkway) marks the Harlem–Manhattan Valley border. The junction, Frederick Douglass Circle, is named for the great abolitionist and educator; Central Park West's (Eighth Avenue's) northward continuation is Frederick Douglass Boulevard.

56. At the start of the eighties these blocks were a burned-out war zone of derelict tenements. Today the neighborhood west of the park is still a very chancy environment, but the expansive, post-1900 apartment houses extending eastward along Central Park North are restored, and Reuben Glick's brand-new Towers on the Park condominiums west of Central Park West (sponsored by the New York City Partnership, Inc.) are a model of affordable new housing. The chunky design with girderlike spandrels and money-saving prefabricated slab-lift floors (Caudill, Rowett & Scott, architects) reflects a candidly utilitarian aesthetic. On the other hand, the top price for a three-bedroom apartment in mid-1988 was only $110,000.

- - - - - - - - - -

Tour 2 ends at the 110th Street stop of the IND K local. Other transportation options: no. 10 bus north or south on Central Park West; no. 4 bus east or west on 110th; no. 11 bus south at Columbus Avenue (one block west); or no. 1 subway or M-104 bus at Broadway and 110th. If you do hike westward, pause at Manhattan Avenue for a look at the strangely shaped tenements on the southwest corner, designed to fit into the S-curve of the now vanished el—or you may extend your tour to take in the Cathedral Church of St. John the Divine at Amsterdam and 112th (visitor information: 316–7540).

ALONG THE BLOOMINGDALE ROAD: BROADWAY, COLUMBUS CIRCLE TO COLUMBIA UNIVERSITY

The commissioners laying out Manhattan's street grid in 1808–11 considered eliminating Broadway, but it was already too well established. It's still here, the world's best-known thoroughfare, a crosstown slash following the general route of the Bloomingdale Road, which followed the general route of an ancient Indian trail, which in turn followed the high ground around swamps and over primeval ridges. The Upper West Side's section, part boulevard, part Casbah, agora, or inferno, unfurls northward from Columbus Circle like an immense canvas crowded with images from every conceivable source, Norman Rockwell, George Bellows, Childe Hassam—or Hieronymus Bosch.

1. Despite Gaetano Russo's 1892 statue of the Navigator on its Florentine pedestal, and that pious fraud, the 1913 *Maine* Monument (Attilio Piccirilli, sculptor; H. Van Buren Magonigle, architect), Columbus Circle (called The Grand Circle when it was first laid out in 1868) seems less an urban plaza than a misbegotten highway interchange. Three mismatched hulks now dominate the scene: the drab, disused Coliseum; the perforated marble facade of Huntington Hartford's Gallery of Modern Art (Edward Durrell Stone, 1965), now headquarters of New York's Cultural Affairs Department; and the striped slab of the Gulf + Western building (Thomas E. Stanley, 1967). (A recent survey placed the last two high on a list of buildings New Yorkers would most like to see demolished.)

The embattled Columbus Center development, with its three overlapping towers, may soon rise over the Coliseum site. (Or not; see chap. 13). If so, the circle could become "a gay place" again,

with a total of (as currently projected) nine movie theaters and a galleria of shops, galleries, and a food court with several restaurants. In addition, if the city's traffic and parks departments follow through on current reconstruction plans, Columbus Circle may even finally realize its potential to be one of Manhattan's grandest public spaces.

2. Broadway's planted central mall begins at West 61st Street and continues, with interruptions, until the subway pokes aboveground at 123rd. The original Tweed-era mall had a double row of elms, with a continuous walk up the center. Subway construction in 1901–4 tore up Broadway curb-to-curb. Today's mall is necessarily more modest, with tiny fenced-in lawns (some of which serve derelicts as a summer campground) and benches at the cross streets.

3. No. 1845 Broadway (west side, between West 60th to 61st streets) is an aging, gable-roofed business building of a type now rare: Martin's Bar downstairs, Jon Devlin's Dancercize, Darvash Ballet School, and similar low-budget enterprises above. Between here and 96th Street, fifteen thousand people still practice ballet, tai chi, jazz dance, yoga, and modern dance in cheap old studios like this. No one expects them to last much longer; the land under the buildings is too valuable.

4. No. 1865 Broadway, northwest corner, West 61st Street, houses the American Bible Society. World's largest bible collection within.

5. The twenty-eight-story condo-office building at the southwest corner of West 62nd Street is "Chequers," the first Up-

per West Side project (1988–89) by Eli Attia, the flashy Israeli architect of the Republic Bank building on Fifth Avenue at 40th Street.

6. The Automobile Club of New York (AAA) at 1881 Broadway (northwest corner of West 62nd Street) occupies a building that was a Cadillac dealership back when this part of Broadway was New York City's Automobile Row.

7. Harkness Plaza, a 1979 apartment tower, occupies an L-shaped plot wrapped around 1881 Broadway; the site once held the Colonial (later the Harkness) Theatre, whose stage was hallowed by Chaplin, Houdini, Walter Hampden, and—among many others—Walter Winchell, whose nightly broadcast originated here in the forties.

8. At 63rd Street and Broadway, at the southwest corner, is the Empire Hotel, the second structure (circa 1926) of the name on this site, both popular with musical and theatrical folk. Cross Columbus Avenue via Dante Park with its statue of the poet by Ettore Ximenes, erected in 1921, and continue to . . .

9. The Lincoln Center for the Performing Arts. Left to right, the view takes in the New York State Theatre (Philip Johnson and Richard Foster, 1964), the Metropolitan Opera House (Wallace K. Harrison, 1966; lobby paintings by Marc Chagall), and Avery Fisher Hall (Max Abramovitz, 1962), grouped around the fountained plaza. All are clad, unfortunately, in travertine, a fine-grained, "holey" limestone that forms in caves and, alas, weathers poorly. Call about free guided tours of Lincoln Center (877–1800, ext. 512) and the enormous backstage facilities of the Metropolitan Opera (582–3512), or 877–2011 for current program information.

10. One Lincoln Plaza (on the east side of Broadway, West 63rd to 64th streets) is one of the earliest (1971), highest (forty-three stories), and biggest (seven hundred units) of the West Side's recent crop of high rises (Philip Birnbaum, architect). It is also home to ASCAP, the American Society of Composers, Authors & Publishers, a group founded in 1915 to protect the interest of popular music's creators, with Victor Herbert as its first president. (Peer around the corner to see an architectural footnote. After long negotiations, the elderly owner of the five-story tenement at 33 West 63rd Street refused at the last minute to sell to One Lincoln Plaza's developers; the holdout seriously cramped the larger building's design, pushing it back from West 63rd Street and forcing the architect to put a windowless bathroom at the southwest corner of each floor—right where the view would have been most spectacular.)

11. Another Automobile Row relic: the brick commercial building with terracotta trim and green windows at 1926 Broadway (east side, West 64th to 65th) was designed by Frank W. Andrews in 1909 as a garage for a member of the land-wealthy Goelet family. Later it housed the curious publishing empire of nature-faddist Bernarr Macfadden (chap. 10). Today it is a lone reminder of Lincoln Square's days as a hustling commercial center. Behind it on West 64th, note the Statue of Liberty atop the former Liberty warehouse building (chap. 5).

12. Continue up the west side of Broadway past Juilliard School of Music and Alice Tully Hall (Pietro Belluschi, with Eduardo Catalano and Westermann & Miller, 1968) on the site of the old Lincoln Arcade Building. Across Broadway, Richard Tucker Park, with its portrait bust of the beloved tenor by Milton Hebald, marks the crossing with fabled Columbus Avenue. This was the first section of the Upper West Side to be rejuvenated following the completion of

Lincoln Center. At West 65th Street, in no. 2 Lincoln Square/125 Columbus Avenue is the eastern headquarters of the Church of Jesus Christ of Latter-Day Saints (Mormons to you) with exhibits and tours. Cramming the block of Columbus from 66th to 67th are the gaggle of new buildings that make up the "corporate campus" of the Capital Cities/ ABC, Inc. broadcasting empire, topped by the rounded twenty-three-story twin facades of the 1988–89 block-through headquarters building (Kohn, Pedersen, Fox, architects).

13. No. 1965 Broadway, Empire Building (west side, West 65th to 66th streets). The ground floor houses the giant Tower Records store (curiously, one of only two record shops in this musical neighborhood). Upstairs is the Penthouse Organization, publishers of *Omni, Forum,* and the pioneering *Penthouse,* the nation's first girlie magazine to show models' pubic hair.

14. Until 1987 the Regency Theatre (1987 Broadway, above West 66th) was the last survivor of the great trio of West Side movie revival houses: Thalia, New Yorker, Regency.

15. The twenty-eight-story Copley (at the northeast corner of West 68th Street; Davis, Brody & Associates, architects, 1987) is one of the more opulent new apartment towers. The Food Emporium on the ground floor represents an important compromise between the developer and the community: the Copley itself replaces an old supermarket (housed in another one-time auto showroom) that was judged an important neighborhood amenity.

16. The Nevada Towers (west side, 69th to 70th; Philip Birnbaum, architect) is another early product of the New Gilded Age. The original builder was too early to catch the wave of eighties prosperity, and the building stood half-finished

throughout the recession years of the late seventies until a new owner could finance its completion in 1977. The little concrete triangle just to the north is officially Sherman Square, a skimpy memento of the general who ended his days a block east on West 71st Street; his real memorial is the St. Gaudens statue at Fifth Avenue and 59th Street.

17. Visible to the east from Broadway are the flamboyant Graeco-Egypto-Babylonian colossi and terra-cotta doodads of the Pythian Temple at 135 West 70th (Thomas Lamb, architect, 1911). Manhattan Community College took over the building in the sixties. When it was converted to condominiums in 1983, the reconfiguration of interior spaces was so complex that the conversion itself is considered an engineering marvel.

- - - - - - - - - -

Seventy-first Street and Broadway marks roughly the center of Harsenville (chap. 3). Harsen's Lane, that "lonely country way," wound eastward through what is now Central Park. The block-long bulk of 201 West 70th, with its Pathmark and McDonald's, covers the rise that once held Jacob Harsen's Dutch-style farmhouse "mansion."

18. The Dorilton, 171 West 71st (Janes & Leo, 1902). At the dawn of the century the *Architectural Record* deplored the Dorilton's "gross excess of scale" and its design in which "everything shrieks to drown out everything else." Today the shriek seems more of a murmur; it still shouts, "Look at me!" but the handsome iron gateway, abundant cartouches, and the remains of the copper-clad mansard roof seem relatively genteel, the overblown statuary endearingly naive.

19. At the southwest corner of West 72nd Street is the once-handsome 1892 building designed by Henry Kilburn for the prestigious Colonial Club, which, alas, folded in 1903. Converted in 1906

to the Lincoln Trust building, it's now overrun with a welter of typical West Side enterprises (Ecuadorian mission, detective agency, fruit market) and is a rumored target for demolition.

20. West 72nd Street was once a decorative boulevard and the main carriage route from Central Park to Riverside Drive (which is why it was still unpaved till after the turn of the century.) The 1904 IRT Subway Control House on its island at 72nd and Broadway–Amsterdam, with its buff-colored Roman brick and limestone quoins and stringcourses, is the last of its kind in Manhattan (others were at 103rd and 116th streets). The architects, Heins & LaFarge, also designed the playful Elephant House at the Bronx Zoo and the original portions of the Cathedral of St. John the Divine.

21. Above West 72nd Street, the junction with Amsterdam Avenue bounds Giuseppe Verdi Square (triangle, actually). Pasquale Civiletti's marble portrait was dedicated in 1906, five years after the composer's death. Characters from *Aida, Falstaff, Otello,* and *La Forza del Destino* surround the base. A flourishing OTB parlor nearby helps populate the spot with Runyonesque types. Needle Park (the only name the locals use) has been notorious since the 1960s as the major hub of the local drug traffic; the 1970 film *The Panic in Needle Park* was partly shot on location here. A designated scenic landmark.

22. Rutgers Church formerly occupied the southwest corner of Broadway and West 73rd; now, as with many similar sites, the church is down the street and a bank (Chase Manhattan, in this case) occupies the corner. A far better bank building is the Apple Bank (originally Central Savings Bank) on the east side of Broadway at West 73rd to 74th, a 1928 building by York & Sawyer, architects of the Federal Reserve Bank on Maiden Lane and of the north and south

wings of the New-York Historical Society (see Central Park West tour, no. 20). The elaborate decorative lanterns and grills are by the great Philadelphia ironsmith Samuel Yellin (it's even better inside).

23. The Ansonia (west side, West 73rd to 74th streets) looked even better before its thirty-foot-tall rooftop lanterns were removed in the early thirties, but what's left isn't half bad: massive leering satyrs' heads, scrolls, brackets, iron and masonry balconies in an ebullient jumble (see chap. 6, and visit the lobby for a well-labeled selection of period photos). (Graves & Duboy, 1904.)

24. The unimposing facade of the Beacon Theatre (2124 Broadway, above West 74th Street) belies the grandeur of the landmark interior: one of the last (1928) and most lavish of New York's movie palaces (Walter Ahlschlager, architect). Threatened with conversion to a disco, it has been the focus of neighborhood protests and (appropriately) fund-raising concerts.

25. The trio of copper cornices on the Astor Apartments (west side, West 75th to 76th streets) were one of Broadway's crowning glories. They were removed following passage of Local Law 10. The block-long building was erected by William Waldorf Astor, whose family began buying West Side land in 1860 and soon owned some ten million dollars' worth of property in the neighborhood. Other Astor blocks included Broadway, west side, West 76th to 77th and 78th to 79th streets and the full blocks on both sides of Broadway, West 90th to 91st and West 92nd to 93rd streets. This one is actually two buildings: the two shorter, southerly wings, by Clinton & Russell, opened in 1905, the year after the IRT subway, the third, by Peabody, Wilson & Brown, four years later.

26. The Promenade Theatre and Second

Stage Theatre (east side, above West 76th Street) occupy part of a thirty-story L-shaped condominium building with crenellated towers. Built as Manhattan Church Towers (Tillion & Tillion, 1928), it is one of several "church-hotels" erected in Manhattan in the twenties as churches sought ways to exploit their real estate holdings. Snuggled in at the corner, battleship-gray 2160 Broadway is an older commercial loft building (Townsend & Oppenheim, 1907) now used for studios, with dancers and calisthenes often visible through large windows.

27. The Belleclaire Hotel at the southwest corner of West 77th Street is the first New York City building (1903) by the young Emery Roth. Note especially the elegantly proportioned window mullions and carvings, frieze of intricately carved leaves above fourth-floor windows, and expressive faces beneath the rooftop chimneys. Even minus its original bulbous tower it's a striking and evocative presence, and one of New York City's best surviving Art Nouveau buildings.

28. The former Seventy-seventh Street Theatre (east side, north of West 77th Street) now houses a Crazy Eddie electronics outlet. (In between, like many Upper Broadway theaters, it became a supermarket.) Other buildings on this block make it a turn-of-the-century time capsule, with typical commercial buildings that predate the subway, opened in 1904. No. 2194 Broadway, at the southeast corner of West 78th (M. C. Merrit, 1901) is still in excellent shape.

- - - - - - - - - -

If you haven't yet done so, detour left to see some of West End Avenue's finest surviving mansion–row houses and the Collegiate Church (Riverside Drive tour, no. 7).

29. Still a coveted address, the full-block Apthorp Apartments on the west side of Broadway, West 78th to 79th streets

(Clinton & Russell, 1908), was W. W. Astor's most grandiose apartment house venture, with luxurious suites in every French, English, and American historical style. The name honors Willie's great-grandfather Charles Ward Apthorp(e), whose daughter and son-in-law, the John C. van den Heuvels, had their country seat (later Burnham's tavern) on this block in the early 1800s (chap. 3).

30. The First Baptist Church (at the northwest corner of West 79th Street, 1892) is by an imaginative but little-known architect, George Keisler, who seems to have been allergic to symmetry: no two elements in this intricate facade are in precise balance. The building was built by (and still belongs to) the first and oldest Baptist congregation in the United States, founded 1817.

- - - - - - - - - -

For all its unruliness, Broadway in the West 70s and 80s is softened and lightened by the planted mall and the sprinkling of venerable one- to three-story buildings. The street's zig-zag route is marked by tall buildings—the Ansonia at 73rd to 74th, the green-roofed Regent at 104th—that close off the vista and make this part of Broadway seem confined and companionable.

31. The Broadway Studio Building at 2237 Broadway (southwest corner of West 80th Street; William W. Howe, architect) has been a home to artists and teachers (Robert Henri and Frank A. Parsons, among others—see chap. 9) since it opened in 1906. The Robert Louis Stevenson School was here in the late forties; current occupants include artists Joyce Abrams, Paul Resicka, the Office for Metropolitan History, and, on the ground floor, one of the city's essential culinary establishments, H & H Bagels.

32. Broadway, east side, West 79th to 80th streets contains two of the low

"taxpayer" structures that once filled many blocks. Both are by the distinguished apartment-house architect George F. Pelham and date from 1906–7: the 79th Street building was originally the fashionable Oliver Olsen's furniture emporium. Now they house a typical gaggle of upper-Broadway ventures: Woolworth's; a rug merchant; cut-rate dress, shoe, and drug stores; "City Music Schools"; Congregation Morya; the Women's Body Awareness Center; West Side Dance Project; and a second-hand bookshop on the upper floor. Cheap, temporary structures, supposedly, but look closer: their materials and workmanship far exceed standards for today's *luxury* housing.

33. The ten-story apartment building at the northeast corner of West 80th Street was formerly the Hotel Varuna, where W. E. D. Stokes was assaulted in 1911 (see chap. 6). Designed by John H. Duncan, architect of Grant's Tomb, and opened in 1905.

34. Starting from a mid-block location above West 80th Street, Zabar's, that Matterhorn of delicatessens, now fills a half block of Broadway, starting with the mock-Tudor building at no. 2245 Broadway (northwest corner of West 80th Street). Upstairs was an eighty-five-room SRO hotel in the seventies, a haven for prostitutes and addicts and a home of sorts for elderly and disabled pensioners; now it's the Zabar's housewares department. ("Half-timbered" tenement renovations like this building were the rage in the late twenties; another good example is 2276 Broadway/230 West 82nd, one block uptown.)

35. One bookstore or another has flourished in the nicely proportioned three-story commercial building at the southwest corner of Broadway and West 81st Street since the 1960s; currently in residence: Shakespeare & Company Booksellers. (1905; designed by Charles

Volz for Morris K. Jesup, banker, philanthropist, and president of the American Museum of Natural History.)

36. The terra-cotta-trimmed 81st Street Theatre (at the southeast corner, Thomas Lamb, architect, 1913) was formerly part of the Keith-Orpheum vaudeville circuit, later housed second-run RKO pictures and a TV sitcom set in the neighborhood ("Love, Sidney," with West Sider Tony Randall). Its *real* glory: this is where "Sesame Street" originated. The remodeled front is now part of a subtly designed twenty-one-story luxury condominium tower, the Broadway, with duplex residences in a connected seven-story structure along West 81st Street. (Beyer Blinder Belle, architects, 1988.)

37. Another two-story taxpayer (west side, West 82nd to 83rd streets) dates from 1897–99 and includes the former theater (subsequently a Schrafft's restaurant and now a Red Apple supermarket) where the first color TV network broadcast—by Jackie Gleason—is said to have originated in 1953.

38. The Bromley, east side of Broadway, West 83rd to 84th streets (Philip Birnbaum & Associates, 1987). One of the most pretentious—and most successful—of the new Upper West Side luxury apartment buildings, with two-story-high atrium shops, pyramidal setbacks, and eight-foot-diameter porthole windows; the limestone base and "classically inspired" details were meant (said the developer) to "echo the distinguished apartment buildings of West End Avenue and Riverside Drive." One of the first large buildings to go up under the new Upper West Side zoning, its low bulk keeps it in scale with the neighborhood's older structures. A puzzle: why wasn't the facade of the Loew's 84th Street movie house, developed at the same time, integrated into the larger building's design?

39. Charivari store, originally West Side Republican Club House, 2307 Broadway (west side between West 83rd and 84th streets; J. A. Schweinfurth, architect, 1897) has an elegant American Georgian design in pink "wash brick" with a graceful second-story loggia and Indiana limestone trim.

40. Forget the street level, but the upper floors of the Broadway Fashion Building (at the southwest corner of West 84th Street, Sugarman & Berger, 1931) combine glazed terra-cotta, metal, and glass into what once was a sleek, *moderne* curtain wall.

41. Eagle Court, an early 1980s condo project, extends eastward from the northwest corner of West 84th Street, ingeniously recycling a variety of industrial buildings: the 1897 corner loft building (note the date in wrought iron); a onetime Borden Dairy (bearing the eponymous gilded eagle); and a former Con Edison substation (W. Weissberger, Jr., 1911).

42. Early in its career, the venerable Bretton Hall Hotel (east side of Broadway, West 85th to 86th streets) was a genteel showplace, with a palm court, soft music for afternoon tea, and elegant shops: a custom milliner, and couturiere Hattie Carnegie (Harry B. Mulliken, architect, 1903). Across Broadway is a smaller but similar establishment of the same vintage, the Euclid Hall Hotel (George Hill, architect, 1903).

43. Despite its bulk, the block-long Boulevard apartments, west side of Broadway, West 86th to 87th streets (Schuman, Lichtenstein, Claman & Efron, architects, with Alexander Cooper & Partners, 1988), sits lightly on its prominent site. Triple setbacks, rounded corner treatment, and bands of gray brick against salmon-red are, for a change, respectful of the location and the older buildings nearby. Like other buildings of recent vintage, it would have been improved by more carefully selected (read "costly") details, e.g., curved instead of flat bricks at the 86th Street corner.

44. Look westward to West 86th and West End Avenue for the Church of St. Paul and St. Andrew, with its red-tiled roof and open octagonal corner tower (R. H. Robertson, architect, 1897). The trustees of this landmarked structure are among the most devout enemies of the city's landmarking process: they not only sued to tear down their own building, but have spearheaded—with other clerical groups—a movement to invalidate the landmarking of any such church properties.

45. No. 257 West 86th Street is one of the Upper West Side's early studio apartment buildings, with double-height windows on the uptown side to catch the steady north light. (Pollard & Steinem, 1901)

46. The landmark Belnord Apartments, east side of Broadway, West 86th to 87th streets (H. Hobart Weekes, 1908) is a massive Renaissance Revival courtyard building, once purportedly the world's largest apartment house. Not as sumptuous as the Apthorp, with which it is often compared, but many special touches—e.g., the "eaves" over the fourth-floor windows and the double entrance arches facing 86th Street—help keep it in scale. Beyond the Belnord on Amsterdam Avenue, the Romanesque Revival West-Park Presbyterian Church (Henry F. Kilburn, 1890) is clad in a rich red "brownstone." The original chapel, now part of the church's West 86th Street facade, is the only surviving uptown work by Leopold Eidlitz.

47. The block-long Montana Apartments (east side of Broadway, West 87th to 88th streets; The Gruzen Partnership, 1984), deliberately evokes Central Park

West's twin-towered apartment skyscrapers of the 1920s. The architects intended the building to have a more sumptuous skin, but the uncertain economics of the early eighties dictated a relatively drab cladding of khaki-colored brick.

48. To the west on West 88th Street is the B'nai Jeshurun synagogue, fifth home of the oldest Conservative Jewish congregation (1825) in the United States. The massive Byzantine-Romanesque sandstone facade (Henry B. Herts & Walter Schneider, architects, 1918) has been called "the greatest extant architectural example of Semitic art"; it would probably look more at home in the Sinai Desert than on a crowded city street. The mile of Broadway from the upper 80s north, formerly a district of SROs, head shops, and more dubious enterprises, has gotten a partial face-lift in the 1980s: the "new" Broadway is (or tries to be) an avenue of glossy homes and pricey shops—safer, more predictable, and ordered, but relatively short on chaos and color. Prime contributors to the change:

49. At the southwest corner of West 89th Street, the seventeen-story, red brick and limestone-trimmed Savannah apartment house (Schuman, Lichtenstein, Claman & Efron, architects) has been praised by critic Paul Goldberger for its "urban responsibility and civilized good sense." It occupies the site of the legendary New Yorker revival movie house. The double-height windows here do not proclaim painters' studios, but the duplex apartments beloved of 1980s co-op buyers.

50. At the southwest corner of West 90th Street, the New West (Philip Birnbaum & Associates, 1988) is another new arrival, this time with stacked balconies and pale trim setting off salmon-colored brick.

51. The block-long, thirteen-story Astor Court apartments, east side of Broadway, West 89th to 90th streets, was another elegant courtyard apartment building developed by William W. Astor (Charles A. Platt, architect, 1915), originally with tennis courts on the land adjacent to the east. The topmost floor is a little hard to make out from the street; the tiny windows indicate their original use as servants' rooms.

52. Early in the century the Clark estate planned a greenhouse for the northwest corner of Broadway and West 90th Street. (The entire block to the south was then a garden.) Instead, the Cornwall apartments blossomed on the site in 1910 (Neville & Bagge, architects) with its unique vertical cornice of pierced "brocade" polychrome terra-cotta.

53. The Off-Track Betting parlor, west side of Broadway about ten paces above West 91st Street, occupies a tiny rhomboidal, not rectangular, plot—a short segment of what once was Apthorpe Lane (chap. 1). The bounds of that ancient byway have also shaped the floor plans of several buildings west of Broadway: 75 West 92nd; 639, 640, 645, and 646 West End Avenue; and 190 and 194 Riverside Drive.

54. The fourteen-story Greystone, at the southeast corner of West 91st Street, dates from 1924, a typical second-rank, "second-growth" upper Broadway apartment hotel. (Schwartz & Gross, architects.)

55. Evangelical Lutheran Church of the Advent, at the northeast corner of West 93rd Street recently got a thorough scrubbing that lets its unpretentious facade shine: limestone trim setting off the walls of Flemish-bond red and black brick. (William A. Potter, 1902.)

56. At West 94th to 95th streets, west side, the celebrated Symphony Space occupies a drab yellow two-story building with a red-lettered marquee. Erected as a market by W. W. Astor in 1915, the building served as an indoor ice skating rink (Thomas Healy's Crystal Carnival) and a movie house with a downstairs restaurant (the Sunken Gardens, later a long-running neighborhood institution, the Thalia revival house) before Allan Miller and Isaiah Sheffer turned it into "a cultural 'town square' for the neighborhood" (see chap. 13).

As of mid-1988 the only other surviving business on the block was At Our Place, a Mid-Eastern restaurant at 2527 Broadway with a facade by Gamal el Zoghby. The original name, Cleopatra, had to be altered when the restaurant changed hands. The new owner, having just paid for an expensive sign, recycled as many letters as possible: only the "U" is new.

57. Pomander Walk, a unique enclave of twenty-four two-story cottages, nestled about a private walk between West 94th and 95th streets east of West End Avenue (King & Campbell, 1923). Restaurateur-developer Tom Healy (see above and interlude following chap. 7) fell in love with the stage set of the English play *Pomander Walk* and replicated it here in 1922; residents have included critic Ward Morehouse and actors Barnard Hughes, Frances Sternhagen, Gloria Swanson, Victor McLaglen, Madeleine Carroll, Rosalind Russell, the Gish sisters, and Humphrey Bogart.

58. The seven-story apartment house at 251 West 95th (northwest corner) was one of several Upper West Side residences of Damon Runyon, the Bard of Broadway. It overlooked the corner of 96th and Broadway, where some of his favorite hoodlums hung out (chap. 11), and so far it hasn't changed all that much, though it probably will soon. In the 1940s Edward Mueller, the coun-

terfeiter known to the Secret Service as Mr. 880, lived on the top floor of 204 West 96th, near the southwest corner of Amsterdam Avenue.

59. Another typical new apartment building, this one a cut above most, is the Princeton, at the northeast corner of West 95th Street (Schuman, Lichtenstein, Claman & Efron, 1987).

60. The block on the west side of Broadway, West 96th to 97th streets, has a colorful history. The Riverside Theatre, the first U.S. movie palace, went up in 1915, and a few years later *four* theaters filled the block. By the 1970s they had degenerated into porn houses and were demolished after doomed efforts to make them a community arts center (as the Symphony Space later became). Community groups took over the empty blockfront in the seventies as a flower and vegetable garden, until construction of the thirty-five-story, orange-brick apartment tower, the Columbia, in a style a neighbor calls "industrial Bauhaus modern." (Liebman Williams & Ellis, architects, 1983.)

61. Visible at the northwest corner of West 96th Street and Amsterdam Avenue is the tall copper-clad steeple of the Holy Name of Jesus Church, a barnlike structure in German Gothic style with a magnificent beamed interior. (T. H. Poole, architect, 1891.)

62. The curious copper-roofed, one-story building occupying Broadway's central mall above 96th Street is a former public toilet. Abandoned since the 1960s, in 1986 it was turned over to the Westside Arts Coalition, an umbrella group for about three hundred artists, dancers, and theater people and thirty arts organizations. The Coalition runs it as the Broadway Mall Center, with exhibits and information for the public on weekends and Wednesday evenings.

63. Look eastward along West 99th Street.

The pyramidal green-copper roof on the 180-foot bell tower at the corner of Amsterdam Avenue and West 99th Street belongs to St. Michael's Church (Protestant Episcopal), the Upper West Side's oldest surviving institution (founded 1815). The present church building (Robert W. Gibson, 1891) is the third on the site; the rectory building occupies the bed of the old Bloomingdale Road.

64. The Metro Cinema, formerly the Midtown Theatre, at 2626 Broadway between West 99th and West 100th streets, was designed by Boak & Paris in 1933 as a twin to the (now-demolished) New Yorker at 88th to 89th and Broadway. Identical facades featured terra-cotta medallions with figures representing the performing arts.

65. The Riverview (later the Keystone) Theatre occupied the long, narrow building at 2633 Broadway in the post–World War I era. Before its conversion to a Red Apple supermarket it was a popular dance hall.

66. The Whitehall Hotel (250 West 100th Street, southwest corner; Charles Meyers, architect) replaced the elegant little Carlton Terrace restaurant in 1923. Two years later, when he found his family's nearby apartment too noisy for work, George Gershwin took a room in the Whitehall to finish his *Concerto in F*.

67. The three-story wood building at 2641 Broadway (northwest corner, West 100th Street) is a unique survivor, built in 1871 by Henry Grimm, who rented out the upstairs and ran a tavern on the ground floor. Note the Italianate bracketed cornice, diamond-patterned fascia, and round-headed windows, woodwork equivalents of brownstone-era masonry. Grimm kept the place only five years, but the saloon, with old fashioned swinging doors in front and a genteel "family entrance" at the rear, survived till Prohibition. (Another wood building, its clapboards now covered with metal siding, also survives at 248 West 106th.)

68. Hungarian-born architect Emery Roth designed the gray fifteen-story building at 210 West 101st (southeast corner of West 101st and Broadway; 1927) and occupied its penthouse in the early 1930s.

69. Nos. 2660–66 Broadway (215–17 West 101st). An overlooked masterpiece, with rich limestone and terra-cotta trim, *two* ornate cartouches stacked over the entrance with its dark, polished granite columns, and twisted colonnettes on the upper windows.

70. At 103rd Street, Broadway veers slightly to the left, at the point where a steep-banked stream once led down to Striker's Bay. Commanding this curve today is the seventeen-story Regent Hotel, 2720 Broadway (northeast corner of West 104th Street), with its green two-story mansard roof (originally copper, now painted) visible from as far downtown as 76th Street. (Novelist Herman Wouk once lived here.) The three-story building at the southeast corner of West 103rd Street, with an Art Deco frieze above the third story, was formerly home to the Equity Library Theatre. The green-painted row house west of Broadway at 245 West 103rd was Humphrey Bogart's boyhood home.

71. The Marseilles Apartments at the southwest corner of West 103rd Street, with its massive mansard roof and rehabilitated Beaux Arts masonry (H. A. Jacobs, 1902) was a crime-ridden welfare hotel in 1978. It has since made a comeback as a decent renovated building with 134 units for the indigent elderly, a social room, and a resident social worker, sponsored by the West Side Federation for Senior Housing. On the ground floor at 2693 Broadway is the One Stop Senior Services Center, where member organizations include the Japanese Association for Help to the Aging

Inc., the Manhattan Valley Golden Age Senior Center, the West Side Inter-Agency Council for the Aged, Holy Name R.C. Church, West Side Jewish Community Council, and Phelps House, among others.

72. The recently renovated Columbia Cinema, 2706 Broadway (between West 103rd and 104th streets) originally opened in 1913 as the Essex; later, as the Nuevo Edison, it was the only theater in New York showing historic Spanish films of the thirties and forties.

73. The Clebourne apartments, 924 West End Avenue, fills the short block of West 105th Street (north side) at Broadway to West End Avenue. Notable features include the recently restored marble lobby and brick-paved, arched porte cochere entrance. (Schwartz & Gross, architects, 1911.)

74. Jazz composer-bandleader Edward Kennedy (Duke) Ellington had a mansion at 333 Riverside Drive around the corner from West 106th Street, in an area long popular with jazz musicians. Ellington's state funeral was at St. John the Divine in 1974; three years later West 106th Street was rechristened in his honor: Duke Ellington Boulevard.

75. Straus Park, Broadway and West End Avenue, West 106th to 107th streets, was briefly known as Bloomingdale Square, but renamed for Ida and Isidor Straus of West 105th Street after the *Titanic* disaster claimed them (see chap. 5). The memorial fountain is by Evarts Tracy, architect (1914), with sculpture by a neighbor, H. Augustus Lukeman. Inscription is from 2 Sam. 1:23: "Lovely and pleasant were they in their lives and in their death they were not divided."

North of 107th Street Broadway, tamed at last, surrenders to the Manhattan grid and follows the northward route of Eleventh (West End) Avenue. The district from here north to around 123rd Street was known as Asylum Hill in the 1840s, when the Bloomingdale Lunatic Asylum was new. Now it is Morningside Heights, a felicitous name coined by Frederick Law Olmsted, architect of the verdant park (Morningside Park) that cloaks the Heights' steep eastern escarpment.

76. Proposed West 108th Street Historic District (see Riverside Drive tour, no. 34).

78. The Manhasset (Janes & Leo, architects, 1904) fills the west side of Broadway at West 108th to 109th streets with two back-to-back apartment buildings, which at first glance seem to form a mirror image. Look closer. An elegantly proportioned two-story mansard roof with corner volutes tops off and controls a lively, asymmetrical profusion of cornices, stone and wrought-iron balconies, windows, and broken and triangular pediments.

79. The La Ronda bar and a variety of humble enterprises occupy a one-story taxpayer at the southeast corner of West 109th; this one was built for John Jacob Astor IV in 1908, and retains its original cornice on the north wall (C. H. Cullen, architect).

80. The fate of old West Side theaters is to become supermarkets; the D'Agostino's store at the southeast corner of West 110th Street occupies the premises of what was once the Nemo movie house.

81. At the northeast corner of West 110th Street (Cathedral Parkway) is another two-story taxpayer building (Walker & Hazzard, circa 1909) in vaguely Spanish style with green, orange, and white terra-cotta decorations. The Chemical Bank branch next door at 543 Cathedral Parkway was mentioned in chapter 11 in connection with bank robber Willie Sutton.

82. The College Residence Hotel at 601 Cathedral Parkway (northwest corner) was formerly the Hendrick Hudson Annex, designed by the same architect (William Lawrence Rouse) and completed in 1908 (see tour 1, no. 35).

83. Between West 111th and 112th streets, on the west side of Broadway, note the sharply angled walls of 2867–69–71 Broadway, marking part of the southern boundary of James De Peyster's colonial era estate.

84. No. 542 West 112th (southeast corner of West 112th Street) is a red brick building with an ornate, two-story limestone base and an imposing entrance arch. (Neville & Bagge, architects, 1908.)

85. The private, seventy-three-year-old Bank Street College of Education, now in sleek brick and glass quarters at 610 West 112th (west of Broadway; Harry Weese & Associates, architects, 1970) is nationally recognized as a leader in early childhood education.

86. Conspicuous to the east on West 112th Street is the elaborately ornamented portico and immense rose window of the Cathedral Church of St. John the Divine, known to generations on Morningside Heights as St. John the Unfinished. A program is now under way to complete the west towers, transepts, choir roof, and great central crossing, using traditional methods and materials. A master stonemason was brought from England to train a corps of local, mainly minority youths, who have been laboring since 1980 in a stoneyard off Amsterdam Avenue. Optimists hope to see the work done by the Cathedral's hundredth birthday: St. John's Day (Dec. 17) 1992.

87. The twelve-story building at the northwest corner of West 113th Street is one of many in the area by the brothers George & Edward Blum (1912). Part of the ground floor is occupied by the West End Café at 2911 Broadway, famous as a hangout for Allen Ginsberg, Jack Kerouac, and other Beat writers of the forties and fifties and for local political types in the sixties. Now dispenses fine jazz.

88. Between nos. 600 and 604 West 114th Street, a massive rock outcrop occupies what would have been no. 602 West 114th—a unique geological relic, and a reminder of what early builders contended with.

89. The Broadway Presbyterian Church (northwest corner of West 114th) moved to this location in 1912 after sojourns on Bleecker Street and Fourth Avenue. (Louis E. Jallade, architect, 1912.)

90. Columbia University occupies the old Bloomingdale Asylum site from Broadway east to Amsterdam, 114th to 120th streets, as well as many nearby properties. Robert F. McKim of McKim, Mead & White was mainly responsible for the original (upper) campus, north of 116th Street, with its Italian Renaissance classroom buildings grouped around paved and planted courts and centered on the monumental, domed Low Memorial Library. Prominent among many other features: Daniel Chester French's bronze statue of *Alma Mater*, centered before Low Library (notice the owl of wisdom concealed in her robe); colonnaded Butler Library at the campus's south end (James G. Rogers, 1934); St. Paul's Chapel at Amsterdam and 117th, with its richly polychrome Guastavino vaulting (Howells & Stokes, 1907). The red-brick building between Low Library and St. Paul's, now the Temple Hoyne Buell Architectural Center, is a survivor from the asylum era, when it was called Macy Villa. Campus tours start daily from Dodge Hall, room 201 (information: 280–2845).

91. The three massive eleven- and twelve-

story buildings at 2931–39, 2941–47, and 2949–59 Broadway (West 115th to 116th streets) all date from 1910–12 and were designed by the reclusive architect Gaetan Ajello. (Other Ajello buildings nearby include nos. 25, 29, and 35 Claremont Avenue, 420 and 452 Riverside Drive.) The freshly patched walls on the upper floors of his Regnor Court, 601 West 115th (northwest corner of Broadway) have a rather grisly significance. The evening of May 16, 1979, a chunk of masonry from a seventh-floor window fell and killed Grace Gold, a Barnard freshman. The immediate result (besides a ten-million-dollar lawsuit against the owner, Columbia University) was Local Law 10, requiring immediate inspection of all building facades. Fearful of similar suits, many other owners hastily amputated acres of cornices, balconies, gargoyles, scrolls, and brackets, a collective act of vandalism that left many fine old buildings bandaged in concrete and tin—and often *less* trustworthy than before.

92. From 116th to 120th, Broadway is a placid (sterile?) passage between imposing institutional buildings. The copper-domed building at 117th Street is Earl Hall, which houses several of Columbia's religious counseling and social outreach groups; just beyond it, a bronze plaque set into the corner of the Mathematics Building commemorates the Battle of Harlem Heights (chap. 2). Across Broadway is Barnard College, originally Columbia's undergraduate women's division. Its earliest buildings, by Lamb & Rich, mirrored the McKim, Mead & White work nearby; later additions by Vincent Kling & Associates and others gives the campus a sleeker, corporate look. Other world-famous (and some architecturally striking) institutions nearby include the Manhattan School of Music, originally the Juilliard School, Claremont at West 122nd Street, east side (Donn Barber, with additions by Shreve, Lamb & Harmon; 1910) and

the Jewish Theological Seminary, Broadway at West 122nd to 123rd streets, east side (Gehron, Ross, Alley, with David Levy, 1930).

93. From 120th Street the view to the northwest is dominated by two Gothic turrets: the nearer is Union Theological Seminary (Allen & Collins, 1910); the further, taller one is the spire of Riverside Church (tour 1, no. 41). Teachers College, a division of Columbia, fills the entire block from 120th to 121st streets, Broadway to Amsterdam. The early buildings are warmly clad in red brick and brownstone. At the northeast corner of Broadway, Horace Mann Hall, with its frieze of eminent names (Columbus, Washington, etc.) was originally the Horace Mann School (Howells & Stokes and Edgar H. Josselyn, 1901); halfway up the block is Gothic-arched Main Hall, T.C.'s original building and the oldest academic edifice on the Heights (1892; William A. Potter, architect).

94. You could follow The Greatest Street In The World as far as Albany, but stop instead at Pupin Hall, Columbia's original physics building (1925), east of Broadway on 120th. Lots of history here. This land was the buckwheat field where Continental and British troops traded shots in 1776. Pupin Hall itself—named for Michael Idvorsky Pupin, the Croatian-born physicist who wrote *Romance of the Machine*—is where the nuclear age started on January 25, 1938 (Carl Sandburg called it "a sad day for our earth"), when scientists first split uranium in the basement cyclotron. The Manhattan Project, which created the first A-bomb, also started here. On Pupin's roof behind the copper gargoyles is nestled the dome of a tiny astronomical observatory: there, in the late 1970s and early 1980s, astronomer Patrick Thaddeus and his team swept the Milky Way with a four-foot radio telescope. They discovered immense clouds of exotic chemicals in interstellar space, hundreds

of millions of light years across, the
most massive objects in our galaxy—
and incidentally changed our view of
the universe.

Come to think of it, that should be
enough exploration for anybody.

ACKNOWLEDGMENTS AND BIBLIOGRAPHY

New York history, happily, is a shared addiction. This book would have been very different (shorter, probably) if not for many hours arguing and swapping yarns with (and picking the brains of) fellow enthusiasts Marvin Gelfand, Val Ginter, Sidney Horenstein, Barry Lewis, Joyce Mendelsohn, John Tauranac, Dick Shepard, Gerard Wolfe, Joe Zito, and especially three former Upper West Siders who seem to have encyclopedias in their heads: architect-historian Andrew Alpern; architectural historian Christopher Gray of the Office for Metropolitan History; and theater historian Miles Kreuger.

I am also deeply grateful—

To Guy Bolton, Irving Caesar, Edward Downes, Herb Grossinger, Ruth Hurwitz, Antoinette Kraushaar, Emma DeLong Mills, Lewis Mumford, Raphael Soyer, W. E. D. Stokes, Jr., Arnold Vollmer, and Helen Worden for helpful interviews.

To the unfailingly helpful professional staffs at the Museum of the City of New York; the New-York Historical Society; the New York Public Library (particularly the Local History and Genealogy Division, at 42nd Street, and the Performing Arts Research Center at Lincoln Center); and especially the New York Society Library.

And to Esther Brumberg, a dear friend of this book and its author—and the best damn photo-researcher in the business.

The following bibliography lists the chief printed sources for this book, but several authors deserve special mention. Bruce Bliven, Jr.'s lively little volume *Battle for Manhattan* provided many details and two-thirds of the title for chapter 2. The discussion of pre-1880 West Side life owes much to Hopper Striker Mott for both his manuscripts, now in the New-York Historical Society, and his elegiac 1908 history of the Bloomingdale Reformed Church, a loving tribute from a son of Bloomingdale to his vanished boyhood home. Lloyd Morris's *Incredible New York* provided sidelights on many aspects of nineteenth-century social life. My discussion of row-house architecture is indebted to Sarah Bradford Landau, who surveyed the subject admirably in an article in the *Journal of the Society of Architectural Historians*; and the Central Park West tour owes a similar debt to Alexandra Cushing Howard's 1975 inventory for the New York State Division for Historic Preservation. Howard Taubman's *Maestro* yielded irresistible anecdotes on Toscanini, as did Richard Rodgers's *Musical Stages* for himself, Larry Hart, and Oscar Hammerstein II; W. A. Swanberg's *Citizen Hearst* and *Dreiser* for their respective subjects; Maurice Zolotow's *Stage Struck* for the Lunts; Jablonski and Stewart's *The Gershwin Years* for George, Ira, and their associates; Alfred Kazin's *New York Jew* and

Susan Edmiston and Linda Cirino's *Literary New York* for a variety of Upper West Side writers; and Charles Higham's *Ziegfeld* and Billie Burke's autobiography, *With a Feather on My Nose*, for information (if that's what it is) on the Great Glorifier. Articles by the *New Yorker*'s St. Clair McKelway led me to the irrepressible Stephen Weinberg and Mr. 880; J. Bryan III provided the tale of Robert Benchley and Ulysses Grant. Apologies in advance to anyone inadvertently omitted.

Anyone delving into the city's long and complex past is soon grateful to I. N. P. Stokes, architect, nephew of the Ansonia's builder, and compiler of the monumental, indispensible *Iconography of Manhattan Island*, published in six oversize volumes in 1915–28. Having already taken so much from so many, I will compound the felony by appropriating something Stokes later wrote about his masterwork, since it applies pretty well to this book too: "It was a labor of love, and brought me a good deal of pleasure, and some satisfaction, although I now realize that it involved an expenditure of time, energy, and money, which was probably out of proportion to the results achieved, and consumed many hours which should have been devoted, not only to my office, but to my family, and to social amenities, so that, on the whole, I suspect that it has proved a rather selfish, perhaps even a narrowing, influence in my life."

Amen!

Alpern, Andrew. *Apartments for the Affluent*. New York: McGraw-Hill, 1975.

Alpern, Andrew, and Seymour Durst. *Holdouts!* New York: McGraw-Hill, 1984.

Asser, Solomon, and Hilary Roe. "The Development of the Upper West Side to 1925, Thomas Healy and Pomander Walk." Masters Thesis, Columbia University Graduate School of Architecture and Planning, 1981.

Atkinson, Brooks. *Broadway*. New York: Macmillan, 1970.

Barrows, Sydney, with William Novak. *Mayflower Madam: The Secret Life of Sydney Biddle Barrows*. New York: Arbor House, 1986.

Bennett, Joan, and Lois Kibbee. *The Bennett Playbill*. New York: Holt Rinehart and Winston, 1970.

Bertensson, Sergei, and Jay Leyda, with the assistance of Sophia Satina. *Sergei Rachmaninoff: A Life in Music*. New York: New York University Press, 1956.

Birmingham, Stephen. *Life at the Dakota*. New York: Random House, 1979.

Bliven, Bruce, Jr. *Battle for Manhattan*. New York: Henry Holt & Company, 1956.

Brandon, Ruth. *A Capitalist Romance: Singer and the Sewing Machine*. Philadelphia and New York: Lippincott, 1977.

Bryan, J., III. *Merry Gentleman (and One Lady)*. New York: Atheneum, 1985.

Buek, Charles & Co. *Semi-annual list of Choice New Dwellings Constructed and for Sale by Charles Buek & Co., architects, successors to Duggin & Crossman*. New York, 1887.

Burke, Billie, with Cameron Shipp. *With A Feather on My Nose*. New York: Appleton-Century-Crofts, 1948.

Burns, William J. *The Eagle's Eye*. New York: George H. Doran & Co., 1913.

Cavett, Dick, and Christopher Porterfield. *Cavett*. New York: Harcourt Brace Jovanovich, 1974.

Chapman, John Jay. *John Jay Chapman and his Letters*. Boston: Houghton Mifflin, 1937.

Chappell, G. S. *Restaurants of New York*. New York: Greenburg, Inc., 1925.

Churchill, Allen. *The Great White Way: A Recreation of Broadway's Golden Era of Theatrical Entertainment*. New York: E.P. Dutton & Co., 1962.

Collins, Frederick L. *Homicide Squad: Adventures of a Headquarters Old Timer*. New York: G.P. Putnam's Sons, 1944.

Considine, Bob. *The Remarkable Life of Dr. Armand Hammer*. New York: Harper & Row, 1975.

Cook, Clarence C. *A Description of the New York Central Park*. New York: F.J. Huntington and Co., 1869.

Coward, Noel. *Present Indicative*. Garden City, New York: Doubleday, Doran and Company, 1937.

Danckaerts, Jasper. *Journal of Jasper Danckaerts, 1679–1680*. New York: Charles Scribner's Sons, 1913.

Dau's New York Blue Book. New York: Dau's Publishing Company, 1893–1937.

Dayton, Abram C. *Last Days of Knickerbocker Life in New York*. New York: G.P. Putnam's Sons, 1897.

Dimmick, Ruth Crosby. *Our Theatres To-day and Yesterday*. New York: H.K. Fly Company, 1913.

Dunlap, William. *Diary of William Dunlap (1766–1839): The Memoirs of a Dramatist, Theatrical Manager, Painter, Critic, Novelist, and Historian*. New York: New-York Historical Society, 1929.

Edmiston, Susan, and Linda D. Cirino. *Literary New York: A History and Guide*. Boston: Houghton Mifflin, 1976.

Ellis, Edward Robb. *The Epic of New York City*. New York: Coward-McCann, 1966.

Ernst, Jimmy. *A Not-So-Still Life*. New York: St. Martin's/Marek, 1984.

Erskine, John. *The Memory of Certain Persons*. Philadelphia: J.B. Lippincott & Co., 1947.

Freeman, Don. *Come One, Come All!*. New York: Rinehart & Company, 1949.

Gilbreth, Frank B., Jr. *Time Out for Happiness*. New York: Thomas Y. Crowell Company, 1970.

Glazer, Nathan, and Daniel Patrick Moynihan. *Beyond the Melting Pot: The Negroes, Puerto Ricans, Jews, Italians, and Irish of New York City*. Cambridge: MIT Press, 1963.

Goldberger, Paul. *The City Observed: New York. A Guide to the Architecture of Manhattan*. New York: Random House, 1979.

Goldstone, Harmon H., and Martha Dalrymple. *History Preserved: A Guide to New York City Landmarks and Historic Districts*. New York: Simon & Schuster, 1974.

Green, Benny. *P.G. Wodehouse: A Literary Biography*. New York: Rutledge Press, 1981.

Harris, M. A. "Spike." *A Negro History Tour of Manhattan*. New York: Greenwood Publishing Corporation, 1968.

Heinl, Robert D. "The Woman Who Stopped Noises." *Ladies' Home Journal*, April 1908.

Hellman, Lillian. *An Unfinished Woman*. Boston: Little, Brown & Co., 1969.

Henderson, Mary C. *The City and the Theatre: The History of New York Playhouses—A 235-year Journey from Bowling Green to Times Square*. Clifton, N.J.: James T. White & Co., 1973.

Hershkowitz, Leo, and Isidore S. Meyer, eds. *Letters of the Franks Family*. Studies in American Jewish History, no. 5. Waltham, Mass.: American Jewish Historical Society, 1968.

Higham, Charles. *Ziegfeld*. Chicago: Henry Regnery Co., 1972.

Hill, C. T. "The Growth of the Upper West Side in New York." *Harper's Weekly*, 25 July 1896, 730–34.

Hovey, Richard B. *John Jay Chapman: An American Mind*. New York: Columbia University Press, 1959.

Howard, Alexandra Cushing. *Central Park West Building-Structure Inventory*. Albany: New York State Parks and Recreation Department, Division for Historic Preservation, 1975.

Hyams, Joe. *Bogie: The Biography of Humphrey Bogart*. New York: New American Library, 1966.

Jablonski, Edward, and Lawrence D. Stewart. *The Gershwin Years*, 2d ed. Garden City, N.Y.: Doubleday, 1973.

Jenkins, Stephen. *The Greatest Street in the World*. New York: G.P. Putnam's Sons, 1911.

Johnson, James Weldon. *Black Manhattan*. New York: Arno Press, 1968.

Josephy, Helen, and Mary Margaret McBride. *New York Is Everybody's Town*. New York: G.P. Putnam's Sons, 1931.

Kazin, Alfred. *New York Jew*. New York: Alfred A. Knopf, 1978.

Kerfoot, F. B. *Broadway*. New York: Houghton Mifflin Co., 1911.

Kouwenhoven, John A. *The Columbia Historical Portrait of New York: An Essay in Graphic History*. New York: Doubleday, 1953.

Kreuger, Miles. *Show Boat, The Story of a Classic American Musical*. New York: Oxford, 1977.

Lamb, Mrs. Martha J. *History of the City of New York: Its Origin, Rise, and Progress*. New York and Chicago: A.S. Barnes & Co., 1877.

Lamb, Martha J. "Riverside Drive." *The Manhattan* 4, no. 1 (1884): 52.

Landau, Sarah Bradford. "The Row Houses of New York's West Side." *Journal of the Society of Architectural Historians* 34 (March 1975): 19.

Laurie, Joe, Jr. *Vaudeville: The Honky-Tonks to the Palace*. New York: Henry Holt & Co., 1953.

Liebling, A. J. *Back Where I Came From*. New York: Sheridan House, 1938.

Lockwood, Charles. *Bricks and Brownstone*. New York: McGraw-Hill, 1972.

Lockwood, Charles. *Manhattan Moves Uptown: An Illustrated History*. New York: Houghton Mifflin Co., 1976.

Lyford, Joseph P. *The Airtight Cage: A Study of New York's West Side*. New York: Harper & Row, 1966.

McCabe, James D. *New York by Sunlight and Gaslight*. Philadelphia: Douglass Brothers, 1883.

McClave, John. *Communication from John McClave to the West Side Association, at the Request of Property Owners*. New York, 1871.

McIntyre, Oscar Odd. *White Light Nights*. New York: Cosmopolitan Book Corporation, 1925.

McKelway, St. Clair. *The Big Little Man From Brooklyn*. Boston: Houghton Mifflin Company, 1969.

McKelway, St. Clair. *True Tales from the Annals of Crime and Rascality*. New York: Random House, 1951.

Mannes, Marya. *The New York I Know*. New York: J.B. Lippincott, 1961.

Marks, Edward B., as told to A. J. Liebling. *They All Sang: From Tony Pastor to Rudy Vallee*. New York: Viking Press, 1935.

Morell, Parker. *Diamond Jim*. New York: Garden City Publishing Company, 1934.

Morell, Parker. *Lillian Russell: The Era of Plush*. New York: Random House, 1940.

Morris, Lloyd. *Curtain Time: The Story of the American Theatre*. New

York: Random House, 1953.

Morris, Lloyd. *Incredible New York: High Life and Low Life of the Last Hundred Years*. New York: Random House, 1951.

Morton, Frederic. "Bohemia, Such As It Is, On the West Side." *New York Times Magazine*, May 9, 1971.

Mott, Hopper Striker. *Bloomingdale: The New York of Yesterday*. New York: G.P. Putnam's Sons, 1908.

Mumford, Lewis. *The Brown Decades*. New York: Harcourt, Brace and Company, 1931.

Mumford, Lewis. *Sketches from Life*. New York: Dial Press, 1982.

New York Fall Renting Guide to High Class Apartments. New York: The Star Company, 1909–11.

New York City. *Minutes of the Common Council, 1675–1776*. 8 vols. New York: Dodd, Mead and Company, 1905.

Osofsky, Gilbert. *Harlem: The Making of a Ghetto*. New York: Harper & Row, 1966.

Peters, William. *Annals of St. Peters*. New York: G.P. Putnam's Sons/ Knickerbocker Press, 1908.

Phillips' Elite Directory of Private Families and Ladies' Visiting and Shopping Guide for New York City. New York: W. Phillips & Co., 1880–1903.

Pintard, John. *Letters from John Pintard to his Daughter, Eliza Noel Pintard Davidson, 1816–1833*. 4 vols. New York: New-York Historical Society, 1937–40.

Porter, Luther H. *Cycling for Health and Pleasure*. New York: Dodd, Mead, 1895.

Proceedings of Meetings of the Property Holders of the West Side District of New York. Held at the Museum Building, Manhattan Square, October 3 and November 26, 1878. New York: P.F. McBreen, Printer, 1878.

Real Estate Record Association. *A History of Real Estate, Building, and Architecture in New York City during the Last Quarter of a Century*. New York: Record and Guide, 1898.

Real Estate Record and Builders' Guide. *A History of Real Estate, Building, and Architecture in New York City*. New York: Clinton W. Sweet, 1894.

Records of New Amsterdam, from 1653 to 1674 Anno Domini. Edited by Berthold Fernow. New York: The Knickerbocker Press, 1897.

Reeves, William Fullerton. *The First Elevated Railroads in Manhattan and the Bronx of the City of New York*. New York: New-York Historical Society, 1936.

Rice, Julia Hyneman. "Our Barbarous Fourth." 1908.

Rideing, William H. "Croton Water." *Scribner's Monthly* 14, no. 2 (June 1877): 161–76.

Riker, James. *Revised History of Harlem (City of New York), Its Origin and Early Annals, Prefaced by Home Scenes in the Fatherlands; Or, Notices of Its Founders Before Emigration. Also, Sketches of Numerous Families and the Recovered History of the Land-Titles*. New York: Harlem Publishing Company, 1904.

Robinson, W. G. "New York's Open Air Restaurants." *Town and Country*, September 8, 1906.

Rodgers, Richard. *Musical Stages: An Autobiography*. New York: Random House, 1975.

Sabine, Lorenzo. *Biographical Sketches of Loyalists of the American Revolution*. Boston: Little, Brown, 1864.

Schell, Jonathan. *The Fate of the Earth*. New York: Knopf, 1982.

Schuyler, Montgomery. "The Romanesque Revival in New York." *Architectural Record* 1, no. 1 (September 1891): 7–38.

Sims, Dorothy Rice. *Curiouser and Curiouser: A Book in the Jugular*

Vein. New York: Simon & Schuster, 1940.

Sloan, John. *John Sloan's New York Scene.* Edited by Bruce St. John. New York: Harper & Row, 1965.

Smith, William. *Historical Memoirs of William Smith from 16 March 1763 to 9 July 1776 (William Sabine, ed.).* New York: New York Public Library, 1956.

Stokes, I. N. P. *The Iconography of Manhattan Island.* New York: R. H. Dodd, 1915–28.

Stokes, I. N. P. *Random Recollections of a Happy Life.* Typescript, 1941. New York Public Library Manuscript Collection, New York, New York.

Swanberg, W. A. *Citizen Hearst: A Biography of William Randolph Hearst.* New York: Charles Scribner's Sons, 1961.

Swanberg, W. A. *Dreiser.* New York: Charles A. Scribner's Sons, 1965.

Taubman, Howard. *Maestro: The Life of Arturo Toscanini.* New York: Simon & Schuster, 1951.

Tauranac, John. *Essential New York.* New York: Holt, Rinehart & Winston, 1979.

Tauranac, John, and Christopher Little. *Elegant New York.* New York: Abbeville Press, 1985.

Thompson, Craig, and Allen Raymond. *Gang Rule in New York.* New York: Dial Press, 1940.

Towne, Charles Hanson. *This New York of Mine.* New York: Cosmopolitan Book Corporation, 1931.

Trow's New York City Classified Business Directory.

True, Clarence. *Riverside Drive.* New York: Press of Unz & Co., 1899.

Tucker, Sophie. *Some of These Days.* Garden City, N.Y.: Doubleday, Doran & Company, 1945.

Valentine, Lewis J. *Night Stick.* New York: Dial Press, 1947.

Van Rensselaer, Mariana. *History of the City of New York in the Seventeenth Century.* New York: The Macmillan Company, 1909.

Viele, Egbert L. *The West End Plateau.*

Walker, Stanley. *The Night Club Era.* New York: Frederick A. Stokes Company, 1933.

Walsh, Raoul. *Each Man in His Time.* New York: Farrar, Straus & Giroux, 1974.

Ward, Maria E. *Bicycling for Ladies.* New York: Brentano's, 1896.

Wertenbaker, Thomas Jefferson. *Father Knickerbocker Rebels: New York City during the Revolution.* New York: Cooper Square Publishers, 1969.

"West Side Is Itself a Great City." *New York Times,* March 10, 1895.

"West Side Number." *Real Estate Record and Guide* 46. Supplement. (July–December 1890).

White, Norval, and Elliot Willensky. *AIA Guide to New York City* (revised edition). New York: Collier/Macmillan, 1978.

Williams, Tennessee. *Memoirs.* New York: Doubleday & Company, 1975.

Wilson, James Grant. *The Memorial History of New York.* New York: New York History Company, 1892–93.

Witmark, Isidore, and Isaac Goldberg. *From Ragtime to Swingtime.* New York: Lee Furman, 1939.

Wodehouse, P. G., and Guy Bolton. *Bring on the Girls! The Improbable Story of our Life in Musical Comedy, with Pictures to Prove It.* New York: Simon & Schuster, 1953.

Worden, Helen. *The Real New York.* Indianapolis: Bobbs-Merrill Company, 1932.

Worden, Helen. *Round Manhattan's Rim.* Indianapolis: Bobbs-Merrill Company, 1934.

Zabar, Lori. "The Influence of W. E. D. Stokes's Real Estate Career on West Side Development." Masters thesis, Columbia University Graduate School of Architecture and

Planning, 1977.
Zeckendorf, William, with Edward McCreary. *Zeckendorf*. New York: Holt, Rinehart and Winston, 1970.
Zeisloft, E. Idell. *The New Metropolis*.

New York: D. Appleton & Co.,1899.
Zolotow, Maurice. *Stage Struck: The Romance of Alfred Lunt & Lynn Fontanne*. New York: Harcourt, Brace & World, 1965.

PICTURE CREDITS

INDEX

Numbers in italics indicate pages on which entry appears only in caption or photograph.

Fuchs, Renée, 200
Fulton, Robert, 45. *See also* Hudson-
  Fulton celebration of 1909
Funny Girl (film), 155
Furniss, William P., 44, 52, 212–13
Futterman, Lewis, 292

Galiano, Henry, 280
Garden of Allah, The (play), 190
Gatti-Casazza, Giulio, 136, 142
Gehrig, Lou, 90
Genth, Lillian, 199
George, Grace, 155
Gershwin, George, 89, 147, 153–54,
  193
Gershwin, Ira, 147, 152, 153–54, 215
Gilbert, Charles P. H., 205
Gilbreth, Frank, family, 86–88
"Gilded Age," 71
Gillette, William, 181
Ginger Man (saloon), 275
Ginsberg, Allen, 221, 223, 267
Girofle-Girofla (play), 154, *166*
Glackens, William, 203
Glasgow, Ellen, 213
Glass, Bonnie, 199
Glazer, Nathan, 255
Glick Organization, 292
Goddard-Riverside Community Center,
  290
Goderis, Joost, 15–16
Gold, Herbert, 222
Goldberg, Rube, 203
Goldberger, Paul, 245, 293
Golden Glades (cabaret), *171*, 182,
  202, 243
Goldman, Henry, 82
Goldwyn, Samuel, 156–57
Gompers, Samuel, 218
Gonsalves, Paul, 207
Goodbye Columbus (restaurant), 288
Goodman, Andrew, 256
Goodman, Benny, 207
Goodman, Paul, 272
Gordon, Ruth, 228, 248
Gorky, Maxim, 211–12, 223
Gorme, Edie, 208
Gottschalk, Ferdinand, 188
Gould, Bruce and Beatrice, 218
Goulet, Robert, 194
Graham, Martha, 275

Grand Circle. *See* Columbus Circle
Grant, Ulysses, *35*, 121
Grant's Tomb, 16, 26, 45, *110*, 121;
  architect of, 70; visitors to, 211, 216,
  278
Grauer, Bill, Jr., 207
Green, Andrew Haswell, 59, 227, 298
Green, Hetty, 85
Greengrass, Barney, 279, 288
Greengrass, Moe, 288
Greenleaf, Jonathan, 47
Greenspun, Roger, 267
Greenwich Village, 16, 32, 45, 198
Grey, Zane, 213
Griffin, Percy, 71
Griffin, "Pop," Pelican Inn, 32, 50, 51
Griffin, Theresa, 65
Griffin, Walter, 199
Griffith, D. W., 156, 157, 267
Groff, Joseph D., 89
Grogin, Harry, 219
Gruwe, Emile, 69
Gruzen, Jordan, 291
Guggenheim, Meyer, 82
Guggenheim, Murry, 82
Guinan, Texas, 190
Gumbs Brothers, 286
Gurney, J. R., 280
Gusweller, James, 255
Gutterman's Funeral Home, 294

Haggin, Ben Ali, 199
Hale, Nathan, 26
Hale, Ruth, 215
Hall, Thomas, 14–15, 17
Halleck, Fitz-Greene, 50, 51, 198
Hamersley Forge (iron works), 41
Hamilton, Alexander, 42, 43, 44, 48,
  122
Hamilton, Chico, 268
Hamilton, Eliza, 48
Hamilton, Robert Ray, 122
Hammer, Armand, 84–85
Hammerstein, Oscar, 145, 160
Hammerstein, Oscar, II, 90, 147, 152,
  153
Hampden, Walter, 190, 199, 275
Hampton Apartments, 94
Hancock, John, 26, 27
Hardenbergh, Henry J., 66, 71
Hardwick, Elizabeth, 221, 237

85, 124, 243, 277
Hudson River Yacht Club, 124
Huerta, Victoriano, 137–38
Hughes, Charles Evans, 9, 86, 91, 141
Hughes, Langston, 150, 222
Hurok, Sol, 136
Hurst, Fannie, 216, 248, 273
Hyde, James Hazen, 188

Inca (hotel), 66
Ingraham, Rex, 160
Interborough Rapid Transit Company,
   124
Inwood Village, 32
Irving, Washington, 58, 64;
   Knickerbocker's History, 13, 15
Ives, Charles, 205

Jacobs, Jane, 272
Jagger, Mick, 209
Janes & Leo, 70, 126
Japanese Tea Garden, 156
Jasper, John, 32–41
Jay, John, 42
Jefferson, Joseph, 182
Jefferson, Thomas, 44
Jessel, Georgie, 149
Jesup, Morris K., 60
Jewish Theological Seminary, 90, 285
J. G. Melon's (restaurant), 278
Joan of Arc, statue, 122
Jobs, Steve, 245, 287
Joel, Billy, 209
John, Augustus, 198
Johnson, Jack, 249
Johnson, James P., 150
Johnson, Philip, 273
Jones, Hugh Bolton, 199
Jones, Humphrey, 19, 44
Jones, James, 42
Jones, Nicholas, 19, 26
Journal (newspaper), 87, 121, 130
Journal-American (newspaper), 274
Juilliard School of Music, 90, 202, 206,
   273
Jumel, Betsy, 32
Jumel, Stephen, 32

Kael, Pauline, 267
Kahn, Otto H., 188, 192
Kalikow, Peter, 292

Karno, Fred, 150
Kaufman, Bea, 152
Kaufman, George S., 147, 152, 153,
   215, 228, 247
Kazin, Alfred, 222–23, 294
Kean, Edmund, 49
Keaton, Buster, 149, 159
Keaton, Diane, 245
Keepnews, Orrin, 207
Keith, B. F., 156
Keith's 81st Street Theatre, 149, 158,
   249, 294–95
Kelly, Harry, 193
Kent, Rockwell, 202
Kern, Jerome, 147–48, 152, 153, 193
Kerouac, Jack, 223, 267
Kester, Vaughan, 213
Keystone (theater), 156
Kinney, Troy and Margaret, 199
Knickerbocker families, 64–65, 219
Knopf, Alfred A., 218
Knowlton, Thomas, 26, 27, 44, 56, 296
Koch, Edward I., 279, 292, 293
Kohn, Robert D., 70
Kreuger, Miles, 268
Kroll, Leon, 198
Krupsak, Marianne, 206
Kuhn, Walt, 202
Kuniyoshi, Yasuo, 202
Kurtz, Swoozie, 294
Kusch, Polykarp, 90

La Farge, John, 71
LaGuardia, Fiorello H., 251, 271
Lamb, Martha J., 44, 49; quoted, 31
Lamb, Thomas, 294–95
Lamb, Willis E., Jr., 90
Lamb & Rich, 68, 70, 73
Landmarks Preservation Commission,
   295
Landmark West!, 294
Laredo, Jaime, 206
La Rocca, Nick, 184
La Rochelle (apartment house), 68, 91
Lasky, Jesse, 156
Laurents, Arthur, 254
Lawlor, Charles B., 151
Lawrence, Carol, 194
Lawrence, Steve, 208
Lawson, Ernest, 203
Lawson, Louise, 228

Nordica, Lillian, 84
Normandie (ship), 252
North River, The (painting; Bellows), 202
Norworth, Jack, 151
Notlek's (miniature golf course), 243
Notre Dame High School, 265
Nuevo Edison (movie theater), 251, 287
Nugent, Louise, 96
Nygaard, Jens, 284

Oak Villa (Henry Brockholst Livingston estate), 42, 43
O'Brien, Pat, 158
Ochs, Adolph S., 218
Odd Couple, The (film), 159; television series, 245
Ogilvy & Mather, 278
O'Hanlon, Philip F., 84
O'Hanlon, Virginia, 84, 94
Oh, Boy! (musical), 87, 148
Oh, Lady, Lady! (musical), 148
Old Bloomingdale Inn and Tea Garden, 50
Olmsted, Frederick Law, 58, 60, 64, 65, 298
Olson, Oliver A., Co. (store), 78
O'Malley, Frank, 215
Onassis, Jacqueline, 293
O'Neal's Baloon (saloon), 275
O'Neill, Eugene, 202
Ono, Yoko, 208
Oppenheimer, J. Robert, 252, 256
Orange Riot of 1870, 180
Osborn, Henry Fairfield, 90
Ostrow, Steve, 142
Ovington, Mary White, 94

Pabst's (beer hall), 181, 184, 202
Pacino, Al, 159
Painz, John, 229
Palmer, Thomas, 50
Panic in Needle Park, The (film), 159
Panic of 1873, 56, 57
Papanastassiou, John, 285
Papp, Joseph, 256
Paramount Pictures, 156
Park, Anna, 41
Park & Tilford, 68
Park Avenue, 244–46

Parker, Dorothy, 89, 148, 215, 228
Park Plaza (hotel), 266
Park Theatre, 149, 249
Parsons, Frank A., 203
Pasteur Institute, 83
Patterson, Floyd, 249
Pavarotti, Luciano, 206
Pavlova, Anna, 181
Peale, Charles Willson, 198, 205
Peary, Robert E., 91
Peck, John E., family, 234, 235–37
Pei, I. M., 245, 287
Pelican Inn, 32, 50, 51
Penn Central, rail yard, 291. *See also* New York Central Railroad
Perlman, Itzhak, 206
Perugini. *See* Chatterton, John
Peters, John, 69
Peters, Thomas McClure, 47
Peter Stuyvesant Apartments, 218
Phelps, Isaac N., 60
Phelps, William Lyon, 188
Philharmonic Hall. *See* Lincoln Center: Philharmonic Hall
Philo Vance series (books; Van Dine), 214, 227
Phipps, Henry, 94
Phipps Houses (apartment house), 94, 207
Pickford, Mary, 158, 159
Pinza, Ezio, 136
Plato's Retreat, 143, 289
Platt, John R., 227
Plaza Memorial Chapel, 284
Plimpton, George, 221
Podhoretz, Norman, 221
Podolsky, Zenek, 286
Poe, Edgar Allan, 51, 198, *210*, 212
Pollard, George Mort, 199
Pollock, George, 44
Pollock, St. Clair, 44–45, 216
Polshek, James Stewart, 293
Pons, Lily, 136
Ponselle, Rosa, 228
Pontiac (club, 81st Street), 181, 182
Pontiac (club, 104th Street), 92
Pope, John Russell, 90
Porter, Edwin S., 159
Porter, Horace, 130
Post, George B., 45
Post, Joel, 45, 53; family, 27, 52

Westinghouse, Herman, 81
West Park Presbyterian Church, 43, 280
Westpride, 294
West Side Association, 55, 56–57, 60, 61
West Side Highway, 123, 291; 79th Street interchange, *261*
West Side Republican Club, 92
West Side School for Boys, 89
West Side Seniors for Action, 291
West Side Story (musical; film), 159, 194, *253*, 254, 272
West Side Tennis Club, 92
West Side Urban Renewal Plan, 288
West Side YMCA, 292
Wexler, Irving "Waxey Gordon," 230, 231
Wharton, Edith, 213
White, Aleck, 41
White, George, 153
White, Stanford, 71, 125, 135, 143; Sherman Square Hotel, 69, *119*
Whitehall Hotel, 153
Whitney, Harry Payne, 188
Whittemore, Mrs. Richard, 160
Widow's, The (roadhouse), 179
Wiggins, Guy, 199
Wilhelm II, Emperor of Germany, 137
Willard, Frances, 181
Willard, Jess, 139, 249
William IV, King of England, 45
Williams, Andrew, 46
Williams, Bert, 153
Williams, Cornelius, 227
Williams, Percy G., 149
Williams, Tennessee, 220
Willow Bank (Meier estate), 44
Wilshire, H. Gaylord, 86, 211
Wilson, Edmund, 213
Wilson, Lanford, 280
Wilson, Teddy, 207
Wilson, Woodrow, 137
Winchell, Walter, 9, 149, 150, *169*, 217, 219–20, 233
Wise, Stephen, 249
Wiseman, Joseph, 159
Witmark, Isidore, 192
Wizard of Oz, The (musical), *146*, 148
Wodehouse, P. G., 147–48, 153, 188, 193

Woman's Hospital, 83
Women's Health Protective Association, monument, 122
Women's University Club, 92
Wood, Fernando, *36*, 55, 58
Woodhull, Nathanael, 28
Woodlawn (Heyward house), 44, 51–52
Woods, Arthur, 229
Woods, Florence E., 133
Woodworth, Samuel, 51
Woollcott, Alexander, 155, 215, 217, 246
Woolrich, Cornell, 138, 214–15
Worden, Helen, 79, 222
World (newspaper), 81, 121, 127, 211, 215, 234
World-Telegram (newspaper), 217
World War I, 137–38, 193, 213
World War II, 251–52
Wouk, Herman, 217, 250
Woutersen, Egbert, 14, 15
WPA Guide, 250
Wright, Wilbur, 124
Wright, Willard Huntington, 214

Ximenes, Ettore, 121

Yip! Yip! Yaphank (musical), 193–94
Youmans, Vincent, 147, 151
Yourkevitch, Vladimir I., 252
"Your Show of Shows" (television show), 249

Zabar's (delicatessen/gourmet shop), 160, *264*, 279, 283, 290
Zanker, Bill, 283–84
Zeckendorf, William, 250, 272, 292
Ziegfeld, Florenz, 9, 84, 136–37, 147, 154, *163*; *Follies*, 87, 151, 192–93, 228
Zinsser, Hans, 90
Zion Church, 47
Zuckerman, Eugenia, 206
Zuckerman, Mortimer, 292, 293
Zuckerman, Pinchas, 206
Zukor, Adolph, 156, 160

ABOUT THE AUTHOR

Peter Salwen has been well known to lovers of New York history for more than ten years as a writer and tour guide. He has led tours for the Municipal Art Society and other groups, and his annual downtown walking tour of "Mark Twain's New York," on or near the humorist's birthday, has become an annual tradition. Mr. Salwen's articles on New York's neighborhoods, personalities, history, and architecture have appeared in the *New York Times, Newsday, Daily News,* and other publications. He heads a New York public relations agency and has lived on the Upper West Side since 1957. The late Elliot Willensky praised *Upper West Side Story* as "everything that a book about a great New York neighborhood should be."

UPPER WEST SIDE STORY

------------ A ------------

HISTORY
AND GUIDE